RETURN TO THE THINGS

Husserlian Neurophenomenology and the
Scientific Anthropology of the Senses

by

Charles D. Laughlin, Ph.D.

DAILY GRAIL PUBLISHING

Return to the Things: Husserlian Neurophenomenology and the Scientific Anthropology of the Senses

ISBN: 978-0-6452094-7-1

Daily Grail Publishing
Brisbane, Australia
publications@dailygrail.com
www.dailygrail.com

CONTENTS

ACKNOWLEDGEMENTS

Many friends and colleagues have helped me along the way leading to this book. Not all of them agree with my conclusions or theories, but all were supportive and fed me with ideas, criticisms, and suggestions over the years. My heartful thanks to Ivan A. Brady, Eugene D'Aquili, John McManus, Robert A. Rubinstein, Jon Shearer, John Cove, Ian Prattis, Brian Given, Adam Rock, Vincenza Tiberia, Michael Winkelman, Stan Krippner, Melanie Takahashi, Tracey Prentice, Margaret Stephens, Jason Throop, Mark Webber, Robbie Davis-Floyd, Paul Devereux, Charla Devereux, and Klaus-Peter Köpping. I would like to extend my thanks to my Buddhist meditation teachers over the many years, Ven. Namgyal Rinpoche, Ven. Kalu Rinpoche, my preceptor Ven. Chogye Trichen Rinpoche, and Tarchin Hearn. Bless you all, wherever you be.

In Memoriam
Edith Stein (1891 – 1942)
phenomenologist extraordinaire

CHAPTER ONE

Introduction: Science and the Anthropology of Experience

This is not a "view," an "interpretation" bestowed upon the world. Every view about…, every opinion about "the" world, has its ground in the pregiven world. It is from this very ground that I have freed myself through the epoché; I stand above the world, which has now become for me, in a quite peculiar sense, a phenomenon.

– Husserl (1970[1936]: 152)

What, then, does the future hold? In total with the postmodernists, I have come to the regrettable but obvious conclusion that there is no easy accommodation of the scientific and hermeneutic intellectual frames. Since the hermeneutic frame is for me fatally damaged by its denial of objective truth and the possibility of scientific anthropology, my solution is to proclaim that it is not anthropology at all in any reasonable sense of the term. The wave of the anthropological future that I hope for is a scientific anthropology taking into full account the human capacity for discriminating among highly complex combinations of circumstances and reacting systematically to their similarities and differences. Scientific archeology will benefit from such an anthropology, and it will contribute to it in turn. More properly, it will be a part of this anthropology because a properly scientific anthropology searches for significant relationships among all possible sets of variables at all times and places.

– Albert Spaulding (1988: 270)

Anthropology has long resisted becoming a nomothetic science. Every time our beloved discipline gets close to a theoretical paradigm, it recoils as from a plague. Anthropologists repeatedly miss any opportunity to build upon relevant theoretical constructs and back away into a kind of natural history of sociocultural differences

(Dow 1996, Jarvie 1967, Kuznar 2008, Lett 1997, Spaulding 1988). For a discipline to attain the status of a paradigmatic science, it must eventually discover its foundations in the structures of reality. Until then, it remains a pre-scientific, naturalistic exploration of the surface of things, an "artificial" science as cognitive psychologist Herbert A. Simon (2019[1981]) called it. Contemporary anthropology is like biology before Darwin, chemistry before the periodic table, or astrophysics before Newton. Anthropology has come close to this paradigmatic Rubicon in the past, only to rebound from fully acknowledging the roots of its scope in the structures of reality—that is to say, the evolutionary biology of the human organism, and the neurophysiology of the human brain.

The irony is that the founder of anthropology as a full-on scientific discipline, the great German ethnologist Adolf Bastian (1826-1905), sought an anthropology grounded in the psychophysics of our species (see Adams 1998: 291-292, Koepping 1983, 1995, König 2007, Laughlin 2011: 38-43, Throop and Laughlin 2007). He reasoned, and I think correctly, that the variety of ways of life of different peoples was generated by the same hidden "psychic unity" of the species (read: structure of the human brainmind). It was the task of anthropologists *qua* ethnographers to do intensive, long-term Malinowski-like field research among many traditional peoples (as Bastian himself did over many years) before "civilization" had completely corrupted their lifeways. However, it was not his vision to collect all the weird and wonderful ways that humans carried out their affairs, but rather by collecting the surface manifestations of variance among many peoples, to inductively produce accurate empirical generalizations that in turn might be deductively explained by theories about the underlying structure—the *Elementargedanken* or "elementary ideas"—operating within the neuropsychology of humanity. Alas, British social anthropology failed to apply Bastian's injunctions and preferred to rely upon second-hand reports from others who had dealings with traditional folk "out in the colonies." Only after the example set by Malinowski's famous exile to the Trobriand Islands did British ethnography gain a hold on ethnology, and by that point the earlier notions of a structural underpinning of "psychic unity" beneath apparent variation of lifeways was repudiated.

This repudiation of a structural basis of human mentation and behavior was compounded by one of Bastian's students, Franz Boas, who famously migrated to the United States to escape virulent antisemitism in Germany. In the United States he established himself at Columbia University in New York and from that platform, essentially founded American style "cultural anthropology." In historical perspective, it is understandable why American cultural anthropology originated in the anti-racist, anti-social Darwinist polemics of the early 20th century (Bunzl 1996). To acknowledge even the slightest biological heritance of social and cultural forms was to leave open the door to claims of inherited and abhorrent racial characteristics, be they Jewish or African or Aboriginal American. This rather reactionary and scientifically naïve sociopolitical stance, understandable as it might be in hindsight, generates empirically unsupportable claims of the "it's culture all the way down" sort that effectively denies any biogenetic origins of mind, experience, cognition, judgments, ethics/morals, or sociality. Everything of interest to the anthropologist is supposedly a cultural or historical construct (see e.g., Geertz 1985, 2017, Knorr-Cetina 2013, Schweder 1991).

NEUROANTHROPOLOGY

In order for there to be no structural basis for apparent individual and cultural variations, logic requires that the organ of learning, the brain, be a blank slate, a tabula rasa, at birth. The human newborn must, if the constructivist account is correct, be born without any inherent structure to their brain, just waiting as it were for society to pour it full of beliefs, concepts and behaviors. Now, in the age of neuroscience, we know this is not the case (Rochat 2001). However, the emergence of anthropology during the first three quarters of the 20th century occurred during a time when science was burgeoning, but neuroscience was in its infancy and very much limited to neurological medicine (Casper 2014). Neurologists at the time generally steered clear of addressing the relations between brain and mind, and few drew any interdisciplinary connections between neuroscience and the social sciences. But by the 1980s, interdisciplinary neuroscience had begun what some now refer to as a *global neuroscientific turn*, or simply the *neuro-turn*, an engagement with research and theoretical issues in the purview of the social sciences and humanities (Allman 1989, Churchland and Sejnowski 1992,

Claffert, Baker and Winkelman, 2019, Littlefield and Johnson 2012, Samson 2015, Wajman 2010). This movement led to several new sub-fields in neuroscience resulting in new journals such as *Culture and Brain, Social Cognitive and Affective Neuroscience, Social Neuroscience,* as well as numerous related books and articles (e.g., Cacioppo *et al.* 2002, Chiao *et al.* 2016, Han 2017, Lin and Telzer 2018), including cross-cultural neuropsychology (Fernández and Evans 2022).

Biocultural perspectives began to emerge mid-century and later-on may be seen as one early manifestation of the neuro-turn in anthropology (see Dufour 2006, Saniotis 2009, Zuckerman and Martin 2016). Physical anthropology of course has had an abiding interest in the evolution of the hominin brain, especially reflected in the work of Ralph L. Holloway (see Broadfield *et al.* 2010). Although the roots of anthropological interest in the brain of living peoples dates back over a half century to at least the 1970s (Chapple 1970, Count 1973, Laughlin and d'Aquili 1974), it may be viewed as a more direct outgrowth of *neuroanthropology,* a movement my colleagues and I developed in the 1980s and thereafter (Laughlin 1989a, 1997a, Laughlin, McManus and d'Aquili 1990, Rubinstein and Laughlin 1977), in synch with other scientists (Armstrong 1991, Blonder 1991, Falk 1992, TenHouten 1991), in an attempt to engage cultural anthropology with the neurosciences.[1]

Neuroanthropology is the study of how the brain *mediates* (i.e., produces, generates, "functions to," organizes, portrays; in Husserl's term, "constitutes") experiences, social relations, techno-skills, histories and social learning among *Homo sapiens,* and incidentally other large brained social animals, especially other primates. We now know that we share many of the neural structural features, including structures mediating conscious experience, with our fellow creatures with big brains, and that there is much to be learned from comparative neuropsychological studies (Allen and Trestman 2017, Birch, Schnell and Clayton 2020, Edelman and Seth 2009, Feinberg and Mallatt 2016, Griffin 2013). Like other animals we individually exhibit both invariant structures of experience and considerable variation within our stream

---

[1] I created and edited *The Neuroanthropology Network Newsletter* which was a self-published monthly from 1988-1992. All issues of this newsletter are available online at http://www.biogeneticstructuralism.com/nnn/nnn.htm.

of consciousness (Van den Bos 2000). Given evidence from modern neuroscience and comparative psychophysiology, the scientific debate about whether or not infrahuman animals experience consciousness is in my opinion passé (see Feinberg and Mallatt 2016, Hunt 1995: Chap. 5). The interesting questions now revolve around what animal experience is like compared with our own, and how various species' brains mediate their experiences.

The neuroanthropological approach is also inherently and inescapably linked to evolutionary theory, for it insists that accounts of human behavior and neuropsychological processes be amenable to coherence with neurobiological and evolutionary psychological knowledge from related sciences. As such, neuroanthropology stands as a necessary alternative to what might be called the "naïve culturological position" described above—the notion that upon inventing "culture" humanity somehow left biology behind. If you think about it a moment, neuroscience produces a field of limiting factors upon any theoretical model of human mental, cognitive, or psychological processes. If what we know about how the brain is organized and functions cannot support a model, then it is probable that the model is wrong. The classic example is linguist Noam Chomsky's (1965) *language acquisition device* (LAD) which was put forth as a black-box model of how children develop language skills. We now know there is insufficient support from neuroscience for the existence of such a mechanism. In short, the brain does not work that way to either acquire or utilize language/speech skills. Chomsky cannot be blamed for his errors in modeling, for at the time he was working on the problem, there was scant neuroscience upon which to evaluate his thinking—hence the necessity at the time for a black-box model.

It is my belief that only through integrating the psychophysical aspects of human nature with ethnographic data on variation of lifeway can we establish a structural basis of a science of anthropology—in other words, follow Bastian's project. A nomothetic science of human sociality, adaptation, consciousness, and behavior cannot be grounded on the ephemeral notion of "culture," for "culture" does not exist save as a shorthand concept for shared patterns in the social learning and lifeways of intragroup individuals. As with Chomsky's LAD, anthropological models—especially those of *cognitive anthropology* (Bowerman and

Levinson 2001)—now must face the limiting factors of neuroscientific findings. If we find that the brain cannot process information, thought, language, feeling, etc. in the ways we anthropologists model them, then we must scrap the models, not ignore the neuroscientific evidence. When cognitive anthropologists speak of a "cultural model" as a *schema*, meaning "a generic version of (some part of) the world learned from experience and stored in memory" (Strauss and Quinn 1997: 4), that schema must refer to a possible or actual neural network, or its formulation as an explanatory concept is invalid. Again, schemas as black-box models of how the human mind functions were the best we could do before the neuro-turn, but we now must build our models of mental acts upon how we know the brain works. In case you may think I am dumping on cognitive anthropologists unfairly, consider that of the 30 articles in a recent compendium, *A Companion to Cognitive Anthropology* (Kronenfeld, Bennardo, De Munck and Fischer 2015), only one article makes any mention of the brain or neuroscience. Contrast this remarkable neglect of the neurosciences with anthropologist Roy d'Andrade's cogent and prescient attempt to link cognitive cultural and neuropsychological processes:

> In my view, the cognitive part of cognitive anthropology is in its concern with the way in which cultural content "interfaces" with psychological processes. Cognitive anthropology and cognitive psychology are both concerned with the interaction between processing and information, except that the cognitive anthropologist wants to know how cultural information is constrained and shaped by the way the brain processes such information, while the cognitive psychologist wants to know how the machinery of the brain works on all types of information, including cultural information. ...An important assumption of cognitive anthropology is that in the process of repeated social transmission, cultural programs come to take forms which have a good fit to the natural capacities and constraints of the human brain. Thus, when similar cultural forms are found in most societies around the world, there is reason to search for psychological factors which could account for these similarities. (d'Andrade 1981: 182)

I am reminded of something one of my teachers at the University of Oregon, the late Professor Homer Barnett, taught us students: Being a student of A. L. Kroeber, Barnett entered his first fieldwork venue among a west coast Aboriginal group where he expected to see a "superorganic" culture, but all he found were people. I might add, he found people with brains pretty much like the brains of people in other groups. The point is, anthropological theory grounded upon an unreal and fuzzy abstraction is at best an empirical generalization about similarities and differences among groups of people, or at worst just an ephemeral idea. Still, "culture" is a useful umbrella term for the products of social learning, as long as we acknowledge that: (1) the organ of culture is the brain of a social animal, thus making it of use in referring to intragroup shared learning among social animals, including humans, and (2) we model lifeway elements ranging from minimal cultural input to maximal cultural sharing, thus recognizing both biogenetically transmitted elements and elements influenced by social learning. The latter acknowledgment dispenses with the "culture all the way down" fiction and leaves open the possibility of a "cultural" theory grounded upon psychophysical, and more directly, neurophysiological structures. I hasten to add that "culture" is not an indispensable ingredient of a nomothetic theory of human lifeways.[2]

EXPERIENCE, EMBODIMENT, AND PHENOMENOLOGY

Beginning in the 1970s and continuing to the end of the century, American and British anthropologists turned their backs on the potential theoretical sea change promised by Levi-Straussian, linguistic and Piagetian structuralist theories—all of which emerged before the neuro-turn took effect in the social sciences—and began to embrace so-called post-structuralism and then postmodernism. Granted, Levi-Strauss' structuralism failed primarily because he could not point to the mechanisms mediating his homologies (Ardener 2017: 171). The rejection of structure underlying apparent variations in cultural forms effectively rendered theory-building in anthropology all but moribund.

---

[2] If I had chosen to do so, I could have written this book without a single reference to "culture."

Yet despite this aversion to the biological, some anthropologists were exploring new approaches to studying human lifeways. On the one hand, the early work leading to the field of *evolutionary psychology* began to appear, spearheaded by Canadian anthropologist Jerome Barkow and his colleagues (Barkow 1989; 1992). They reasoned that modern peoples are actually operating from a brainmind that evolved during the upper paleolithic, and many "cultural" features we encounter among living peoples begin to make sense when viewed as ancient adaptations to a physical and social world much changed (Davis 2009, Over 2003).

Hominin cognitive processes have emphasized increasing flexibility in integrating information both retrieved from sensory experience and stored in memory[3] in unique ways to address dynamic contingencies in the *environing world* (alternatively the *surrounding world*)—that is, that part of the real world that an animal senses and acts within, the part of the world that includes the animal's niche (Ger.: *Umweld*; Sebeok 1991, Sebeok, Umiker-Sebeok and Young 1992, Sheneman, Schossau and Hintze 2019, Von Uexküll 1909, 2018[1926]). The physiological nature of a species determines its environing world; thus, the environing world of a woodpecker is different than that of a whale or a human even though their respective geographical ranges may overlap and sample the same reality. Incidentally, Husserl made this point quite forcefully in insisting that: "As a person, I am what I am (and each other person is what he is) as *subject of a surrounding world*. The concepts of Ego and surrounding world are related to one another inseparably" (Husserl 1989[1952]: 195).

Other anthropologists began to ground their understanding of human lifeways upon subjective and intersubjective experience (Turner 1982, 1985, Turner and Bruner 1986). With a significant stimulus from earlier theorists such as Durkheim, Levi-Straus, and Levy-Bruhl (Throop 2003a, Throop and Laughlin 2002) and the tantalizing cybernetic psychological theorizing of Gregory Bateson (1972, 1979), Victor Turner (1977, 1982), and others began shifting focus from social systems (people viewed from the outside, as it were) to the everyday experience of people going about their daily lives (people viewed from the inside, so to speak).

---

[3] Research suggests that memories are laid down, modified, rearranged, and lost by minute changes in the brain at the level of the synapse (see Dempsey *et al.* 2022).

This shift in focus led to the *anthropology of experience* approach to doing ethnography, as well as understanding the sociality of humans from an intersubjective standpoint (see e.g., Brereton 2009, Harris 2007, Naidu 2013, Throop 2003b, Willen and Seeman 2012). The reorientation of perspective towards the lived experience of people in different societies raised interesting methodological issues about how the ethnographer should or could go about "getting into the heads" of their hosts—i.e., how is one to access the privacy of consciousness (Csordas 1994a)? This is not a new challenge by any means, but rather requires an expansion of what it means to do "participant observation" into the first person, intersubjective mode (Moeran 2009; Tedlock 1991).

The anthropology of experience approach and its quest for appropriate methods led quite naturally to interest in the contemplative methods used in phenomenological philosophy (Desjarlais and Throop 2011 Knibbe and Versteeg 2008 Laughlin and Throop 2008, 2009, Petrus 2006, Ram and Houston 2015a, Throop 2000, 2002, 2010, Throop and Laughlin 2002), especially the formative work of Edmund Husserl (Kockelmans 1967, Spiegelberg 1983, Zahavi and Stjernfeld 2002). The blending of the anthropology of experience with phenomenological methods led quickly to the recognition, either explicitly or implicitly, that experience is always *embodied*—a realization already well established in early 20th century Husserlian phenomenology (Husserl 1989[1952]: 152-154). *Embodiment* thus rapidly became "a thing" among psychological scientists (see e.g., Glenberg 2010, Sheets-Johnstone 2009, Varela, Thompson and Rosch 1991) and soon was fundamental to the anthropology of experience (Csordas 1990, 1993, 1994a, 1994b, Elkholy 2016, Kulenović 2021, Mascia-Lees 2011, Seligman 2014, Throop 2010), for it is easy to prove using even casual introspection that everyday experience is had from within an embodied standpoint. I am staring at this screen with my eyes open, from a posture of sitting, and typing with my fingers on a keyboard. Embodiment is as simple and yet as profound as that—as the old saying goes, "wherever you go, there you are," taken there in and by your body, even when you may be "out of body" in a dream. Yet as physician and phenomenologist Drew Leder (2010) has shown, we are usually oblivious to the functions of our bodies that mediate our experiences of the world.

Yet with all this concern by some anthropologists with embodiment, scant attention has been paid to that part of the body that mediates experience, namely the nervous system (see Bartra 2014, Immordino-Yang 2013, Lende and Downey 2012 for exceptions), this persistence of cultural constructivism has gradually alienated anthropology from mainstream post-neuro-turn science (Domínguez Duque *et al.* 2010, Shore 1998; see especially Laidlaw 2014 on this issue). Even among phenomenological anthropologists, researchers tend to base their findings upon those phenomenologies that support the "culture all the way down," constructivist bias (see Čargonja 2013, Desjarlais and Throop 2011, Ram and Houston 2015a for summaries).

Even a casual reading of Husserl will show you that embodiment of experience is fundamental to his understanding of sensory perception:

> The Body is, in the first place, the *medium of all perception*: it is the *organ of perception* and is *necessarily* involved in all perception. In seeing, the eyes are directed upon the seen and run over its edges, surfaces, etc. When it touches objects, the hand slides over them. Moving myself, I bring my ear closer to hear. Perceptual apprehension presupposes sensation-contents, which play their necessary role for the constitution of the schemata and, so, for the constitution of the appearances of the real things themselves. (Husserl 1989[1952]: 61)

If you are feeling a bit puzzled by the emphasis placed upon the "body" as a central concept here, try this exercise. Take a walk somewhere safe with little chance of stumbling over something—perhaps a sidewalk or familiar path. Become aware that you are viewing a slowly changing vista, listening to a field of changing sounds, and perhaps smelling various odors wafting by. Now, without losing awareness of these "external" sensations, become aware of the breeze caressing your face and hands, the feeling of changing pressures on the bottom of your feet, then work your way into your body to connect with interoceptive sensations—movement of your arms, pivoting of your joints, the swaying and shifting of your backbone, the rise and fall of your chest, and turning your head and eyes. If you are like most of us, you will naturally pay attention either to the external sensations or discursive thoughts and fantasies "in your head" when you are out for a normal walk and in either case will lose awareness of your body. Aware of your body or not, your somatic processes continue to mediate your experiences of the environing world. Also notice that your natural tendency when you—as Watcher—turn your gaze inwards is to lose touch to some extent with the external sensations. What I suggest you do in this exercise is for most of us unnatural, *balance your attention upon both external and internal sensations.* When you are able to do this for an extended duration, notice how external sensations relate to internal ones and vice versa, how the kinesthetic feeling of turning of your eyeballs and head correlates with changes in external sensations derived from looking here and there, turning your head to track the direction of sounds, the movements of your muscles under your skin propelling you forward, and so forth. Become conscious of how your body mediates every experience of the environing world around you. You will now better realize how and why it is crucial to understand that all experiences are mediated and facilitated by your body. With realization of this sensuous embodiment surely must lead to curiosity about your brain and its role in bringing about your experiences.

It should be obvious that the anthropology of experience with its understanding of embodiment and its increased reliance upon phenomenological methods would lead to both a sharper focus upon the role of the senses in experience—a primary focus of Husserlian methods (Classen 1997, Howes 1991a, Pink 2009, 2010, Throop 2016)—and to a closer proximity to psychobiology. Entire books—indeed, hundreds of them—have been written about human social organization, kinship, ritual, behavior, and social institutions with no reference at all to people's experiences, their bodies or brains. However, it is much harder to avoid human physiology when focusing the ethnological gaze upon the ineluctable embodiment of experience and the senses. In fact, it is downright silly not to take the neurophysiology of the senses into account, considering the fact that all animals with brains are conscious and live through a stream of experience informed by each species' array of senses (Feinberg and Mallatt 2016). While anthropology up until now has succeeded in shying away from grounding "culture" in the structures of the body, even filling journals with the silliness of postmodernist political polemics (Carrier 2016), some insightful practitioners of the discipline have ventured into human interiority where ignoring biology, physiology and neural structures becomes ridiculous.

READING HUSSERL

A major method by means of which we can bridge from experience to structure is that of Husserlian phenomenology. But here's the rub: Husserl is notoriously hard to read and understand, whether in German or in English translation, especially if the reader has no background in meditation and contemplation (Natanson 1981). Moreover, many of Husserl's descriptions of sensory experience are controversial in philosophy and even among philosophers calling themselves "phenomenologists" (Natanson 1973: 192-193). It helps to remember that Husserl was classically educated in the German tradition and was well versed in ancient Latin and Greek, and with many of the terms he uses the literal ancient meanings are resurrected and intended. However, what Husserl was on about becomes relatively transparent if one reads him, as I did, with a background in *mature contemplation*—by which I mean a person who has mastered a path of self-realization requisite to carrying out certain fundamental reflexions (Laughlin, McManus and d'Aquili 1990: Chap. 11, 1993; see also Lusthaus 2014: Chap. 2, Whitehead 2015)—for instance, ascertaining the impermanence of the "empirical" or "psychological" ego, harboring the body's energies in service to intense introspection, capable of focusing upon elements of experience without being distracted by noise and chatter, able to directly perceive the processes elemental to time-consciousness, capable of entering into so-called "mystical" absorption states leading to the realization of Totality, or as Eugene d'Aquili liked to call it, *Absolute Unitary Being* (AUB; see d'Aquili 1982).

Edmund Husserl was a mature contemplative and, from a Buddhist point of view (Laycock 1994, Lusthaus 2014), a mature *mindfulness* contemplative. He was able to focus his attention upon any object, any element of experience, and "reduce" it—suspend or disassociate all the ideas, meanings, theories, ontologies, beliefs, biases, emotions, and all the other cultural detritus associated with the object—and study how "pure" moment-by-moment experience is constructed ("constituted")—or, as I would claim, *mediated by the nervous system*. What he discovered, among other things, is that experience is comprised of sensory qualia (*hyle* or "stuff"), forms (*morphé*), ideas (*eidos*), interrelations and intuitions that are mediated by *essential structures* (or *essences*) of perception—i.e., in short, the sensuous and the sensuously associated intuitive. But because his approach to studying consciousness was totally subjective and introspective—indeed, what meditation tradition is not perfected in solitude—he came under fire for neglecting the importance of empathy, social engagement and social learning, a claim made only by writers like Sartre who were philosophizers, not contemplatives (see Harding 2005, Hutcheson 1980 on this issue). Those who approach Husserl as one would to an advanced meditation master with experience and wisdom to offer will be enriched immeasurably by their efforts.

CAUTIONARY NOTES

It is not my intention to write another introduction to Husserl and his philosophy. This has been done by others far more competent than I in tracing the subtleties and changes in Husserl's thinking. His approach and understanding of what he was on about grew over the course of his life and he never really penned a comprehensive manual to his approach. He was very like Carl Jung in that respect. This is the hallmark of a contemplative, because each intuitive leap is but another flagstone to step on along the path to the teahouse. I will make little effort to track these changes, for I am more interested in showing the reader how to do pure and transcendental phenomenology than to sketch its history.

In working through Husserl's writings, with a prior background in Buddhist mindfulness meditation, I find that I do not always agree with Husserl's results (I never disagree with his methods). Like virtually any philosopher you can name, Husserl exhibits ethnocentrism at every turn, e.g., in his assessment of the grandiose role he assumes for Western philosophy in the global march to enlightenment. That said, I do not intend to be another of his critics. There is plenty of that elsewhere in the literature. Rather, I wish to apply his methods, combine them where possible with what we know about how the brain works, and contribute the effort to forwarding a genuinely scientific anthropology.

Most of Husserl's writings have not yet been published, even in German. Taken as a whole, Husserl's oeuvre is called his *Nachlass* ("estate," "legacy;" see Leuven 2007). His major works have now been translated into English, but there remain some critical writings, though published in German, remain untranslated into English. The untranslated material is full of gems that only gradually seep into the English-speaking student's awareness. I am highly reliant upon scholars who have consulted the German language archives and report their discoveries in English.

ANTHROPOLOGY AS A SCIENCE AFTER THE NEURO-TURN

The anthropology of experience with its increasing focus on the senses, and the relationship between direct perception and cultural factors like interpretive frames, systems of belief, worldviews, *alternative states of consciousness* (ASC) and transpersonal procedures, institutional practices, etc., would seem to cry out for a full engagement with interdisciplinary neuroscience. After the neuro-turn, the neurosciences have developed models of the nervous system and the body that can provide the *neural correlates of consciousness* (NCC) upon which a biogenetic grounding for anthropological theories about the structures, evolution, adaptive value, and limitations of cultural patterns can be based (Koch 2019, Koch *et al.* 2016, Metzinger 2000, Seth 2021: 28, Sieroka 2015, Tononi and Koch 2008). Such an approach in no way privileges neurobiology, nor "reduces" anthropological theories to biological ones. Quite the reverse in fact, and as Husserl showed, the natural and social sciences must logically be grounded in the accurate description of acts of experience (Crowell 2013: 32-33). If anything is to be privileged in this engagement, it is the evidence of direct experience (see Husserl 2002[1910]). All sciences must touch base with the experience of the objective world routinely, or they are not "sciences" as most of us understand the term. After all, this is what differentiates science from classic philosophy, and why the sciences split off from their parental discipline generations ago.

Husserl (2008[1906-1907]: 116-122) essentially came to the same conclusion as did William James who grounded his psychological work in an epistemology he called *radical empiricism*, a method of doing psychological science that requires: (1) that all of the ideas and theories in science be grounded in direct experience, and (2) that no experience be excluded from the scope of scientific study (Taylor 1994: 353-354; see also Laughlin and McManus 1995). James presented the core of his ideas about radical empiricism in two key articles entitled "Does 'Consciousness' Exist?" and "A World of Pure Experience," both published in 1904 in the same journal. These articles and supporting papers and documents were collected in the volume entitled *Essays in Radical Empiricism* (James 1976 [1912]). From the anthropological view, the important emphasis on James' part was that no experience, however common or outré, can be excluded from the purview of science. And as ethnographers routinely carry out fieldwork among peoples who consider ASC as part of their epistemological engagement with the world, ethnological theories must perforce include accounts of such "extraordinary" experiences in our reports and theories.

This book will explore the prospects of applying a *Husserlian neurophenomenology* to anthropologically relevant issues. As far as I know, Husserl himself never suggested a merger of his methods with those of neuroscience. Again, his project was the production of a "pure" subjective study upon which to rest the findings of the natural sciences, including psychologies of various sorts (Husserl 1977[1925]: 166-170). In short, Husserl showed that if we wish to understand how we come to know what we claim to know about the world, a close and extraordinarily disciplined scrutiny of the structures of experience is fundamental, for even the most cursory study of consciousness from the "inside" demonstrates that at the most rudimentary level, the primordial sensory given at the center of experiences, is accompanied by intuitive knowing, that is independent of higher cognitive processes (see Hardy 1999).

The neurosciences of Husserl's day were incapable of the fine determinations required to discover the NCC that might be mediating the essential structures Husserl uncovered introspectively. However, Husserl was not ignorant of the fact that his consciousness was somehow being generated by the brain:

The main point to be examined here is the question of whether or not the essence of consciousness, which expresses itself a priori in essential laws, resists such a universal [psychophysiological] regulation. The essence of consciousness in general does raise claims and demands. For example, is it possible, we are asking, for the matter here at issue to be understood in such a way that the cerebral states (states of the B) precede, in an Objectively temporal sense, the corresponding conscious lived experiences, or must not, for reason of principle, the brain state and its conscious accompaniment be simultaneous, in conformity with the absolute sense of simultaneity? Thereby is not a parallelism given *eo ipso*? Namely, in this way: to every conscious lived experience in *my* consciousness Cm there corresponds a certain state in my B, a certain organic state [read: NCC]. On the other hand, to everything without exception that comprises the B there correspond real events of a certain kind in *every* subject, and consequently also in me: certain real perceptual possibilities, which, if not corresponding to the state of the brain B, then to another state in connection with it in a natural-scientific nexus. (Husserl 1989[1952]: 305)

In the above quote Husserl raises the question of whether there is a lawful connection (be it simultaneous or over some short "objective" duration) between brain states and states of consciousness. More specifically, do the essential laws of consciousness and experience correspond with laws of psychophysical functions (Horst 2010)? Hence, what I will be doing in this book in part is a lengthy answer to Husserl's own queries, as others have also done (see Engelhardt 1977, Sieroka 2015). Incidentally, in direct answer to Husserl's question pertaining to the temporal relations between brain states and states of awareness, the "regulation" between brain state and psychological state may be nearly simultaneous in some circumstances and may exhibit significant lags in others (see Libet 2004).

The phrase "Husserlian neurophenomenology" was coined in an article by neuropsychologist Francisco Varela (1997) who was himself a mature contemplative. Varela was influenced by Husserl's writings and seems to have agreed to some extent with Husserlian methods (see

Rudrauf *et al.* 2003). He contrasted Husserlian neurophenomenology with his own approach which he called "experiential neuroscience." Varela, of course, was a practitioner of Tibetan Tantric Buddhism, being a follower of the late Chögyam Trungpa Rinpoche, and the methods Varela used in this regard were different than those used by Husserl. To my knowledge, Varela never applied Husserlian methods in any systematic way.

THE INTENTION OF THIS BOOK

The purpose of this book is to point out the advantages of a Husserlian neurophenomenology for the anthropology of sensory experience and embeddedness in the fullest sense. Husserl's phenomenological writings are vast and explored far more elements of consciousness and experience than I could possibly survey in this book. But then, such an effort would defeat my purpose. What I will do is present a summary of Husserl's methods and results in sufficient detail to show how his efforts can be combined with neuroscience in a way that can ground sociocultural anthropology[4] in reality. By combining the phenomenological methods of Edmund Husserl with studies of the neural correlates of the structures of sensory experience, an ontological and epistemological grounding can be constructed to aid in the normalization of anthropology as a science of human experience and variations in experience conditioned by social learning (i.e., "culture"). To do this, I must explore Husserlian phenomenology with an emphasis upon *how it is actually accomplished* and how we can make sense of essences with the help of neuroscience. Where we are successful in blending phenomenology and neuroscience, we can then describe how this approach might contribute to a scientific anthropology.

I am going to assume most of my readers are at best casually familiar with Husserl's work, and do not actually have experience in carrying out any phenomenological research. We will come to see that

---

[4] By "anthropology" I will always be referring to *sociocultural* anthropology of the American and European traditions, and not the *philosophical anthropology* to which Husserl and other philosophers address comments, the latter being an entirely separate discipline within philosophy and theology (see Lombo and Russo 2014).

the linchpin of doing phenomenology and effectively applying it to ethnographic issues requires becoming a *mature contemplative*—that is, becoming skilled at altering one's own state of consciousness to what Husserl called the "phenomenological attitude." Because I came to Husserlian phenomenology via a circuitous route before I had read a word of Husserl's writing, I will have to treat the reader to a tidbit of autobiography that, trust me, will make sense in the long run.

It is my contention that combining Husserlian phenomenology with evolutionary and neurobiological approaches to consciousness produces a solid standpoint to explore how evolution resulted in a primate with a complex brain that is exquisitely oriented toward *adaptation*[5] to its environing world. The relevance of Husserl's discoveries placed in an evolutionary and ecological interpretive frame amounts to a powerful account of how mind and world interpenetrate and continues the work of such giants as Jakob von Uexküll (1864-1944), James J. Gibson (1904-1979), and Roger Barker (1903-1990) in understanding the relationship between experience of the world and action in the world (see also Fuster 2002, 2014, Hurley 1998, B. Smith 1997, 2001).

At a certain point (Chapter 7) I will introduce a theory about how and why hominins became extreme "culture-bearers" and language speakers. Much of what we discuss before then is fundamental to comprehending the theory and its repercussions. As an enticement perhaps, I will be arguing that hominin evolution reached a watershed era when the expanding cognitive capacity of the brain endangered sociality and the adaptive advantages of social cooperation and action. But a lot of water must pass under that bridge before we can cross it.

INTRODUCING THE SENSORIUM AND SOME INITIAL AXIOMS

Humanity's ability to adapt to its various environing worlds by way of sensory experience and behavior comes at the end of a lengthy and ongoing process of evolution that began some 14 billion years ago with the Big Bang, eventually leading to the formation of our planet Earth four-plus billion years ago, and to the beginnings of Earthly life over 3

---

[5] When I say that something is "adaptive," or speak of "adaptation," I intend the strict biogenetic meaning of the term. To adapt is to survive selective pressures.

billion years ago. Almost from the emergence of life, animals developed physiological structures by means of which they experienced their species-specific environing worlds and responded to events in the real world with themselves at the center of things. Biology is notoriously conservative of mechanisms that work well, and sensory faculties were built, retained, and evolved to ever more complex systems for detecting objects and events in the environment and using such information to act adaptively within the world. The evolution of sensory systems is a fascinating study in itself, and I would recommend Ivan R. Schwab's remarkable book, *Evolution's Witness: How Eyes Evolved* (2012), in which the author traces the evolution of the visual sense from its inception in single cell organisms that may have had photoreceptive capacities over 3 billion years ago. This grand perspective reminds me of physicist John Wheeler's wonderful cosmogram depicting this entire process of evolution from the Big Bang to the universe's self-reflection at the present moment (see Figure 2).

With evolution of sentience, a process no doubt occurring all over the universe, *the cosmos becomes aware of itself.* Whether we live on Earth or on some exoplanet orbiting a star in a far galaxy, we sentient beings are the universe organizing its material into systems of self-awareness and environmental-awareness of those bits of the universe that most concern us in our perpetual struggle to adapt, survive and promote our kind—our species-specific environing worlds (Von Uexküll 1909).

Each of us is an organism that is designed to do two things: (1) Adapt to our environing world by way of sensory experience, memory, feeling, cognition, and action, and (2) maintain a viable internal organization and functions requisite to remaining an organism (Piaget 1971). In other words, our individual challenge is to simultaneously find sustenance without becoming sustenance for other organisms, and we have to use some of the energies we ingest to grow, maintain, and repair our internal organs and their functions. One of the main mechanisms for carrying out both operations is our stream of conscious experience. In this respect, we are no different than any other animal on this planet, or any other planet for that matter.

Our best information from the neurosciences indicates that the brain is neither "hardwired" or totally "neuroplastic" with respect to childhood or adult neural development. Rather, we inherit structures

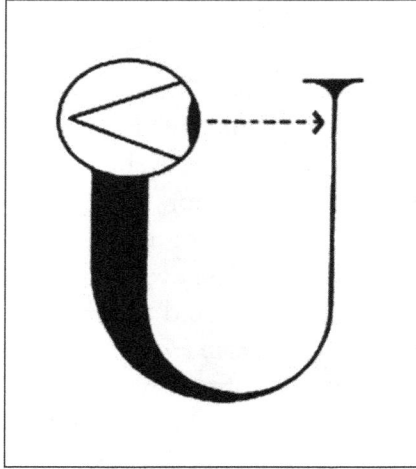

Figure 2. John Wheeler's Self-Perceiving Universe. The universe is formed in the upper right with the Big Bang and eventually evolves living beings who are able to witness the universe while being themselves a part of the universe. Reproduced with alteration and with permission (Wheeler 1983, Laughlin, McManus and d'Aquili 1990: 236).

that begin life as an initial platform for environmental and social learning, and that all structures are plastic to some extent depending upon the developmental stage and environmental contingencies (see Fox, Calkins and Bell 1994). When we speak of brain or neural plasticity, we are usually referring to *synaptic* plasticity—that is, changes in the structure and organization of synapses, the feature of neural cells that allow electrochemical transmissions between neurons (Mateos-Aparicio and Rodríguez-Moreno 2019). There has been a tendency among some neuroanthropologically inclined writers to over-emphasize the extent and fluidity of neuroplasticity, thus seeming to biologically support cultural constructivist accounts of human variation (Bartra 2014, Lende and Downey 2012, Prat 2022). In my opinion, the neuroscience data do not support their views. In contradiction to the erroneous, but still very popular view of William James that the baby's sensory consciousness is a "booming, buzzing confusion," babies are in fact born with a well-ordered sensory reality already there, and a reasonably competent perceptual learning system (Arterberry and Kellman 2016. Slater 2002). Moreover, humans are not unique in exhibiting synaptic plasticity. Indeed, plasticity is characteristic of the development of nervous systems in all animals with brains. Moreover, there are limitations to plasticity in whatever network or region of the brain it is found—i.e., no part of a normal nervous system is continuously or totally plastic. In addition, neural systems tend to exhibit *critical periods* of enhanced plasticity during their development (Kolb, Harker and Gibb 2017). Much of plasticity during development is biogenetically predetermined in anticipation of an "expected environment," and violations of expected conditions can lead to untoward neurophysiological consequences (Nelson and Gabard-Durnam 2020).

Regarding the neural structures of sensory experience, I will be following the lead of Horace Barlow and John Mollon in their hugely influential book, *The Senses* (1982) and agree with them in assuming as axiomatic the following propositions about perception formulated by Horace Barlow (1972: 380-381; labels altered, my additions in brackets):

Proposition 1: Neurons are fundamental. A description of the activity of a single nerve cell which is transmitted to and influenced by other nerve cells, and of that cell's response to such influences, is complete enough for functional understanding of the nervous system. [With the possible exception of the role played by so-called support cells, which at the moment is poorly understood,] there is nothing else necessary to account for how the brain controls sensory input, cognition, and behavior.

Proposition 2: Neural systems are hierarchically organized. At progressively higher levels in sensory pathways, information about the physical stimulus is carried by progressively fewer active neurons. The sensory system is thus organized to achieve as complete a representation [of the environing world] as possible with the minimum number of active neurons.

Proposition 3: Sensory neurons are activated by redundant patterns in the world. Trigger features of neurons are matched to the redundant features of sensory stimulation to achieve greater completeness and economy of representation. This selective responsiveness is determined by the sensory stimulation to which neurons have been exposed, as well as by genetic factors operating during development. [It is by this mechanism that the organism *samples* energies in the environing world.]

Proposition 4: Patterns of neural activity at each level trigger those above them. Just as physical stimuli directly cause receptors to initiate neural activity, so the active high-level neurons directly and simply cause the elements of our perception. [This is the mechanism of *penetration*.]

Proposition 5: The more intense the neural activity, the greater certainty that the stimulus is real. The frequency of neural impulses codes subjective certainty: a high impulse frequency in a given neuron corresponds to a high degree of confidence that the cause of the percept is present in the external world.

In every animal there is a neural system where the animal's sensory representation of its environing world all comes together. In animals with brains, that place is constituted by organizations of neural cells or networks. The technical term for that place is the *sensorium*, about which I will have a lot to say. The sensorium has been called the "seat" of sensation, the place to which energetic impressions from the external world are conveyed and perceived. The sensorium can also refer to the entire sensory apparatus of the body. In medicine, the "sensorium" refers to those structures that may be injured producing aberrations of perception. Like many terms in physical science, "sensorium" and "sensation" derive from the Latin *sensus*, meaning "the faculty of perceiving." It is a time-honored term in science that dates back to Newton and beyond (see Connolly 2014).

Sensorium is considered fundamental, real, and experienceable for the purposes of the current work and is most likely located in the prefrontal cortex where cross-modal sensory information is integrated with cognitions, memory, emotions, and motor responses and social cooperation (Brown, Lau and LeDoux 2019, Fuster and Bressler 2012, LeDoux 2020b, LeDoux and Brown 2017, Miller and Cohen 2001, Picton, Alain and McIntosh 2002, Rolls 2018, Schmidt and Polleux 2022, Senkowski *et al.* 2008, Tang, Shin and Jadhav 2021, Zoh, Chang and Crockett 2022). The prefrontal cortex is profusely interconnected with the posterior secondary sensory association areas, as it is with limbic structures mediating emotion (including fear learning), hippocampus mediating memory, inferior parietal areas mediating concept formation, and motor areas mediating behavior (Arbib, Érdi and Szentagothai 1998, Chen *et al.* 2021, Fuster 1993, 2002, 2015, LeDoux 2020b, LeDoux and Brown 2017, Machado *et al.* 2010, Stuss and Benson 1986, and various sources in Stuss and Knight 2002). This hypothesis makes sense as the prefrontal cortex of our brain is the place where our conscious experience "comes together" *in toto* (see Kapoor *et al.* 2022, Xu *et al.* 2022 for experimental support for this hypothesis).

For our purposes, the sensorium will usually refer to the totality of neural systems that mediate our *conscious* sensory experiences, whether or not we are perceiving objects in the environing world "outside," or perceiving imagery generated internally within the brain (fantasy, dream). Our sensorium portrays the page in front of you as you gaze at it, and it also portrays the afterimage of the page if you close your eyes. Your sensorium is quite active in generating dream imagery, as well as hallucinations, psychedelic imagery, creative imagery, and fantasies. In a word, *the multi-modal movie that is your world of experience is mediated by your sensorium.* Your sensorium does not depend upon extrinsic sensory input from sense receptors to produce scenes in the movie, for intrinsic stimulation may come from elsewhere in the brain. After all, this is how the unconscious layers of the psyche express themselves in dreams, fantasies, and memories.

We know that several kinds of information come together in each moment of our experience, information that is processed in different areas of the brain nearly simultaneously. Patterns of sensory activity at the periphery—from the retinae of the eyes, the cochlea of the ear, pressure receptors in the skin, chemoreceptors in the mouth and nose—are sent inwards toward the brain and to the cortex such that topological organization is retained at each level. In vision, the spatial relations in the environing world are retained as *retinotopic* mapping which is projected inwards to the primary visual association areas in each cerebral hemisphere. Vision is our dominant sense, and the retina of each of our eyes has roughly 110 million photoreceptor cells that send gigabytes of information into the brain each moment (Schwab 2012: 241). For the auditory sense, the pattern of frequencies detected by the hair cells of the cochlea are retained *tonotopically* as they are projected into the brain to the primary auditory association area in the temporal cortex. The sensory system is thus designed to operate upon patterns impressed upon our senses that penetrate inwards in such a veridical way that those patterns act as keys to unlock apperceptive, cognitive, affective, intuitive, and motor associations which are the "meaning" of the patterns.

OUTLINING THE BOOK

In Chapter Two, I will introduce the reader to Husserlian neurophenomenology by summarizing Husserl's project in general terms and show how these methods can be combined with neuroscience. The emphasis of the chapter will be to impress upon the reader who is only casually, if at all, familiar with Husserl's work that we are not dealing with just another brilliant philosopher who dispenses learned wisdom. In fact, in this book I will avoid philosophizing, even when Husserl happens to be the philosophizer. In my opinion, Husserl's great contribution to science is in his unique introspective method of exploring and describing experience from the inside-out. Husserl was a profound contemplative, and in this book, we are interested in what he found out about experience and how we can replicate his efforts in a way that can be utilized in building a scientific anthropology, as well as allied disciplines. The chapter will clarify several issues including why Husserl was able to carry out contemplative work without first using calming techniques to quiet and center his mind—a process that most of us have to pass through before we are able to enter that phenomenological "attitude" so fundamental to Husserlian methods. We will also discuss why philosophizing alone will not avail us much in grounding any science, and we will begin to sketch in Husserl's model of "intentional acts" within which he unpacks sensory essences and universal processes of consciousness. We will briefly introduce some of Husserl's main concepts such as epoché, reduction, intentionality, noema and noesis, intuition, and embodiment of experiencing.

Chapter Three is possibly the most important chapter in the book, for what I try to do is show the reader how to accomplish the state of consciousness requisite to performing phenomenological research. It is the *failure* to follow Husserl's lead into that meditative state that hinders many of Husserl's critics who, because they are not meditators, much less mature contemplatives, typically misconstrue what Husserl was on about. Husserl's task was simply to reach a state of consciousness within which he could study the universal essential structures that ground all of human knowledge, be that knowledge scientific or "pre-scientific." I will proceed in this chapter to move from exercise to exercise illustrating how Husserl's principal method, the "pure phenomenological reduction," is accomplished. The exploration of "pure" phenomenology in this chapter will be limited to sensory experiences excluding those experiences involving other people. It is fair to say that *if the reader cannot follow these steps, they will be very limited in how well they can comprehend Husserl's project and his results, as well as the results of other contemplative phenomenologists who followed Husserl's lead.*

Chapter Four moves us into Husserl's phenomenology of intersubjectivity and the hugely important concept of the "lifeworld." This "turn" in Husserl's project is perhaps of greater interest to anthropologists, although basically the same contemplative methods are used in both "pure" and intersubjective reductions, so this chapter should be considered a follow-on from the previous "how it's done" chapter. We will discuss how we include the experience of the Other into our meditations, and via that route we learn that we share the same a priori world with other humans, regardless of cultural background. When we reduce our experience of the Other, we find that at root is the experience of empathy, about which we now have ample neuropsychological research that gets us into "mirror neuron" networks of the brain. It is clear from both Husserlian phenomenology and from neuroscience that we humans have social brains that are "wired" to perceive the Other as "like-me"—a fellow "monad" within a "community of monads."

Chapter 5 takes up the phenomenology of "qualia," or to retain Husserl's terminology, the *hyle*. A fundamental distinction is made in direct experience of primordially given sensory perception between the form of objects and the qualia or hyle that "fill up" the forms—i.e., sounds, colors, brightness, textures, odors, tastes, etc. In Husserlese, the hyle constitutes the "matter" that fills forms. We know from neurophysiological research that information about form and information about hyle are processed in separate parallel cortical areas. I also carry our explorations further than intended by Husserl by addressing the "atomic" question of how sensory hyle is constructed by the brain, not just by the human brain, but by all animal brains. Here I begin to introduce the evolutionary pressures that assured that the a priori sensory world and species-typical lifeworld optimized concordance with reality.

Chapter 6 continues from the previous chapter to show how the brainmind structures the perception of duration. We will see that Husserl showed how the naïve, natural attitude experience of the temporal "now" is really a melding of the recent past, the real now-point and anticipated near future experience. The real now fades into the past but is retained in short term memory while the system "feeds forward" into the future by way of intuitive anticipations. Within the phenomenological attitude, however, the contemplative can easily discern the past and future bits within the intentional act, bracketing them, and leaving for study the real now-point, the now-moment. Our human ability to anticipate the future, and in some cases predict the causal relationship between events in the past and the now moment and the now moment and anticipated now moments are conducive to the constitution of plans which bind time into chunks with plan formulation at one end and goals at the other.

Chapter 7 marks a pivotal shift in our discussion, for it combines Husserl's efforts with a theory of mine that explains why humans have language and other animals do not—namely the theory of the "crisis of expanding consciousness." But more on that later. The chapter recognizes the importance of the evolution of signs and symbols in hominin phylogeny and applies Husserl's methods to uncovering the essential structures of symbolic acts. We come to see why we are called the "symbolic species" with a "symbolic brain." It becomes clear from the reduction that all intentional acts of consciousness are essentially a symbolic process. The sensory object "penetrates" through neural tracts into the cognitive, affective and memory networks of the brainmind to become fully meaningful.

Lived experience is chockablock with knowledge. In order to adapt to the world, it is insufficient that the brainmind portray mere sensuous things. As we see in Chapter 8, the things must be rendered meaningful in order for appropriate judgments and actions to be assigned. All knowledge for Husserl is subjective, that is, objectivity is an accomplishment of subjectivity. Subjective knowing is rooted in intuition. Husserl began his career as a logician and mathematician (e.g., Husserl 2003[1887-1901]). He was looking for the roots of logic in experience. This led him later to broaden his scope of inquiry to all knowledge and the structures of knowing, including thought, reason, and conceptualization.

Chapter 9 begins our expansion of Husserlian methods applied to alternative states of consciousness, some of which cause us to discuss what Husserl called "limiting" problems. We begin by looking at his conception and phenomenology of the unconscious. He was influenced, as was his contemporary Sigmund Freud, by the psychology and philosophy of his day. The unconscious for Husserl was the place conscious material "sinks into" out of awareness. Moreover, he was aware of hidden brainmind functions that rarely if at all become conscious, and obviously if the data are unconscious, pure phenomenological methods become limited. We will see that Husserl's findings are more congruent with Carl Jung's understanding of the unconscious than with Freud's. In particular, dream experiences offer us a wealth of material for phenomenologically exploring image consciousness.

Chapter 10 continues our discussion of limit problems and states of consciousness, and the value of Husserlian methods in the study of transpersonal experiences. This is another area of intersection between doing phenomenology and enriching our understanding of issues relevant to anthropology. There is a growing consensus that the origins of religious institutions across cultures are to be found in lived experiences, especially experiences had in extraordinary states of mind. We will examine how different societies value transpersonal states and see how far Husserl's methods can apply in those situations, and in particular dreams, absorption states, and so-called mystical experiences.

Our final substantive Husserlian discussion before wrapping up, Chapter 11, is about Husserl's engagement with natural axiology, that is with the ethical and aesthetic attitudes. Both require the phenomenology of value. We will see that applying the epoché to ethical (moral) issues reduces experience to the essences involved in evaluation within the intentional act, as is also the case with aesthetic judgments. In many societies, ethics and beauty are experientially and conceptually linked. Husserl's perspective supports the view that "axiology" is not merely a type of subdiscipline of philosophy, but that it is a natural and culturally universal process.

We summarize the important elements of Husserlian neurophenomenology in the concluding Chapter 12 and relate them back to bolstering a science of anthropology, especially an anthropology grounded in the neuroethnology of the senses. We will scrutinize how Husserl dealt with "culture" in a way that can be used to redefine the concept without the historical baggage of the erroneous "culture all the way down" bias. The chapter closes with some suggestions as to how to operationalize Husserlian methods in the ethnographic setting, a much-needed corrective both to integrate phenomenology into ethnographic fieldwork and to eliminate the ethnocentric biases found in Husserlian and other types of phenomenology.

CHAPTER TWO

Edmund Husserl's Project

One of the main virtues of phenomenology—though many there may be—is that phenomenology is an opening to "the matters themselves." This requires of those practicing phenomenology a flexibility of mind, and a genuine open disposition to follow the course of the phenomena as they give themselves, no matter how they give themselves. Certainly, this does not mean that one just talks about the things willy-nilly, as if this openness were arbitrary speculation about whatever comes to mind; there is a rigor to phenomenological methodology.

– Anthony J. Steinbock, (2017: ix)

Having reached Coutances, we entered an omnibus to go to some place or other. At the moment when I put my foot on the step, the idea came to me, without anything in my former thoughts seeming to have paved the way for it, that the transformations I had used to define the Fuchsian functions were identical with those of non-Euclidean geometry.

– Henri Poincaré, *Science and Method* (1914[1908])

I have written a great deal about various approaches and methods for applying phenomenology both in the context of transpersonal anthropology and within the approach Professor Jason Throop and I have called *cultural neurophenomenology* (see e.g., Laughlin 1988a, 1992a, 1994a, 2011, 2020a; Laughlin, McManus and d'Aquili 1990: 24-33; Laughlin and Throop 2006, 2008). Along the way I have offered examples of exercises and thought experiments to illustrate my points. All along the way I have known that only those readers who had accrewed direct experience of contemplation through one practice or another would fully comprehend what I was discussing.

To put it bluntly, and in philosopher Don Ihde's words: *"Without doing phenomenology, it may be practically impossible to understand phenomenology"* (2012: 3). This is as much the case for Husserlian phenomenology as for, say, Buddhist *vippassana* meditation or any other esoteric contemplative path leading to enlightenment (or the truth of things). There are of course many phenomenologies to choose from (see Kockelmans 1967; Hanna, Wilkinson and Givens 2017) and they range from shorthand for "paying attention to experience" and "becoming more aware of the body," through experience-oriented metaphysics and philosophical discussions of phenomenological issues, to one form or another of full blown disciplined contemplation. I am only interested in the contemplative phenomenologists, *for talking about phenomenology is a long way from doing phenomenology* (Albertazzi 2018, Laughlin 2020a). In this book, I specifically exclude the phenomenological philosophies of Heidegger, Sartre, and Derrida, among others, none of whom were mature contemplatives and all of whom, despite their lack of the requisite contemplative abilities, rejected to one extent or another the methods of Husserl's pure phenomenology (see Inkpin 2016: 12; Lee 2010). I may rankle my reader by the strictness of this course, but proceeding in this way will: (1) allow me to discuss Husserlian phenomenology more fully, (2) result in a shorter book, (3) avoid getting bogged down in philosophical rhetoric and debates, and (4) allow me to make my points with the reader's full participation—full participation by actually *doing* phenomenology while reading about phenomenology.[6]

EDMUND HUSSERL'S PROJECT

As I made clear in the Introduction, the anthropology of experience and the senses cries out for a *contemplative* phenomenology which naturally

---

[6] Please keep in mind that most of what passes for phenomenology in anthropology and sociology is either of the *hermeneutic* variety (e.g., "phenomenology of interpretation;" Conroy 2003) or of the "put yourself in the other guy's shoes" approach (Gieser 2018, Jackson 1996, Knibbe and Versteeg 2008). These perspectives are useful as intellectual and methodological strategies in "doing" fieldwork, especially in carrying out "participant observation" in the ethnographic sense, as well as grounding consciousness in the body, but it is not "doing" phenomenology in the Husserlian contemplative sense, which is what will solely concern me in this book (see Albertazzi 2018, Ihde 2012, Inkpin 2016: 12; Laughlin 2020a, Lee 2010).

impels us toward the phenomenology of Edmund Husserl (1859-1938).[7]
Husserl's project was and still is radical. He intended nothing less than
to found a new science:

> A new fundamental science, pure phenomenology, has developed
> within philosophy. This is a science of a thoroughly new type and
> endless scope. It is inferior in methodological rigor to none of
> the modern sciences. All philosophical disciplines are rooted in
> pure phenomenology, through whose development, and through
> it alone, they obtain their proper force. Philosophy is possible as a
> rigorous science at all only through pure penomenology. (Husserl
> 1981[1917]: 10)

Husserl's intentions are clearly set out in his article "Philosophy as
Rigorous Science" (Husserl 2002[1910]), in his set of lectures from 1902-
1903 published in a short book as *The Idea of Phenomenology* (Husserl
1999), his book *Ideas: General Introduction to Pure Phenomenology*
(commonly called *Ideas I*; Husserl 1982[1913]: 41-47), and is described
as a "new science" that reveals and analyses the essential structures
of "pure experience". As Czech philosopher Jan Patočka (1907-1977)
described Husserl's project so succinctly:

> Husserl defined his phenomenology as a fundamental
> philosophical discipline, a *prima philosophia*, with the help of
> the idea of the phenomenological reduction. That is a distinctive
> methodological approach aimed at rendering all of our experience,
> of things, of ourselves, of others, accessible in the full scope of its
> significance just as it naturally functions, as it puts us in contact
> with all such realities. Experience, that is, is to be seized in its
> primordial, original meaning, *without any interpretation, without
> any theorizing*. Our experience, on the other hand, contains
> all assertions and theories within it. If it is to be seized in its

---

[7] If you wish to read about Husserl's life and his relations with other thinkers who
influenced him and whom he influenced, see Husserl 1997, Kockelmans 1967: 17-20,
Moran 2000, 2005: Chap. 1, Moran and Cohen 2012: Introduction, Smith 2013:
Chap. 1, Spiegelberg 1983, Tougas 2013.

integrity, then such seizing of our experience must not presuppose any theory of either what experience or of what the world really is. Everything has to flow solely from following our experience itself. (Patočka 1998: 89)

Phenomenology on Husserl's account is a discipline of inquiry, a direct contemplative *seeing* experience as it unfolds and passes away within our stream of consciousness—*as it really is*. When we do this work, we find, as Husserl claimed, that phenomenology amounts to an *eidetic science*; the term "eidetic" deriving from the Greek *eidos* or "essence" (see Welton 2000: Chap. 2). Phenomenology is also an a priori science—that is, it is not "empirical" in the sense of collecting facts from scientific research tools (participant observation, questionaires, interview schedules, fMRI protocols, statistical analyses, measurement devices, etc.), and testing ideas in light of consensus statements of facts:

> …as when [Husserl] talks about the dangers of modern scientific methods and methodologies when they take on "typical, learnable, and habitually exercised forms. That represents progress, but also a danger: ever greater intellectual work is saved, but ever greater portions of thinking come to lack insight through a mechanization of the method: external rationality, the confirmation through mutually confirming results no longer corresponds to inner rationality, the comprehension of the inner sense and goals of such thinking and the fundamental methodological elements" (p. 6). (Nenon 2013b: 232-233; Husserl quote from *Natur und Geist:Vorlesungen Sommersemester 1919, Husserliana Materialien Band IV*).

By contrast with highly instrumental methods used especially by the "natural" and "empirical" sciences, phenomenology is an approach that seeks a first-hand introspective exploration and description of the essential structures of experience leading to an analysis of essences upon the basis of which scientists can build inductive theories about the world inside and outside the body.

> At every step the [phenomenological] analysis is an analysis of essence and an investigation of universal states of affairs that are

constituted within immediate intuition. The entire investigation is thus an a priori investigation—but not, of course, in the sense of mathematical deduction. What distinguished it from the "objectifying" a priori sciences is its method and its goal. *Phenomenology carries out its clarafications in acts of seeing, determining, and distinguishing sense.* It compares, it distinguishes, it connects, it places in relation, it divides into parts, it separates off moments. But it does all this in the act of pure seeing. (Husserl 1999: 43)

What I am going to do in this chapter is follow Husserl's lead about how we can do "pure phenomenology" in such a way as to ground a phenomenological anthropology (Albertazzi 2018, Spiegelberg 1975: Chap. 14). But first let me share how I got into Husserlian studies in the first place, for that has direct influence upon how I read and interpret Husserl's methods.

HOW I CAME TO DO HUSSERLIAN PHENOMENOLOGY

My experience with contemplation ranges over decades of practice and a variety of systems, both Eastern and Western, including Buddhist *vipassana*, Tibetan and Japanese *vajrayana*, and Zen, as well as esoteric Tarot and Kabbalah, Western Mysteries group meditations and other phenomenologies of various sorts. Working through the Eastern systems was fortuitous, for I had become what Gene d'Aquili, John McManus and I called a *mature contemplative* (d'Aquili, Laughlin and McManus 1993; Laughlin 2020a, Laughlin, McManus and d'Aquili 1990: Chap. 11) as a consequence of Buddhist practice. When I later began, not just to read *about* Edmund Husserl's phenomenology, but to read Husserl himself, his method was immediately transparent to me. Like all phenomenologies, it is far more complex to talk about, describe or teach than it is to realize in practice. It is one of the limitations of language that words must operate via concepts, and concepts are not the truth of the nature of mind—the finger pointing at the moon is not the moon itself, notes an ancient Buddhist parable. Whether the methods be those of Tibetan *mahamudra* or *dzogchen* (Schmidt and Tweed 2012), Theravada *vippassana* (Paravahera Vajiranana Mahathera 1987), esoteric Kabbalah (Matt 1995), or Husserlian pure phenomenology, when the core insights about the nature of mind intuitively arise and are realized by the aware mind, the "seeing" is *always* simpler than the language of the texts or teachings leading to the insights. As the old saw goes, the realization of the true nature of mind is closer to you than your nose.

Anyhow, I found it easy to slice through the stilted language of the English translations and antiquated jargon of Husserl's *Cartesian Meditations, Ideas I*, and *The Crisis of European Sciences and Transcendental Phenomenology* and to parse out his intentions and "pith instructions"[8] for those wishing to do phenomenology themselves. Equally interesting was the ease with which I could separate the mature contemplatives from the naïve phenomenologists who read Husserl casually and who have critiqued his project without actually learning his methods. This is not to say that Husserl's intentions were the same as the Buddha's or the Kabbalah's—far from it (see Laycock 1994, Lusthaus 2014). While the Buddha was on about uncovering the causes of suffering and the causes of liberation, and esoteric Kabbalah a unity with the godhead, Husserl founded a movement and method for making philosophy scientific, and sciences grounded in the direct experience of the real world (see Husserl 1981[1941], 2002[1910], Farber 1943: 3, Nenon 2013b).

At the time I first seriously encountered Husserl, it was a commonplace claim that Husserl had not studied Buddhism, or the Pali Canon, for he never mentions Buddhism in his major writings. Still, a few scholars had already acknowledged the similarities and differences between Husserlian phenomenology and various forms of Indian philosophy (e.g., Mohanty 1972). It turns out, however, that Husserl did engage with the Buddhist literature—the Pali Canon had just been translated into German—and even wrote a brief note expressing his feelings about what he had read. Thanks to Fred Hanna (1995), we have an English translation of that 1925 note entitled "On the Teachings of Gotama [Gautama] Buddha."

---

[8] "Pith instructions" (Skt.: *upadeśa*) are narratives or "manuals" that show how to accomplish something, and not merely talk about that something. Pith instructions about meditations show you how to go about doing the meditations.

In that note Husserl seems to thoroughly identify with the aims and methods of Buddhist phenomenology:

> That Buddhism—insofar as it speaks to us from pure original sources—is a religio-ethical discipline for spiritual purification and fulfillment of the highest stature—conceived of and *dedicated to an inner result of a vigorous and unparalleled, elevated frame of mind, will soon become clear to every reader who devotes themselves to the work.* Buddhism is comparable only with the highest form of the philosophical and religious spirit of our European culture. It is now our task to utilize this (to us) completely new Indian spiritual discipline which has been revitalized and strengthened by this contrast. (Hanna 1995: 367; emphasis added)

Husserl's methods of contemplation—"bracketing," "reduction," the *epoché*, returning "to the things," and so forth—were already familiar to me, for I had experienced them all before, but encountered under different labels (see Laughlin 2020a). Indeed, as Hanna (1995: 366) reports: "Eugen Fink once told Dorion Cairns 'that the various phases of Buddhistic self-discipline were essentially phases of phenomenological reduction'" (Cairns 1976: 50). This statement is especially significant since Fink was Husserl's chief assistant and was considered by Husserl to be his most trusted interpreter (see e.g., Fink 1981a, 1995; see also Bruzina 2004). It is thus also significant that Husserl considered the effort of and dedication to attaining the phenomenological attitude inevitably impacts the contemplative's psychological development. Again, as Hanna (1995: 369) notes: "Husserl claimed side benefits of phenomenological seeing in terms of self-exploration and self-development. He said that the insights gained from performing the transcendental phenomenological method of seeing brings about 'a complete personal transformation'" (Husserl 1970[1936]: 137). Neuropsychological research has confirmed this kind of permanant alteration of the organization of consciousness in long-term meditators (see e.g., Kilpatrick *et al.* 2011).

HOW ABOUT CALMING BEFORE DOING PHENOMENOLOGY?

Think about this for a moment. Imagine you are a Zen monk sitting and staring at a blank wall for two hours. Would you be able without any training to retain your focus on the wall without giving in to the myriad distractions demanding your attention—the sounds around you that come and go, the pain in your joints, the itch in the middle of your back, the feeling of boredom and anxiety to be up and doing something, the incessant chatter of the voice and images in your head? Well, if you are honest with yourself you would probably answer that your mind would be all over the place, everywhere *but* the blank wall in front of you. This is the irony of Zen, it is at the same time the simplest of contemplative exercises and the hardest to accomplish for most of us. It is difficult for us because we do not know how to calm and center our brainmind in preparation for the task at hand, namely, controling our awareness so that real contemplation upon a single object can occur undistracted. There are traditional paintings done by Buddhist artists that depict the path of *samatha*, or calming of the mind, which begins at the bottom of the mountain with the monk running after an elephant being led by a monkey and ends with the monk riding and controling the elephant and giving the monkey a ride. The elephant is a metaphor for the mind, the monkey for the conditioned "natural attitude" mind and the monk of course for the person wishing to be liberated from suffering caused by the lack of control one has over one's mind and its habitual greed, aversion, and cultural conditioning. For most of us, contemplation is thwarted by lack of control over our minds such that disciplined contemplation requires some method of calming our mental processes before we are able to get down to work.

Thus far, I have found no reference in Husserl's writings to the need to calm the brainmind before entering the phenomenological attitude. In Eastern traditions, *samatha* ("mind-calming") is used to relax the brainmind and shut off the energies supporting distracting chatter—discursive thought, slideshow imagery, dialog with fantasy, etc. (together known as the *Saṅkhāra*, mental "formations," in Buddhist psychology)—so that singleminded focus (*vipassana*) upon the object of contemplation (breath, heart, belly, passing of sensations, etc.) becomes progressively easier to sustain. Clearly, Husserl was one of those rare individuals who could carry out mindfulness contemplation without precursor calming exercises. My hunch is that this ability served him well in the contemplation of experience, but was a stumbling block in getting his method across to those who are too involved dialoging with their internal chatter to get the point of the discipline—and here I am thinking specifically of Heidegger, Sartre, Schutz, and Merleau-Ponty among many other less famous critics (Crowell 2013: 31-32), most of whom never studied with him, and those who did, like Heidegger, did not keep up the work long enough to realize and perfect the phenomenological attitude. Please forgive me for sounding arrogant, but what I am saying is nothing but the bare fact of the matter.

Most meditators must calm the brainmind and its formations before we have any chance of entering this attitude. A simple exercise will make this clearer to you. Sit quietly, breathing naturally through your nose and mouth (neither blocked) and let the discursive thoughts, subvocalizations, feelings, objects, desires, plans, fantasies—all the mentally constructed distractions in the moment—arise and pass away in the flow of your consciousness. Clinging to no thought, feeling, inclination, whatever—just be in the moment and watch how quickly your body and mind relax. With dilligent practice, your level of calm can become deeper than you thought possible. As the mind calms and formations slow down and eventually cease altogether, it becomes easier to perform phenomenological studies. This is the Eastern way of entering phenomenology. An agitated and distractible mind simply cannot realize Husserl's epoché (see below). In Buddhist phenomenology (see Laughlin 2020a; Lusthaus 2014; Suzuki 1970; Austin 1998) it is recognized that a period of disciplined tranquility meditation (*samatha*) usually (although not always) precedes contemplation (*vipassana*; see Thanissaro 1998), and performing phenomenological reductions is distinctly a contemplative effort.

I will be suggesting that you try some exercises I mention along the way, and if you find them difficult, do not despair. *Try calming meditation before you try performing any of Husserl's methods.* I suspect some of you will find doing phenomenology easy, but many more of you will struggle to maintain focus at the level of intense awareness necessary to perform a pure phenomenological reduction. One reason for the struggle is that the brainmind is designed to feedforward, rather than focus on the now (Soltani and Koechlin 2022). What I mean is that our natural way of going about things is acting in the world *in anticipation* of what will happen next. We naturally operate on plans—how to walk from here to there, how to get food, how to satisfy urges, scanning for interesting or threatening events. Meanwhile in the background our brainmind is generating noise and chatter, dialoging with fantasied happenings, conversations, problems to be solved. Doing the phenomenological reduction takes us into the actual now moment of experience, the "real" now, what is right before our senses *now* (Chapter 6). To maintain this now-orientation requires a certain level of calm centeredness in the body and mind. Thus, I am adding this preparatory step to the reduction process that we will discuss in the next chapter, for its necessity is immediately obvious to any practitioner of Buddhist phenomenology. The simple fact is, the more excited the body gets, the more fragmented becomes the brainmind. There is no such thing as a calm mind in an excited body, nor an excited mind in a calm body.

In a sense, I set you up, dear reader, for a self-test. If you wish to practice phenomenology and are not able to accomplish a sustained focus such as I described above, then you must learn to "calm the formations"—relax your brainmind so that you can stop the chatter, scatter, and anxiety sufficient to do the work. There are all sorts of tranquility methods out there: hatha yoga, autogenic training, breath work, tai chi, so forth. Take your pick. I will leave the calming method up to you. Henceforth, I will assume you are capable of chilling-out sufficiently to follow the exercises that I will suggest as we go along. We will return to this issue in later chapters when discussing the role of "absorption" experiences in Husserl's phenomenology of the unconscious and spirit.

DON'T WASTE TIME PHILOSOPHIZING!

I personally, in the excellent company of Husserl, find little value in philosophizing, much less calling my theoretical ruminations "phenomenology." Referring to doing the real work of investigating the life of consciousness, Husserl noted, "But there is no use in philosophizing about it from on high and veiling it even in the finest-spun thoughts, instead of forcing one's way into its huge concreteness and making it actually fruitful philosophically (1969[1929]: 244).

Husserl's phenomenology is not a scientific theory of perception. It is a method for studying and describing perception via introspection that produces data about what is happening when we experience. It is not an invitation to philosophize, although lots of professional philosophers make it their business to do so. You can easily find this kind of "phenomenological philosophizing" throughout the literature. Some of it may even be interesting to you. But no one ever realized the phenomenological attitude by merely reading about it or thinking about it, and it is the practice of phenomenology that is so valuable to science—especially to the social, psychological and behavioral sciences—as well as to developing scientists in various fields who can "see" in a contemplative way.

The trouble is, one can easily get bogged down in discussing the numerous controversies, philosophical arguments, ideological hermeneutics, and so on that punctuate the history of professional philosophy's treatment of Husserl's project. Does phenomenology lead inevitably to solipsism? Is existence more primordial than essence? What is the ontological status of essences and the hyle? What constitutes intuitive insight? What did Husserl really mean by *noesis* and *noema*? And what exactly do we mean by "phenomenology?" These and other questions too numerous to mention can be quite engaging, especially if the reader is interested in the many ways that Husserl's methods can be misread, distorted and misunderstood by those who do not practice them, but merely philosophize about them. An example might be Swedish philosopher Ulf Drobin's criticisms of Husserl's "philosophy" with respect to the *phenomenology of religion* (Fujiwara, Thurfjell and Engler 2021: 32-34). For Drobin, "phenomenology" amounts to being value-neutral when comparing the various traits present in a sample of different religions. There is nothing contemplative about his notion of phenomenology. As a result, he spends his efforts doing trait analysis, which American anthropologists will recognize in the methods of Boas and Kroeber. While this is a very valuable methodology in studying world cultures, it has nothing whatever to do with Husserl's phenomenology. Another example is David Bell's (1990: 194-197) handling of "eidetic variation" and "intuition." It is clear to me that Bell's take on Husserl's methods is philosophy, not contemplation. He shows none of the nuances that are a tipoff to the results of meditation. In short, he has not actually done the eidetic variation method to the point where he intuitively "gets it"—he just finds the method silly and moves on.

To make matters more difficult, when the notion of the *lifeworld* (Ger: *Lebenswelt*; see Husserl 1970 [1936]) is introduced into discussions, writers (e.g., Berndtsson *et al.* 2007) as often as not mangle various phenomenological concepts and lose sight of the original project, *which quite simply is to find a method by which experience of the Other can be studied and described scientifically* (Husserl 2002[1910]; see Cairns 1939 for the many results of Husserl's contemplations). Husserlian phenomenology is not a group project, but criticisms directed at his seemingly introverted approach to contemplation—indeed, contemplation is *always* a solitary pursuit, even when practiced in a group context—led him to discuss the social aspects of both beliefs about the world and the primordial sensory given, as well as empathy, intersubjectivity, and other matters that in my opinion tended to obfuscate the simplicity of his initial scientific approach, his pure phenomenology. We will get to the phenomenology of intersubjectivity later on (Chapter 4).

LEARNING TO PRIVILEGE PURE PHENOMENOLOGY BEFORE DOING SCIENCE

Before we get into the process of actually doing phenomenology, let me emphasize something that Husserl argued, but many somehow ignore or misunderstand. Phenomenology is designed not only to precede science, to ground science in the truth accessible via sensory experience, but also to critique the taken-for-granted grounds of sciences that are, after all is said and done, dependent upon perception.

> Let us make this clear to ourselves in detail. At the natural standpoint we simply *carry out* all the acts through which the world is there for us. We live naively unreflective in our perceiving and experiencing, in those thetic acts in which the unities of things appear to us, and not only appear but are given with the stamp of "presentness" and "reality." When we pursue natural science, we *carry out* reflexions ordered in accordance with the logic of experience, reflexions in which these realities,

given and taken alike, are determined in terms of thought, in which also on the ground of such directly experienced and determined transcendences fresh interfaces are drawn. At the phenomenological standpoint, acting on lines of general principle, we *tie up* the *performance* of all such cogitative theses, i.e., we "place in brackets" what has been carried out, "we do not associate these theses" with our new inquiries; instead of living *in* them and carrying *them* out, we carry out acts of *reflexion* directed towards them, and these we apprehend as the *absolute* Being which they are. We now live entirely in such acts of the second level, whose datum is the infinite field of absolute experience—*the basic field of Phenomenology.* (Husserl 1982[1913]: 155)

This is why treating pure phenomenology as just another philosophy is wrongheaded (see Johnson 1980). The intent of Husserlian phenomenology is to strip away all of the taken-for-granted-ness about the world, bundle it all up and store it in a mental closet until next it is needed, leaving the Watcher free of beliefs, ontological assumptions, instrumental methods, and other hindrances to studying their own intentional acts.

In the unbroken naïveté in which all psychology, all humanistic disciplines, all human history persists, I, the psychologist, like everyone else, am constantly involved in the performance of self-apperceptions and apperceptions of others. I can of course, in the process thematically reflect upon myself, upon my psychic life and that of others, upon my and others' changing apperceptions; I can also carry out recollections; observingly, with theoretical interest, I can carry out self-perceptions and self-recollections, and through the medium of empathy I can make use of self-apperceptions of others. I can inquire into my development and that of others; I can thematically pursue history, society's memory, so to speak—but all *such reflection* remains within transcendental naïveté; it is the performance of the transcendental world-apperception which is, so to speak, ready-made, while the transcendental correlate—i.e., the (immediately active or sedimented) functioning intentionality, which is the universal apperception, constitutive of all particular apperceptions, giving them the ontic sense of "psychic experiences (*Erlebnisse*] of this and that human being"—remains completely hidden. (Husserl 1970[1936]: 209)

The implication of this approach to understanding the roots of experience is revolutionary, both in the sense of its implications for the grounding of philosophy and the sciences in the a priori structures of experience, and in the sense of the self-transformation of the contemplative. Rest assured that as with any full-on contemplative path, Husserlian phenomenology will not only change how you understand your perceptual processes, it will inevitably change *you* (Goleman and Davidson 2017).

CONSCIOUSNESS AND INTENTIONALITY (NOESIS AND NOEMA DEFINED)

A reasonable first entre into Husserl's phenomenology is via his conception of consciousness. For Husserl, *consciousness*[9] (Ger.: *Bewusstsein*) is a broad umbrella term for all of the mental faculties involved in constituting the flow of experience through time—indeed, for Husserl time *is* consciousness. He mentions for instance the "flow" of consciousness and the "stream" of experience (see Husserl 1982[1913]: 112-116). The internal structure of consciousness is that of intentionality. That is to say, everything that "I" am aware of is constituted and organized by *eidetic laws* within my consciousness (Husserl 1970 [1900-01], II: 94-102). Elsewhere I have modeled consciousness as an n-dimensional phase space that at any given moment includes all the neural processes mediating experience, and this model seems to describe Husserl's conception of consciousness. In modern terms, experience arises in a complex entrainment of neural networks (the sensorium), which is not so much a physical location as a neural phase space—or what some neuroscientists call

---

[9] If you wish to read more about Husserl's concept of *consciousness*, see Husserl 1970 [1900-01], II: Investigation V, 1982[1913]: §34, 2008[1906-1907]: 244-258, 1973[1939]; see also Barua 2009, Giorgi 2009, Levinas 1995, Moran 2005, Natanson 1973: 13-14, Staiti 2017.

a *cortical* workspace (Mashour *et al.* 2021). The concept of the *phase space* was introduced by scientist Willard Gibbs (1839-1903) in the early twentieth century (see Nolte 2010) and is a model in which all possible states of a system are represented. The concept has been used in mathematics, mechanics and physics for decades, and has more recently been applied to the neurophysiology of functional organization and experience (e.g. Calitoiu, Oommen, and Nussbaum 2012, Laughlin 1988a, Werner 2013).

A neural phase space is made up of all the various functional areas of the nervous system that may potentially become connected to the network mediating the brain's dynamic "stream of consciousness" (see Brown, Lau and LeDoux 2019, Koch 2004, 2019). The moment-by-moment shift in consciousness is the place where sensory materials arise to meet the cognitive functions mediating the meaning of things. The prime directive of the experiencing brain is to seek out sensed patterns and then render those patterns as meaningful. Of course, we all realize that most of the mental activities of the brainmind occur outside of the stream of consciousness (i.e., they are subconscious or unconscious). Consequently, many of these processes never actually rise into consciousness.

Husserl understood that within any act of intentionality what we are aware of is never more than a tiny bit of reality, and the only bit of reality that is "determinate" within the context of our experience—all the rest of the universe is "indeterminate." One of the central terms he uses in describing the structure of consciousness is the word *act* which in modern psychological terms we call "state"—an act of consciousness is more or less the same as a state of consciousness. Acts are distinguishable (also labeled) by their qualities, functional characteristics and significant parts of an experience, all being elements within the overall intentional act. The quality of an act defines the act's general nature. Intentional acts may be judgemental, emotional, meditative, reflective, assertive, and so on (Husserl 1970 [1900-01], II: 119-122). In modern-speak, we would say that a certain state of consciousness is characterized by feeling, thought, curiosity, expression, communication, etc. When Husserl speaks of the intentional act, he is saying the same thing as if we refer to the structure(s) of a state of consciousness. To give an extreme example, what we would call a psychedelic state of consciousness, Husserl might have referred to as a psychedelic act.

The bit of reality that is determinate is given a priori as the primordial sensory data at the concrete base of experience. Borrowing from his teacher, Franz Brentano (2014[1874]; see also Bell 1990: Prolegomenon, Føllesdal 1978), Husserl's model of conscious acts is one of *intentionality*, meaning that every act of consciousness is organized around the awareness of something (Husserl 1982[1913]: 241-244, 1973[1939]: 77, 1997[1907]: 11-12).[10] In every act of perception there is an object and a *Watcher* (my term, or in Husserl-speak, an "absolute transcendental ego" or "pure ego;" see Husserl 1993[1931]: 89). This inevitable relationship is fundamental to all experience, whether the object be a sensuous thing out in the world, an idea in the mind, an act of imagination, a feeling, a sensation in the body, and so forth. The relationship may be initiated by the object in the environing world (e.g., something—a thing, event, quality—catches my attention) or by the Watcher (e.g., I desire a sip of coffee and reach for the cup). By shifting my attention to the object, however initiated, I *intend* the object and the object is *intended* by me. Moreover, the object, the "sensory given," *fulfills* my intentional act. Until I perceive the object I desire, my intention remains "empty" in Husserl's view. Indeed, an intentional act may remain empty if in fact the object it intends does not exist (I desire to ride a dragon), or is not available to me at this time (I want to drive a Maserati). This will become important when we later discuss the emptiness of signitive or expressive acts (Chapter 7). It is also important to our later discussion of lucidity of sensory experience and real-ness of the object (Chapter 5) that there is an experienced gradation of sensory fulfillment (Husserl 1970 [1900-01], II: 238-240). That is, we can experience the object vaguely, or over a short duration, or we can experience the object clearly and more richly filled with qualities and over a sustained duration. In any event, in fulfilling the intention, my mental faculties reorganize around that object as it is given in perception, including all of the essential structures that attend it and make it possible. Those essences include the causal relationships with the object's surround, its characteristic form, color, sound, etc., and all the other relationships that obtain within the *horizon* (Husserl 1982[1913]: 101-103, 1993[1931]:

---

[10] If you wish to read further about *intentionality*, see Husserl 1982[1913]: 241-244; see also Brentano 2014[1874], Gurwitsch 1967, Hanna 2013, Ihde 2012: 24-25, Kersten 1973, and Zahavi 2005: 11-13.

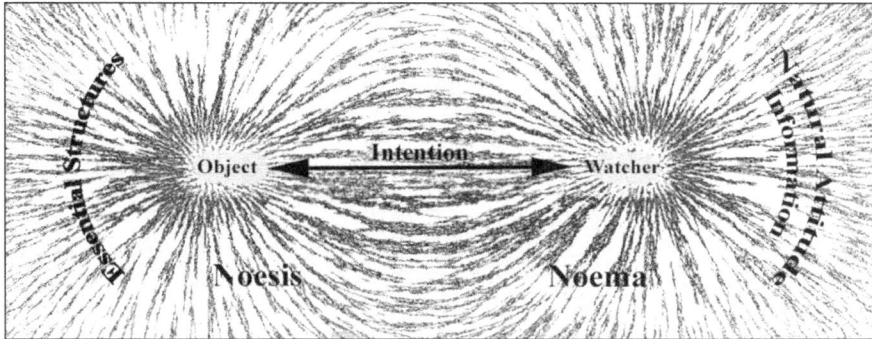

Figure 3. Intentionality. A two-dimensional model of a four-dimensional intentional act (occuring over time). The object of consciousness on the left, the Watcher (ego) on the right are in an intentional relationship. Surrounding the object are the essential structures available within the horizon of perception (form, relations, intuition). On the right are the modes (desire, interest, judging, wishing) of our intentions. The two sources of information blend to produce meaning. The object may be said to "penetrate" into the field of knowledge about the world. *Noetic* information merges with *noematic* information within the total act.

44; see also Geniusas 2012, Welton 2000) of the perceptual act, all of which are primordially given.

In the simplistic model of an intentional act in Figure 3 I have imagined the relationship between the Watcher (the pure ego) and the object as being *like* the field produced by electromagnetic waves between the two poles of a bar magnet as seen by sprinkling iron filings on a piece of paper covering the magnet. One pole is the object, the other the Watcher. Each is surrounded by and associated with information of various kinds. From the object as a primordial given is provided all the irreducible essential structures that attend the object within its horizon. In the model the horizon of the object includes all the visible and invisible structures within the boundary limits of the illustration, and that are essential to the intentional act in that moment. The horizon also includes the possibilities of alternative perceptions, other ways of encountering the object, and broadening and shifting the limits of perception (Husserl 1993[1931]: 44, Geniusas 2012, Welton 2000: Chap. 15). In the dialogue between Watcher and object the two sources of information blend, we might even say become tangled, to produce the meaning of the object in that moment. With respect to meaning, philosopher Maurice Natanson tells us:

...there is another, equally urgent side to the "I"-"object" relationship: its logical aspect. There, the meaning of the world which is chronologically prior to our existence must be disclosed and interpreted. That disclosure consists in an active dimension of phenomenological work: a building up of meaning, step by step, a putting together of elements which compose the unities of meaning through which a coherent world emerges. The primordial phenomenological stratum in which the source of that "building up" of meaning structure has its locus is a universal, pure structure in which the "becoming" of the "I"-"object" correlation has its ultimate ground. The "building up" proves to be an ordering or construction of essential elements which form the "I" and its "object" correlate. In a way the concrete life of the individual may be traced back phenomenologically to a source which is transindividual and transobjective; that source is pure subjectivity understood as the meaning-builder of the human world. (Natanson 1981: 110)

Contrary to the phenomenologically naïve constructivist view shared by many anthropologists, it is primarily the relations and structures to the left of the intentional act that provide the universal, biologically inherited information (objects, relations and intuitions)—the "eidetic morphology" (Husserl 1982[1913]: 402)—that provides the ground for the "building up" of meaning grounded in reality. The noesis includes the mechanisms in the body and nervous system—particularly the sensory systems—that ground us in the real world while much of the noema involve thoughts, ideas, judgments, etc. mediated by the brain's *cognits*; knowledge stored in memory "in the form of distributed networks of neurons of the cerebral cortex" (Fuster 2013: 62; see also Fuster 2003: 14-16, 2013: 62-71). As we blend Husserl's discoveries with modern neuroscience, we have to keep in mind that the noesis and noema are elements of the intentional act, but they are not mediated by the same neural structures. Indeed, noesis and noema can be psychodynamically dissociated in top-down intentionality. The noesis can be virtually ignored when the effort of intentionality is to bolster interpretations, beliefs, theories, etc. (see Di Gregorio *et al.* 2022, Prat 2022).

Of course, Husserl had his own way of talking about intentionality (see Hopp 2008). For him, the Watcher and the object "correlate"—as we have seen, they literally *co*-relate (the two-pointed arrow in Figure 3). He also made an important distinction within the correlative intentional act between what he called the *noematic* (meaning "what is thought" in ancient Greek) and the *noetic* ("to see, perceive" in ancient Greek) operations of sensory systems upon the genuine object (see Husserl 1982[1913]: Chap. 3, Cairns 1940, Kersten 1973, Held 2003b: 8-9). Put simply, the noema provides the idea of the thing in all its possible occurrences (I can see it, touch it, imagine it and fantasize and dream it) while the noesis is the genuine, concrete object the senses present us in the moment. The sensory object is in a sense a bundle of attributes (colors, textures, properties, forms, position, relations, intuitions, etc.) that are all concrete, objective, original, and of a piece with the whole. This bundling of attributes Husserl called the *noetic mode* of perception. The gathering up and applying to the object all the faculties of consciousness (beliefs, categories, information, uses, values, terms, emotional reactions, ontological assumptions, etc.) is the *noematic mode* of apperception (see Husserl 1980[1952]: 73-77, 1982[1913]: 282-295, Held 2003a: 37-40).

Natural intentionality is a correlation of noetic information with noematic information. If either pole changes, both sides change and the configuration of entangled noetic-noematic information[11] changes. Also, as strange as it sounds, the noema can be said to go seeking the noesis. If the urge for an update on the news enters my stream of consciousness— my "Hericlitean flux" as Husserl occasionally called it referring to its constant change—I will tune in to NPR, and the news fills my auditory perception. The noema can anticipate, seek, necessitate, require, desire *perceptive fulfillment* (or *primordial filling-out*; Husserl 1982[1913]: 398) in a concrete given yet to arise within the stream of consciousness. To put this in common-speak, I desire the news and take actions that get the news—I switch on the radio and voila! There it is. On the other hand, the noesis may insist upon the noema by popping up in my sensorium. This happens all the time when objects appear in my stream of consciousness

---

[11] When I speak of *information*, I mean the literal, physical/biochemical in-forming or re-organization of the neural tissues mediating the entire intentional act (see Maturana and Varela 1980, Varela 1979), not the specialized and more recent cybernetic meaning of the term defined originally by Bell Lab's Claude E. Shannon (see Laughlin and Throop 2006).

and demand my attention—or speaking more accurately, demand my neural processing. Indeed, that is one of the adaptive functions of consciousness, to scan for novelty and to attend objects until they become redundant by way of noematic closure.

EMBODIMENT

A mature contemplative—in the present case a practitioner who has mastered Husserl's methods through extensive practice—will inevitably reach a number of conclusions about the a priori, primordial givenness of sensory experience, including that there exists no such thing as a permanent ego, that no object of experience is independent of surrounding objects and events, that there is an ideality (eidetics) to knowing objects, that objects are experienced as wholes (gestalts or "monads") rather than a collection of observed bits, and that the primordial given is replete with intuitive insights (see Chapter 8). One of those ineluctable conclusions is that all experiences are both intentional and embodied. Interestingly, these and other conclusions are routine for practitioners of Buddhist *satipatthana* or "foundation of mindfulness" meditation because one of the first domains of essential structures revealed is that of awareness of the body: *kayanupassana*, the Pali word for body being *kaya* (Mahasi Sayadaw 1994). Considered strictly as a constituted physical "thing" in spacetime (Husserl's German term is *Körper*), my body is an object much like other concrete objects (houses, cars, keyboards), and as such is subject to causation (gravity, mass, form, causation, etc.) and enduring substantiality. This is my body in nature and as a subject of biological science and medicine (Paci 1970: 227). However, my body is also a "lived Body" (Ger.: *Leib*), a "constituted unity"—or what Jan Patočka (1998: 6th Lecture) interestingly termed a "personal situation"— that is the epicenter, orienteer, and mediator of all my experiences (Husserl 1977[1925], 1989[1952]: Chap 3).

> The Body is, in the first place, the *medium of all perception*; it is the *organ of perception* and is *necessarily* involved in all perception. In seeing, the eyes are directed upon the seen and run over its

edges, surfaces, etc. When it touches objects, the hand slides over them. Moving myself, I bring my ear closer in order to hear. Perceptual apprehension presupposes sensation-contents, which play their necessary role for constitution of the schema and, so, for the constitution of the appearances of the real things themselves. *To the possibility of experience there pertains, however, the spontaneity of the courses* of presenting acts of sensation, which are accompanied by series of kinesthetic [proprioceptive] sensations and are dependent on them as motivated: *given with the localization of the kinesthetic series in the relevant moving member of the Body is the fact that in all perception and perceptual exhibition (experience) the Body is involved as freely moved sense organ, as freely moved totality of sense organs,* and hence there is also given the fact that, on this original foundation, all that is thingly-real in the surrounding world of the Ego has its relation to the Body. (Husserl 1989[1952]: 61)

To elaborate this in neurophenomenological terms, my big-B "lived Body" (*Leib*) contains a nervous system with its sensory systems and sensorium, and all of my acts of perception are mediated by those systems. Wherever I go, there's my lived Body. My lived Body gets me where I want to go, gets me what I desire, and gets me away from anything I fear or abhor. All my interactions with, and feedforward tests of, the environing world are via my lived Body. I am constantly adjusting my Body to produce the perspective I desire (Powers 2005), or to respond to stimuli as they crop up. My lived Body is the "zero point" (Ger.: *nullpunkt*) center of perception of the environing world, as well as my proprioceptive and interoceptive awareness of my own physical interiority (my "inner attitude;" Husserl 1989[1952]: 168; see also Carvalho and Damasio 2021). It is interesting that viewed visually, our body appears as more or less a *Körper*, a "thingly-real," concrete object in the environing world. Also interestingly, upon my death, I am no longer my Body, no longer a *Leib*, no longer constituted as a "subject," but merely as a "corpse."

As Husserl demonstrates (1989[1952]: 155-156), things get really interesting if we shift focus to the tactile sensing of our Body. When I palpate the surface of my arm or belly or legs, I produce a binary sense-channel, one being my hand feeling my arm, and the other my arm feeling my hand. It does not take much effort for the contemplative to shift awareness from one to the other. Moreover, I find that my Body— the living locus of my will, my awareness, my action, and physical causality operating upon me (1989[1952]: 159-169)—is endowed with these and many other properties that do not belong to a "thingly-object." The primordial givenness of my Body includes both physical aspects and psychological aspects. I simultaneously and intuitively know my Body from the outside-in and from the inside-out. Indeed, I am an object in the environing world that is aware of myself surrounded by that world (Zahavi 2019: 11).

Husserl injects a critical distinction relative to perceptions of outer objects and perceptions of inner ones; namely, *"external perception is deceptive, inner perception evident"* (Husserl 1970 [1900-01], Vol. 2: 336):

> However widely I may extend my critical doubts regarding knowledge, I cannot doubt that I exist and am doubting, or again, while I experience them, that I am having presentations, am judging, feeling or however else I may designate such inwardly perceived appearances: to doubt in such a case would evidently be irrational. We accordingly have absolute "evidence" regarding the existence of the objects of inner perception, we have that clearest cognition, that unassailable certainty which distinguishes knowledge in the strictest sense. It is quite different in the case of outer perception. It lacks "evidence," and the frequent conflicts in statements relying upon it point, in fact, to its capacity to deceive. We have therefore no right to assume from the outset that the objects of outer perception really and truly exist as they seem to us to be.

This difference is why the *apodicticity* of inner knowledge is so fundamental to any contemplative path—indeed, of great interest to transpersonal anthropology (see Laughlin 1994b). For what Husserl is driving at is that inner perception is our brainmind coming to know itself, and neuropsychologically speaking, as we come to know more about ourselves, the self we know changes as a consequence (Goleman and Davidson 2017).

Essence and essential structure

Every time we are conscious of the world around us, we project our beliefs, attitudes, habits, biases, and other conditioned views upon what we see. Giving this the ancient Greek name for all this cultural and developmental detritus, Husserl wrote of the *doxic* elements pervading our "natural attitude" toward events in the environing world.

> I am aware of a world, spread out in space endlessly, and in time becoming and become. Without end. I am aware of it, that means, first of all, I discover it immediately, intuitively, I experience it. Through sight, touch, hearing, etc., in the different ways of sensory perception, corporeal things somehow spatially distributed are *for me simply there*, in verbal or figurative sense "present," whether or not I pay them special attention by busying myself with them, considering, thinking, feeling, willing. (Husserl 1982[1913]: 101)

Husserl wanted to suspend all *doxa* in experience and take a look at what is left over. What is left are the essentials of perception. We will be exploring Husserl's notion of *essence* or *essential structure*[12] repeatedly over the course of this book. Put simply, an essence is a universal structure of experience that is the same for everybody, regardless of cultural upbringing. This is a very controversial idea, and yet an old one dating back at least to Plato and other early philosophers, experimentally confirmed by modern cognitive neuroscience (Atran 1998, Atran and Medin 2008), and familiar to anyone steeped in Carl Jung's concept of the *archetype* (Tougas 2013). As we saw in Chapter 1, my colleagues and I have written about similar issues under the concept of "neurognosis." These structures exist solely in the brainmind of the perceiver—in biogenetic structural theory neurognosis refers to universal perceptual structures and nascent cognits in the nervous system—and they contribute to how we see the world in a very natural, human way. The entire stream of consciousness exhibits a "law of essence." For example,

---

[12] Essence is also sometimes termed "moment" as in "a moment of red" (Husserl 1970 [1900-01], II: 4).

as we shall see, the mind is interested in objects of perception that are instances of *eidos*, or "ideas" in the Platonic sense.

Objects are of two types, "simple" and "complex." A simple object cannot come apart—literally, for it has no parts to separate. A complex object has parts and can thus "come apart" mentally or physically. Most objects of interest to humans are complex objects. A flower can be plucked apart into pedals, stamens, peduncle, and so forth. A car can be disassembled into doors, wheels, engine, transmission, etc. Mind you, Husserl is referring to *experienceable parts*, parts that can be seen. He is not referring to theoretical parts like atoms and molecules that are not present to experience. Notice that we have names for both the whole and the parts of anything of interest to us. If a part of an object is separated from it and cannot itself be taken apart, it is a "simple" object (see Husserl 1970 [1900-01]: Chap. 1). Parts of objects are said to be "non-independent objects," while whole objects (a flower separated from its plant, a car) are considered "independent objects." We are usually interested in independent objects and relations among independent objects in our everyday stream of consciousness.

The experienced relationship between parts and wholes is determined by the law of essences and is considered an essential structure of consciousness. A "cup of coffee" is a whole thing, a totality or monad, although it is made up of the cup and the coffee, or the cup, its lip and handle and the coffee it contains—or even the ceramic, glaze, design in the glaze, affording quality of "liquid substance container-ness," lip, handle and contents. The uniting of parts within wholes is done automatically, primordially, within our sensorium: "Thus: to bring an object in general, an objective unity, to intuition means *successively* to intuit, from out of the Ideal union of constituents to whose conceptual synthesis the object owes its unity, those constituents (parts or properties) which provide a completeness that satisfies our interest" (Husserl 1994: 318). And all sciences depend for the truth of their facts and theories upon these initial intuitively rich experiences of the world: "All discoveries and inventions of the experts move within the framework of an absolutely intransgressible a priori that one can draw not from their doctrines but only from the phenomenological Intuition" (Husserl 1980[1952]: 20).

Intuition

We know essences intuitively. We recognize (identify) objects of intentional acts intuitively—Husserl termed this *categorical intuition*. Intuition is the a priori, primordial act of knowing the object of direct experience and its relations within its horizon (set of limits) that is the field of perception at any given moment (Husserl 1994: 313-344, 1982[1913]: Chap. 1):

> Every science has its own object-domain as field of research, and to all that it knows, i.e., in this connexion, to all its correct assertions, there correspond as original sources of the reasoned justification that support them certain intuitions in which objects of the region appear as self-given and in part at least as *given in a primordial (originärer)[13] sense*. The *object-giving* (or *dator*) intuition of the first, "natural" sphere of knowledge and of all its sciences is natural experience, and the *primordial* dator experience is *perception* in the ordinary sense of the term. *To have something real primordially given, and to "become aware" of it and "perceive" it in simple intuition, are one and the same thing.* Husserl 1982[1913]: 51; emphasis added)

The object of consciousness does not just pop up as total novelty, it is known to be there and what it is—categorical intuition is "the first natural sphere of knowledge" that accompanies any object of consciousness before any higher cognition, ratiocination, or higher level, non-sensuous intuition occurs (Husserl 1970 [1900-01], 2: 281-283). Seeing something entirely novel is a rare but instructive act. Cast your mind back to any experience of something that happened to you like this: Something catches your gaze, you look at it, but what it is does not immediately "compute"—it is something for sure, but you don't know what it is. Your interest intensifies until suddenly you "recognize" it. Thereafter when you look at it, it is no longer novel, it is identified. Recall the sense of puzzlement that accompanied the failure to automatically know the thing for what it was. This was your brainmind

---

[13] The German term *originärer* means "original."

working to match thing with idea, sensory given with percept, object with intuition.

Most of the time, we gaze at something and the history of our encounters with similar things automatically comes into play. We not only perceive the object as it is given in form and hyle, the object before us instantiates a category of object. This is primordial knowing and is prior to any act of higher cognition, conceptualization, reason, thought, or prior to any projection of doxic elements from cultural conditioning, concept, ideology, memory, affect, imagination, or such. In biogenetic structuralist terms, the sensory system of our brain is "wired" to pair objects and foundational knowing in this way, often incorporating emotional associations (e.g., "gut-feelings," sense of danger, feeling of being watched). Compared with the slow process of conscious deliberation, intuitive knowing occurs rapidly, experienced as virtually being simultaneous with the appearance of the object. Neuroscientists have shown that different parts of the cortex are active in mediating deliberation (which is bracketed in any reduction) and intuition (Kuo *et al.* 2009).

The relationship of sensuous intuition to conceptualization is a foundational one. We can, of course, produce concepts that have nothing to do with experience of the environing world, that have no foundation in a priori sensation or intuition. But concepts about the real world must, on Husserl's account, be founded in intuitive knowing:

> ...it is necessary to make clear to oneself the following: no matter what the much-discussed, even ambiguous, "stemming from experience" may mean—and no matter how, whether in our sleep or by a miracle, we have acquired the disposition to use general words in identical signification—the word-significations can *be valid* as logical essences only if according to ideal possibility the "logical thinking" actualizing them in itself is adaptable to a "corresponding intuition," if there is as corresponding noema a corresponding essence that is graspable through *Intuition* and that finds its true "expression" through the logical concept. (Husserl 1980[1952]: 23)

For you to comprehend Husserl's reliance on intuition, I suggest you play around with intuiting things. Look around you. Scan your environment. Notice that as soon as you light on an object, you not only see it, you know it in some automatic, nearly instantaneous way. There is seemingly no delay between sensing and knowing. I am looking at my coffee cup, not an object before my eyes that I somehow have to figure out and identify eventually as a coffee cup. As we will see in the next chapter, the sensory patterns adumbrated from the sensory field penetrate imediately to intuitive knowing. There is no ratiocination involved, no discussing the object among opinionated bits inside your head, no application of formal logic, no need to talk about it. There is just sensory giving and giving intuition in the act of intentionality. It is one of Husserl's greatest contributions that he showed, unequivocally in my opinion, that all human knowledge of the environing world is based upon "originary giving intuition." As we shall see in Chapters 8 and 10, intuition can present problems, especially when dealing with our Self and experiences had in ASC.

The neuroscience of intuition is problematic (Laughlin 1997b). Generally speaking, intuition refers to knowing something without awareness of how we know that something. Intuition is an umbrella term covering subconscious or unconscious cognition that produces conscious knowing, and depending upon the type of intuition may be mediated by various cortical structures.

> Intuition is an inductive skill. It is the ability to "see the big picture," to sense the possibilities and implications of any particular situation or potential decision by looking at the whole problem rather than each of its component parts. It is the ability to come up with a workable solution to a problem even when data for making that decision is inadequate or unavailable. (Agor 1985: 15)

There are no studies to my knowledge that specify the sensuous intuition to which Husserl is referring. As of now, we do not know what neural structures mediate sensuous intuition. What we do know is that like other forms of intuition, the process is very rapid and that there is no conscious thought involved. Wolf Singer (2007) has shown that general intuitions pertaining to how our brains work are often distinctly wrong, imposing linear causation to an essentially non-linear brain, and imposing a belief in a fixed ego when there is no such thing.

Turnbull (2018) demonstrates how general intuition can lead to beliefs about the world that endure even in the face of contradictory evidence from reality. But sensuous intuition is rarely wrong, so rapid and precise are the associations. We do occasionally get it wrong. We can pass by a shop window and briefly mistake a mannequin for a real person staring out at us. If you have ever explored ambiguous figures (like the Necker cube in Figure 4 on page 79), you can experience the effort it takes to shift from your first intuitive resolution of the figure to its alternative. Such exercises teach us, among other things, the effort it takes to will a change in sensuous intuition (see Wimmer and Doherty 2011 on the developmental issues surrounding ambiguity of object identification).

A WORD ABOUT NEUROGNOSIS

Those readers familiar with my colleagues and my theoretical works will be aware that we have argued that the initial organization of what we know about the world and experience in perception is mediated by inherited neural structures. We have called these nascent knowledge systems *neurognostic structures* or simply *neurognosis* (Laughlin 1992c, 1996, Laughlin and d'Aquili 1974, Laughlin and Loubser 2010, Laughlin, McManus and d'Aquili 1990, Laughlin and Throop 2003; see also Krippner and Combs 2002, Saniotis 2010b, Winkelman 2006, Zimmer 2000). Neural development is not a matter of the environment, including culture, externally imposing structure on a "blank slate" brain. Brains are already structured such that the world of experience, including intersubjective experiencing among social animals, is already present in its nascent form by the time those structures are called upon. They grow to become pre-adapted to the environment into which they are born and which they interact (Vandervert 1988, 1995). Because neural structures are living cells, they are active from the time they are formed. In other words, neural structures are not like microchips that lay dormant until "switched-on."

Research has shown that sensory structures in the nervous system are automatically activated *before* they are called into serious use—a process that Martin Seligman (1975, Seligman and Hager 1972) called "preparedness" in the development of the brainmind's cognitive and sensory systems.[14] For instance, we now know that neonatal mice dream about the visual world before their eyes are open, thus preparing sensory structures and sensorium for their roles once the visual system comes into action when their eyes open:

> Our results show that spontaneous activity in the developing retina prior to vision onset is structured to convey essential information for the development of visual response properties before the onset of visual experience. Spontaneous retinal waves simulate future optic flow patterns produced by forward motion through space, due to an asymmetric retinal circuit that has an evolutionarily conserved link with motion detection circuitry in the mature retina. Furthermore, the ethologically relevant information relayed by directional retinal waves enhances the development of higher-order visual function in the downstream visual system prior to eye opening. *These findings provide insight into the activity-dependent mechanisms that regulate the self-organization of brain circuits before sensory experience begins.* (Ge *et al.* 2021; emphasis added)

When Husserl speaks of essences and essential structures, he is referring in his own terms to perceptual neurognosis. When we combine his descriptions of essences, available for replication by anyone willing to follow his methods, with neuropsychological research, we have a powerful approach to the nature of universal brainmind structures, or at least those that reveal themselves via trained introspection. However, this is not a book about biogenetic structuralist theories of neurognosis and the development of neurognostic structures under influence of social and ecological learning. Rather, the book is an exploration of just how we can use Husserl's work and his methods to further explore the interaction between biogenetic and enculturative factors influencing the nature of the adult brainmind, and how these researches can ground a scientific anthropology in reality.

---

[14] If you wish to follow-up on the spontaneous, endogenous activation of visual networks and the role played by this process in developing an adaptive sensorium, see Ackman, Burbridge and Crair (2012), Gribizis *et al.* (2019), Huberman, Feller and Chapman (2008).

A WORD ABOUT SPACE AND TIME

Much is made about Husserl's "static" and "genetic" phenomenologies. Some authorities consider his turn toward the genetic—that is, the temporal (historical, developmental) dimension of experience—an improvement in his methods. I do not agree, and those that make this claim are likely unable to reduce their own experiences to the stratum of absorption into the "real now" moment. Absorption into the real now is essentially timeless, almost durationless, yet dynamic and animated. We will get to this distinction when we discuss time consciousness in Chapter 6 and will explain the advantages of both the static and the genetic methods of reduction.

SUMMARY AND SEGUE

Even a cursory engagement with Husserl's writings will show you that his challenge to philosophers and scientists alike is to learn how to transform their states of consciousness in such a way that they can experience from a phenomenological standpoint. This challenge involves the application of disciplined concentration of an extraordinary sort that not everyone can or will wish to master. But the payoff for answering the challenge is great, for one comes to realize more about how their own brainmind produces the movie of the mind which is our stream of awareness about the world and the things in it, including ourselves. Moreover, the promise of Husserl's project is that the phenomenologist lays the groundwork within their own direct experience for knowing what is real and what is added as "meaning" by their mind. The challenge requires effort and dedication on the reader's part. In the next two chapters I will describe how to do Husserlian phenomenology and show how the addition of a neuropsychological ingredient makes the work just that much more powerful.

CHAPTER THREE

Doing Phenomenology Husserl-Style

Now phenomenology, in point of fact, is a pure descriptive discipline which studies the whole field of pure transcendental consciousness in light of pure intuition.

– Edmund Husserl (1982[1913]: 176)

Husserl's method of bracketing and eidetic description is possibly the most thoroughgoing philosophical attempt of modern times to disclose the universal structures within human experience. The phenomenological epoché is intended to suspend the prejudices of our "natural" way of seeing the world in order to allow pure description of the meaning structures that are universal in human experience.

– Galen Johnson (1980: 78)

Husserl called phenomenology "scientific" by which he meant that one studies one's experience with rigor, using explicit methods that lead to descriptions which in turn can be replicated by others *who follow the same methods*. Husserl was saying the same thing that psychologist Ken Wilber suggests in his book, *A Sociable God* (2005[1983]: 156), that one begins the process of phenomenological inquiry with the injunction "If you want to know this, you have to do this." When one does "this" (meditate on the breath, conduct a "reduction," tour Cincinnati, etc.) then certain experiences, insights and realizations consequently arise, and then perhaps the contemplative has a conversation with one's fellow colleagues to compare notes. Obviously, one cannot compare notes if one has not done "this."

How to do "this," exercises in pure ("static") PHENOMENOLOGY

Sources in the Western phenomenological literature that actually offer pith instructions for accomplishing a Husserlian "phenomenological reduction" are thin on the ground, but some sources are more useful than others in this respect (see Held 2003a, Ihde 2012, Spiegelberg 1975, Luft 2004, 2011: Part 1, 2015, Zahavi 2019, Vagle 2018, Welton 1999). On specific methodological issues, see Jansen (2005) on Husserl's approach to fantasy and Luft (2004) on performing the phenomenological reduction. In this chapter, I want to bear down on the question of how one accomplishes Husserlian pure phenomenology. Notwithstanding the enormous literature that preceded Husserl's work and that has grown from Husserl's philosophy, replete with supporters and critics, Husserl's original project was simple: "'Phenomenology' is, in the 20th century, mainly the name for a philosophical movement whose primary objective is the direct investigation and description of phenomena as consciously experienced, without theories about their causal explanation and as free as possible from unexamined preconceptions and presuppositions" (Spiegelberg 1975: 3). Or as Husserl himself put it:

> We, therefore, speak of "experiences" to begin with, a term that, therefore, indicates an experiencing I, an experiencing individual, an individual with a mind. I want to know what knowledge's relationship to an objectivity means and how such a relationship to an objectivity is possible. So, I take knowledge, I meditate on it, I examine it thoroughly. I go back to my experiences of knowledge. I separate perceptions, memories, expectations, etc. I experience them. While I am meditating on them, in this meditating, I am meditating on inner experience, the consciousness of their being my experiences. I grasp them in relationship to myself, as my mental acts or states. They stand before me experientially as such, i.e., in believing, in conviction, in the broadest sense of the word, in judgment. (Husserl 2008[1906-1907]: 207)

ENCOUNTERING EXPERIENCE

If you happen to be in a situation right now that allows you to focus entirely upon what you are experiencing this moment, then try out what I will suggest. If you are not in such a situation, postpone carrying on until you can do this safely. Pause and reflect upon the experience you are having right now. Describe to yourself what is before your consciousness, and only before your consciousness—what Aron Gurwitsch (1964, 1966) called your "field of consciousness." Discovering how to clearly describe what you are seeing is fundamental to doing phenomenology (Williams 2016). You are reading this book. But that is not all that is happening. There are your hands holding the book, a view of your arms, the frames of your glasses (if you wear them), the color and texture of your clothing, the hissing in your ears if, like me, you suffer from tinnitus, itches in the scalp and back, pressure of your rear and back on the chair, your feet on the floor, air passing in and out of your nostrils, your body posture, light source from window or lamp, myriad colors, fragrances, etc. in your immediate surround. Hold still with your gaze fixed on the book and note everything coming in from each and every sense, both external and internal. What visuals, sounds, smells, tastes, touches, internal feelings, and so forth are present to you this moment? Now focus upon each sense and ignore as much as possible the other senses—examine all the things you can see without turning your head, and what discernable parts make up each thing (book has pages and fonts, hands have veins and spots and wrinkles, clothes have pockets, buttons, textures, colors, seams, and so forth). Do that for every sense that is before your consciousness—within your field of consciousness.

Now consider what Douglas Harding wrote in his marvelous little book, *On Having No Head*:

> What actually happened was something absurdly simple and unspectacular: just for a moment I stopped thinking. Reason and imagination and all mental chatter died down. For once, words really failed me. I forgot my name, my humanness, my thingness, all that could be called me or mine. Past and future dropped away. It was as if I had been born that instant, brand new, mindless, innocent of all memories. There existed only the

Now, that present moment and what was clearly given in it. To look was enough. And what I found was trouser legs terminating downwards in a pair of brown shoes, khaki sleeves terminating sideways in a pair of pink hands, and a khaki shirtfront terminating upwards in—*absolutely nothing whatever! Certainly not in a head.* (1961: 1-2; emphasis added)

Let us work with this brief excursion into phenomenology of the experience we can call "reading the book." You have done pretty much what Harding did when he described his experience of "having no head." You did not find a head there either, did you. Maybe you could see a bit of your cheek, mustache, eyebrow, even itching above or behind the level of your eyes, but no head at the top of your shoulders. What you do have before your consciousness is a sphere of sensory awareness comprised of different things, perhaps ringing in your ears, an itch where your head should be, as well as all the things you already catalogued.

Now, *what you likely did not find was anything novel*—that is, you found nothing you could not immediately identify, anything that was not familiar. Another way to say this is that your experience was full of meaningful things, your hands are hands, your itch is an itch, the lines of font on the page of the book are words and they are meaningful. If something were to pop-up unexpectedly, chances are it too would be familiar and meaningful.

STEP ONE: REPLACING YOUR NATURAL ATTITUDE WITH THE PHENOMENOLOGICAL ATTITUDE

The first lesson in doing phenomenology is that most of the complex information that constitutes meaning—the hand-ness of your hands, the itch-ness of your itch, the dog bark-ness of the sound you might be hearing, the word-ness and font-ness of the ink on the page—is contributed by your mind, not the real world (Husserl 1989[1952]: 248). In a word, no meaning in the cognitive/linguistic sense whatever is given in sensations, but only sensory form, hyle (*hyletic matter*, or *hyletic data*; see Chapter 5), relationships (configurations, topological relations) among parts and objects, and intuition (Husserl 1982[1913]:

246-248). As Jan Patočka (1996: 89) notes: "thus *mere perception* is to become the absolute, self-certifying source of cognition, drawing on nothing else, sustaining itself solely from itself, in *pure immanence.*" Mere, or pure perception is of *absolute being* which is meaningless in and of itself (in the normal, everyday, and fuzzy sense of the term meaning) until patterns in perception are matched with apperceptive, cognitive, affective, imaginary, and action schema stored in your brainmind (see Azzouni 2015).[15] That does not mean that experience is chaotic until heaped in layers of meaning. Quite the contrary. The process of reduction *never* uncovers a layer of sensory chaos down to and including pure immanence.

Consciousness and brainmind are on about order from the git-go. At no time from womb to death is experience a "booming buzzing confusion." As I mentioned above, this was William James' big mistake (see Pinker 2003). The body and its brainmind are ordered and operate to impose order upon the environing world via projection and activity. As the great physicist Erwin Schrödinger once wrote in his book *What Is Life?,* "An organism's astonishing gift of concentrating a 'stream of order' on itself and thus escaping the decay into atomic chaos—*of 'drinking orderliness' from a suitable environment*—seems to be connected with the presence of the 'aperiodic solids,' the chromosome molecules, which doubtless represent the highest degree of well-ordered atomic association we know of—much higher than the ordinary periodic crystal—in virtue of the individual role every atom and every radical is playing here" (1946: 77; emphasis added). Babies of all animals with brains are born with the exquisitely ordered sensorium ready to mediate an "already there" world of experience, an order that has evolved in each era to be adaptively veridical.

This inherent order pervades psychophysical processing from the "bottom to the top." For Husserl, the structure of intentional acts, and thus the structure of meaning is a hierarchically constituted layering process by which the sensuous (Ger.: *Sinn*, "simpliciter") is the primordial foundation upon which layers of meaning are stacked (Husserl 1969[1929]: 244-245, 1982[1913]: 282-290, Moran 2013b, Nenon 2013b). By "primordial" Husserl means that it is already there in my experience as a

---

[15] I am assuming that you are not considering primordial intuitive knowing as "meaning" in the normal sense of the term.

type of perceptual intuition—the primordial sensory given is irreducible, presented a priori, and as we shall see, mediated by the essential structures of the nervous system's sensory systems (see Taipale 2012). The meanings of the words you are reading now are not provided by your eyes (Azzouni 2015). Just reflect a moment, if you were suddenly "reading" ancient Greek chances are all the meanings of the words would stop. Your brain could not supply the meanings because you "do not read Greek;" i.e., you do not "recognize" the Greek sign-meaning code—for example:

Διαβάζω

It gets stranger than that, for even your assumption that what you are experiencing is "real," is "out there," that it "exists," is an assumption you bring to the experience from your conditioning. To give you a well-documented example: We Westerners tend to assume that the world we experience while awake is real, while the world we experience while "dreaming" is unreal. But far more non-Western traditional cultures hold that both waking and dreaming worlds are part of the same reality (see Laughlin 2011).

All of these assumptions—words are meaningful, the sensation in my hand is an "itch," my hand really exists—whether conscious or unconscious, are part of your *natural attitude* (Ger.: *die natürliche Einstellung*; also "general thesis") as Husserl (1982[1913]) labeled it.[16] What Husserl meant was that this is the orientation toward everyday lived experience that is natural to you, that you grew up learning and believing in, and given all the conditioning you have undergone as a member of your society (see Prat 2022 for a neuroscience take on this process). In anthropologese, you are a culture-bearer in good standing, naïvely "seeing" the world through your "participation mystique" (Levy-Bruhl 1966[1923]). Your natural attitude is everything you bring into the experience from memory, except for what is given by the senses each moment. All the meanings, identifications, familiarity, interpretations, beliefs about the reality or unreality of what

---

[16] If you wish to read more on the *natural attitude* (aka: "natural standpoint," "natural concept of the world," "natural subjectivity," etc.) and its complimentary phenomenological attitude, see Husserl 1982[1913]: 101-114, 1999: 15-16, 2006[1910-1911]: 10, 2019[1923/24]: 286-295; see also Kohak 1978: 29-35, Moran 2000, 2013a, Landgrebe 1981: 18-19, Natanson 1973: Chap. 2, Zahavi 2005, and Färber 1967.

you are experiencing, and so forth comprise your natural attitude. Speaking for himself, Husserl wrote:

> The General Thesis according to which the real world about me is at all times known not merely in a general way as something apprehended, but as a fact-world *that has its being out there*, does *not* consist of course *in an act proper,* in an articulated judgment *about* existence. It is and remains something all the time the standpoint is adopted, that is, it endures persistently during the whole course of our life of natural endeavor. (Husserl 1982[1913]: 107)

If you think in anthropologese, your "enculturation" (process of learning your culture as a child) supplies the meaning of things. As fast as your senses deliver sensations before your consciousness, you have laid on layer after layer of meaning and interpretation upon those sensations so rapidly that the two merge before your unreflective consciousness— pure perception becomes apperception—one meaningful experience, a mandala of sense and meaning that we are conditioned from birth to take as real. Here Husserl uses the term *constitute* for how the brainmind builds objects according to a priori eidetic laws of pure perception and continues to build layers and processes that mediate the meaning of the object for the natural attitude. In neuroscience we would use the term "entrain" to refer to the same process of "constitution" or construction. I will retain Husserl's term as I have previously done and emphasize the importance of understanding that this *constituting occurs so automatically and so rapidly, we are unaware of the complex processing involved* (Husserl 1982[1913]: 411-415, 1969[1929]: 245-250; see also Sokolowski 1964, Zahavi 1992).

Notice that I said one must *realize* the distinction between primordial sensory given and natural attitude. "Realize" in the present sense means to see it directly with intuitive certainty, not just thinking about it after the fact. Realize the actual distinction between the sensory given and the laying on of meaning *while it is happening*. This realization is the first step toward attaining the *phenomenological attitude* which is requisite to "seeing" as a true phenomenological contemplative (Kohak 1978:119-120). More precisely, it is an ASC in which your awareness is very sharp, focused, and able to discern what is right before your mind's eye and pay attention to nothing else (see Natanson 1973: Chap. 3). Following Harding, your head is no longer there, but neither is the usual taken-for-granted, largely uncritical engagement with the world. If you work with this exercise and other similar exercises over a period of time, it will become as familiar to you as your natural standpoint, and you will eventually be able to flip between the two ways of "seeing" with ease. The difference between the two states involves your heightened awareness and persistence of practice. Presumably, you at least tried the mind-play in step one and are able to make the discrimination between sensory given and natural attitude interpretations. You simply cannot do phenomenology without being able to willfully intuit the distinction while experiencing it.

STEP TWO: REDUCING WHILE EXPERIENCING

Here we come to the really interesting part. You will want to learn how to make a special discernment using the method called *reduction*,[17] also known as *epoché* or "bracketing." Husserl uses the term "reduction" in its original Latin sense of "lead back" or "bring back," or to "restore or return to a previous state." He often says, "return to the things" or "return to the things themselves." What he is getting at is that the mind needs to discern the original pre-cognitive, pre-natural attitude sensory given, the sensory material prior to the layering of meaning (imagination, thoughts, feelings, memory associations, identifications, etc.) that complete the "natural" act of apperception. For Husserl, the sensory given comes first and is the bit of apperception that cannot be "set aside" and cannot itself be reduced. The sensory given is thus "primordial," meaning the "beginning," or "origin" of the acts of recognition (literally *re*-cognition or "knowing again"). All that is left

---

[17] If you wish to read more about the *reduction* (aka: the "phenomenological reduction," the "transcendental phenomenological reduction," the "*epoché*," the "setting aside," the "bracketing," the "returning to the things," etc.), see Husserl 1982[1913]: 107- 111, 1997[1907]: Chap. 3, 2006[1910-1911]: 39, 2008[1906-1907]: 206-211; see also Cairns 1976, Føllesdal 2006, Färber 1943: 20, Funke 1987, Giorgi 2007, Hart 1992, Ihde 2012, Kohak 1978: 35-46, Landgrebe 1981, LeVasseur 2003, Moran 2000, Patočka 1996: 89-106, 1998: 90-93, Schmicking 2010, Schmitt 1967, Welton 2003: 259-260, Spiegelberg 1975: 10-11 and Zahavi 2019.

over when you have "bracketed" all the layers and set them aside is "the thing itself," the original trigger for, or fulfillment of the apperceptive act (Moran 2013b).

> Thus, to every psychological experience there corresponds, by way of the phenomenological reduction, a pure phenomenon that exhibits its immanent essence (taken individually) as an absolute givenness. All positing of a "non-immanent reality," a reality not contained in the phenomenon and therefore not given in the second sense, even if it is intended in the phenomenon, is shut off, that is, suspended. (Husserl 1999: 34)

So, let us try this out. It really is simpler to do than to talk about. Let us use the fact that you are reading this book as a start. Your eyes are scanning lines on this page from left to right because it is written in English. You are conditioned to read from left to right. If this book were written in Arabic, you would be naturally reading right to left, and if it were in traditional Japanese *tategaki* script, from top to bottom in columns written from right to left. As a starter exercise, pick a line on this page and read it from right to left. Let us pick this line for instance:

Instance for line this pick us let.

How much sense does it make? Not much, although the individual words "retain" meaning—we categorically intuit the meaning of each word, but not the "sentence." But now, if you were to focus more sharply in reading not only the line right to left, but also each word, I suspect almost all meaning would stop. You perceive the patterns of letters, but the categorically intuitive meaning of words stops:

Ecnatsni rof enil siht kcip su tel.

Of course, you can eventually make sense of the words and the sentence by reading it all backwards, but in the process, you can sense how slow the matching of symbols to meaning has become. And if, instead of playing with a sentence in English, I started writing in Navajo:

Ndi dziłbigháa'di honeezk'ází yee'.

You may recognize the font as phonetic and broken up into words, but all other categorical intuitions fail to appear. It would not make any difference how you read the line, all the meaning of words would stop popping up in your head to match the signs and the sense of meaning of the sentence would be beyond your grasp and would no longer automatically flow along doing its thing in your stream of consciousness. You can more easily see now, if you did not know it before, that your "reading a book" is a ritualized activity that is second nature to you. You do not have to remember to read the lines in the right direction. You just do it, and the meaning flows along quite naturally and intuitively.

Now, let us look more carefully at what "reading" involves. As your eyes scan the text on the page, you are conditioned to lump words into phrases and sentences, and sentences make up blocks of text called paragraphs, and eventually those paragraphs comprise a full text we might call a "story," "letter," "essay," "poem," "article," "chapter," or "synopsis." For me to be able to communicate with you, I have to write in the same form that you are conditioned to read and interpret the relations between words in a sentence, sentences in this paragraph, the relationship between this paragraph with those that have come before and that will follow. The same would be the case if you were reading me in Arabic or Japanese, though the ritual elements would be different.

It is interesting that written language has to unfold in time, as does speech. A duration passes between when you begin to scan a sentence and when you reach its conclusion at the period. Yet as your eyes scan the sentence, you do not actually scan the letters in each word (unless you are learning to read). You actually take in written words and even phrases as a gestalt, as a single act of recognition that takes little time. In fact, there are speed-reading courses that teach you to take in whole sentences as gestalts. Using this fact, we can continue to hone our focus upon a single word. Choose a word on this page which we will now call the "target." Focus in on that target and notice that you recognize the word. Perhaps you subvocalize how the word sounds in speech. You have seen it perhaps thousands of times. If you were to choose a word you had never encountered before, you would know it is a word but would not know its meaning. Say I note that a lot of political shenanigans are going on in the Althingi this month, you would not know what I was talking about because, unless you know a bit about Iceland, you would not recognize the name of that nation's parliament. You would know that Althingi is a word, that it is a noun and, because it is capitalized, it is probably an institution of some kind. All of these assumptions are supplied quickly from your memory banks.

But here is the trick when performing a reduction: Focus on the target (in this case a written word) and study what is given by your visual sense and exclude everything else. In other words, ignore all that is not given in your visual sense—that is, ignore the meaning, cognitive and imaginative associations, your feelings, so on and so forth. In proper phenomenologese, bracket meaning and everything else that pops up in your consciousness except what is before your eyes. As distinctly as you can, make the effort to see only what can be seen sensuously. Now, describe to yourself what you actually see while in this phenomenological attitude.

What I see is a pattern of black lines separated and surrounded by white background. The lines seem non-random, and some patterns repeat themselves:

imagine

The "i" pattern is repeated twice. The bodies of each pattern form a string with some bits above the string (e.g., "i") and some below the string (e.g., "g"). I notice that when I scan over the field of black patterns on white background that the black patterns are repetitive. There seem to be a finite number of these patterns that are mixed to form strings, many of which are repeated and many of which are unique. Some of the individual patterns are lineal while others are rounded. Etcetera, etcetera, etcetera—on and on we could describe what is before our eyes, but not supplied out of memory. *We have thus performed a reduction.* We have returned to the "thing itself," returned to just what is offered in our sense of sight. We are conditioned to even recognize and name all the black patterns—an "i" followed by an "m," and so on, spelling out the word. But in our reduction, we do not even re-cognize letters, for that comes from our memory. Letter-ness is not given, nor is word-ness. They are interpretations of the given.

We can take this investigation much further of course. Notice that during these reductions we have been able to direct our attention upon one object (a "word," a "meaning," or just patterns of black on white background) to the exclusion of all else. The object is the "phenomenon," hence the term for the method, "phenomenology." You really must be able to control your focus upon the phenomenon like this to perform reductions. This ability of consciousness to direct focus is what phenomenologists call *intentionality* (see Arvidson 1996 on the phenomenology of attention). Intentionality is at the root of the structure of consciousness. In the natural attitude, our intentionality carries with it all the pre-interpretations, anticipations, expectations, meanings, assumptions, plans, etc. into the experience of the given. Please remember, it is not my intention here to do an exhaustive reduction of the printed page, but rather to show you how it is done.

EXPANDING THE SCOPE OF REDUCTION

Of course, one may practice the phenomenological reduction on any object before the mind. Any object whether sensuous, imagined, conceptual, relational, etc., can be reduced as long as it is susceptible to intuitive knowing or insight (Spiegelberg 1975: 11). I happen to choose words because they are before my mind and your mind at the moment:

> The application of this method allows phenomenologists to view virtually anything with a refined state of consciousness that results in more clear, unbiased perception. The "phenomenon" in this context could be a physical object, concept, mental image, being, entity, process, or relationship. Phenomenology is thus meant to illuminate the foundations of human experience by providing a research method for exploring how human consciousness engages the world.... (Hanna, Wilkinson and Givens 2017: 145)

More than this, it is the intent of Husserlian phenomenology to explore how much of our flow of experience is provided by the world and how much is provided by the mind. How accurately do we perceive the real world, including our own actual being? The only way to do that, Husserl argued, is bracket all presumptions about the object (the phenomenon), no matter what that object might be, and for as long as the exploration might take. The necessary bracketing most especially includes one's metaphysical/ontological *worldview* (see Landgrebe 1949, Berndtsson *et al.* 2007, Bostar 1993), a central feature of all cultures (Kearney 1975).

If you were able to hold the state of mind in which the words on this page were reduced to just what is presented before your consciousness—black geometric patterns on white background—and you were able to sustain that attitude long enough to study the visual sensations without thought, feeling, identifications, interpretations, etc., then you should be able to do the same thing with other sensations, whether they be visual, auditory, tactile, or otherwise. So, let us play with this new-found ability. If you practice these exercises seriously, and apply the methods throughout your scope of experience, your brainmind will eventually "learn set" (as psychologists like to say) and will be able to enter the phenomenological attitude at will. Try out these exercises and see where they take you.

1. Tactile distinctions. Turn to your sense of touch. Shut your eyes and place your index finger on your opposite arm. Focus your attention on the sense of touch. Move your finger up and down your arm. Try to distinguish between the feeling of your finger touching your arm and the feeling of your arm touching your finger—you will have tactile sensations deriving from both your fingertip and the skin of your arm. Can you make that distinction? Can you "put your mind" into first your finger and then into your arm? Try this with one index finger touching your other index finger. Can you discriminate the feelings, one from the other? Keep this exploration going until all that is before your consciousness are these tactile sensations.

2. The effort of focus. Sit calmly with your eyes gazing upon a field of visual objects. Focus upon one object directly in front of you (tree, book on the shelf, word on this page, whatever). Study it intently. Then, without moving your eyes or body, change your attention to another object distant from the first object. Describe to yourself the experience of shifting focus while not moving eyes or body. Then shift attention back to the first object. Keep "moving" your attention from the first object to other objects, including those in your peripheral field, and back again. Notice that among other things, you may be able to experience the effort it takes to shift focus to a different object, even when your body remains still.

3. Speech sounds. Tune-in to a talk radio program or an audio book, some source of speech with which you need not converse. Focus your attention strictly upon the flow of sounds. If the speech is in a language you understand, you will be aware that there is an on-going flow of meaning. Your natural attitude toward speech is the meaning of the sounds, not the sounds themselves. You know upon reflection that the meaning of the sounds is all in your head. You are not hearing meaning, but sound patterns you render meaningful in your brainmind. Just as with writing, if the speech suddenly changes to a language you cannot interpret, the meaning stops. In a way it is easier to focus on the sound of speech from a language you do not understand but stick with English or whatever language you do understand and focus your attention so intensely that you become aware only of the constantly changing tones of speech. These sounds are the primordial auditory given. All else is bracketed as natural attitude apperception. If you can do this with sufficient focus, nothing remains but the flow of changing tonal frequencies and textures of the voicing. With sufficient intensity of awareness, you may experience the flow of sounds slowing down and becoming more detailed.

Once you are comfortable with tracking the changes in the flow of speech sounds, explore other attributes of the flow of sound. Notice perhaps that in normal everyday speech the flow of sound is continuous. If I were the speaker you are hearing, I would not break up my speech to form words. I would not say, "I [] would [] not [] break [] up [] my [] speech" where the "[]" are tiny durations of silence. Rather, I would say, "Iwouldnotbreakupmyspeech" with no discernable breaks in the flow. Hence, somehow your mind projects meaning on recognizable sound durational patterns within the string of vocalizations creating meaningful worlds and a meaningful phrase.

There are many other ways to play with sounds in this way. Try it with a piece of orchestral music. Focus in on the flow of sounds to the point where you lose track of themes, melodies, and repetitions. Study to what extent your mind has to project an a-temporal pattern on the temporal flow of music for it to mean something. Try various objects in this way. If you have a handy snowbank near you, focus not on "snow" but upon what is given. Is the snow really "white"? In fact, you may find it is rich in colors you never noticed before.

4. Multistability. Philosopher Don Ihde wrote a book entitled *Experimental Phenomenology* (2012) in which he has the reader explore ambiguous figures and asks the question, how much of the ambiguity of interpretation is given and how much supplied by the pre-interpretive structure of the mind. Here is a famous ambiguous figure that Ihde uses called a Necker cube (Figure 4).

The Necker cube is named after the Swiss geographer Louis Albert Necker de Saussure who created this drawing in such a way that there are no visual clues as to how it might be apperceived, with the left square facing front or back. You can resolve the cube in either direction. Play with it yourself and experience the effort necessary to change from one to the other. Then try to see both at the same time. Finally, notice that seeing the drawing as a cube in either direction is a projection of your mind. Bracket this projection and see the figure as it is given in two dimensions, lines on a page. It is not easy, is it?

Notice among other things that each part of the object, in this case the cube drawing, is distinct and yet is interdependent upon other parts of the drawing, all parts are relative to the whole, and the whole is in a relationship with the Watcher's point of view. Each part can, of course, be studied independently of the other parts, but when we reflect upon the whole drawing, the resolution of "cube-ness" requires all the parts to be located where they are in relation to each other and the Watcher as subject. This is true of any object we reduce. This is the "expansion" aspect of the object; its features are distributed spatially (also temporally) within

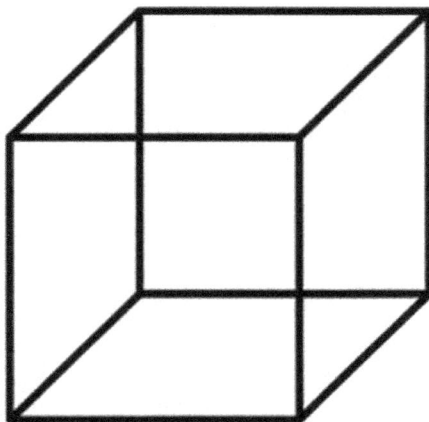

Figure 4. Necker Cube. One of many ambiguous figures used in psychological research which can be seen in two perspectives.

a boundary (Farber 1943: 296). If you would like to pursue this kind of reductive exercise, get a copy of Donald Hoffman's book, *Visual Intelligence* (1998) which is replete with such "illusions" and ambiguous figures, all of which demonstrate that there is more to the given than sensory form and hyle. Relationships among objects within the horizon influence how we perceive the object, and how we perceive the object so automatically is due to intuitive knowing.

Ihde (2012) uses this illusion and others as examples of what he calls *multistability*, a common aspect of our interpretation of objects and events in the world. In these drawings, and in many cases in the real world our mind has been conditioned to interpret the given in a specific way. Ihde has argued that all technologies are multistable because how they are used depends upon the conditioning of the people using them. A Paleolithic hand ax could be and likely was used to both cut up food and brain an enemy. Its meaning and use were determined by the people that handled them. Their use(s) are not primordially given, but imposed, just as the resolution of the Necker cube is imposed by the viewer. This is but another way to experience the crucial distinction between given and natural attitude. Working with the Necker cube is another set of reductions.

5. Object and horizon. Pick any object in your environment. Use any sense you wish, even introspective senses (a feeling, image, itch, etc.). When you focus on the object—perhaps a paperclip on your desk—notice how the object becomes the center of your sensory world at that moment. In a very real sense, the object becomes the center of a multisensory perceptual mandala. When you focus on an object, the rest of the world does not vanish, but rather becomes the context within which the object is positioned—the object's perceived environment. No matter what object you focus upon, the rest of the sensory world reorganizes itself around that object as a material context. The context of the object of scrutiny is part of what Husserl called the *horizon*.[18] Every object is experienced within its horizon.

This perception, with its modifications (remembering and other "re-productive" acts), became [the contemplative's] theme.

---

[18] If you wish to read about Husserl's notion of the *horizon*, see Husserl 1982[1913]: 101-103, 2019[1923/24]: 347; see also Geniusas 2011, 2012, Ihde 2012: 38-39, Welton 2000, Zahavi 2019, Bachelard 1968: 102-103, Landgrebe 1981.

Analysis of the perception of a particular thing—analysis of the syntheses in which the perception of a thing comes about— show that one cannot confine oneself to the thing as an isolated phenomenon, if one intends to discover the concrete sense of such a perception. The perceptual thing is always a thing in front of its objective background, a background of objects consciously and more or less explicitly co-meant along with it. Such co-intentions are always involved in the concrete nature, the *what* of the thing standing before our eyes: the table is "a table in the room," "in front of the window," "in my house," the house "on the street," "in this town," etc. (Landgrebe 1981: 123-124)

More than this, the horizon includes unsensed aspects of both the object and its context that you cannot actually perceive at the moment. Your attitude provides you with an extension of your field of perception to include unseen but known objects around you. You may be glancing at this page, then the wall clock and at the same time you know your children are playing in the yard, your spouse is out gardening, your toilet is in the other room. All these known but invisible objects may be within your horizon at the moment (Husserl 1982[1913]: 101-103). Alternatively, you may think of your horizon being the boundary (or "fringe") of those things included within your moment-to-moment awareness (Ihde 2012: 38-39).

Try this exercise. It is best done in nature but can be done anywhere if you cannot go outside. Sit quietly *with your eyes closed*, focusing on the field of sounds around you. Listen to all the sounds around you without focusing on any particular sound. Imagine that you are sitting at the center of a sphere of sound. When you are relaxed and able to ignore any impulse to focus on any particular sound, then choose one sound to focus upon (like the bird singing, the wind in the trees, the gurgling of the stream, the ticking of a clock) as intensely as you can, excluding all other sounds as background. Note how the selective abstraction of one sound over alternative sounds changes the whole field of your consciousness (Husserl 1973[1939]: 77). Now let go of the focus and return to tracking all sounds equally (with "bare attention" as Buddhists call it; see Nyanaponika 2005). Notice how sensory awareness changes again, back to a kind of resting state. Practice focusing and unfocusing on sounds around you. Oscillate back and forth between intense focus and relaxed focus. This is in fact a powerful meditation and is worth spending a lot of time on, especially when out of doors. It is in effect playing with objects and their horizon and can be done with any of the senses. This kind of flipping back and forth between global and specific focus is known as "sword and stream" meditation in Buddhist practice, "sword" being a metaphor for attention and "stream" a metaphor for flowing consciousness. Throughout this exercise, be mindful of the urge to identify sounds. Enter the phenomenological attitude and parse the auditory given from any natural projections upon and presumptions about the given.

6. Perspectives on the object. Any three-dimensional object you perceive has unperceived aspects (Husserl 1997[1907]: 37-46, 1982[1913]: 130, see also Kohak 1978: 67). Dan Zahavi (2019: 10-13) uses a clock as a prop here. When we look at a clock, usually at its face, we make the intuitive assumption that there is a back to the clock—that the clock is a three-dimensional thing, that it is "all there"—although in fact we cannot see the back of the clock while gazing at the face. You see the part or aspect of the thing, but the whole thing is intuitively present to you simultaneously. In philosophy and psychology, this is called *perceptual* or *object constancy*—no matter how our perspective changes on the object, it is perceived to be the same object. Using instead the perception of a house, Husserl shows: "The front side refers to the back side; the back side to the front. In other words, the *perceptual* presentation of the front side is bound up with components of apprehension, ones which refer beyond it to a back side, and the imaginative presentation [of the back side] is bound up no less to components which refer to the front side" (Husserl 1997[1907]: 48). Perhaps you will remember those old Western movies filmed in mocked-up towns made of false-front props. Viewing these movies, we did not perceive false-fronts, we perceived a main street with real buildings. Our perception automatically completes the object, although we can only perceive the object from one perspective at a time.

Indeed, you probably look into a mirror every once in a while, but you rarely, if ever, see the back of your head. And yet, you apprehend your whole head. If you want to, you can touch the back of your head, or you might feel it if it itches, or a breeze ruffles some hair back there. The point is that part of the horizon we take for granted when we focus on any object is that it is all there whether we can see all of its aspects or not. This too is part of the primordial sensory given. This is part of the hidden world that we naturally fill in with intuitive knowing.

Choose an object near you, say a coffee cup. Focus upon just what sensory information you are receiving about that object. Get into its colors and textures. If you have chosen a 3D object instead of a word on the page, then try studying it with both eyes open and then with one eye closed. Notice that with one eye closed the object "flattens." You can see clearly that it is the parallax provided by two perspectives afforded by two retinae that somehow produces the illusion of 3D-ness in the object and the "puffed-out," spacious nature of the visual world. Bear down on this exercise. Study the object with first one eye and then the other and analyze how one perspective differs, however slightly, from the other. Notice that when you open both eyes, you do not see two perspectives on the object, but rather one 3D image. What happened to the two distinct perspectives in the process of constituting the experience before the Watcher?

7. Duration. Perhaps the most profound and influential reduction carried out by Husserl was his phenomenological exploration of the sense of duration or time (Husserl 1964a). Reflecting on the exercises I have suggested above, you will recall that each took "time" to complete; that is, each object had duration. As you study the primordial given over time, you find the given is durable, unlike for instance a momentary flicker of light (due perhaps to photopsia or phosphenes) that come and go unbidden in your retinae. Husserl recognized that there is a temporal aspect to all objects and that the presumption of durability is part of the horizon of the object. Indeed, from Husserl's point of view, time-consciousness *is the stream of consciousness*. We will return to time consciousness in detail in Chapter 6.

8. Intentionality. Phenomenology makes the claim that every experience is *intentional*; that is, every experience you have *is an experience of something*.[19] There is no such thing as an experience without an object, even if that object is a blank space, a relationship, a horizon, a fantasy, a

---

[19] If you wish to read about *intentionality*, see Husserl 1982[1913]: 241-244, 1997[1907]: 11-12; see also Brentano 2014[1874], Ihde 2012: 24-25, Zahavi 2005: 11-13, Gurwitsch 1967, Hanna 2013, Kersten 1973, Kohak 1978: 121-131.

thought or concept, or even aspects of consciousness itself. Each and every moment of consciousness is constituted between the Watcher as subject and the percept as object. Don Ihde describes intentionality nicely: "... every experiencing has its reference or direction toward what is experienced, and, contrarily, every experienced phenomenon refers to or reflects a mode of experiencing to which it is present" (Ihde 2012: 25). Experiencing is thus a correlation—literally a "*co*-relation"—between Watcher and watched. This is the "subjectivity" of experience. There is no experience without someone experiencing. This *co*-relation, this intentionality, is (in philosophy jargon) a priori, meaning that intentionality is wired-in to the structure of experience—it is inherent, not chosen (Føllesdal 1978). The object of your intending may change, but the intentional relationship is inevitable, as are the associations within the relationship of relevant mental processes that produce "meaning" of the object. The structure of the intentional relationship is the same for everyone, regardless of their sociocultural background.

If you will reflect upon the various exercises you have explored above, you can repeat any one of them and notice that each object, each primordial sensory given, and each horizon is experienced from a standpoint. That standpoint is "you" the experiencer, the Watcher. The given (black line, coffee cup, red patch, feeling, verbal chatter, itch, belly ache, whatever) is not there and then you come along and discover it. You in fact produce it and it reflects your intentional act by its perspective. This reminds me of the ancient Sufi story of the eight blind men sent to explore and describe an elephant which none had encountered before. Each described the object from their standpoint, one feeling only the trunk, one a tusk, one a side, one a leg, one a tail, and so forth. Each comes back to describe an "elephant" from their respective standpoint. The intent of the story since antiquity has been to teach about intentionality and subjectivity.

Take one of the exercises above and play with intentionality a while. Reduce the given of a word on this page. Gone are the word-ness, font-ness, page-ness, meaning, etc., and all that is left is the given black pattern on white background *as seen by you at this moment*. Now, shift your head around a bit and watch how the perspective on the black patterns change. Move your eye to the side slightly and note how the black patterns change. You are reducing the word to the given from your unique point of view, *your standpoint*. Reduce the coffee cup or some other 3D object around you to what is primordially given. Move your head around, in and out, side to side, and notice how the perspective changes. The experience incorporates both the reduced coffee cup with its horizon and you the Watcher.

9. Attention. You might think that intentionality is another word for attention, but when you get into the phenomenology of the matter, you will discover this is not the case. Intentionality labels the inevitable relationship between the object and the Watcher and encompasses all of the mental processes that are brought to bear on the object, including attention. Attention has to do with your ability to direct focus within the field of your consciousness, your ability to "turn towards or turn away" from the object, whether that object is a thing, an event, a horizon, or the entire field of consciousness.[20] Return to the exercise of intentionality in the last section and note that you are directing your attention and thus controlling the intentional relationship. You can change your standpoint and thus change the relationship between "you" the Watcher and the object. Not only does the polarity between you and the object change, so too do the mental processes engaging in the intending. This time, explore the range of objects you can "turn towards" and "turn away from." Notice that the "turning" requires effort and the mental processes involved must change. You may have to reorient your body, or just shift your gaze, or merely pick out one sound from among the auditory surrounds. Notice also that you can attend things "out there" and things inside your mind (images, sensations, feelings, body postures and movements, etc.). Notice also that you must exercise attention-control in order to reflect upon anything, including your inner states. Training the searchlight of attention upon an object to the exclusion of any other object yammering for your attention is what learning to contemplate is all about. With increased concentration upon the focal object, other sensations fall away from your notice. Yet many of the sensations are stored in memory, as experiments in hypnosis and hypermnesic recall have shown—although the accuracy of recall is questionable (Mazzoni, Laurence and Heap 2014).

---

[20] If you want to read more about the phenomenology of *attention*, see Husserl 1982[1913]: 267-270; see also Arvidson 1996, Gurwitsch 1964, 1966, Zahavi 2005: 53-54.

10. Willing. Another term that gets muddled with intention and attention is *willing* (Ger: *wollen*).[21] For Husserl (1982[1913]: 329), willing is an act of positing, an act of intentional experience, and thus an essence (below). But it is hard to tease out much description of willing in Husserl's works, at least those available in English. His close friend and colleague, Alexander Pfänder (Pfänder and Spiegelberg 1967), is another matter entirely, for Pfänder gave much attention to the role of willing in experience, *grounding his conclusions upon direct contemplative methods.*

Let us return to the things with our increasingly proficient phenomenologist's hat on and reduce acts of willing. If you have reached the point where you can experience your field of consciousness like Harding did, as a sphere of perception atop your shoulders instead of a head, you have noticed that you can direct your focus of attention toward anything whatever in that sphere whether the object be a sensation or a relationship or a qualia. Notice now that you "direct" attention toward whatever you desire to attend. You *will* your attention to move without any body movement, or by turning your head, moving your eyeballs, shifting from one sensory mode to another, etc. Behind each willful act is a conscious "motive." Notice the difference between consciously blinking your eyes and the automatic subconscious eye blinks that happen all the time with no conscious intent. Notice the difference between consciously directing your attention to something and having your attention attracted by a sudden noise or movement. In one case you consciously will and in the other you do not consciously will. Because you always have a motive behind your conscious willing, you can see that willing is inseparable from cognition and feeling.

The really important realization with respect to willing and the primordial given is that no act of willing will change the sensory given. You can will your body to move, but only in ways it is architecturally (primordially) prepared to move. You cannot will your hand to grasp backwards, only forwards. You cannot will the green patch to turn red in the reduction. You can will a change of perspective and thus change the light penetrating your retinae, but if you stand still and focus on the blue siding on a building, you cannot will it to become red or speckled or

---

[21] If you wish to read more on the phenomenology of *willing*, see Husserl 1982[1913]: 329, Melle 1997, Pfänder and Spiegelberg 1967, Uemura and Salice 2018.

vanish. This is your willing in relationship to the "obduracy" of the real world purveyed before you in the sensorium.

Notice also that unless you step back into your natural attitude, the question of the *cause* of willing does not arise. Notice also that the mechanisms that intervene between your act of willing and the changes in body orientation or attention are also absent. That is the magic of willing, for all you have to do is willfully initiate an act and the act happens. No switch is thrown, no plan is contrived, hardly any duration occurs between thought and act. You will also discover perhaps that willing changes intentionality, or the relationship between Watcher and object.

11. Essences. One of the most controversial topics in Husserlian phenomenology is his concept of the *essence(s)* or the various primordial structures of consciousness.[22] Much of the historical controversy over essences derives from critics who have never themselves committed to a meditative discipline. One obvious example was the philosopher Moritz Schlick's rejection of essences in support of his logical positivist agenda (Livingston, 2002). Schlick's objections were on logical and theoretical, not phenomenological grounds—whatever his value has been in the history of the philosophy of science, there is no evidence the man ever meditated in any formal sense, and hence missed the reality of essences.

Husserlian phenomenology comes closest to Buddhist mindfulness contemplation with the isolation and study of essential structures of experience (see Laycock 1994). Not only this, but Husserl's treatment of essences or essential structures is of prime importance to neurophenomenology as well as anthropology, as we will see later on. As usual, Husserl begins with the given, the "turn to the things themselves"— that which appears in our perception with nothing added from the natural attitude. He then asks what about the object is essential to being that class of object. Following Zahavi (2019: 45), let us take for example this book:

> ...I might change the color and design of the cover; I can add or subtract its number of pages; I can change its size and weight, etc.

---

[22] To read more about *essences* and *essential structures*, see Husserl 2002[1910], 1982[1913]: 51-58, Held 2003a: 13-17, Levinas 1967, 1995, Mohanty 1959, 1978, Moran 2005: Chap. 5, Smith 2013: 135-141, Spiegelberg 1975: 6-7, Thomasson 2017, Zhok 2011.

In performing this exercise, I am relying on both my previous experience of books and on my imagination. The end result is the delimitation *of a certain set of properties that belong to the book as such*, and which, if changed, would make the book cease being a book. The imaginative variation can, consequently, help us disclose the invariant structures that make up the essence of the object. (Emphasis added)

The essence(s) of a book constitutes the *eidos* of book-ness supplied from intuition. And the use of imagination to explore the possible variations covered by the idea is called *eidetic variation*. Eidetic variation is an exercise—a kind of thought experiment—that eventually leads to an *eidetic intuition* about the essence of the object's class membership ("types of objectivity"):

The character of the activities of consciousness is not dependent on the empirically given objects that happen to be there, but instead on *"Essence,"* that is, on the universal determination of types of objectivities. Thus, there are areas of objectivities, *"regions of being,"* as Husserl says, that are differentiated according to the special characteristics of their being, their *"Eidos,"* that is, the mental view that they offer in a corresponding originary intuition. (Held 2003a: 14-15)

One of the easiest ways to quickly engage intuitive essences is the study of illusions. Like many illusions, the Kanizsa Triangle (Kanizsa 1955) gives visual cues that the sensorium intuitively completes to form an object, in this case the white triangle in the middle of the drawing (Figure 5). Notice that there appears to be a brightness variation at the borders of the triangle where no real variations exist. In this manner, the sensorium "invites" meaning; that is, invites recognition, cognitions, lateral imaginative associations, etc.

Let us carry this farther by reducing, say, a paperclip. What is essential to the object being a "paperclip?" Imagine that you straighten out the wire that forms the paperclip. Same wire, but where is the "paperclip?" All we have now is a "straight" wire. If you think to yourself, "that's a straightened-out paperclip," you have actually fallen back into your natural attitude, applying memory of how the wire got into its present shape. There is nothing about the wire before you that signals "paperclip." Remind yourself over and over again, "return to the thing itself."

Now bend the wire in the middle to a 90° angle. Still no "paperclip," but we now have a "bent" wire—is it an "L-shaped" wire? Yes, but there is nothing given by the object that relates it to a letter of the alphabet. You have supplied that association from your cognition and memory, from your natural attitude. Add another 90° angle going the opposite way. We have a "Z-shaped" wire, but again, you are supplying that from memory and cognitive associations. Now, bend the wire back until it resembles a "paperclip" again. What is it about this given that makes it a "paperclip"? Stretch your imagination here. This paperclip is made of steel wire. If it were made of pure silver, gold alloy, aluminum, brass, would it still be a paperclip? What happens if we imagine a paperclip made of plastic, glass, butter, wood? Is the given still a paperclip? What is the difference between "looking like" a paperclip and "being" a paperclip? After playing with this exercise for a while, try it on another object, say a pencil, a marble, a fork, whatever. The object here is to reach an intuitive understanding

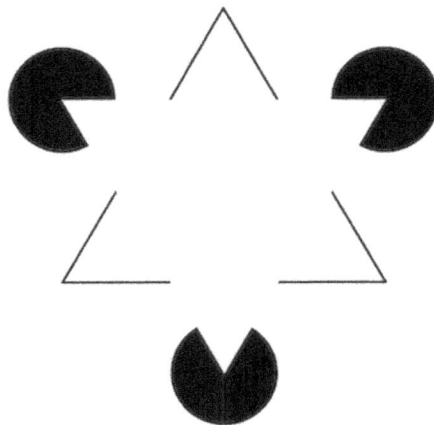

Figure 5. Kanizsa Triangle. In this illusion, the triggers for the illusion of a white triangle are presented in the given, but the sensorium completes the triangle intuitively by creating apparent but unreal color gradations at the border of the illusory triangle. Sensory hyle suggest an object and the sensorium completes the perception.

of what constitutes the intuited class to which the given belongs within the horizon of your direct perception. You should also have associated form and function to paperclip-ness. The form of the object affords the "clipping" of paper together.

Recalling once again that Husserl's project was to create a disciplined science of the essential structures of consciousness (2002[1910]), what are the essences that we have uncovered? We have seen that form and hyletic content are given but meaning is suspended while in the phenomenological attitude. Stripping away all presumptions still leaves objects characterized by their boundaries and class characteristics. The class characteristics are an *eidos* provided by intuition. Every experience is focused upon an object, whether a thing or a horizon, and as focus changes the context reorganizes around the object of attention (Husserl 1973[1939]: 77). Experiencing the object is a given relationship between the object and the intending Watcher. The object of awareness is seen from a perspective, the perspective can change, and we automatically account for unseen perspectives upon a whole.

12. Transcendence. Husserl often speaks of certain things as being *transcendent*, by which he means that there is some aspect of the thing that "goes beyond" subjectivity. When we reduce an object completely so that all we are focusing upon is the primordial sensory given, and when we realize that we cannot willfully alter the form, hyle, or relations within the perceptual field to change (green patch to red, curved form to straight) without physically manipulating the object, we sense the transcendental "objectivity" of the object. Things that participate in our stream of consciousness, but that also have the quality of transcendental objectivity are essential structures, the sensory object from the real world, the Other, and even my being (as a thing in the world) and the Watcher. As we track our stream of consciousness, we learn intuitively that a major function of consciousness is engagement with the transcendental world, the real world in which things exist whether we are aware of them or not. This is why Husserl often characterizes his work as discovery of the *transcendental phenomenology* of consciousness.[23]

---

[23] If you wish to read more about *transcendence*, see Husserl 1993[1931]: 103-108, 1982[1913]: 133-135, 212-215; see also Bruzina 2004, Moran 2000, Welton 2000.

PHENOMENOLOGY OF THE INVISIBLE

If you were to continue practicing as a pure phenomenologist, what other essential structures might you uncover? A direction that is very productive vis-à-vis the anthropology of religion is what might be called the *phenomenology of the invisible* (Zahavi 1999, 2019: 60-62; Serafin 2016). Recall that invisible aspects of the object and relations within the given are also included by Husserl in the horizon (Carr 1974: 92-93). Moreover, most causal relations are invisible to perception and that leaves great scope for imagined and projected causations to fill the natural attitude—the stuff of what religions are made. One of the functions of the natural attitude with its cognitions and worldviews is to fill in the invisible aspects experienced in the given, a role taken up by theory in the empirical sciences (Laughlin 2020b; Merleau-Ponty 1968).

PHENOMENOLOGY OF THE EGO

One of the most important reductive exercises you will ever carry out will be of your own *"empirical" ego* (see Husserl 1977[1931], 2019[1923/24]: 555-558, van Peursen 1959, Spiegelberg 1965, Bachelard 1968: 181-184).

> When I, the meditating I, reduce myself to my absolute transcendental ego by phenomenological *epoché* do I not become *solis ipse* ["I alone," the root of "solipsism"]; and do I not remain that, as long as I carry on a consistent self-explication under the name phenomenology? Should not a phenomenology that proposed to solve the problems of Objective being, and to present itself actually as philosophy, be branded therefore as transcendental solipsism? (Husserl 1977[1931]: 89)

Husserl distinguished between the "concrete," "empirical," or "psychophysical" ego of everyday natural existence and the "pure" or "transcendental" ego—the *solis ipse*, the "impartial spectator" (*unbeteiligter Zuschauer*)—of the subjective center after the bracketing of the natural "me."[24] Stating this more clearly, and pointing to the method for reducing the ego, every "thing" you might point to as being part of "me" (e.g., sensation, boundary, spatial extension, quality, feeling, thought, image, belief, status, attitude, etc.) can become, each in its turn, an object of phenomenological scrutiny. Thus, if that bit of me is an object, who is the subject observing that bit of "me?" Exactly! The *transcendental ego* which is non-reducible and structurally given in every experience—what I call the Watcher, which is no "thing" at all— appears as the irrepressible subject. The Watcher is only and always just the subjective pole of intentionality. For some (e.g., Zahavi 2005: 32-36), Husserl seems to be saying that your transcendental ego is virtually synonymous with your stream of consciousness. Watcher and watching are certainly properties of a structural essence.

PHENOMENOLOGY OF PHENOMENOLOGY

Finally, it is inherent in Husserl's methods, and has been clarified by his collaborator, Eugen Fink, that the phenomenological reduction *itself* can be reduced, thus in effect allowing a phenomenology of pure phenomenology (Fink 1995: 8). That is, not only can we reflect upon the reduced primordial given (say, a pattern of black squiggles on this page), or upon the correlation of Watcher and the word on the page, we can reflect upon the reflexive process itself—the Watcher watching itself operate within the intentional act—being aware of being aware, so to speak. The completion of phenomenology, "…is to submit the phenomenologizing thought and theory formation that functions anonymously in phenomenological labors to a proper transcendental analytic, and thus to complete phenomenology in ultimate *transcendental self-understanding about itself.* In other words, the transcendental theory of method intends nothing other than a *phenomenology of phenomenology*" (ibid: 8). This is nothing surprising to any mature contemplative who automatically comes to realize knowledge of themselves contemplating the process of meditation (Laughlin 2020a). If you will repeat any of

---

[24] William James (1890) distinguished between the "empirical self" and the "pure ego."

the reflections I have suggested above and not only carry it out until the reduction is complete, you will realize that within the reflection you are also aware of the process by which you carried the exercise out. Indeed, symbolically this amounts to the contemplative *uroboros*, the snake eating its own tail. Perhaps you might reflect again on Professor Wheeler's wonderful cosmogram in Figure 2. Neuropsychologically speaking, this is the brain becoming aware of its own processes.

EIDETIC FREE VARIATION AND ESSENCES

Among other things, what we have been doing above is playing-around with what Husserl called *eidetic free variation*.[25] This is Husserl's principal method for isolating and describing essential structures of experience. In effect, "free fancy" is a kind of contemplation, or what Husserl calls "reflexion."

> Reflexion [...] is an expression for acts in which the stream of experience (*Erlebnis*), with all its manifold events (phases of experience, intentionalities) can be grasped and analyzed in the light of its own evidence. It is, as we may also express it, the name we give to consciousness' own method for the knowledge of consciousness generally. But in this very method it becomes itself the object of possible studies. (Husserl 1982[1913]: 219)

Contemplation, in other words, takes advantage of the ability of consciousness to study objects, relations, events, and intuitive insights in the sensuous world by turning the selfsame ability upon its own

---

[25] If you wish to read more about Husserl's method of *eidetic free variation* (aka: "free variation," "eidetic variation," "free fancy," "imaginative free variation," "free arbitrary variation," etc.), see Husserl 1982[1913]: 57-58, 198-201, 1977[1925]: 53-65, 1980[1952]: 26-27, 1973[1939]: 329-330, 373-377; see also Mohanty 1991, Natanson 1973:67-71, Smith 2013: 312-322, Zahavi 2019: 45. Husserl's "imaginative free variation" is similar in many respects to Jung's "active imagination," a method of inviting communication with the unconscious by setting up fantasy scenarios and watching what the unconscious mind does to the imagery as it communes with the ego (see Hannah, 2015[1981]; see also Chapter 9).

operations. And a principal way of doing that is to use "fancy" or fantasy to experiment with objects and such to see what is universal about the experiential variations. This is a wholly mental exercise or "thought experiment" that leads inevitably to intuitive discernment of universal properties or essences.

> [...] under this title [free variation] we carefully described a certain purely mental activity and therein a chain of purely mental products, as *the final product of which an eidos becomes our own in pure seeing.* We understood by this that it is a universal like the species "red" or the higher genus "color" taken universally, but as a pure universal, something trans-empirical, raised above all factuality of existence, if it is gained in such a way that every presupposition of any factuality at all is thereby cancelled. The species "red," e.g., or the genus "color," is an *eidos,* an essential universality, but as pure universality. That is, pure of all presupposition of any factual existence at all, therefore of any red, or any colored, factual actuality. (Husserl 1977[1925]: 63; emphasis added)

Using this method, we take the given—any sensory object as it is given a priori—and treat it as an example of an infinite number of other examples we may iterate in our imagination. Eventually we directly intuit the *pure* essence of the object and the limits it imposes on the possibility of occurrence in the real world.

> [...] in our imagination we may vary without limit the shapes of any material object; we may also imagine it at various times and places. Our imagination here is absolutely free; it is not limited by anything; and the object we consider remains concrete, i.e., capable of existing. Now, if we try to imagine a material object without any shape at all, then we lose its concrete character, its capacity to exist. The essence of an independent object determines the limits between which we may vary its contents. A variation which steps over the limit imposed by the essence takes away from the object its concrete character, its independence, its capacity to exist. (Levinas 1995: 112)

When Husserl says something is "pure," it usually means that it is independent of any of the natural attitude presuppositions, including ontological assumptions, actual empirical evidence from the sciences, etc. The isolated and discerned *eidos* (eidetic structures or essences) are the building blocks of the a priori elements of experience. Incidentally, the objects we may select for free variation treatment includes the ego and those attributes that in the natural attitude one identifies as part of the ego (DeSantis 2020).

INTERPRETATION HAS TO START SOMEPLACE

As with any skill, the more you practice doing pure phenomenology by applying reductions (bracketing the natural attitude ingredients, reaching and sustaining the epoché) and exploring eidetic variations, the better at it you will become. The goal is to perfect your ability to enter the phenomenological attitude about any and all experiences until it becomes second nature. This process is no different than learning to use a microscope to view tiny things, to test substances for their chemical composition, to study the sociality of water voles, to isolate and describe black holes, or to test for the authenticity of vintage postage stamps. There are unique problems faced in developing each of these skills, and with doing pure phenomenology, the learning curve may be steep, depending upon how easily you can calm the chatter and center the mind on increasingly subtle tasks of introspection.

All I have offered here are a few beginner's steps, introductory exercises, invitations to explore an alternative way of studying your own consciousness—i.e., "if you want to know this, do this," right? These steps can lead you into the ASC Husserl and other true contemplative phenomenologists depend upon to obtain phenomenological data for analysis. After all, you have to start someplace, and if you do not learn to see in a phenomenological way, it is unlikely you will ever really understand what Husserlian phenomenology is on about. At the simplest level, there is direct experience and there is interpretation. Experience is structured at a primordial level while interpretation involves cognition at the highest level, involving a lot of social learning, cultural knowledge systems and so forth. At the level of experience, two people from different cultures can have more or less the same dream, and yet how they interpret their dreams may be worlds apart. Moreover, interpretations can be quite erroneous. Take for example so-called *out-of-body experiences* (OBE) in which a person experiences themselves leaving their corporeal body and floating around above the body or taking a journey and having adventures (Blanke *et al.* 2004). One might conclude (people in fact commonly do) that consciousness must be somehow separate from the brain. They would be wrong, for as neuropsychological research has shown, changes in certain areas of the brain can lead to radical changes in first person perspective (see Seth 2021: 164), or what Husserl would call an ego "displacement" (Husserl 2005[1898-1925]: Chap. 1; see also Chapter 3).

ESSENTIAL STRUCTURES OF EXPERIENCE

You have already uncovered several essential structures of experience using the methods of pure phenomenology. Here are a few that you may recognize from your reflections while carrying out the exercises above:

1. Pattern. Each and every object you reduce to its primordial given is ordered, never random, shapeless, or chaotic. Suspending the natural attitude therefore does *not* produce a "blooming, buzzing confusion" of qualia. It is easy to see how the mind apprehends the sensory and intuitive patterns supplied by the primordial given and projects meaning upon those patterns. You might say that the given is inherently salient within the context of the intentional act.

2. Things. Our experience is full of things, "thingly-real" objects with stable boundaries and duration. Things are filled with apparent qualia (*hyle* in Husserl's terms as contrasted with form or *morphé*: colors, textures, tones, tastes, etc.), relations among objects, and intuitions (class membership, position within the horizon, aesthetics, pragmatics, etc.).

3. Part-whole relationship. If the object is a three-dimensional thing, we never perceive it in its entirety at the same time. We intuitively infer the whole from the perspectives we take upon its parts. We never "see" part of the clock per se, we see the clock as a whole.

4. *Eidos* ("form," "type," "species"). Things before our gaze are intuited within direct experience as exemplars of a class, an idea, an *eidos*.

5. Entanglement. Objects always are given within the context of an environment of other objects with which they relate and with which they interact.

6. Horizon. Objects always present within the context of a horizon (limits to what can be perceived at the moment).

7. **Impermanence.** No matter the object of our focus, it is impermanent. It was not there to your perception before you experience it, and it will not be there at some point in the future. This includes any aspect of the "I am" or "empirical" ego ("my" opinion, "my" belief, "my" feeling, etc.).

8. Naïve now. The stream of our experience under the natural attitude occurs as a flowing duration, part retention of past moments from short-term memory, part protention of near future moments, and part the real reducible "now" point.

9. Object-Watcher discrimination. Reduction of the relationship between the object and the Watcher. The object only arises before a subject, the subject intends the object.

10. Intentionality. Every moment of consciousness is constituted as a system of essential structures linking an object and a subject perceiving the object.

11. Attention. You may exercise control over your relationship with the object, or the object may "draw" your attention. This is the function within consciousness that allows for willful control of focus and modification of intentionality.

12. Willing. You perhaps reduced your willful acts in all the exercises and discovered the relationship between willing and intentionality. We can will an intentional act and we can will within an intentional act.

Many other essences are detectable and describable within the scope of pure phenomenological methods (see Cairns 1939 for a long list). We have worked with only a few so as to get the flavor and the technique of reducing aspects of experience and playing with them using free variation. Indeed, once you are skilled in entering the phenomenological attitude, you can rely upon it in any state of consciousness, including ASC such as psychedelic (entheogenic) drug trips, lucid dreams, hypnagogic and hypnopompic states, meditative states, absorption states, and so on (see Chapter 10). In my own work and writings, I have relied heavily upon both my own experiences enriched by phenomenological methods, and the reports of other mature contemplatives that have mastered these skills from various traditions.

THE BURNING QUESTION OF ONTOLOGY

We need to address the common and controversial topic often referred to as "the ontological status of the essences" problem. There are many opinions about whether, and to what extent you can or do carry your ontological thinking with you into pure phenomenology (Landgrebe 1949, Berndtsson *et al.* 2007, Bostar 1993). Frankly, many of these discussions reveal an author's lack of experience in performing reductions rather than clarify the actual doing of phenomenology. If you took me up on my invitation to play with reductions in the exercises above, then you should have realized you can keep your *thoughts* about "reality" out of the process. Performing a reduction upon a paper clip does not require any information whatever as to the ontological status of the paper clip. All you need is what is already present a priori, including the intuition that the sensory object as a whole is "real" (Ger.: *real*) and its parts too are "real" (Ger.: *reell*). Of course, the implication that you can somehow ablate your natural attitude from your brainmind is ridiculous. Nor was that Husserl's intention, as Berndtsson *et al.* (2007) make clear. Husserl called for the suspension, not the eradication, of the natural attitude while performing reductions (Husserl 1982[1913]: 110-111). You have seen where that takes you. It takes you to that ASC in which you can observe and analyze the given without dialoguing with assumptions, judgements, concepts, thoughts, theses, theories, and presuppositions. When ontological chatter arises, you just "return to the things themselves." Retaining the results of those experiences in memory you can later compare them to ontological, conceptual, and theoretical material if you choose. Indeed, to develop a phenomenologically grounded science you must eventually do so. As Erazim Kohák (1978: 70-72) showed, Husserl's conclusion after his extensive meditations was that *experience is our absolute datum*:

> All claims about transcendence—say, that not only do I *see* a
> chair but that *there is* a chair, not only that murder *is* wrong but

that a given act *is* a murder—represent a second, hypothetical level of awareness and so are not a datum but a conjecture. It may be very well-warranted conjecture indeed, but its givenness is always a matter of contingent fact, not an essential necessity. Only the immanent, the awareness of the I and its stream of lived experiences, is given absolutely. Even if all the objects of my experiences were fictions, *they would still be the reality to which I respond*. Imaginary guilt can drive humans to suicide; "objective" guilt, never experienced as *Erlebnis* ["lived experience"], cannot. (Kohák 1978: 71)

Perhaps one of the most intriguing puzzles about perception has to do with how the brainmind mediates intuitions. For example, the awareness of *numerosity* is ubiquitous to animals with brains, ranging from fishes to elephants and monkeys (e.g., Brannon and Terrace 2000, Bryer *et al.* 2022), and of course humans (Gebuis, Kadosh and Gevers 2016). This makes perfect sense evolutionarily speaking. This system is called the *approximate number system* and includes operations ranging from how the pupils of the eyes work (Castaldi *et al.* 2021) to higher cortical processing. This research offers us information about the neural correlates of intuition, one of Husserl's types of essences.

SUMMARY AND SEGUE

If you have followed along and tried the various exercises, you will have at least the beginnings of an appreciation of how one may do pure phenomenology, apply the method of reduction, and enter the ASC we call the phenomenological attitude. This can really be a finicky process, for at every turn you are required to see clearly what is given to us primordially and what we add on to the experience out of higher processing. If you have reached the point when carrying out a reduction is fairly straightforward and easy, then you will by now realize that essential structures of perception are ubiquitous to intentional acts. Regardless of the object before you, you can now parse out the various elements that must come together in the sensorium in order for a gestalt view to arise. Some of the elements are essential while others are imposed from above. In no case however is experience "culture all the way down." By application of the epoché you can accrue more than sufficient evidence that the cultural constructivist take on consciousness is fundamentally wrong.

As I mentioned, we have been focusing upon doing "static" pure phenomenology on material objects to the exclusion of living beings. Husserl was criticized for this approach by some authorities that wanted to know, "What about our experience of other people?" But Husserl was already aware of the issue of intersubjectivity. His early concern was to lay the foundations of more formal ways of knowing—logic, arithmetic, mathematics, so forth. In the next chapter we will examine how Husserl eventually took up the study of intersubjectivity and lay the framework for his transcendental phenomenology and the phenomenology of the lifeworld.

CHAPTER FOUR

Intersubjectivity and the Lifeworld

*Every I finds in its surrounding, and more often in its surrounding of
immediate interest, things which it regards as lived bodies but which it
sharply contrasts to its "own" lived body as other lived bodies. It does this
in such a way that to each such lived body there belongs again an I, but
a different, other I. (It regards the lived bodies as "bearers" of I-subjects.
But it "sees" the other I's not in the sense that it sees itself or experientially
finds itself. Rather it posits them in the manner of "empathy;" hence other
lived experiences and other character dispositions are "found" too; but
they are not given or had in the sense of one's own.)*

– Husserl (2006[1910-1911]: 5)

*...how can we explain the fact that not only does every individual
consciousness have an experiential world that is exclusively its own, but
together they also possess an experiential world that is common to them
all, that is, a universal horizon that surrounds their subjective horizons?*

– Klaus Held (2003a: 48)

Those readers more familiar with the history of the
phenomenological movement will have noticed I have thus
far avoided issues related to intersubjective experiences and
the so-called "lifeworld." Husserl was goaded into emphasizing
humanity's social nature by various critics, and in response developed
his approach to intersubjectivity, begun early in his meditations, and
culminating in the publication of his now famous book *Crisis in
European Sciences and Transcendental Phenomenology* (1970[1936]). I
had three reasons for avoiding a discussion of this aspect of Husserlian
phenomenology previously: (1) Doing phenomenology and developing
the phenomenological attitude is no different when the object is a

person or social relationship—the reduction operation is the same when you are actually *doing* phenomenology (Husserl 2006[1910-1911]: 82, Landgrebe 1981: 177). Husserl used the same method of reduction for any object that arises within the stream of consciousness. (2) Most discussions of the phenomenology of intersubjectivity amount to philosophical, existential, or social scientific theory, and *not* reports of the results of doing phenomenology. (3) This would take us into the murky area of "transcendental" phenomenology which would confuse the fundamental question of how to do pure phenomenology. But now it is appropriate to add the intersubjective ingredient into the epoché, and to explore what Husserl found out about intersubjective consciousness.

THE LIFEWORLD

One of the most important concepts in Husserlian phenomenology from the standpoint of anthropology or any other social science is the *lifeworld* (Ger: *Lebenswelt*).[26] Husserl borrowed the term from philosopher Richard Avenarius (1843–1896) and others to characterize the interpersonally shared, pre-scientific, primordial givenness of our experience of the environing world, and to emphasize the role of intersubjective experience in performance of the *transcendental epoché*—that is, realizing that the environing world I am experiencing within the horizon of the primordial sensory given is the same transcendental world you are experiencing via the same essential structures of primordial perception (Husserl 1982[1913]: 130-137, Luft 2011, Overgaard 2002). Husserl used the term lifeworld in the same way as Adolf Bastian used the term "psychic unity of mankind" (see Chapter 1). However, there was nothing new about the lifeworld in the later writings of Husserl, for "lifeworld" was just a new term he inserted into his writings for an intersubjective expansion of what he earlier called the pregiven sensory world (Husserl 1982[1913], Duranti 2010, Haney 2002, Landgrebe 1981: 186, Luft 2011: 120). We have seen that my natural attitude is a mish-mash of primordial data plus everything I bring into my experiences from cognition, feeling, and memory. The primordial

---

[26] If you wish to read more about *lifeworld* phenomenology, see Husserl's *Crisis*; see also Embree 1972, Kern 2019, Lee 2019, Nenon 2013a, Schutz 1967[1932].

object blended with all the meanings that I bring to my experience of the object comprise my natural attitude (see Prat 2022 on the neuroscience of "building" one's unique brain from a lifetime of experience). From an anthropological standpoint, Husserl was talking about "culture" from the subjective perspective of an individual's direct experience.

> While the content of particular experiences is contingent and particular, the structure of subject experience as such is universal. Thus, while laws and customs may differ, the experience of a rightful due and of injustice is universal. Any world, even that of a different culture, is in principle understandable by any subject and so by any anthropologist, *qua subject,* sharing a common subjectivity—"humanity"—with the humans from whom he is separated by cultural differences. Contrary to the popular misconception, the epistemological puzzle about cross-cultural understanding is not how we can grasp the "mentality" of a culture far removed from ours in space and time. As subject beings dealing with other subjective beings, we can, in principle, understand the pattern of their needs, hopes, and fears. The problem is to understand the specific ways in which another culture *acts out*, in particular, the pattern of being-human which, in principle, we understand by sharing it. But, epistemologically speaking, that is only a problem, not a mystery. As the patterns are in principle shared, the particulars, though hitherto unknown to us, are in principle experienceable. (Kohak 1978: 88)

The course of Husserl's phenomenological project from the start was to suspend ("reduce," "set aside," "bracket;" see Luft 2011: Chaps. 2 and 3, 2015) everything that is not directly given to perception by the senses and by intuitive ("primordial," "a priori") knowledge—as Husserl noted, culture (including scientific concepts and theories) drapes over our everyday experience like a "garment of ideas" or "garment of symbols" (e.g., Husserl 1970[1936]: 51). This of course refers to or implies at least all your *enculturation*[27]—everything you learn from other people while

---

[27] "Enculturation" is anthropology-speak for the process by which we learn to be a "culture-bearing" member of our society (see Mead 1963).

growing up as a member of a group, especially those many experiences you share vicariously with other members of your group (Husserl 1989[1952]: 365-366). Husserl (1999, 2002[1910], 1982[1913]) argued that only by application of the phenomenological method can the sciences and philosophy be grounded in direct knowledge of how the mind constructs the reality we experience. It is the failure of sciences to retain awareness of the pregiven world of the senses that requires a distinction between phenomenology and science:

> It is this [pregiven] world that we find to be the world of all known and unknown realities. To it, the world of actually experiencing intuition, belongs the shape of space-time together with all bodily shapes incorporated in it; it is in this world that we ourselves live, in accord with our bodily..., personal way of being. But here we find nothing of geometrical idealities, no geometrical space or mathematical time with all their shapes. (Husserl 1970[1936]: 50)

Husserl paid attention to criticisms from other philosophers and social scientists that claimed he had not paid enough attention to intersubjective experiences—to social life (e.g., Habermas 1992)—despite the fact that he had in fact done so from the very beginning (see Duranti 2010, Haney 2002, Hutcheson 1980, Weiss 2016, Welton 2000 on this issue). This claim is the root of many of the criticisms over the years that he was a "solipsist" and a rank "idealist," neither of which is true (see e.g., Van de Pitte 1977, Fink 1972). This issue was thoroughly addressed by the writings of the Munich Circle, realist movement, during the early years of Husserl's career (see B. Smith 1997). In any event, the natural attitude includes all the meaning we bring into our experiences, whether or not those experiences be of things or people. In other words, the natural attitude is inherently symbolic, cultural, and social, and thus applies equally to meanings of the physical and social worlds (Chelstrom 2012, Hutcheson 1980). Moreover, the natural attitude knowledge changes over time in each society, while retaining the same universal lifeworld rooted in the pregiven sensuous world of perception (Husserl 1989[1952]: 365-366).

Intersubjectivity

In deciphering Husserl's understanding of lifeworld phenomenology, it is critical to understand that his perspective is always subjective—that is, doing phenomenology of social relationships is always from the standpoint of the individual, not the group. "Group," "couple," "society," "company," "band," "community," etc. are all abstractions for social coordination among individuals. As Anthony Steinbock notes:

> There are acts that by their very nature are individualizing acts: self-refection, examining one's conscience, introspection, and the like have this quality. This does not mean that they are isolating acts. However, it is to say that even if you and I did this at the same time, or a group of us did this, it would not change these acts into social acts. There are, however, acts which by their very nature are social acts: trusting, being sincere, ordering, promising, obeying, and admiring are social acts in the sense that they posit some other for that act to have any meaning at all. (Steinbock 2021: 30)

This distinction must be kept in mind especially when dealing with misdirected critiques of Husserl's methods as being solipsistic. Moreover, it is both non-Husserlian and empirically sloppy to speak of a group as having a "phenomenology." Cultures and societies do not practice phenomenologies, people do. Cultures and societies do not experience, people do. One may accurately speak of a community intersubjectively sharing individual phenomenologies (Welton 2000). Husserl never lost track of the fact that the people that I am experiencing are a special type of object of consciousness that, like all other objects before the mind, can be reduced to the level of perceptual given and, from that phenomenological attitude, studied. Let me quote Husserl on the matter of intersubjectivity:

> To introduce the matter of intersubjectivity, what we have said also holds true if another person tells me about his past experiences, communicates his memories: what is recalled in them belongs to the same objective world as that which is

given in my and our common present lived experience. The remembered environing world of the other, about which he tells us, may certainly be another world than that in which we find ourselves at present, and likewise the environing world which I myself remember may be another world; I can have changed my place of residence, have come to another country, with other men and other customs, etc., or this same geographical neighborhood with its inhabitants may have so changed in the course of a human life that it has simply become another; but, despite all this, all these different remembered environing worlds are *pieces of one and the same objective world*. This world is, in the most comprehensive sense, as the *lifeworld* for a human community capable of mutual understanding, *our earth*, which includes within itself all these different environing worlds with their modifications and their pasts—the more so since we have no knowledge of other heavenly bodies as environing worlds for possible human habitation. In this unique world, everything sensuous that I now originally perceive, everything that I have perceived and which I can now remember, or about which others can report to me as what they have perceived or remembered, has its place. Everything has its unity in that it has a fixed temporal position in this objective world, its place in objective time. (Husserl 1973[1939]: 163; emphasis added)

Let us unpack Husserl's statement. The key concept is "environing world," which we saw earlier is an English translation of the German *Umwelt* (also "surrounding world"). Some have loosely translated this as "environment" or "milieu," but this is not strictly correct (Cairns 1973: 115), for Husserl wished to retain a direct reference to the "world" (notice he sometimes speaks of "our earth"). My environing world is the "world around me" that may contain rocks, coffee cups, plants, wild animals, pets, books, and people. Environing world is somewhat similar to anthropologist Roy Rappaport's (1984) concept of "operational environment" that our biogenetic structuralist group borrowed and applied for years in our own theoretical writings (e.g., Laughlin, McManus and d'Aquili 1990). The environing world is *not* a euphemism for the planet or the universe. Rather, it is the world that I experience and interact with daily. It is the world from my subjective point of view, moment by moment, within my stream of consciousness. In terms of *niche theory*, the environing world is that part of the real world that involves my adaptation (Godsoe *et al.* 2017, Hutchinson 1965).

In doing intersubjective phenomenology, Husserl notes that my environing world overlaps with your environing world, for how else could we communicate, encounter, interact, and coordinate with each other. I might encounter you in person within my environing world. Also, I am writing this sitting at my desk and perhaps you are reading this sitting at your desk. Perhaps we both have—at different times of course—a coffee cup before us, we are sitting in our respective chairs, communicating via a mutually understandable code, electric lights illuminating our desks and pages. We share a lifeworld here on the same planet earth. At the same time, you and I may be in different locales, I in Seattle (at the moment of this writing), and you perhaps in New Delhi, Miami, or London. Yet when we actually do pure phenomenology, we come to the same conclusions about the essential structures of experience, and because we pretty much share the same lifeworld, we can communicate these conclusions (Chapter 7). Moreover, each of us can remember other environing worlds we have inhabited, and none of them may overlap in our respective memories.

I am an experienced scuba diver, and you may have never dived underwater. Yet I am able to describe my experiences to you and you can understand me. Let me share an example. I have dived in the St. Lawrence River hundreds of times, and while underwater have drifted along with schools of bass, many of whom had been the victims of "catch and release" fishing. Catch and release is based upon the belief that the method is "humane" and does no harm to the fish. But what I saw *from my vantage point* swimming amongst schools of bass were holes in their cheeks which hampered easy breathing and that had become infected with fungus and other parasites. Eventually the infected fish can no longer eat and gradually starve to death. Perhaps you are an angler and never heard this before, and perhaps my sharing this experience may influence how you evaluate catch and release methods in the future, and perhaps not. The point is that I am able to inform your brainmind by experiences that you now may vicariously share with me. Quoting Husserl above, "[...] despite all this, all these different remembered environing worlds are *pieces of one and the same objective world.*" We share a lifeworld because it is part of the range of human experience here on planet earth.

EMPATHY

When we encounter each other, I know you for the physical being that you are in this "objective" world, within the perceptual horizon of my environing world. Your physical body is given within my *primordial* experience, just like the coffee cup, paper clip, or the keyboard. I do not have to add your body to my experience out of cognition, memory, or imagination because it is *already there* a priori in both its morphic/ hyletic fullness within a horizon of relations with other objects and relations, and its associated intuitive knowing. This is not the case, however, with your mind and your feelings, for your experiencing mind is not a primordial given for me:

> We "behold the living experiences of others" through the perception of their bodily behavior. This beholding in the case of empathy is indeed intuitive dator [intuitively "given" or "donated"], yet no longer a *primordially* dator act. The other man and his psychical life are indeed apprehended as "there in person," and in union with his body, but unlike the body, it is not given to our consciousness as primordial. (Husserl 1982[1913]: 51-52)

My grasp of your consciousness and experience derives (Husserl 1993[1931]: 120, 135) from a special type of intentionality Husserl called *empathy* (Ger: *Einfühlung*; see also Jardine 2014, Stein 1989 [1917], Zahavi 2007, 2019: 92, Welton 2003: Chap. 6). This is not to be confused with our everyday, fuzzy notion of empathy that refers to feelings (compassion, pity, concern, kindness, the urge to help) or identification with someone's plight (Jardine 2014, Batson 2011). My empathy in the phenomenological sense is a generalized intuition associated with the primordial given in my experience of your body, behavior, and expressions (Husserl 1982[1913]: 210, 2006[1910-1911]: 149, Stein 1989 [1917]: 11, Throop 2008). In other words, I do not just experience your presence as a physical thing, or even a body behaving, but I experience you intuitively as a class of "person" and that you, like me, are experiencing a stream of consciousness. "More specifically, what counts in the strict sense as empathy are those experiential acts in which a foreign subject is not merely hypothesized or inferred, but rather given and experienced herself" (Jardine 2014: 274). In the same way, when my dog Luke is present to my perception, I experience not only his physical being, but as an exemplar of a class "dog" and that, like myself, he is experiencing a stream of consciousness in which I am an object (see Smuts 2001). In neither case can I experience the content of Luke's or your stream of consciousness *in the same primordial way I experience your respective bodies, behaviors, and expressions.*

My empathetic act is directed at the physical object given in my perceiving—your visage, your activities, but my intuition of *your* pain can never be a given, and yet it is part of the noesis of your being:

> Needless to say, I have no outer perception of the pain. Outer perception is a term for acts in which spatio-temporal concrete being and occurring come to me in embodied givenness. This being has the quality of being there itself right now; it turns this or that side to me and the side turned to me is embodied in a specific sense. It is primordially there in comparison with other sides co-perceived but averted. ...*The pain is not a thing and is not given to me as a thing, even when I am aware of it "in" the pained countenance.* I perceive this countenance outwardly and the pain is given "at one" with it. ...Thus, empathy does not have the character of outer perception, though it does have something in common with the outer perception: In both cases the object itself is present here and now. We have come to recognize outer perception as an act given primordially. But though empathy is not outer perception, this is not to say that it does not have this "primordiality." (Stein 1989[1917]: 6-7; emphasis added)

We know now that the brains of advanced social mammals are "wired" to apprehend the emotional states of conspecifics (Hecht, Patterson and Barbey 2012). Dolphins and other social animals are empathetic beings, although the communication of pain in another may be received via other senses (Bekoff 2002). It is clear that we have inherited the capacity for apprehending the emotional state of another person, even in fellow non-human creatures. Indeed, it is hard to imagine a functioning society without such a faculty.

Some researchers in psychology attribute this intuitive grasp of you as a conscious person to an inherent "theory of mind," a kind of mental module that automatically attributes mental faculties to other people or animals (Frith and Frith 2005, Gallagher and Frith 2003), a faculty that in fact can be lost or even fail to develop properly (Baron-Cohen 1997). There have been discussions of whether animals operate on a neuropsychological theory of mind (see e.g., Premack and Woodruff 1978). My own position is that there are no "black boxes" in the brain and that the issue is more complex than can be accounted for with a neuro-modular explanation. Moreover, even in phenomenological circles, this issue has generated controversy (see Zahavi 2008).

In any event, to put this issue in Husserl-speak, as phenomenology is strictly descriptive of experience, and not an exercise in theory building, I cannot describe your stream of consciousness, but I can describe the intuition that you are a conscious being. If I could directly experience and describe the contents of your consciousness by, say, telepathy (image of Mr. Spock mind-melding with someone, "My mind to your mind..."), there would be no reason for us to communicate using behavior, nor for any selective pressures over the course of phylogenesis leading to the evolution of language in our species. In short, you are to my experience "self-evidently" a conscious being (Husserl 1982[1913]: 210, 390). Not only that, but my experience of you is a given of a *purely generalized* class associated with having a stream of consciousness, although none of the contents of those streams are given to me, save my own (Husserl 1973[1939]: 352, 1982[1913]: 58). Experiencing you and all others like you as being as conscious as am I is *essential generalized eidetic knowledge* that is intuitively and immediately given in any experience of a person, or a dog or bird for that matter, and without the necessity of theories or simulations. By reducing our experience of the other to its primordial sensory given, we see clearly that there is no time lag between my perception of your physical body and the intuition that you are a conscious being of a class to which I also belong (Costelloe 2003: 77). We can only suppose that social animals experience others in much the same way as we do and consequently treat group members and non-member conspecifics in this special intuitive way.

Please note, I am not talking about a culturally/historically derived and learned "theory of mind" (see Lillard 1998). It may well be that we find that the brainmind of most people do generate a theory of mind grounded upon this primordial intuition, but that is an empirical question we will not get into here. What I am talking about is an inherent system of knowledge, intuitive in its subjectivity and primordially present in experience, given without thought. Explaining human sociality in such a way that it implies at least that sociality is learned is antithetical to what we know about social animals (Call and Tomasello 2008). We are born with social brains, just like chimpanzees, elephants, penguins, starlings, voles, and the like. What this means for subjectivity is that we intuit that the conspecific is "same-as-me."

Also please note that I am writing out of my own phenomenology. Of course, there are people who deny that animals are conscious, deny that animals suffer, feel joy or love. Their experiences of animals will be different than my own. There are people in certain traditional cultures who experience trees and rocks as conscious. I do not. I can project anthropomorphic qualities onto rock formations, mountains, and clouds—so-called "simulacra" (see Devereux 2013)—but unlike folks in animistic cultures, I do not experience simulacra as conscious beings. By way of contrast, we know there are people incapable of much if any empathy—e.g., extreme narcissists and psychopaths—and their lack of empathy is of great interest to neuropsychologists (Decety *et al.* 2013).

Social neuroscience research relating to the neural systems mediating intersubjectivity have burgeoned in the last two decades, including studies of empathy (Batson 2011, Bernhardt and Singer 2012, Decety and Ickes 2009). Singer *et al.* (2004) got the ball rolling by showing that the experience of pain and the experience of another person in pain was mediated by overlapping areas in the cingulate and insular cortices of the brain. There followed other studies (see Bernhardt and Singer 2012 for a review) that together tend to show that the areas of the brain responsible for mediating emotions also mediate the perception of those emotions being experienced and expressed by others. Our understanding of the neuropsychology of empathy took a huge leap forward with the discovery of *mirror neuron* systems in the brain that are made up of neural cells that are active when mediating a behavior and when perceiving that same behavior in another (Hayman 2016). They also "fire" when one experiences feelings and when one perceives those feelings expressed by others (Arbib 2012, Ferrari and Rizzolatti 2014, Gallese *et al.* 2007, Keysers and Fadiga 2017, Kilner and Lemon 2013). The role of the orbitofrontal portion of the prefrontal cortex in mediating empathy is now known (Rolls 2018: 89).

In summary, empathy—a special type of intentionality—is from the neuroanthropological point of view the result of millions of years of evolution, reaching its most important adaptational significance in social mammals, including humans, and birds. Empathy is wired-in to the *social brain* (Dunbar 2003, Dunbar, Gamble and Gowlett 2010, Dunbar and Shultz 2007, Graziano 2013, Gazzaniga 1985). The primordial sense of empathy is inherent in the experienced given with the given's sensory hyle and complex order of form, class, and relations. There are people with psychological disorders where empathy is not within the horizon of the given, posing an interesting thought experiment: imagine a human society made up solely of psychopaths. Our empathy attributes consciousness to the other but cannot "read" the contents of the other's consciousness. There is always a layer of alterity to the other, even others within a family or local social group, and even more so with others from different cultural backgrounds. But these are layers of interpretation (including erroneous interpretations that may lead to conflict) that permeate the natural attitude. When bracketed, natural attitude elements cease to impinge upon the primordial given. And the presence of empathy in the given does not necessarily require the application of a cognitive "theory of mind," although such a theory may develop on the foundations of empathy.

INTERSUBJECTIVITY AND THE SOCIAL BRAIN

Within Husserlian phenomenology, Klaus Held's question in the epigraph at the start of this chapter reigns paramount, and is of considerable interest not only to social philosophy and social phenomenology, but also to cultural neurophenomenology. It is crucial for the latter because it focuses the twin beams of the phenomenology of intersubjectivity and neuroscience upon the everyday experience of the social Other. And because of what is discovered in those investigations, the inclusion of evolutionary and comparative evidence of sociality and social learning among non-human beings becomes relevant to explaining the evolution and adaptive functions of the primordial given in human social relations. When we reduce intersubjective experiences, we discover how the inherent structures of perception—the essences—contribute to forming a community-level lifeworld. In short, we humans are, just like dolphins, chimpanzees, and crows, born as social animals with social brains (Blakemore and Frith 2004, Feinberg and Mallatt 2016). The raw sensory and perceptual information which is the ground of all social experiences is virtually the same for everybody, regardless of sociocultural background. Many of these inherent structures are already evident in infancy (see Laughlin 1991, Legerstee, Haley and Bornstein 2013, Meltzoff and Kuhl 2016, Rochat 2001, Robinson 2007, Van Manen 2018).

Husserl was perfectly aware that it was by way of intersubjectivity that the charge of rank solipsism was to be answered, for if your consciousness is not part of mine, and all I can be certain of is my own conscious existence, then how can I know I am not alone in a world of my own making (Haney 2002: 147, Hutcheson 1980, Overgaard 2002)? Husserl in fact developed his approach to pure phenomenology of intersubjectivity throughout his career. The problem of intersubjectivity is already engaging his attention in *Ideas I* (1982[1913]: 165) and is later addressed more fully in the fifth meditation of his *Cartesian Meditations* (1993[1931]), in his so-called *Ideas II* (1989[1952]), and in *The Crisis of European Sciences and Transcendental Phenomenology* (1970[1936]).[28] Most of the criticisms of Husserl's lifeworld explorations I have read are philosophical, not methodological, and much less contemplative. As we saw before, it is this single failing that has led to much of the confusion about Husserl's phenomenology of the lifeworld (see Fink 1972 on this issue).

How does one do a phenomenological reduction of intersubjectivity? How do you "bracket" your natural attitude involving social Others?

---

[28] Iso Kern edited a series of three collections of Husserl's writings on the issue of intersubjectivity that was published by Springer in German as *Zur Phänomenologie der Intersubjektivität*. Thus far these volumes have not been translated into English. Kern's (2019) summary of these writings in English is a must-read if you are interested in Husserl's insights on intersubjectivity, empathy and language.

In exactly the same way that you would proceed if you were reducing your natural attitude about anything else (see Costelloe 2003: 79, Haney 2002). In what follows, I am going to assume you know how to do a reduction, and that you have practiced doing so on people or animals in your environing world. If you are an ethnographer, you might want to perform a reduction of your experience of people from your own culture and your hosts from another culture—a kind of phenomenological compare and contrast, a study of your own cross-cultural mindsets. Interestingly enough, it was Margaret Mead (1952) who strongly urged nascent ethnographers to get involved in practices that trained them to grasp their own ethnocentrism, and the influence of their own childhood experiences upon how they perceive the cross-cultural Other. This training under certain circumstances might even involve undergoing psychoanalysis.

One important conclusion from performing an intersubjective reduction is that perception of the Other as a member of the class "person" (or "like me") and as a conscious being is immediate and primordial. It is part and parcel of the given. It cannot be reduced further. The information that the object before me is presenting as a physical human (or animal) body, and thus by empathy a conscious being, is part of my perceptual horizon. Apperception of the Other as the same as me *does not require inference or any other rational, cognitive, or logical act* (see Husserl 1993[1931]: 111, Gallagher 2008, Flings 1978, Stein 1989 [1917]: 11, Zahavi 2019). Indeed, there is evidence that this intuition is shared with other social animals and that we inherited this faculty from our primate past (Voland 2007). Of course, the a priori givenness of the Other may eventually contribute to and ground our natural attitude view of reality. Also, we are not speaking of a relationship that can be empirically perceived from outside, but rather phenomenologically adumbrated from within the horizon of my own experience (see Schnell 2010: 11).

As we saw above, my brain is inherently social in its organization. My brainmind is "wired" to apprehend the Other in a mode of intersubjectivity. This is precisely what it is like for a social brain to apprehend the Other and phenomenologically reduce its own social experience to the primordial sensory given. This helps us understand phenomena like *emotional contagion* (Hatfield, Rapson and Le 2011), as when we sit next to an anxious person and find ourselves becoming up-tight. If you are like me and have a slight tendency to acrophobia, you not only get that twinge in your genital area when you stand on a precipice, you also get the same feeling if you see another person standing on a precipice, or even a picture of someone standing upon the edge of the roof of a building. By means of eidetic variation (see Chapter 3) we can also appreciate the difference between our "normal" act of empathetic intentionality and the lack of this act in a psychopath. Try a thought experiment by imagining a number of psychopathic personalities forming a functional hunting and gathering band. How would they fair? What would their social structure, ritual gatherings, families, and jurisprudence look like? Compare these conclusions with what we know about the real life of hunter-gatherer peoples (see e.g., Marlowe 2005, Meschiari 2009). You may conclude as I and others (Arnhart 2001) have done that a society of psychopaths would not survive for long.

Another important conclusion we may reach, with Husserl, is that by reducing the other person within my environing world, I see with direct clarity that my environing world is inherently intersubjective, *not solipsistic.* I am unable to reduce the other to the status of a physical thing like a light bulb or toilet plunger—again, unless I am a psychopath. After bracketing the natural attitude about beings, the irreducible result of the primordial other is still an empathetic intentional act (see Reynaert 2001). What this means in neurophenomenological terms is that the Other-as-conscious-being is already there full blown. Indeed, we know that at a rudimentary level, the Other-as-conscious-being is already there in infancy. We are born with an inherent interest in faces and facial expressions, as well as nurturing behavior and sensations (see Husserl 1980: 129; see also Cole 1998, Southgate *et al.* 2008).

Still another conclusion we must acknowledge is that my "ap-presentation" of you within my primordial horizon is as an *alter*-ego. You are within my intentional act, not as a thing, but as an *alter*-own-self. What is primordially present about myself in this intentional act is intuitively associated with my perception of your body—in short, I know you through knowing my embodied self (Husserl 1989[1952]: 60-61). You are thus "co-present" with me within my primordial horizon, in many (but not all) respects my analogue. In Husserl's own words:

What is specifically peculiar to me as ego, my concrete being as a monad [unit], purely in myself and for myself with an exclusive ownness, include (my) every intentionality and therefore, in particular, the intentionality directed to what is other [...]. In this preeminent intentionality there becomes constituted for me the new existence-sense that goes beyond my monadic very-ownness; there becomes constituted an ego not as "I myself," but as mirrored in my own ego, in my monad. The second ego, however, is not simply there and strictly presented; rather he is constituted as an "alter ego"—the ego indicated as one moment by this expression being I myself in my ownness. The "Other," according to his own constituted sense, points to me myself; the other is a "mirroring" of my own self and yet not a mirroring proper, an analogue of my own self and yet again not an analogue in the usual sense. (Husserl 1993[1931]: 94)

The conclusion reached by Husserl in the fifth of his *Cartesian Meditations* (1993[1931]) is that I know myself as a *monad* (my ego as a whole unit) and then "constitute" you as a similar monad, a member of the same class of persons as am I, plus endowed with a stream of consciousness, subjectivity, and intentional acts.[29] We can say that intersubjectivity is a communion of monads, and if we are part of a social group, we are both members in good standing of a *community of monads* (Husserl 1993[1931]: §56). What I intuit about myself I then intuit about you, a kind of *assimilative apprehension*. You are as I am, a being with consciousness who is experiencing the same *real world* as am I. If we are both members of the same community of monads, then my knowledge of you is likely to be more veridical than if we belong to different communities (i.e., different "cultures"). But, of course, even if we belong to the same group, our empathetic intentions can be wrong—in fact often are, and this can be revealing as well:

Meaning input or empathy occurs when, for instance, we quickly pass by a store window and momentarily mistake a dummy for

---

[29] Husserl borrowed the term "monad" from Leibniz (Sieroka 2015: 7). If you wish to read more about Husserl's *monadology*, see Husserl 1993[1931]: §56, 2001[1920/24]: 627-634; see also Bruzina 2004: 442, Donohoe 2016, Kjosevik, Beyer and Fricke 2019, Moran 2000: 174, 2005, Sieroka 2015, Welton 1999.

a human being. In cases such as this there takes place a bestowal of an embodied meaning through an assimilative apprehension originating from the primal instituting of my own body and lived body-ego. One perceives the dummy but wrongly as human, while the meaning input into the dummy holds "true" before the empathetic intentionality expathizes. *This expathy, if I may use this term, is tantamount to the cancellation of the other there for me.* (Frings 1978: 145; emphasis added)

When this kind of mistake happens, we do not process it by thought and reason ("It's a stupid dummy and not appropriate for projecting my empathy, so I shall 'expathize' it."). The correction is automatic and at the primordial level of the given. And yet, people can be quite blind to assimilative errors. Because narcissists and psychopaths are so good at mimicking how a "normal" person behaves, those they interact with can be fooled, sometimes for years (see Jones 2014, Book *et al.* 2015)

Naturally enough, Husserl's contention that I know you (presumably correctly) as a conscious person—like me, you are a "lived body"—because I know myself as an embodied conscious person has been criticized. The phenomenologist Jan Patočka has made the opposite argument, that I know myself through you, the *alter*-ego (see Čapek 2017). The relevant ethology and neuroscience currently do not support the primacy of either argument. As we have seen above, empathetic intentions seem to be simultaneous via mirror neurons and other neural systems that mediate empathy, imitation, and mimicry (Lohmar 2006). I am "wired" to apperceive the other, attribute my own self-awareness to the other, and to assimilate the other into my inherently social horizon.

Summarizing again, the important message from a Husserlian neurophenomenological standpoint is that my experience of my primordial environing world is *inherently social.* You are not a physical object like a bicycle or pair of jeans; rather, you are a transcendental being of the class "person" who presents within my experience as "like me," a body with a mind and a stream of consciousness (i.e., a monad) that I cannot directly apprehend. If I am a "normal" human being, my intentional acts with you as object are empathetic, and we have seen that our brains are "wired" for that kind of intention. We have noted that there are people who are incapable of empathy, and this deficiency poses for them an intersubjective and cognitive challenge. My experiential world is not a "mind-only," solipsistic and narcissistic paradise, but is replete with other beings with minds who operate upon the same real world as do I. I do not have to think about this or theorize about others with minds. All of this is noetically given in my reduced horizon—and relevant science tells me that I was born this way. Just as I realize myself as an embodied monad, I noetically intuit that you are the same kind of being as am I. I thus realize by virtue of entering the phenomenological epoché that my environing world is social, and that what I experience of this world is shared by similar intentional acts of others.

MORE ABOUT THE LIFEWORLD

The serious development of the lifeworld concept came late in Husserl's career—best represented in his books *The Crisis in European Sciences and Transcendental Phenomenology* (1970[1936]) and *Experience and Judgment* (1973[1939]). In the former he wrote:

> The lifeworld is pregiven to us all…as persons within the horizon of our fellowmen, i.e., in every actual connection with others, as "the" world common to us all. Thus, it is …the constant ground of validity, an ever-available source of what is taken for granted, to which we, whether as practical men or as scientists, lay claim as a matter of course. (1970[1936]: 122)

The lifeworld is the primordial sensory given level of our everyday world of experience, whether we are scientists, lawyers, nurses, factory workers, and yes, even philosophers and anthropologists, and whether we are infants, children, or adults. My lifeworld includes the perceptually given data about things like computers, carrots, rocks, my dog Luke, my family members, and on and on—hundreds and hundreds of meaningful things, beings, and people—all instantiating ideas (*eidos*) in my head. My lifeworld is the inherited, primordial sensory underpinning for all sorts of historical residues picked up over a lifetime of enculturation (e.g., Red light stop! Green light go!). "The original givenness of the world—

our 'lifeworld'—depends on the fact that, as men living in the world, having our experience and carrying on our practical activities in it, we are unities of body and mind, such that all our experience of the world is ultimately mediated by our senses and the functioning of our sense-organs" (Landgrebe 1944: 45). And my lifeworld inevitably places me ("me" the transcendental ego) at its center.

The crucial constituent in Husserl's description of the lifeworld, and the one that is ignored, distorted, or criticized by so many philosophers over the years (see Lee 2020) is *that we all have the same lifeworld because we share the same reality, and our perceptions, after the phenomenological epoché, reveal the same essential structures.* We know this with absolute certainty because after performing the *transcendental epoché*—reducing my perception of you and others—I realize intuitively that we are (primordially speaking) the same. I cannot read your mind, I cannot perceive your stream of consciousness, and I cannot know with certainty the meaning you ascribe to objects, *but I intuit your perception when stripped to the primordial given is the same as mine.* The structure of my intentional acts is the same as your intentional acts. We share the same reality (Husserl 1970[1936]: 139, 151) and the same essences (ibid: 108-110, 184-186). After completing the transcendental epoché, a Maori phenomenologist and an Irish phenomenologist will uncover precisely the same essential structures, the same a priori objects-in-the-world, and the same perception of the other as same-as-me. All that is required is that both complete the appropriate reductions ("you want to know this, do this") and then communicate with each other ("have a conversation and compare notes").

Understanding the nature of this structural underpinning of all human perception helps us appreciate the extent to which all of us on planet Earth can communicate, share information, empathize with each other, and form common bonds of love, understanding, and cooperation across cultural lines. It is only the persistent Boasian resistance to anything even slightly structural that has proved such an impediment to anthropological theory building along these lines. Anthropology still, despite reams of evidence to the contrary, cannot appreciate the very Husserlian contention that the same brains living in the same world will produce the same primordial givens (*noesis*), and similar understandings though varying layers of interpretation (*noemata*).

There is another impediment that confronts many others besides anthropologists. As Husserl makes clear in various places, a transcendental phenomenology of the lifeworld requires nothing less than a total reconstitution of one's own natural attitude (e.g., Husserl 1970[1936]: 148). He is speaking here of a radical reorganization of the phenomenologist's consciousness similar to that which produces a mature contemplative or advanced meditator in other traditions (Laughlin 2020). It would seem that this is not a path that many, in any vocation, wish to travel. Failure to dedicate oneself to a path of self-reflection has placed severe limits upon researchers who are afraid to commit to self-study, or do not wish to be personally changed by their research. In anthropology this has led to ethnographers galore who report on "religious" systems that depend upon evoking extraordinary states of consciousness, often augmented by psychoactive drugs, but who will not subject themselves to their hosts' transpersonal processes. Those ethnographers who have trodden the path of spiritual awakening provided by their hosts produce reports for us of inestimable value (see e.g., Rodd 2002, Young and Goulet 1994).

RETURNING TO THE THINGS – EUGEN FINK AND THE SIXTH MEDITATION

In a real sense Husserl's development of transcendental phenomenology did not stop with his death in 1938. During his last years, Husserl was in deep collaboration with his assistant, Eugen Fink (1905-1975), who, still in his 30's at the time, carried on developing his mentor's transcendental studies (Bruzina 1989, 1990, 1995, 2004, Elden 2008). Fink continued in his own independent direction, despite linking up with Heidegger (who typically misunderstood Husserl's methods; see Moran 2000) later in his career and made some fruitful links between the transcendental epoché and the real world. Although it may seem at first sight to be a tangent, the work of Eugen Fink has been largely ignored by phenomenological social scientists, even when they partially ground their respective thinking on Husserlian phenomenology. I would like to show how Fink's persistence paid off on our account, keeping in mind that Fink had Husserl's blessings in his endeavors.

As Ronald Bruzina noted in his translator's introduction to Fink's *The Sixth Meditation* (Bruzina 1995: xxviii),[30] "Husserl's phenomenology, at least as it reached its maturity in his last years, *was not just Husserl's*—it was Husserl's *and Fink's*." What makes Fink pivotal to our discussion of Husserlian neurophenomenology is that he focused upon the co-relationship of consciousness with the world and the world with consciousness by way of the transcendental reduction (Fink 1995). This in effect strengthens the bridge between pure phenomenology and anthropology, for Fink's findings are amenable to dialogue with science, and especially with evolutionary psychological and neurophenomenological theories.

According to Bruzina, Fink:

> ...takes Husserl's Cartesian theme of the idea of science and explicitly sets it back into the situation of *life in the world*; cognition as such, and therefore science, is an operation oriented in and to the world. The structural condition needing to be thematized and elucidated in order to explicate the significance of the enterprises of scientific reason is therefore that of the *world as pregiven*... . The move of reduction, then, is to be the effort to reach an understanding of the essential place of the world not only in the mundane life of psycho-physical humanity but also precisely in the total ambit of the functioning of subjectivity... . (Bruzina 1990: 171)

There are two ways to think about the world phenomenologically: the world that impresses our perception through the primordial sensory given, and the world as horizon for our intentional acts. "[T]he true theme of phenomenology is neither the world on the one hand, nor a transcendental subjectivity which is to be set over and against the world on the other, but the world's becoming in the constitution of transcendental subjectivity" (Fink 1970: 130). The world is not static, but dynamic. The world "out there" is real, both for Husserl and for Fink, and operates relative to our

---

[30] The "sixth meditation" in Fink's book title is considered a continuation of Husserl's five previous meditations in *Cartesian Meditations* (1993[1931]). Please note that Fink appended a number of Husserl's responses to an earlier version of this work at the end of the current version (see pp. 163-192).

consciousness as a field of playful symbols (Fink 2016[1960]). Fink took up the theme of "play" from one of the surviving fragments of the 5th century BC philosopher Heraclitus of Ephesus' one book, *On Nature* (see Elden 2008). This was fragment no. 52 which reads, "Time is a child playing draughts, the kingly power is a child's" (Burnet 1930). Using "play" in its sense of *metanoia* (see Laughlin 1990)—the sense of change and transformation—Fink argues that "play can become the symbolic theatrical enactment of the universe, the speculative metaphor of the world," that world is "like a child playing a game" (quotes from Elden 2008: 49). For our consciousness, the "world" is symbol and because it is dynamic, it is play (Fink 1960, 1968, 2016[1960]). This organic realization brings transcendental phenomenology into accord with how science actually proceeds (Goldman 2022).

Repeating for emphasis here, the world of my experience is pregiven through my senses and is the same world that triggers your world of experience. Yet each of us provides similar, varied and even quite different meaning to the same things in the world. Thus, things that come and go in the play of a dynamic transcendental world operate relative to our respective intentional acts as symbols, penetrating to layers of meaning supplied by our brainminds, beginning with the level of primordial essences and in a momentary comprehension. This process, in my opinion, begs for a neuropsychological model which I have offered in the notion of *symbolic penetration* from the world to the brainmind (Laughlin 1989b, 1990a, 1990b, 2011, 2020, Laughlin, McManus and d'Aquili 1990: 189-195).

The lifeworld for Fink, as for Husserl, is the layer of primordial given that makes any kind of science, as well as adaptation, possible—indeed, that makes assessing the truth of any opinion, belief or theory about the world possible (Fink 1981b: 63). It is the layer within which the flow of space-time offers our consciousness objects as enduring primordial givens demanding interpretation within the "play" of cosmic events. The lifeworld moreover may be considered as a field of symbols which become meaningful through a layering (Husserl's word was *Verflectung*, "intertwining;" see Moran 2013) of significance, within the intentional act, beginning with the primordial given and its horizon of visible and invisible associations penetrating those hierarchical structures of the brainmind mediating the natural attitude and intersubjective acts of communicating. Those higher levels of meaning (information, emotion, imagination, cognition, etc.) are, of course, not wholly dependent upon the primordial given. We can imagine, hallucinate or dream of objects that are in fact not primordially given from the environing world at the moment, or for that matter, ever. We can think or feel about something we wish to see and go looking for it in the world. In Husserlian terms, the lifeworld "fulfills" our intentions by sensually "filling up" our ideas with form, relations, and hyle. At this moment I think about a word, I type it and, voila! The word is there on the screen, thus fulfilling my creative intention via "primordial givenness" feedback. This playful engagement with the world is fundamental to *spontaneous creativity* (Husserl 1973[1939]: xxviii, 198-199, Bello 2004).

Indeed, I have long argued that the brain of all animals, including us humans, operate as symbolic processors (see Laughlin 1989b, 2011, Laughlin, McManus and d'Aquili 1990, Laughlin and Stephens 1980, Laughlin, McManus and Stephens 1981). In my opinion, only through the phenomenological epoché can one realize this multi-layered processing of information, one that we take completely for granted in our daily lives. We perceive meaningful objects and events moment by moment, and we act in response with those perceptions. Conversely, we act to produce the perception of meaningful objects or events. More than this, we actually feed-forward into the lifeworld anticipating acts that *will happen* (according to our expectations). When we take a stroll, we automatically and unconsciously plant our foot expecting to meet solid ground. We only wake up to our feet if we stumble or step in a puddle. This feeding-forward into the future is only possible because of the automatic, symbolic processing of the primordial given, whether or not we are aware of it. And of course this feeding-forward process is even more complexly the case when the objects in our lifeworld are other people.

Social phenomenology

As I noted above, Husserl's notion of the lifeworld has directly, and more often indirectly, influenced many philosophers and social scientists. Heidegger, Merleau-Ponty, Gurwitsch, Schutz, and other philosophers have devoted tomes to the subject. They in turn have also inspired treatments by various anthropologists and sociologists: see Duarte 2004, Weiner 1992 on Heidegger; Csordas 1990, Fusar-Poli and Stanghellini 2009, Levering and Van Manen 2002 on Merleau-Ponty; and Wagner 1983, Psathas 2004, Lengermann and Niebrugge 1995 on Gurwitsch and Schutz. And, of course, Husserlian lifeworld phenomenology has garnered reams of criticism, usually (in my opinion) by philosophizers without requisite contemplative skill or experience. Naturally, social scientists are interested in social behavior, social relationships, social institutions, and all things social. Hence, social scientists tend to shy away from approaches they believe are wholly psychological. However, they are quick to use the works of social phenomenologists without fully appreciating that many of those philosophers drag us back into empiricism without the mediation of the Husserlian phenomenological attitude and dealing with issues pertaining to history and social processes that lead to conditioning the brainmind.

One of the most influential of the social phenomenologists has been Alfred Schutz (1967, 1970, Schutz and Luckman 1973, 1989). Schutz was not a contemplative, so far as I can tell, but rather a social theorist who combined Weberian sociology with some of Husserl's ideas like the "natural attitude" as well as the lifeworld and emphasized the role of socially shared meanings in mediating the problem of intersubjectivity. So far as I know, Schutz never read Fink's *Sixth Meditation* or understood Husserl's emphasis upon the lifeworld being the post-epoché world to which all of science is focused. In fact, Schutz actively eschewed the epoché and focused his attention upon "phenomenological psychology" and the structure of the natural attitude (see Schutz 1962) and thus misunderstood Husserl's transcendental project in some very critical ways (see Zahavi 2003b, 2005, Dreher 2003, Gros 2017). Once again, Husserl's lifeworld is *not* synonymous with the natural attitude, an error that has seeped into the concept as used by some anthropologists (e.g., Mimica 2010). The lifeworld for Husserl is the primordially structured world that is the same for all of us—what we all will experience if we bracket all the layers of "cultural" conditioning to which we are subjected as members of society. Schutz's focus upon symbolism is, however, very useful, for it is by way of culturally shared meanings that we are able to communicate intersubjectively. This became absolutely critical in human evolution as we will see in Chapter 7.

Social phenomenology typically applies to human societies. However, many of the insights of social phenomenology probably apply as well to the intersubjectivity of other extremely social animals (especially *eusocial* animals) that must develop methods of communicating for social adaptation to the environing world to happen. Sociality is a powerful adaptive strategy for many animals and has been independently "discovered" many times during phylogenesis, influencing adaptive strategies of birds, insects, reptiles, and mammals (Wilson 1975). In this respect, given its full biological weight, Husserl's lifeworld would be part of what Earl W. Count (1973) called the human *biogram*.[31] Thus, from a biological perspective, "ontology" and "epistemology" are two sides of the same process with respect to brainminds evolving and functioning within their environing worlds (Luft 2011: 111).

SUMMARY AND SEGUE

Husserl's greatest contribution to social phenomenology was in discovering that our sense of sociality is rooted in the noetic experience of empathy. Empathy is not the product of reason, feeling, belief or any of the other mechanisms of meaning available at the noematic level of processing. Empathy arises in the primordial sensory given when another being I perceive to be "like me" enters my stream of consciousness. This essence constitutes my initial primordial engagement with the Other as a fellow monad and my participation within a community of monads and is the foundation upon which higher order meaning-building processes operate. Just as inorganic objects in the world that present themselves before my gaze are apprehended as monads, so do other people and perhaps animals. With the perception that the object is of the *eidos* "like me" comes the intuitions of the Other having a stream of consciousness very like mine, and that the primordial sensory given

---

[31] A *biogram* labels the fact "that the life mode of any animal kind possesses a configuration, a pattern, a gestalt, *which is an integral expression of its bodily morphology...* It is grasped best from studies of behavior and of central nervous systems" (Count 1973: xi; emphasis added), and again, "The life cycle of the individual, the life mode of the *coenonia* [a genus of bacteria] or species or even phylum, taken as a cycle, is its biogram." (Count 1973: 7).

perceived by the Other is the same as I am perceiving. This intuition grounds my assumption that when I and the Other communicate about events in the world, we are sharing information about the same world and not about two dissimilar, solipsistic figments of our respective imaginations.

What we also discover is that the concrete form of the Other within my perception is constituted by the same ingredients as coffee cups and paper clips. It is to those ingredients we now turn to better understand how the brainmind produces its movie as it arises and passes away within our stream of consciousness.

CHAPTER FIVE

All About the Hyle

[A] human being's total consciousness
is in a certain sense, by means of its
hyletic substrate, bound to the body.

– Husserl (1989[1952]: 160)

We have just explored what we can learn when we apply the reduction to the problem of intersubjectivity. We discovered that even our perception of social Others is rooted in eidetically given forms, hyletic data, relations, and intuitions. We are "wired" at the primordial level to perceive the social Other as "like me." There is no logical reason, then, that we cannot apply the reduction to the *hyle* ("stuff," "matter," "primary content," "sensuous content," or in modern parlance, "qualia") that "fulfill" forms and ideas, both physical and social, within the sensorium. From my admittedly neurophenomenological perspective, this "movie" is a very special one, for it is produced, not for our enjoyment (although we may enjoy ourselves watching), but for our adaptation to the objective environing world by anticipating potentially significant events (Arbib 1985, Fuster 2014). The movie's veridicality has profound biological consequences. However, from the strict Husserlian point of view, the elements constituting the movie directly perceived within the phenomenological attitude are descriptive categories, not the product of ontological presumptions or theories. As we saw previously, Husserl's account of visual perception makes the distinction between form and hyle which presaged the discovery that in fact the brain processes the edges that constitute forms and the "qualia" filling the forms in separate areas of the cortex more or less simultaneously (Fuster 2003: Chap. 4). For instance, in vision, the color processed in one area of the visual system is layered atop the form of the object processed simultaneously in another area of the visual system (Arbib, Érdi and Szentagothai 1998: Chap. 8, Krug 2012).

Thus far we have ignored the hyle in our procedures, but as with any aspect of experience, the hyle can become the focus of our phenomenological meditations—indeed, to do so proves advantageous to our neuropsychological understanding of how the brainmind portrays the environing world. We are not the only ones to ignore the hyle, of course. Husserl himself gave short shrift to his treatment of hyle relative to other aspects of sensory experience. The explanation for this is fairly simple, I think. Husserl's focus was upon the sensory given noetics as an instantiation of intentional eidetic noemata, and less upon noesis in its own right. He was following Descartes in this pursuit—remember René Descartes' second meditation upon a blob of wax which changed its state but was still the same wax (Descartes 2008). The hyle can and does change, but the *morphé* remains more or less the same. That is why natural intentionality is object-driven in Husserl's account.

When we turn our full attention to the hyle—the sensuous "stuff" that fills up the form of any perceived object—we are shifting the orientation of the reduction in a significant way, taking a turn toward *hyletic phenomenology* only suggested here and there within Husserl's published reports. Indeed, when we do take up hyletic exploration, an entirely new picture emerges as we focus upon *fields of hyle* within our sensory experience: patches of color, spatial distributions and patterns of texture, fields of changing and interrelated tones, powerfully evocative smells and tastes, as well as interoceptive senses such as pain, emotion, kinesthesia, skin pressure, and the like (Husserl 1997[1907]: 135, 257). Each of these fields of hyletic data may be reduced individually and *in toto* within the multisensory sensorium (Calvert, Spence and Stein 2004). It is crucial, however, to note that the reduction of hyle is harder to accomplish than the classic Husserlian intentional objects—i.e., it is easier to apply disciplined attention to a coffee cup than to the fields of sensory hyle that visually fill the "cup" form before our eyes. In truth, hyletic phenomenology demands extraordinary focus of attention that comes with mature contemplation. Before getting into an extension of his methods into the nature of hyle, let us survey what Husserl himself made of this aspect of sensory experience.

Husserl's meditations on the hyle

As we have mentioned before, Husserl was classically educated and used ancient Greek and Latin terms as technical concepts, especially when common terms like "stuff" and "matter" come with unwanted historical and conceptual baggage. His term "hyle" derives from the Greek referring to the material, sensible, changing and enduring "stuff" that fills intentional objects in sensory experience (Husserl 1982[1913]: 246-248).[32] As with many of Husserl's findings, the notion of the hyle is controversial (see Føllesdal 1978, Gallagher 1986). Most of the critiques of hyletic elements are based upon ontological and theoretical grounds and need not interest us here, for once again, we are only interested in findings accrued by contemplation. Speaking literally, there are no colors, no sounds, no textures or smells "out there" in the environing world. These and other sensations exist only in our brainmind. However, by way of these hyletic data we engage the world as it is, and as it is imagined and dreamed to be.

Hyle of whatever mode encountered, be it in the guise of sensory qualia, feelings (anxiety, pleasure, pain), body sensations, phantasms, dreams, and so forth, enliven the noetic presentations in perception. In fact, waking perception of the environing world is typically characterized by hyletic *lucidity* (Husserl often uses the term "vitality") when compared with sensory experiences had in normal dreaming, fantasy, and memory images. Relative to waking perception, these latter are for us Westerners typically hazy glimpses of the "real thing" (Husserl 1970 [1900-01], Vol 2: 304, Bachelard 1968: 216-217). The veridicality, the immanence, the dynamics, and the vividness of the primordial sensory given is due to the object's and the perceptual field's fulfillment in hyle combined with the intensity of awareness—the more focused the attention, the more lucid the hyle.

The importance of the hyle is revealed most fully in the phenomenology of time-consciousness (see Chapter 6), for hyle may be quite dynamic and vary over a series of temporal moments and constitute our sense of

---

[32] If you wish to read more about *hyle*, see Husserl 1982[1913], 1964a, Appendix III: 137-142; see also Held 2003a: 39-43, Levinas 1995: 40, Lusthaus 2002: 14-20, Derrida 2003: 83-89, Landgrebe 1981: 56-60, Føllesdal 1978, Smith 2013: 247, Moran 2005: 154.

dynamic duration of the object. We know duration via the hyle before us in the moment compared with that of short-term memory of the recently passed moments and in our anticipation of near-future moments. Indeed, for Husserl, hyletic data *is time-consciousness* (Husserl 1964a: 48, 62, (Appendix III): 137-142; also see relevant discussions by Lockwood 1989: 261–293 and Kortooms 2002). Husserl was not the first to note the importance of hyle or "qualia" to sensory consciousness. In this respect his views are similar to late 19th century physicist Ernst Mach (1959[1897]) and early 20th century philosopher/social scientist Friedrich Hayek (2014[1952]). It is only over duration that changing tones reveal a melody (Husserl 1994: 313, Embree 1972: 161). Music requires duration to unfold its structure, and that structure, once revealed is essentially atemporal (as demonstrated in the early 20th century by music theorist Heinrich Schenker; see Yeston 1977). Incidentally, babies appear to already have this capacity before they are born (Van Manen 2018).

Husserl himself uses the duration of striding towards a tree in his garden as an example:

> The colour of the tree-trunk, as we are aware of it under the conditions of pure perception, is precisely "the same" as that which before the phenomenological reduction we [...] took to be that of the real (*wirklichen*) tree. Now *this* colour, as bracketed, belongs to the noema. But it does not belong to the perceptual experience as a real (*reelles*) integral part of it, although we also find in the experience "a colour-like something," namely, the "sensory colour," the hyletic phase of the concrete experience in which the noematic or "objective" colour "manifests itself *in varying perspectives*."

> But one and the same noematic colour of which we are thus aware *as* self-same, in itself unchanged within the unity of a continuously changing perceptual consciousness, runs through its perspective variations in a continuous variety of sensory colors. We see a tree unchanged in colour—its own colour as a tree— whilst the positions of the eyes, the relative orientations, change in many respects, the glance wanders ceaselessly over the trunk and branches, whilst we step nearer at the same time, and thus in different ways excite the flow of perceptual experience. Let us now

start sensory reflexion, reflexion upon the perspective variations: we apprehend these as self-evident data, and are also able, shifting the standpoint and the direction of attention, to place them with full evidential certainty in relation with the corresponding objective phases, recognize them as corresponding, and thereby also see without further difficulty that the perspective colour-variations, for instance, which belong to some fixed colour of a thing are related to that fixed colour as continuous "variety" is related to "unity." (Husserl 1982[1913]: 283-284)

If you can grasp the distinction between the "objective" color of the tree and the sensory variations we experience through time, you will go a long way toward understanding what Husserl is getting at in general (and as supported by vision neuroscience; see Varela, Thompson and Rosch 1991: 165). What he is saying is that the naïve "natural attitude" observer is experiencing an objective tree defined as having a brown trunk and green leaves (the noematic imposition upon the intentional object), while at the same time glossing over as insignificant the variety of colors that are actually occurring in our sensorium as we change our orientation relative to the tree, and as light conditions change. The role of the hyle is to fulfill the empty eidetic intention "tree." The "objective" tree is the same regardless of the variety of sensory colors we perceive changing through time. We do not have to think about this variety/ unity correspondence, it is instantaneous, intuitive, and automatic. "Hyletic and noematic adumbrations have in common their being manifolds: the former are multiplicities over against the unitary objective properties that are displayed through them; the latter are multiplicities over against the unitary, identical object itself" (Rabanaque 2003: 208).

Our brains operating in the natural attitude are *usually* interested in the tree as a thing in the world, not in the variations of its appearances from moment to moment. Sometimes of course we can enter an aesthetic attitude toward a tree in which the role of hyle changes from pragmatic data to value data (see Chapter 11). Putting the matter simply, under the natural attitude, the tree is an intentional object, but the various hyle we experience are not (Husserl 1982[1913]: 246-247). Hyle only become noematic as limiting factors in identifying the intentional object. For Husserl, form is intentional, matter is not. Matter merely instantiates the form.

Apply this perspective to other visual experiences you might encounter. Perhaps you enjoy watching sunsets over the ocean. You go out to the beach every day to watch the sun "go down" in the west. A sunset never stays the same hyletically. It is dynamic in the extreme. Every second or so brings a change in colors and relations among colors in a continuous cascade of hues. Now, you have a friend who, when you mention your love of sunsets, responds, "Oh well, if you've seen one sunset you've seen them all!" Your friend is reacting out of noematic certainty that all our sunsets are objectively the same, and hyletic variation be damned. No matter what you are enjoying, they are all just "sunsets." We might say you are a noetically inclined color-variety junkie, while your friend is a concrete noema-head. For you, catching that elusive green flash is ecstasy, while for him it makes little difference as it is just another sunset. The difference here is profound, for it refers to no less than two states of consciousness. Husserl was aware that one may focus on hyle-as-being-hyle as when we appreciate the color grammar in an abstract painting, the texture of a lovers skin, a bird song, a golden sunset, and so forth (see Chapter 11).

Let us recall that intentionality is a kind of dance between hyletic data on the one hand and ideas on the other (see also Hayek 2014[1952]). If we draw a tree with a pencil, as we all did as children, we create the boundaries of the trunk, branches, and leaves, with lines on the paper. Then we probably color in the different shapes with crayons, finger paints, or watercolors. But perception at the level of the primordial sensory given doesn't work that way. The brain does not draw figures and then color them in. Rather, the boundaries between things are produced via contrasts between patches of light and color. If you study the methods of the pointillist artist George Seurat (Foa 2015; see below), you will discover that he drew few sharp lines as edges, but rather created the edges between patches of color filled-in with dabs of paint. In Husserl-speak, the brainmind is interested in the *eidetics* of things—things presented in primordial givenness are instances of ideas. The hyle "fulfills" the form, the morphé, or the thing. For the purposes of higher levels of cognition, we crispify edges and boundaries, simplify the details, and "chunk" (Miller 1956) variations in the instantiating object into a class of thing (Rosch 1977, 1978, Rosch *et al.* 1976)—which, incidentally, may become signified by a noun.

In the natural attitude, I am normally not aware of the hyle-qua-hyle. I do not experience the world as "I am having sensations," but rather as "I am perceiving the object—the chair, coffee cup, my dog Luke, my daughter Kate" (see Husserl 1970 [1900-01] II: 102-103). However, as we shall see below, the role of hyle in identifying the real, "objective" object upon which I gaze is profound and adaptively crucial. I am not an inherent solipsist or idealist who automatically realizes I am producing this movie I call "the world." I am "wired" to perceive the transcendental environing world as it presents itself to my gaze, and I know about objects and relations in the world as being "out there," not "in here" within my brainmind. By inference, I also intuit that the sensorium and consciousness of other animals operate in much the same way. Without being too flippant about it, the phenomenological attitude is richly productive of insights into the nature of my experience but could well prove disastrous for me in adapting to danger from the environing world if I spend too much time appreciating the hyle and forget about the form, the object—perhaps the venomous snake, stalking predator, or yawning chasm.

We can appreciate the role of hyletic variation relative to invariant morphé by realizing the importance of multimodal processing. As Husserl notes, I can recognize my dog Luke in a variety of circumstances: In bright light where his beautiful Chihuahua fur appears radiant, in subdued light where I can see him in only shades of gray, and in hearing his bark from downstairs where I cannot see him. Many hyletic variations, but only one Luke. More than this, I can walk around Luke, or toward or away from him and despite the different perspectives, he's the same Luke (Husserl 1997[1907]: Chap. 8). And no matter the light conditions, I know that Luke has an "objective" fawn coat. In everyday perception, we are not aware of hyle as discrete, but as a part of a tapestry of interrelated hyletic data within the horizon of our perceptual field throughout the duration of the experience. Tones occurring over time (across epochs; see Chapter 6) are conditioned both by simultaneous tones and tones coming before and after the tone of the moment (Lusthaus 2002: 14-15). Husserl was astute in emphasizing this aspect of perception, for we now know that much of the "wiring" of the brain supports this perceptual function (Arbib 1987: Chap. 4).

Another function of hyle is to limit the possibilities of the idea they instantiate and fulfill. In Husserl-speak, the hyle imposes limitations upon the noema:

> We undergo certain kinds of experiences when our sense organs are affected. These experiences Husserl called hyle. But the hyle are not objects of experience, they are not data that we see, hear, feel, smell, or taste (although they become data thanks to the noema which makes the hyle be appearances of the object). The hyle are what I like to call "boundary conditions" on the noema, in that they put restrictions on what noemata we can have when we are perceiving in a given situation. If we merely imagine something, only our fantasy puts a limit on the noemata we can have. However, when we perceive something, only some noemata are possible, the others are eliminated because they are incompatible with our hyle. (Føllesdal 1990: 267)

Although Husserl did not explain the relevance of the noetic-noematic intentional structure of perception in biological terms, it is clear that if a brainmind in any animal were structured such that every act of perception was novel, perception itself would be maladaptive. To build a hierarchy of meaning sedimented atop the patterns adumbrated from raw perception, hyletically filled forms must be rendered redundant as efficiently as possible. The animal cannot puzzle over the identification of every instantiation of a particular fruit before eating it. The animal's brainmind must be structured so that perception *re*-cognizes this instance as the same as yesterday's edible fruit. To perceive eidetically is what natural selection has produced in animals of all phyla (see Feinberg and Mallatt 2016).

That is not all, of course, for the same evolutionary pressures were brought to bear on the rememoration of techniques (Ihde 1991, 2016). It would be maladaptive for an animal's brainmind to have to puzzle-out how to access the fruit each time the fruit is encountered in experience. Technique (or "praxis") is as important as object remembrance for adaptation. The ideal is that I as an animal within my environing world both recognize an object for what it is and know what to do with it for the benefit of myself or my fellow group members. Our brainminds are designed to construct pathways that facilitate the "prime directive"—

to find food without becoming food (Koch 2019: 16). Hyletic data play a central role in making that initial categorical judgment (Husserl 1973[1939]: 250-252). It is by way of the hyletically filled object as it arises in perception in the immediate present that we know it to be real, genuine, or as Husserl liked to say, *originary* (Ger.: *eigentlich*).

As we shall see in Chapter 10, we are capable of fantasizing or imagining things that are not originary: Klingons, megalodons, dragons, purple dinosaurs, xenomorphs, scrupulously honest politicians, and so on. This system is not perfect by any means. Our experiences in lucid dreams and visions can produce hyletic data sufficient for us to interpret the objects as "real," as originary. This capacity is fundamental to how people come to believe in the reality of "supernatural" beings (Claffert 2019), or as anthropologist A. I. Hallowell (2002[1960]) called them, "other-than-human persons." Husserl eventually recognized different types of hyle, defined in part by whether they have a representational role to play in perception. He was initially interested in the "stuff" filling objects—the colors of a "tree," the sounds of a "bee," the tastes of an "orange," and so forth. In *Logical Investigations* (Husserl 1970 [1900-01], II: 103) these were referred to as "sensational content." By the time he wrote *Ideas I* (Husserl 1982[1913]) they were referred to as hyle.

Husserl also recognized that our experience of ourselves as a living body is, phenomenologically speaking, not a thing made of muscles, bones, hair, circulatory system, and so on, but rather a "freely moved sense organ" (Husserl 1989[1952]: 61, 161-165). By moving my body, I change perceptual perspective, or in W. T. Powers' (2005) brilliant terms, *body movement functions as the control of perception*. Not only this, but sense receptors within my body inform me within the perceptual act about my somatic orientation relative to the object. I know my body as a three-dimensional object both by way of sight and touch (from the outside in) and by way of somatosensory receptors within my body—touch, pressure, balance, proprioception (kinesthetics), nociception (pain, itch), stretch, and so forth (from the inside out; Husserl 1989[1952]: 160-161). For instance, I always know how my body and its parts are oriented to the object of perception automatically and within the perceptual act. Sensing where my left arm is located in space and time is as much primordial sensory given as the red patch on the apple, but the kinesthesis of my arm plays no part in limiting the noematic judgments about the apple. It only comes into play if I reach for the apple or want to change perspective vis-à-vis the apple.

Finally, hyle presents as sensory fields—patches of color, blending of tones, the texture of surfaces, etc. Hyletic fields have extension in space and duration in time (Husserl 1997[1907]: 83-87). Fields may be representative of the current iteration of the object, and may constitute the background, taking its place alongside the parts of things to fill-up the horizon, the perceptual field. Hyletic fields may remain in the background unless and until the focus of attention is shifted to the object they fulfill. On a clear day we may focus on the sky as object and of course we are perceiving a vast expanse of blue fulfilling the sky. Or we may shift our gaze to the tiny patch of blue which, when brought into focus turns out to be representative of a Jay sitting in a tree. In other words, whether a patch of hyle is representative is determined, not by the hyle itself, but by the organization of the entire intentional act. Of course, if we now make the hyle itself the object of scrutiny, as is required in hyletic phenomenology, we can say that the hyle is representative of itself.

THE PIXELATED NATURE OF HYLETIC FIELDS

Using Husserl's methods, we can dig deeper into the phenomenology of hyle. My hunch is that, because Husserl was not a practitioner of tranquility meditation—or in Buddhist terms, *samatha*—there was a limit to the intensity of focus he could apply to the constitution of hyle. It will become apparent to any mature contemplative with sufficient concentration (Lusthaus 2014), and who meditates upon "primordial impressions" (hyle) as sensory "objects," that these impressions are comprised of nearly infinitesimal, conjoined particles. In different traditions, these particles have been variously labelled—e.g., *yod* in Kabbalah, *bindu* in both Hindu and Buddhist traditions—but I will stick with the now commonplace English term and call them *hyletic pixels* (or "picture elements;" see A. R. Smith 2021). I will be using the term "pixel" metaphorically, for the usual use of the term labels the smallest element in an image or picture in a digital array. I am using the term here to refer to the smallest unit of sensation in any sensory mode as experienced in the sensorium by the meditating brainmind. My contention is that the advanced contemplative who turns their focused awareness toward the hyle of any sensory modality can readily ascertain that hyletic data are comprised of pixels (granules, "dots," particles, or what have you). I am describing in Husserlian terms an essential structure adumbrated from the primordial sensory given. Hyletic pixels can be readily and eidetically intuited, much as anyone who cares to look may apprehend the "dots" comprising a television image. And just as the pixels of a TV image are normally invisible to viewers, sensory pixels are normally invisible to naïve perception, or even to the phenomenologist who does not turn their gaze toward the hyle with exceptional awareness.

Hyletic pixels are commonly missed in naive introspection: (1) because most people are not interested in, nor are they trained to concentrate upon the essential features of their perception, and (2) because most people have not developed the depth of calm and steadfast mindfulness requisite to perform the necessary reduction (Lusthaus 2014: 11). While pixels constitute the field of sensation in any sensory mode, they are very tiny. With sufficient incentive and training, however, it is quite easy to become aware of the activity of these minuscule and momentary sensorial events and their patterns of organization within perceptual forms and hyletic fields. Pixels are seen to be the building blocks of objects and movement over time in the sensory field and once apprehended, may be apprehended at any time as long as the requisite intensity of awareness is present to consciousness.

After the requisite reduction has been performed, the sensorium is experienced as a field of pixels that is perceptually and cognitively distinguishable into sensory modes, and within sensory modes into forms producing visual objects (Bar 2004), auditory objects (Bizley and Cohen 2013), tactile objects (Liu, Wu, Sun and Guo 2017), and so on. The fundamental act of perception is the abstraction and reinforcement of invariant features within the order of an arising and dissolving field of pixels (Gibson 1979). Natural perception involves fields of pixels arranged into recognizable configurations, the latter being information of greatest interest to our higher cognitive processes, some of which seek and identify recurrent spatial and topological patterns. Playing with metaphors for the moment, the sensorium is like a backlit screen comprised of a field of pixels. One is normally aware of the "movie" that is the stream of consciousness, but *not how the projector works*—what the Buddha called the "house-builder" (Thanissaro 2003). One intuits the principles of mind that manifest as apparent regularities in the functioning of the projector. But in the case of the sensorium there is no screen. A screen is a "thing" that is still apparent when the cinema stops. There is really no "thing" to perceive when the sensorial movie stops—sensory consciousness just ends, like collapsing a hologram. But there is no "space" either—spatial extension, the "puffed-outness" of spatial relations, taken together being what William James termed the *specious present*—being just an illusion that vanishes with the movie. So, the sensorium is like a magic theatre with no screen, no projector, and no space. In other words, the sensorium is a plenum void constituted by and for the adaptive functions of the brainmind.

Hyletic pixels in experience, ontology, and theory

Of course, I am describing hyletic pixels from my own experience of them, but there is nothing really novel about my subjectivity here. But then, the closest we get to "objectivity" in the real world is intersubjective agreement—more precisely the transcendental lifeworld. Equivalent descriptions are available from various sources. So, before I go further into the neurophenomenology of the pixel, let me place the notion into a broader historical perspective. "Hyletic pixel" is equivalent in some respects to Lonergan's (1958: 442) concept of "prime potency." Potency is the raw "material" of experience, the "stuff" that makes up that about the phenomenal world that is to be known. As such, potency exists as a set of primitive limitations upon form and activity. It is "the potency of the lowest level that provides the principle of limitation [read essence] for the whole range of proportionate being" (Lonergan 1958: 442). Apprehension of prime potency—of fields of pixels—is the result of what Michael Polanyi (1965) called a "logical disintegration" of form into its constituent phenomenal fragments.

The concept of pixelated hyle is also similar to Alfred North Whitehead's (1978) notion of "actual entity" or "actual occasion." But pixel is intended primarily as a descriptive empirical, rather than a theoretical or metaphysical category. Pixels are decidedly *not* our version of McCulloch's (1965: 37) "psychon," the theoretical basic psychic unit. In this respect the pixel is analogous to the ancient Sanskrit concept of *bindu* (meaning "dot" or "drop;" see Woodroffe 1974[1919]) which is the elemental particle of *prana*, the fundamental cosmic energy— again, an empirically derived descriptive concept, not an ontological supposition. Trained yogis come to know the *bindu* by direct experience as the building block of phenomena from the most gross object such as a "table" or a "planet" to the most subtle object like breath or spirit.

Hyletic pixels and theoretical "atoms" are likely to be historically related. I suspect that early atomist theories in Western European metaphysics and science, as well as Eastern ontologies, are grounded in the unconscious projection upon the world by the brainmind of elements of its own essential structure. The idea of something like a "monad" (*not* Husserl's monad) as the ultimate constituent of the universe goes back at least to the early Greeks and, in the 18th century, is specifically referenced by Leibnitz in his *Principles of Nature and Grace*. Many philosophers over the centuries (including Kant, Husserl and Whitehead) have put forward monadologies. The term "monad" derives from the Greek root meaning "one" or "unit," and is used in some cases to refer to a simple, irreducible particle of reality from which all composite things in the universe are constructed. The monad is frequently conceived as a source of power in its own right, and, as in the case of Whitehead's "actual entity," a scintilla of consciousness as well.

The concept of monad used in this sense seems closer to a mental particle than, say, the notions of atom or molecule, but it is usually not clear (and this is the crucial point) to what extent the monad is intended in these philosophies either as a phenomenologically descriptive term, or strictly to apply to consciousness rather than the ontology of the universe. The "atomistic" views of pre-Socratic Greek philosophers like Heraclitus and Empedocles were almost certainly based upon mature contemplation (see Edwards 1967: 477, 496). Empedocles (a physician and in the latter part of his life a confirmed mystic) saw the world of the senses as being in constant change, and as being comprised of a perpetual remixing of tiny entities (Edwards 1967: 497). However, the views of many later philosophers such as Descartes, although also positing atomistic foundations, seem more based upon rational analysis and projection of an "atomist" ontology than upon direct introspection and phenomenological description. A significant difference between early Greek and later European ideas of monads is that the early views—and the ones most akin to direct perception of hyletic pixels by contemplatives—stressed the living and active nature of these particles, often associated with the subtle element "fire" (see Burtt 1954: 87-90), whereas most later philosophers took a more mechanical view of their natures (see Merchant 1980). An interesting exception to this trend was the 17th century philosopher, Pierre Gassendi, who tried with some success to introduce the early Greek conception of the atom as an active particle into science (Merchant 1980).

An interesting artistic example of the projection of the pixelated nature of sensorial events upon reality is to be found in the work of the 19th century neo-impressionists. The painter, Georges Seurat (1859-1891), collaborating with other artists like Paul Signac (1863-1935), used the science of perception of his day as a guide to replicating what he saw in nature (Foa 2015, Homer 1964a: 236). These artists used the "pointillist" technique of painting "tiny dots of pure color" to depict line, shade, and form. This technique was used relatively informally by the earlier impressionists like Monet, Renoir and Pissaro, but it was Seurat and his followers who brought this process to full awareness. It seems unclear just how conscious Seurat was of the pixel-nature of his own perception, but clearly he appreciated the ease with which the observer can lose awareness of the elements making up the picture while fully apprehending its theme and perceptual/aesthetic effects. When criticized of producing patchwork quilts, the neo-impressionist would suggest the critic back up until the eye was no longer attracted to the dabs of paint and could thus appreciate their perceptual effects (Homer 1964: 159). It should again be noted that whereas the pointillist technique often leaves spaces between tiny dabs of paint, there are no such spaces between hyletic pixels in pure perception.

BECOMING AWARE OF PIXELS

As apprehended during contemplation, hyletic pixels have minute spatial extension and are always contiguous within the sensory field.

Even patches or fields of black are constituted by "illuminant" hyletic pixels—i.e., black patches of light in the primordial given are not the *absence* of pixels. If you close your eyes in a dark room, your entire visual field will be filled with "black" light forming a kind of veil. Experienced space-time is an illusion imposed upon topological relations among pixels and the forms they fulfill (Arbib, Érdi and Szentagothai 1998: 223-224). In other words, pixels are perceived to have extension and to make up the entirety of primordial sensory "space" with no gaps between pixels—an extension that is perpetually refreshed producing the universal sense of duration, and hence linear and cyclical time (see Fingelkurts, Fingelkurts and Neves 2010, TenHouten 2005; see Chapter 6). Sensory pixels are not little squares, but tiny energy points with extension into surrounding pixels—pixels merge with each other and have fuzzy (not crisp) boundaries. Extension interpreted as "space" between objects is a relational intuition which nonetheless is in synch in many respects with the environing world. Such "space" or "emptiness" is readily seen by the contemplative to be a "plenum void"—i.e., full of impermanent, conjoined multisensory pixels. Any "place" one concentrates upon within the sensorium, one will find contiguous pixels, be they visual, auditory, tactile, kinesthetic, or other sensory mode. I am speaking here of the topological relations among pixels in the field comprising any given moment of consciousness—topological relations that are preserved as information about the environing world sent inwards via nerve tracts for higher neural processing.

Sensory pixels differ logically from other comparable Eastern cosmological and Western philosophical notions in that they do not entail any ontological claims about the nature of reality apart from the act of perception. Furthermore, in keeping with Husserl's views about hallucinations, fantasies and the like, phenomena are "filled" by pixels whether or not the stimulus initially eliciting the phenomena is internal or external to the body or the nervous system. The perceptions of both a car "out there" and a car "in a dream" involve the constituting of an object within a field of pixels.

Before I retired as a university professor of anthropology, I would explain to students various methods for finding out about hyletic pixels using their own introspection (I called them "dots" at the time). Sometimes I would pass out black cards with a small white dot in the middle. The students' task was to meditate upon the white dot by scanning the card and then closing their eyes and watch the after-image of the white dot deteriorate. If you do this, you will find that the pixels making up the after image drop away randomly over a number of epochs, being replaced by black pixels. This destructuration of the "dot" isolates individual pixels before the mind's eye. One can do this using a tiny bright spot of light in a snowbank, a tiny light at a distance in the dark, etc.

Summarizing thus far, hyletic pixels are intuitively apprehendable elements that are momentary to perception (arise and pass rapidly) and that contribute to enduring objects such as forms, color patches, textures, melodies, etc. All verbalizations, images, percepts, perceptions of physical space, boundaries of forms, and the like, are comprised of pixels. Yet pixels themselves are apprehended as having no enduring form or substance. They are transitory, impermanent and without perceivable internal structure, while being experienced as vibrant, scintillating and alive (hence the early association with the "fire" element). Pixels provide the finest grade of hyletic "texture" of which human awareness is capable of resolving within any sensory modality. It is accurate to say both that without pixels there can be no sensory phenomena, and that there are states of mind within the purview of the phenomenological attitude in which the only awareness of phenomena is awareness of a field of pixels *qua* field (see Buddhaghosa 1976, Lusthaus 2014 on the *arupajhana* states in Buddhist phenomenology).

PSYCHOPHYSIOLOGY OF HYLETIC PIXELS AND PIXELATED HYLE

We know from neuropsychological research that visual pixels are not simply perceived photons, but rather a systematic sampling of wavelengths of electromagnetic energies in the environing world (Arbib, Érdi and Szentagothai 1998: 223-224). To quote Baumgardt (1972), "There is no light, but we may see light. Light is a sensation and thus has no physical existence." I would add that light has no physical existence *apart from the activity of the neural processes mediating visual sensations.* As Husserl noted, the sensory experience and the neural processes mediating them are parallel processes that may or may not occur simultaneously (Husserl 1989[1952]: 205). Our understanding of the "parallel" neural structures mediating the pixel is thus far speculative, but along with Polyani (1965: 806) I would argue that such structures are fairly implastic relative to the plasticity of higher cognitive operations mediated by more complex cognits—hence, the "obduracy" of the primordial sensory given. If you are able to adumbrate pixelated hyle in any sensory mode, you might attempt as an experiment to exercise your will over the arrangement of pixels. I have never succeeded in doing so.

The hyletic pixels of which we become aware are probably produced at the cortical level of organization (see Doty 1975) and are unlikely mediated by the activity of single cells (Powers 2005). It is more likely that pixels are mediated by columns in secondary and tertiary sensory cortex and obtain much of their initial ordering ("primordial givenness") via processing by hypercolumnar organizations.[33] It is now clear that the basic structure of the cortex is fairly consistent across areas and that this consistency facilitates cross-modal communication across cortical space utilizing the same "code." This enables parallel processing over often lengthy durations (Hurley 1998; Singer 2012) utilizing patterns within the primordial sensory given repeated throughout the hierarchical processing system (see Arbib, Érdi and Szentagothai 1998: 46-48).[34] This may also account for the interesting experiences of *synesthesia* (Neckar and Bob 2014) where one may "see" a symphony, or "hear" a painting (mediated by cross-modal cognits).

---

[33] A column is a functional unit of the cortex that may be comprised of 10,000 or more neurons, plus support cells (see Marrocco in LeDoux and Hirst 1986, Molnár and Rockland 2020 and Arbib, Érdi and Szentagothai 1998: 223-229 for reviews of columnar organization). This is a natural level of organizational connectivity which has been demonstrated in living monkey brains during their resting state (Card and Gharbawie 2022). The relationship between sensorial pixels (mediated by cortical networks) on the one hand, and the activity of individual receptor cells at the periphery on the other hand is very complex. It involves a topographical transmission of patterned activity into the brain, a regularity of transmission that functions to maintain an adaptive isomorphism of conscious experience with patterns of stimulation at receptor sites.

[34] This hierarchy may involve, as Karl Pribram (1991) has suggested, storage in a *holonomic* manner—that is, with quantum physical entanglement (see also Laughlin 1996, Persinger and Lavallee 2012).

My colleagues Eugene d'Aquili, John McManus and I—all three of us contemplatives, though from different disciplines—suggested over three decades ago that the hyletic fields we experience within the epoché are mediated in the anterior sensory association area of the prefrontal cortex (Laughlin, McManus and d'Aquili 1990: 112-117). Sensory processing is a complex and hierarchical system with simultaneous parallel activities going on in different areas. It was, and still is, our hypothesis that in the normal course of events, we are not aware of sensory processing occurring in either unimodal or multimodal posterior association areas, even from within the phenomenological epoché.

There are of course states of conscious attained in mature contemplation during which the entire sensorium is experienced as a single field (form-filled or formless, bounded or unbounded, finite or infinite) within which the hyletic fields of different modalities blend into a single monad (the so-called *coincidentia oppositorum*, an advanced absorption-state; see Buddhaghosa 1976, Lusthaus 2014). During this experience consciousness is indistinguishable from the multi-modal sensorial monad, the sensorial monad indistinguishable from consciousness, and which is constituted as Husserl modelled by both noetic and noematic processes. Awareness in this state is of a totality of undifferentiated phenomena—consciousness itself perceived as a plenum void—and perhaps infinitely extended space in which the unfolding field of energy in the being flows without hindrance. Totality and "pure" flow are, of course, the two major attributes of "higher" states of consciousness in various contemplative traditions (Csikszentmihalyi 2008, Goleman 1977). In this ASC (or as Husserl would say, "attitude") the contemplative may focus awareness on the common essential nature of pixels and fields of pixels, without necessarily distinguishing specific modes of sensory experience or objects other than the hyle itself.

Let me reiterate. Unlike the view of the physical world propounded in some atomist theories, pixels are contiguous—there are no "spaces" or gaps between pixels. Pixels are not structured like the lights in a cinema marque which have obvious spaces between the bulbs. The continuity of pixelation constitutes the "plenum" characteristic of "emptiness," or "voidness" noted in some esoteric psychologies (i.e., Skt., *sunyata*; Tib., *stong pa rxyid*, according to some schools of Mahayana Buddhism). Pixels "arise" (Skt., *uppada* in Theravadan Buddhism), have a momentary duration (Skt., *thiti*) and then "dissolve" (Skt., *bhanga*; see Govinda 1974: 133). They thus have momentary occurrence (Skt., *cittakhana*, the so-called "thought moment"). Instead of using Buddhist or other esoteric terms for the iterations of hyle, I will term them *epochs* (meaning "basic interval," not to be confused with Husserl's epoché).

Hyletic epochs are continuously being refreshed—they arise in awareness and pass away (they "sink down" in Husserl-speak) into the unconscious. Although the constituted phenomenon may endure in awareness via short-term memory (John, Easton and Isenhart 1997) and continuous focus on the unfolding iterations of objects, relations, and horizon, the field of pixels constituting momentary epochs do not endure, and in fact may not be held beyond the duration of their momentary occurrence by any act of will whatever—presenting us with yet another example of Husserl's essential structures of consciousness. This is the characteristic known in some schools of Mahayana Buddhism as the "pure voidness" of things. Seeing clearly that all phenomena, including phenomena identified with Self, are constituted from such insubstantial "stuff" is also one aspect of the *anatta* (no permanent soul, self or substance) realization in Buddhist phenomenology, and the realization which is the definitive hallmark of mature contemplation.

This is not to say that the neural network—the *ākāśa*, or unperceived structure of experience—comes into existence and passes away with the hyletic epoch it mediates. Rather, the intermittency of activity of the network is experienced as the momentary occurrence of the pixel field. Nor do I wish to leave the impression that every sensory network is continuously producing pixels in consciousness. Far from it, for a network can only produce a pixel in the sensorial field if it is entrained to the greater intentional network (the noetic-noematic dialog) mediating conscious experience in the moment. Most sensorial networks will remain dormant or active *sub rosa*, excluded from consciousness much of the time.

As I say, pixels are not little LEDs (or audio bits) that turn on and stay on until a switch is thrown. Those contemplatives that are able to discern fields of pixels will also find that they flicker in a synchronized way across the field and over epochs of duration. The refresh rate appears to us as fields of sensation that arise and pass away in unison. Pixel fields are as intermittent in occurrence as are individual pixels. Sensory fields arise and dissolve serially—they "flicker" on and off as discerned by the contemplative—much as a series of photographic frames come and go, producing the illusion of a "moving" picture in the cinema. Sensory fields pulse or flicker over epochs, as does awareness of them.

The importance of this essential feature of hyletic phenomenology cannot be overstated, because sensory epochs are *not readily apprehendable to naive introspection*, and indeed are generally not apprehended until perception of form (i.e., "car," "sound of constant pitch," "taste of sole almondine") has been reduced so thoroughly that concentration is entirely limited to the genetic constitution of hyle itself. When the contemplative becomes fully aware of hyletic epochs and can apprehend the arising and dissolving of fields of pixels as they occur in each of the sensory modes, then they may be said to have performed the reduction to the real, ongoing "now moment" as opposed to the "now" of mundane perception (see Chapter 6). The cognitive mangling of past and future with what is happening in the now moment is well recognized among Western phenomenologists. Paul Ricoeur (1984) noted that this view was a cornerstone of Augustine's philosophy of time. Likewise, Husserl (1964a: 48ff; see also Landgrebe 1981: 59, Miller 1984: 85) saw the "primal impressional datum" of perception as being a synthesis of recently past acts of perception present in short term memory ("retention"), of the streaming present ("now points") and of the anticipated future ("protention"):

> [...]the continuity of running-off of an enduring Object is a continuum whose phases are the continua of the modes of running-off of the different temporal points of the duration of the Object. [...]Since a new now is always presenting itself, each now is changed into a past, and thus the entire continuity of the running-off of the pasts of the preceding points moves uniformly "downward" into the depths of the past. [...]Every primordially constitutive process is animated by protentions which voidly constitute and intercept what is coming, as such, in order to bring it to fulfilment. (Husserl 1964a: 49-50, 76)

As Husserl (ibid: 81) noted, the relations among memories of patterns abstracted from recently past epochs, the "now" or current epoch, and anticipated, soon-to-arise epochs are primordial. These are cognitions that entrain with the sensorial structures mediating the flow of epochs to produce apparently enduring objects and the continuity of events— indeed, the entire sensed horizon of the moment. Obviously, the temporal organization of experience is a complex matter and involves other areas of the brain in addition to those mediating primordial sensory fields. The role of prefrontal cortical intentional processes in selecting, exciting, and ordering sensorial activity into a temporally meaningful "plan" is crucial and has been discussed elsewhere (Laughlin, McManus and d'Aquili 1990: Chap. 4; see also Pribram 1971, 1991).

Sensing reality is not a passive activity—far from it. As I mentioned above, visual sense receptors are not passive microchips waiting for a photon to impinge upon them before they wake up and pass on the stimulation as information for use of higher layers of apperception and cognits. Certain stimuli (forms and hyle) have an "allure" or *gaze* (Ger. *Reiz*) for consciousness (Husserl 1989[1952]: 196-198, 2001[1920/24]: 196-198). In their presence, consciousness is drawn to the object with enhanced focus and interest. The draw might be to the object because of its beauty (an aesthetic allure), or because it involves accessing food, or avoiding noxity (a pragmatic allure). Desire commonly motivates interest in the object, event, or even the entire horizon (Husserl 1989[1952]: 197).

Keep in mind that sensory receptor cells in all sensory modes are living organisms that actively and systematically sample energies within their narrow biochemical purview (see Arbib, Érdi and Szentagothai 1998: 223-224, Churchland 1985, B. Smith 2021). Indeed, the range of electromagnetic or auditory energies sampled by any animal's photoreceptors and auditory receptors amount to a tiny fraction of the energies (the vibes) "out there" in the environing world (Barth, Giampieri-Deutsch and Klein 2012: 91-92). Husserl saw this clearly, though not in neurophysiological terms, for as he emphasized, intentionality is a *transcendental act* (Husserl 1982[1913]: 135-136, 241-244, Levinas 1995: 40)—i.e., intentionality involves a direct engagement with the environing world as it presents itself before consciousness: "Returning then, let us take the position, easily tested, that in physical method the *perceived thing itself is always and in principle precisely the thing which the physicist studies and scientifically determines*" (Husserl 1982[1913]: 159). Indeed, it may be said that the primal function of the brainmind's sensorium is to actively sample the environing world in the interests of adaptation. Were this not the case, truth and *truing*[35] of higher cortical models would be meaningless relative to the objective world (Havlík 2017).

What exactly do the sensory receptors sample? That depends upon the sense mode. We know the most about the human visual system where three types of chromatic cone cells sample frequencies of light (in the red, green and blue range of the spectrum) being reflected from the surface of objects (Schwab 2011). Different experienced colors are produced by graded firing rates (afference) of these three types of photoreceptors as they deliver information into the sensorium. Animals like our family dog only have two types of color receptors while others like the Mantis Shrimp have as many as 12 (Thoen *et al.* 2014). There are some lucky individuals (called "tetrachromats;" see Jordan and Mollon 2019) that, like birds, have four types of cones in their retinae and whose experience of colors is far more nuanced than for the rest of us. What this variety of arrangements tells us is that different species are "wired" to process the frequencies of sampled light in different ways relative to species-specific adaptation strategies. For instance, being mammals, we cannot experience colors in the ultraviolet range whereas honeybees can (Kevan, Chittka and Dyer 2001).

We humans are very dependent upon color vision to detect and identify objects of adaptive relevance. The majority of cone cells in each of our retinae cluster around the fovea, that part of each retina (consisting of about two degrees of arc in our visual field) that processes the object upon which our eyes are focused. If you shift your eyes two inches to the left or right of this page, you will notice you cannot read the words on this page. Also, if you compare a black and white photo of an orchard with a color photo of the same scene, you will see that the fruit of the trees spring out from the background in the color shot. It is also interesting that, as emphasized by Husserl (1982[1913]: 130-131), there is a constancy to color and relations between colors that does not change as the light conditions and our perspectives vary, a feature of great interest to vision scientists today (Gegenfurtner 2001, Gepshtein *et al.* 2021). As Husserl notes, as we walk around a table, we experience the same table regardless of changes in perspective, light conditions,

---

[35] I use "true" as a verb, as in "truing a door to its frame."

and geometric shape. We automatically perceive primordially a shadow falling on an object as something obstructing the light source and not a fundamental color change in the object. This is the importance of the interaction between the iteration of epochs with remembrance in recognizing the transcendental nature of the object.

The sensitivity of sense receptors to waves of external energy is astounding. On a clear moonless night, the most sensitive sensory cells (the rods) in your retinae can detect a candle flame 30 miles away (Okawa and Sampath 2007). If things get really quiet, the hair cells of your inner ear can detect the tick of a clock 20 feet away (Galanter 1962; see also Gescheider 2013). In other words, the truing function of the primordial sensory given is an active one, relying upon the precision of the innate sampling processes as well as maintaining the topography of patterns within sensory iterations into higher processing areas of the midbrain and cortex. Let me emphasize this point, for it is absolutely crucial to understanding truing and, as we shall see, concordance of information at every level of information processing. Real physical properties in the environing world are sampled by receptors that in turn transduce these properties into action potentials (neuron "firings") that are passed on to other neurons and into the interior of the brain where sense is made of them (Churchland 1985, Frings 2012). *The patterns of sensory reception, far from being figments of a solipsistic imagination, do in fact relate directly to the physical surface features and activities of objects and events in the environing world* (for vision, see Degenaar and Myin 2014).

CONCORDANCE AND NEURAL REALISM

The essential structures discovered within the primordial sensory given are mediated by neural processes that evolved over countless generations to actively true the internal cognitive models (cognits) of the environing world such that species fitness is maintained. This view represents a type of *neural realism* (Edelman 1987; Edelman and Tononi 2000) or *evolutionary epistemology* (Callebaut and Pinxten 2012), and runs counter to the old "reactive machine" model of the brainmind (Havlík 2017). These perspectives emphasize the need of selective pressures upon sensuous sampling and the organization of the sensorium to be direct, intense, and dynamic. Our sensory systems do not sample everything in the environing world. In fact, in everyday life we can only focus on a tiny bit of the energy world at a time as represented in perception (Maunsell 1995). The truth is, most of what happens in the real world is either invisible to or ignored by our senses. Natural selection is never supportive of comprehensive sampling within any phylum, for this would prove very inefficient and maladaptive—it would invite a perceptually "over-rich data environment" (Scriven 1977) that could overwhelm processing systems. Rather, those features that are at least minimally present and that result in adaptive judgments and action are selected; those neural features reinforced by biogenetic and Hebbian mechanisms[36] within the phylum (Obermayer, Sejnowski and Blasdel 1995, Arbib, Érdi and Szentagothai 1998: 122-126). These are the species-typical features of an animal's brainmind that are of relevance to successful adaptation to a niche, and often a spectrum of niches (DeSantis *et al.* 2012, Hutchinson 1965). On these grounds, evolutionary psychologists have persuasively argued that the world to which we humans evolved our present brainmind is in fact long gone, lost in the past, and more relevant and adaptive to our Paleolithic lifeways than to modern technocracy (Barkow, Cosmides and Tooby 1992, Over 2003). In other words, there has been insufficient time since the dawn of the Neolithic 12,000 years ago for our Paleolithic brainminds to "catch-up." Mind you, we must disassociate ourselves from the "noble savage" or "primitive communism" bias of a lot of past ethnology. We humans have been an animal that has been capable of all sorts of adaptations to varied and rapidly changing conditions for hundreds of thousands of years. "Cultural" flexibility in adaptive strategies has been the hallmark of our survival as a species, and the ability to fit into various niches as they afforded themselves—a flexibility evidenced by foraging societies studied over the past century (see Singh and Glowacki 2022).

---

[36] Re a Hebbian mechanism: "If the inputs to a system cause the same pattern of activity to occur repeatedly, the set of active elements constituting that pattern will become increasingly strongly interassociated. That is, each element will tend to turn on every other element and (with negative weights) to turn off the elements that do not form part of the pattern. To put it another way, the pattern as a whole will become 'auto-associated'" (Allport 1985: 44).

For neural realism to operate adaptively in the environing world, there must be *concordance* between the primordial level of sensation and subsequent layers of processing up to and including the level of the sensorium. Concordance depends upon a biogenetic system of physiological laws by which each level of processing and each parallel process is *in*-formed by data from lower levels while processing those data differently, especially in establishing broadened associations at the highest level of cognits. The retention of topological information (retinotopic for vision, frequency-topic for sound, etc.) up the layers of processing speaks to the importance of concordance among levels and to the primordial sensory experience by means of which we sample events in the "objective" or transcendental world. Topological information includes the essential structures operating at the primordial level (e.g., the lawful relations between parts and wholes constituting the concrete object) is reiterated throughout the hierarchy of processing. This is not to say that meanings associated with the object must correspond to that essential structure (Husserl 1970 [1900-01] II: 50). It is fair to say that the higher the layer of cognit, the more complex is the processing and the more plastic the organization of cognits become (Maunsell 1995). However, *there is no such thing as a totally plastic cognit* (see Pinker 2003). It should also be noted that concordance may be modelled as a continuum of synchrony that ranges from total harmony at one extreme to dissonance, and even destructive dissociation (Krippner 1997), at the other extreme.

Efforts after Meaning and Truth

The concordance between primordial sensory given and higher cognits operating in everyday life suggests that we can distinguish between two orientations toward knowledge construction in the human brain. These are orientations that require allocation of trophic energy to activate and maintain, and activation of one orientation tends to inhibit the other orientation (Purves 1990, 2010). This holds true at the very highest level of organization, what is now being called a *global state of consciousness*— i.e., "…states of consciousness that characterize an organism's overall conscious condition. An organism can be in only one global state of consciousness at a time" (Bayne, Hohwy and Owen 2016: 406). What is being referred to here is the ASC organized at the highest level where some major functions are "online" and others "offline" (see McKilliam 2020). The recognition of global states of consciousness implicitly incorporates the view that the brainmind of any species is an *intelligent complex adaptive system* (ICAD) wherein each level of complexity of neural organization exhibits emergent properties (see Laughlin n.d., Yang and Shan 2008).

Depending upon the global state of the brain, a person may be driven by an *effort after meaning*[37] or by an *effort after truth* (see Laughlin and Throop 2001, 2003):[38]

> The effort after truth shifts the orientation from attributing meaning to the given to discovering what is novel in the given and then evaluating meaning models by comparison with the given's experienced novelty. In other words, the effort after meaning is a quest for an ordered patterning of experience with a recognition of the correspondence between an experienced given and the instantiation of that given in memory, while the effort after truth is a systematic search for anomaly in our experience of a particular given as it arises in the sensorium. (Laughlin and Throop, 2001, p. 714)

Adults are motivated by the effort after meaning most of the time. It is commonplace to observe adults ignoring anomalies until they become surprising (Jones 1986). The effort after truth can be witnessed by watching small children play—indeed, the function of play among animals is precisely to exercise the effort after truth in the service of truing developing knowledge (Laughlin, McManus and Shearer 1993a). But among adults, the effort after truth tends to diminish with age.

---

[37] In defining the effort after meaning, I am following Bartlett's (1932) usage.

[38] In earlier writings (Laughlin 1992b) I attributed the distinction between "effort after meaning" and "effort after truth" to Ogden and Richards (1923), but the actual origin of the notion of "effort after meaning" originates with Bartlett (1932: 44). The confusion arose in a conversation I had with the late Professor Earl W. Count during which he made use of both concepts. Making the distinction between "effort after meaning" and "effort after truth" was apparently Count's, or at least developed during that conversation.

The healthy brainmind operates in the interests of adaptation by dynamically balancing the efforts after truth and meaning. They really describe two poles of a process of equilibration, now emphasizing truing of knowledge, then emphasizing habitual responses to apperceived redundancy in the environing world (Piaget 1971). The shift from one effort to the other impacts cellular growth, development, and internal organization, the latter occurring mostly during sleep. One can detect in the responses of a person, regardless of cultural background, a style of engagement with respect to distinct domains of reality. At one extreme we find individuals who predictably project a relatively static cognized world of "certainty" upon what is objectively a dynamic world while at the other extreme are individuals who live in a world of perpetual novelty and play. Most of us may be found ranging along the continuum between these extremes. If we are faced with little novelty at the moment, our responses may be routine, but when the novelty quotient "heats-up" to the level of surprise we take great interest ("eustress") in events. Yet if the novelty gets to be noxious, we may slip back into imposing redundancy upon our experiences to reduce distress (see Harvey, Hunt and Schroder 1961, Laughlin 2017a).

Ethnologically speaking, traditional cosmologies tend to be conservative of meaning. Worldviews resist change to a considerable extent, for the principal function of a society's worldview is to assure both a complementarity of experience for the group members, as well as reflect the authenticity of experience in the service of conserving socially shared meaning and viable cooperation. The traditional conservation of meaning is supported by an inherent effort after meaning in the brainminds of group members, often at the cost of the effort after truth. That is, the cognitive processes of the human brain operate to associate what is arising in the sensorium at the moment with patterns stored in memory—as Bartlett (1932: 44) wrote, "...an effort to connect what is given with something else." One can see the effort after meaning operating in institutions in which ritually driven experiences reported to a teacher, leader, guru, or institutional interpreter (e.g., societies that include institutional oneirocritics for dream interpretations) are interpreted in terms consonant with the society's worldview. There are numerous examples of this effort to interpret extraordinary experiences in such a way that the experiences form negative feedback into and instantiations of the group's system of knowledge (see Laughlin 2011: 242-255). The effort after meaning may at times become so intense that potentially anomalous experiences, including even hyletic data, are ignored in favor of supporting the group's worldview. This is not uncommon even in the sciences, as Husserl noted repeatedly when discussing the natural attitude. When this occurs in a systematic way, the worldview, belief system, or scientific paradigm has become an ideology that will resist recognizing or admitting any anomalous data (Turnbull 2018).

The effort after truth shifts the orientation from layering-on meaning atop the sensory given toward discovering what is novel in the given and then evaluating meaning models by comparison with experienced novelty. In other words, the effort after meaning is a quest for an ordered patterning of experience with a recognition of the correspondence between an experienced given and the instantiation of that given in memory, while the effort after truth is a systematic search for anomalies in our experience of the given. The effort after meaning tends to evoke negative feedback, while the effort after truth evokes positive feedback. The former is common to people everywhere, while the latter is less common and is the fundamental impetus behind real science—that is, when the "science" is not marred by an adherence to ideology. It was Husserl's project to *optimize the effort after truth within philosophy and the sciences.*

A disjunction between perception and ideology is an example of *discordance* between the level of primordial sensory given and higher-level neurocognitive processing and memory. Discordance may be superficial as when someone tells a lie—that is, one says something contrary to the actual concord between what the person experiences and knows. But there are more severe instances of discord when one continues to hold to beliefs in the face of potentially disconfirmatory experiences. This occurs when people are afflicted by one form of dissociation or another. *Dissociation* in psychological jargon means that a person is disconnected from parts of themselves—in the present case, disconnected from reality as sampled by the senses. In an anthropological sense, we can posit an existential tension that may arise to some extent between one's system of knowledge held in memory on the one hand and what our senses are telling us on the other (see Almeder 1990, D'Agostino 2009,

Kuhn 1977). In Husserlian terms, this would amount to a tension or disruption between noetic and noematic processes.

PHENOMENOLOGICAL ATTITUDE AND THE EFFORT AFTER TRUTH

Husserlian pure phenomenology *is an extreme example of privileging the effort after truth*. To carry out a reduction, one must dissociate higher cognits mediating information held in memory from any role whatever in the act of perception (Husserl 1970[1936]: 143-147). Bracketing in its most effective form requires dissociation in the psychological sense. In other words, the phenomenological attitude is a positive dissociative state relative to the "natural" attitude. We know from personal experience that dissociation works, and it produces an attitude (an ASC) in which the dynamic primordial given holds sway and fills awareness. And we know from modern neuroscience that affecting such dissociations has a straightforward mechanism, the inhibition of one neural system by activation of another system (Ito 2004, Markram *et al.* 2004). Inhibitory neurons in the cortex of our brains operate to control potential antagonism between neural networks. When working effectively, these inhibitory systems support concordance within the brainmind. Under other circumstances, however, inhibitory systems can produce dissociation between belief and evidence of the senses. Dissociation of those parts of the cortex mediating meaning from the sampling (truing) function of the nervous system's senses facilitates the phenomenological attitude, and makes possible the close scrutiny of those processes, including the hyle, that sample events in the environing world, and present their data as a kind of pixelated, holographic movie of the mind.

SUMMARY AND SEGUE

We have seen that close scrutiny of sensory hyle reveals that fields of sensory data break down into pixels. Pixels in turn are mediated by inherent and irreducible neural structures that "fulfill" the instantiated idea within the structure of the intentional act. This is the case for all sensory modes but is easiest to discern in the visual field. Consciousness trues itself by sampling the energies in the environing world which become hyletic data upon which knowing the world is dependent. The effort after truth requires this entanglement between the environing world and the sampling function of perception. We also see that hyletic fields "flicker" and refresh very rapidly in epochs. This is an ancient structural feature found throughout the phyla and operates to true-up models to a dynamic and constantly changing world. In other words, the activity of hyletic filling unfolds in time, and indeed, are inseparable from our fundamental experience of time-consciousness.

CHAPTER SIX

Time-Consciousness

The thing-appearance is constituted in the primary apprehension of time, the thing-apprehension as an enduring, unaltered phenomenon or as one that is altered. And in the unity of this alteration, we are "conscious of" a new unity; the unity of unaltered or altering thing, unaltered or altering in its time, its duration.

– Husserl (1964a: 118)

A man cannot step in the same river twice.

– Heraclitus

It is readily apparent to mature contemplatives who focus their attention upon the fine structures of experience that consciousness does in fact stream—is directly experienced as flowing—as William James (1890) reported.[39] Under conditions of disciplined meditation, as concentration upon the flow of sensory experience increases and the mind slows its processes, the sensory flow is revealed to present in a continuous sequence of primordial sensory epochs (or "primordial intervals;" Damasio 1999b: 126; Dainton 2006: Chap 5). I have described this process of arising and passing sensory hyle—Husserl (1964a: 48) calls this "running-off" of the hyle into the past—in the last chapter, the results of direct perception after performing countless reductions over many years. It is by studying the discernible fine structure of hyletic epochs, the relations between epochs, and the temporal binding of epochs over durations that we are able to discover the essential and universal nature of time-consciousness—what Maurice

---

[39] Much of this chapter is rewritten from Laughlin and Throop (2008). Many thanks to Jason for his contributions to that paper.

Block (1977: 284–285) called "universal time," the experience of time that underlies the very structure of our subjective life regardless of our particular cultural heritage. When the contemplative becomes fully aware of perceptual epochs and can apprehend the arising and passing of epochs as they occur, then they may be said to have performed a Husserlian reduction to the real, ongoing "now moment" within the stream of time-consciousness.

STATIC AND GENETIC PHENOMENOLOGY

It is curious that some authorities harbor the misapprehension that Husserl's phenomenology of experience before the publication of *Logical Investigations* (Volume Two) in 1921 was "static" relative to temporal considerations, and thus somehow wrongheaded. For instance, Jacques Derrida, referring to Husserl's efforts before that time, notes:

> But all the problems that are studied from this moment on until 1919-1920 still remain problems of "static" constitution, in spite of the great importance that the analyses of the consciousness of time acquired here [*Logical Investigations* II]. It is only after this date that the themes of genetic phenomenology will be unavoidable for Husserl. (Derrida 2003[1990]: 53)

If you are at all familiar with the Husserlian literature, you will have encountered the distinction made between Husserl's "static" and "genetic" phenomenologies (see especially Husserl's *Analyses Concerning Passive and Active Synthesis: Lectures on Transcendental Logic*, 2001[1920/24]; see also Steinbock 2017, Welton 1982, 2000: Chap. 1). Some of Husserl's critics have made much of this distinction, the "static" method being something of a snapshot of a short duration of experience and the more "genetic" method that accounts for temporal phenomena. For example, Schutz (1973) makes the most of this distinction in his critique of Husserl's account of empathy and the primordial sense of the Other. In my opinion, there is an element of misrepresentation involved in such critiques, as though Husserl's "static" method might imply an ignorance of temporality that he somehow stumbled across around 1916 and thereafter concerned himself with the temporal "running off" of hyletic and morphological data, and the history of meaning.

Actually, Husserl was never ignorant of the temporal dimension of experience—how could he be as a student of Brentano and as a great admirer of William James (Spiegelberg 1981)? By utilizing the "static" method, Husserl was focusing, as a competent meditator will do, upon the primordial given within his stream of consciousness. "Genetic" factors like how the essential structures he was describing came to be that way—in other words the developmental personal history (or in Jungian terms, the "individuation" of consciousness), the history of moments of experiencing leading to the present experience, the role of the present moment in opening to future possibilities of experience, or even the biogenetic processes during evolution leading to the psychophysiology of the meditator, were all bracketed during the process of the pure reduction. In short, Husserl's project began with a quest for the eidetic structures operating in every act of intentionality, which, by their very nature are both given a priori and are essentially atemporal even within the context of the stream of consciousness (see Barber 2009, Marbach 2019, Steinbock 2017). Once he completed this grounding, he began to inch outward, so to speak, to examine more complex relations within the dialog between noetic and noematic processes of consciousness, leading of course to his account of the primordial givenness of intersubjectivity (Chapter 4).

Let us be clear about this. Husserl was a meticulous and highly focused contemplative. He knew, as all mature contemplatives know, the value of simplifying the object of meditation, be it the breath, an image, a motion, a feeling, an image, or what have you. One of the greatest traps the world sets for naïve philosophers is starting their ruminations at the top—that is, at the most complex level of cognition, reason, and language. One meditation master I studied under used to say, "complex meditations are for dull minds." Husserl's project was the same as that of any mature contemplative, the injunction to begin with the simple. Let me remind you, intensive meditation along any path will cause the mind to simplify and focus on the "static" dimensions of experience as Husserl saw it. Even toward the end of his career he reminded his readers of this approach and its attendant caution:

To a great extent genetic problems, and naturally those of the first and most fundamental level, have indeed already been dealt with in the actual work of phenomenology [read "actual meditations"]. The fundamental level is, of course, the one pertaining to "my" ego in respect of his primordial own-essentialness. Constitution on the part of consciousness of internal time and the whole phenomenological theory of association belong here; and what my primordial ego finds in original intuitive self-explication applies to every other ego forthwith, and for essential reasons. But with that, to be sure, the above-indicated *genetic problems of birth and death and the generative nexus of psychophysical being* have not yet been touched. Manifestly they belong to a higher dimension and presuppose such a tremendous labor of explication pertaining to the lower spheres that it will be a long time before they can become problems to work on. (Husserl 1993[1931]: 142)

At no time during his career as a meditator was Husserl unaware of the temporal and developmental aspects of consciousness (see Husserl 2008[1906-1907]: 251). He was fully aware that the empirical ego is at any moment a construction of a lifetime of habit, construction of beliefs, changing attitudes, the complexification of identity and meaning. He chose a method that would simplify all of this by removing it from consideration while developing mindfulness of the stream of consciousness as it presents moment after moment after moment. Any mindfulness meditator from any tradition realizes the importance of developing this skill of simplifying and intensifying awareness. Those who have not developed the skill may have opinions to share on the issue, but in my experience, these opinions are of scant value when it comes to actually developing the skill-in-means necessary to follow Husserl's path to revealing the universal structures of consciousness.

With respect to Husserl's distinction between "static" and "genetic" methods, Anthony Steinbock, himself a phenomenologist and a Husserl translator, clarifies this distinction:

When [Husserl] formulated this distinction explicitly, an interesting reevaluation took place: What was described earlier as "lower" and more "basic" and "simple" ("consciousness is absolute," the "now," the noema, etc.) are viewed in light of the "higher," "complex," phenomena ("self-temporalization" as the real absolute, the living-present, the optimal). Now, the "higher" and "complex" phenomena are called "concrete," and the earlier ones that were designated as "lower" and so on are now called "abstract" because they are more formal when they are revealed in a genetic analysis. (Steinbock 2017: xiii)

Steinbock himself opens Husserl's genetic approach out into what Steinbock now calls *generative phenomenology* (Steinbock 1995, 2017), taking off from Husserl's own use of the concept of *generativity* (Husserl 1993[1931]: 142) which Husserl considered an extension of genetic phenomenological methods (see Husserl 1993[1931]: §38). Husserl's genetic methods appreciate the unfolding and concretizing of phenomena in temporal consciousness, and all of his ruminations on genetic processes that come before and make possible the primordial givenness of the moment refer to temporal processes as short as learning a new word and as long as the history and development of a person's natural attitude and "empirical" ego (see Moran 2000, Steinbock 2017, Summa 2014). We will return to Steinbock when we take up excursions into what Husserl called "limit-problems," including engagement with the unconscious (Chapter 9) and spiritually salient experiences and ASC (Chapter 10).

In the meantime, *static methods* are the type of reduction we have carried out in earlier chapters where we analyze pregiven, a priori sensory objects, events, relations and intuitions as though there was no history or development causally impacting those experiences. While some authorities consider Husserl's static approach flawed, the method is anything but flawed, for Husserl knew by intense meditation that if one focuses upon the given with sufficient intensity, one becomes absorbed into the given to the exclusion of temporal factors. But structurally the history and personal development of the experience are implicitly present in the experience whether focused upon or not.

When Husserl introduced more *genetic methods* into his meditations, this was in the interests of capturing more elements of the intentional act. He directed his genetic analyses to the aspect of history and causation involved in experience and especially in the constitution of the ego or subject of the intentional act: "The eidetic laws of compossibility (rules that govern simultaneous or successive existence and possible existence together, in the fact) are laws of causality in a maximally broad sense— laws for an If and Then" (Husserl 1993[1931]: 75). But instead of causality Husserl prefers to speak of *motivation* for constituted acts: "But within this form, life goes on as a motivated course of particular constitutive performances with a multiplicity of particular motivations and motivational systems [systemic and nonlinear causation], which, according to *universal laws of genesis*, produce a unity of *universal genesis of the ego*. The ego constitutes himself for himself in, so to speak, the unity of a 'history'" (Husserl 1993[1931]: 75).

TIME-CONSCIOUSNESS

As we have noted in the last chapter, Husserl (1964a: 48ff; see also Stein 1989: 73, Landgrebe 1981: 59, Miller 1984: 85) described *time consciousness*[40] as a genetically constituted field. Taken all together, duration is what William James termed the "specious present." Husserl extended this view by showing that duration is a synthesis of recently past acts of perception ("retention"), of the streaming present ("now-points") and of the anticipated immediate future ("protention"). The relations among patterns abstracted from recently past epochs, the patterns within the real "now" or current epoch as it is "running-off," and anticipated patterns in soon-to-arise epochs are, as Husserl (1964a: 81) noted, primordial—that is, fundamental to the organization of perceptual acts performed by the perceptual systems of each and every human being on the planet, regardless of developmental and cultural background. Mature contemplation of the fine structures of perceptual epochs is able to clarify some of the confusion we find in the social science, philosophical, psychological, and cognitive science literatures about time-consciousness, as follows:

---

[40] If you wish to read more about Husserl's phenomenology of *internal time-consciousness*, see Husserl 1964a, 1982[1913]: 234-239, 2006[1910-1911]: 54-56; see also Landgrebe 1981: 59, Miller 1984: 85, Kortooms 2002, Zahavi 2003a, Laughlin and Throop 2008, Stein 1989[1917].

1. Duration and epochs

The so-called "now-point" (William James' term; see James 1890) is not a "durationless interface between past and future" (Dainton 2006: 120)—in other words, not instantaneous.[41] We know this as contemplatives because the reduction to the pure "now" involves the falling away of retention and protention until all one is aware of is the intermittent streaming of sensory hyle, as well as patterns and topographical relations among hyletic modes (color, tone, texture, spatial and geometric relations, etc.) as they arise and pass away. In this reduction to the actual now, all gross cognitive and behavioral acts like recognition, anticipation, reaction, rememoration, and so forth, have dropped away from notice. The stream of hyle (e.g., in the case of speech, the vibrations transmitted through the air by the speaker's vocalizations) arise simultaneously within epochs and then pass away. There is clearly some very short duration involved within an epoch, but it would be impossible to measure its duration using phenomenological methods alone. Perceptual epochs are thus not really snapshot-like. They are neither static nor instantaneous. They are themselves what Husserl called "temporal objects;" they are objects of experience that have a durational expanse, however minute. The hyle that arise and pass away in epochal pulsations "take time" to present. But any and all hyle or patterns arising within any one epoch *are experienced as simultaneous* (see Pastor et al. 2004).

Reducing "time" is one of the most challenging, interesting, and rewarding exercises available to the serious phenomenologist. Try this: Go back to a source of continuous speech (radio, audiobook, lecture, whatever), and focus upon the flow of sound until you have reduced the flow to the given and the meaning of speech has been lost to your awareness. Once you can do that effectively, then subtly shift your concentration to the point ("now-point") of actual sound, rather than the flow of sound. Another way to say this is focus upon the arising and passing of sound. Notice that the previous awareness of rising and falling frequencies of sound were actually a retention of what just happened,

---

[41] Some theorists, after William James (James 1890), have called the experience of an epoch the "spacious present," a needlessly controversial topic (see Benovsky 2013, Pockett 2003).

what is happening "now" and what you anticipate happening next. You should be able to experience how the sound that is the real now changes, but all meaning, remembering and anticipation has fallen away. If you are able to do this with sound (speech, then perhaps music), you may want to expand this focus to all sensations. You will come to realize that the entire perceptual field is arising and passing simultaneously. Furthermore, you will see that any sense of duration of any object is an imposition on the part of intentional and cognitive acts, and thus part of your natural attitude.

2. Sensory and sensible time-consciousness

As we have seen, each act of normal, everyday perception is comprised of apperceptive and sensory functions. Sensory data remain meaningless unless and until apperceptive information (what some psychologists call "schemas;" see Arbib and Hesse 1986: 50-54) retained in iconic memory from recently past now-points is imposed upon the sensory field. The very roots of our experience of the world are the arising and passing of sensory perception, and we normally take this process entirely for granted. But when we allow our mental faculties to slow down and our awareness to become more focused and acute, it is quite common to experience a slight lag between the presentation of novel sensory stimuli and the imposition of meaning or "recognition." The new sensation presents, and an instant later there is recognition. The experience is quite distinct and striking. When apperception drops away, as in the case of intense contemplation of the now-point—the now-point is "reduced"—there is no longer either recognition or anticipation, there is just what is arising and passing in the meaningless sensuous epoch. But it is equally obvious to the contemplative that when meaning returns, and apperceptive time-consciousness again predominates, that the rememoration of the past epoch is reiterated in the present, not merely existing in the past or projected into the future (see Dainton 2006: 133; Miller 1984: 109). Thus, anticipated apperception is "fulfilled" by hyle in an integrated perception in each epoch. This integration of apperception and hyle occurs so rapidly that to mundane consciousness the two processes appear to be seamlessly whole—which is why most people cannot distinguish between hyle and recognition of the sensory object;

between sensation and meaning, or, as we will now call them, *sensory* time-consciousness and *sensible* time-consciousness.

3. Inner and outer sensation

Sensations fulfill objects of consciousness whether those objects be stimulated through the senses by the environing world or by internal interoception, fantasy and dream. Hyletic data that fulfill dream and fantasy images operate in the same way, mediated by the same cortical processes; that is, they present to consciousness in epochs as well (see Llinas and Pare 1991, Joliot, Ribary, and Llinas 1994, Llinas and Ribary 1993). Moreover, novel imagery presents first as pure sensation and an instant later become recognized, so the same temporal lag may be discerned, a lag which may require a number of epochs to complete. This fact is confirmable by phenomenologists who are also "lucid dreamers," that is, meditators who have brought their skill of intense awareness into their dream life (Laughlin 2011).

4. Time-consciousness is grounded in perceptual epochs

As Husserl himself emphasized, the flow of sensation *is time-consciousness*—or more properly, the fundamental experiential ground for all temporal experience and judgments, as well as for our sense of time (i.e., duration, planning, recurrence, continuity, cycles, episodes, and so forth). The unfolding stream of perceptual epochs is the target and the ground of all our intentional, interpretive and rememorative acts (Husserl 1964a). Epochs pulse through consciousness, rememorative operations are layered upon and are integrated with them. They are refreshed and retained through sequences of epochs, and anticipations projected from them in search of fulfillment in subsequent epochs— and voilà, *sensible* time-consciousness. All the complex adaptational operations of the human mind are oriented upon the experienced world, the ground of which is the essentially temporal unfolding of these perceptual epochs.

5. Time, sensation, and reality

Husserl is very clear about how cognitive and intentional acts remain grounded in reality. It is because such acts are oriented toward the sensorium (i.e., the whole sensory field), and it is the sensorium that conditions and limits intentional acts. It is sensation that imposes limits to the range of both interpretation and intention. And it is by way of sensation that we know ourselves as embodied beings.

Let us press this matter further. As we have discussed elsewhere (Laughlin and Throop 2003; see also Lonergan 1958), there are two qualities of the sensory world by which our intentionality is conditioned by extramental reality: obduracy and affordancy. *Obduracy* is given a very moralistic definition in the dictionary, but in philosophy the term generally means the characteristic of reality to resist an individual animal's will. If we try to walk through a wall without the benefit of a door, we will come up against the obdurate nature of the material world. While we may imagine or dream that we are flying without mechanical aids, attempts to do so in the objective world may prove disastrous. Much of early child development has to do with exploring the somatosensory limits of obduracy—the obduracy of the baby's environment and of his/her own body (Piaget 1980). The obduracy of sensation, for Husserl, conditions retention in perception and all of the higher intentional acts grounded in perception (Føllesdal 1990).

The other quality of extramental reality by which the sensorium conditions experience is affordancy. *Affordancy* is a term coined by the perceptual psychologist James J. Gibson (1977, 1979, 1982), to label the active interaction between experience and extramental reality. "Roughly, the affordances of things are what they furnish, for good or ill, that is, what they afford the observer" (Gibson 1982: 401). Again, "... the affordances of the environment are what it offers the animal, what it provides or furnishes, either for good or ill" (Gibson 1979: 127). It is by cognitive operations upon sensory data about the world that affordances are recognized and exploited— an object is recognized as "eat-able," "sit-on-able," "lay-on-able," or "swim-in-able." It is affordance that leads us to recognize hindrances and pathways. Perhaps under circumstances of immanent threat, that piece of "firewood" becomes a "club." The development of knowledge about the world is a process of interaction in which things in reality afford the experiencing subject particular qualities relative to the subject's ability to experience and model his or her environment. At the root of any affordancy recognition is an "affording" pattern of sensation presented in the flow of consciousness. This is why Husserl emphasized the role of the eidetic noemata in experience.

Evolutionarily speaking, the relationship between obduracy and affordancy is instructive. Humans more than other animals have specialized in manipulating the obdurateness of the physical world so as to create affording opportunities. We call this *technology*. We are so clever at this process that the environing world around most of us is artificial. In other words, we are the quintessential *stigmergic* animal on the planet because we have to adapt to the world altered by ourselves and others. Coined by the French biologist Pierre-Paul Grassé in the 1950s to label adaptation among termites, the term "stigmergy" refers to animals whose behavior is altered by the effects of earlier behaviors (Beckers, Holland and Deneubourg 1994). With we humans, this means that our brains are capable of feeding forward into the future via plans and behaviors that produce changes in the environing world that inform our later experiences and behaviors, and that may change our patterns of adaptation.

6. Time and the body

Experience of our body derives from data both from interoceptive sensations (sensations from internal body processes, movements, chemical activities, proprioception, etc.) and from exteroceptive sensations (sensations from the external senses: the eyes, ears, haptic sense, and so forth). Sometimes both kinds of data are integrated across epochs, as when we watch a hypodermic needle enter our skin from the outside, and simultaneously feel the "pinch" from the inside. Behavior is fundamentally important in mediating any perceptual act (see Arbib 1972, 1985, Arbib and Hesse 1986, Powers 2005, Richards and von Glasersfeld 1979, Varela 1999 on the role of behavior in the control of perception). What we experience as sensation and sensibility is conditioned by posture, sensory orientation, scanning activity, motor activity, and metabolic processes, as well as proprioceptive and exteroceptive feedback about the efficacy of movement in mediating an anticipated sensory field. Notice if you will how you unconsciously hold this page in just the right position relative to your eyes so that you can focus most easily upon the words you are reading. This demonstrates that we do not know the body merely because of conceptualization at some higher cognitive level; rather, the body is immanent in all acts of perception (Chapter 2; also see Varella, Thompson, and Rosch 1991). We confront and anticipate the extramental world by moving our body, orienting ourselves relative to the object of interest and maintaining that orientation for some duration. We encounter the obduracy and affordancy of the environing world not only by way of sensory sampling and resulting sensory data (i.e., via afference; see below), but also by acting in the world (i.e., via efference). Our body is intermediate between our consciousness and our environing world, and our body is both an experienced and experiencing reality. It is part of both our experienced world and the extramental reality of things. Our body is the prime mediator between perception and the world.

7. Time-consciousness and feedforward awareness

Ordinary consciousness of the "specious present" (James 1890) is essentially a feedforward process (see Neisser 1976, Miller, Galanter, and Pribram 1960, Arbib 1972, Uexkull 1909, Laughlin, McManus and d'Aquili 1990: 107, Soltani and Koechlin 2022). At the root of the adaptation process is the fine structure of the sensory epoch as manifested in sensible time-consciousness. Mundane, natural attitude perception operates to construct, retain, and stabilize a familiar world of experience. As perceptual epochs arise and pass away, the apperceptive/cognitive processes as it were "leap ahead" of the current epoch and seek to fulfill the object with an appropriate hyletic field. The object of our consciousness (say, the words on this page) are simultaneously held in working memory, concretized in the ongoing sensory now, and anticipated by saccadic movements along the line of type. As we saw in Chapter 3, our mundane awareness is upon the meaning, not the sensory material that instantiates the meaning—upon the sense, not the actual sensory data constituting the hyle initiated at our retinae. And our eyes track forward along the line of type so as to complete the anticipated sentence, paragraph, and text. By its very nature, then, perception is a temporal process of binding epochs into an apparently continuous and stable flow of things, relations, intuitions and horizons that renders our experience of the world sensible. Our sense of time—our sense of duration—is thus rooted in this fundamental structure of perception. Perceptual operations are integrated (Pöppel 1988:

90) across perceptual epochs so as to produce the memorable sense of spacetime that is the empirical grounding for higher cognitive operations. We do not think about time and impose it upon a-temporal perception. Rather, we experience in an inherently temporal way, and that experience is unconsciously projected upon higher order cognitions, and upon our understanding of the world—in a very real and subjective way, *experience is time* (see Le Poidevin 2007). We also abstract a-temporal structures from the duration of perception required to constitute them in perception, e.g., melodies, symphonies, stories and myths, plots, rituals, missions, etc.

NEUROPHENOMENOLOGY OF PERCEPTUAL EPOCHS

As we have seen, the temporal organization of experience is a complex matter, and thus far is only partially understood by neuroscience. We do need to keep in mind that time-consciousness evolved, and all animals with brains process time in simpler, but similar ways (Choe, Kwon and Chung 2012). Research upon temporal processing in the human brain has come a long way over the past several decades, and it is fair to say we know a lot more about the NCC of time-consciousness than we did a few generations ago (see e.g., Edelman and Tononi 2000, Fuster 2003, Libet 2004).

First, we are interested in discovering what is known about the NCC of perceptual epochs. There is a lot of evidence now available, although our understanding remains partial at best. There are a number of competing models in the literature on how the brain constitutes perception. For this reason, we will strictly limit the term "epoch" to the phenomenological unit discussed above and not apply it to the possible NCC mediating that unit. So far there is no way to be certain whether there is a precise correlation between perceptual epochs and mechanisms of temporal processing in the brain. But it seems very likely that the known, rhythmic intermittency of sensory processing is a candidate for explaining how perceptual epochs are experienced in the reduction. When neuroscientists refer to how the brain processes perception in discrete temporal iterations, they often speak of perceptual "frames" (Varela *et al.* 1981), perceptual "moments" (Stroud 1967: 624,

Smith, Gosselin and Schyns 2006, Koch 2004: 264–268, 2005), or "integration periods" (Koch 2004: 256).

There is almost universal recognition on the part of neuropsychologists that any act of perception takes time to unfold; in other words, there is a temporal latency to perception (Neisser 1976, Koch 2004: 250–6, Libet 2004, Scharlau 2002, Seth 2021: 138-145), however short the duration might be. The NCC mediating perception appear to operate in a "pulsing" rhythm (Damasio 1999a, 1999b) within which qualia and other features both are mediated by multiple, parallel processes that require different latencies, and are bound together at the cortical level to produce a unified perceptual gestalt in the sensorium (Lehar 2003, 2004, Fuster 2003: 89, Grossberg and Grunewald 1997). Some neuroscience descriptions of temporal processing in the brain appear to be actually congruent with Husserl's phenomenology of time-consciousness (Varela 1999, Vogeley and Kupke 2007, Fuster 2003, see also Laughlin 1992a).

Several decades ago, it was thought that epochs were driven by a central neural "clock" or pacemaker, and that this rhythm was the same for virtually all processes in the brain (see Sanford 1971, Harter 1967, Steriade and Deschenes 1985, Efron 1970, Childers and Perry 1971 for relevant reviews from this period). This central timing mechanism functions to coordinate various processes in time, and lays the foundation in experience for temporal judgements, and sequencing and pacing behavior. These studies led to *scalar expectancy theory* (SET) of temporal processing which holds that there exists somewhere in the brain a central pacemaker that makes it possible for animals, including humans, to estimate time, make temporal judgements, and evaluate the efficacy of behavior in the world (see Gibbon, Church, and Meck 1984; see Pareti and Palma 2004 for a review). There are still adherents to SET and there is very good evidence in favor of something on the order of a central pacemaker function in the brain, perhaps involving the basal ganglia and the cerebellum (see Gibbon, Malapani, Dale, and Gallistel 1997, Ivry and Keele 1989).

However, more recent findings have caused revision in, or criticism of SET (see Lejeune and Wearden 2006, Wearden 2003, Church 1999), and have led other researchers to the opinion that no single "clock" exists in the brain, but rather a context-specific, distributed network of temporal functions involving such areas as the prefrontal cortex, the cerebellum, certain inferior parietal networks, the basal ganglia, etc. (Straddon and Higa 1999, Burr and Morrone 2006, Jantzen, Steinberg and Kelso 2005, Livesey, Wall, and Smith 2007, Buhusi and Meck 2005, Lewis and Miall 2003, 2006, Lewis and Walsh 2005, Harrington *et al.* 1998, 2004, Rao, Mayer, and Harrington 2001). It seems increasingly clear that the mammalian brain processes time in multiple ways, and that the operations of a unitary timing mechanism in the brain, if there is one, may operate more complexly in interactions with different areas of the brain (Merchant, Harrington and Meck 2013).

Not only are there the perceptual epochs, and patterns of rememoration and behavior spanning those arising and passing sensory experiences, there are other ways the body and its brain relate to time. For instance, the day-night cycle here on planet Earth is matched by intrinsic circadian rhythms in the body (Czeisler *et al.* 1999) which are probably driven by a pacemaker function in the suprachiasmatic nucleus of the hypothalamus. This system controls our internal metabolic states, as well as our sleep-wake cycle. As we have seen above, timing processes operating over very short, sub-second durations are fundamental for sequencing various behaviors, including speech, motor coordination, and recognition, while timing durations over seconds and minutes are crucial for making judgements and following behavioral goals (Arbib 1985, Arbib and Hesse 1986). All these different temporal processing systems most likely derive from different organizations in the brain (Hinton and Meck 1997).

How does this confusion about different types and models of timing inform us about the NCC underlying perceptual epochs? The jury is still out on the existence of a single pacemaker in the brain that, among other things, would mediate the rhythm of perceptual epochs, although such a pacemaker is fairly certain for lengthier circadian rhythms. Moreover, there is evidence that there may be a multimodal epoch timer operating in sensory perception (Levitan *et al.* 2015). However, there is near universal agreement that perceptual epochs, whether in perception or in dream and fantasy imagery, seem to oscillate in sub-second intervals in roughly the gamma range—that is, around 40 hertz (40 Hz), or roughly 40 iterations per second (Gho and Varela 1988/89, Allport 1968, Latour 1967, Varela *et al.* 2001, Varela 1999, Joliot, Ribary and Llinas 1994, Singer 1999, Gray and Singer 1989,

Engle *et al.* 1999, Engle and Singer 2001, Neuenschwander *et al.* 2002, Nase *et al.* 2003). These oscillations are the same for perception and for dreaming (Llinas and Pare 1991, Joliot, Ribary and Llinas 1994, Llinas and Ribary 1993). Also, there is evidence that the same neural structures mediate attention to inner and outer stimuli (Singer 2001). In addition, neural oscillations are crucial in explaining the retention and rapid decay of working and iconic memory that is integral to the perceptual epoch, presumably regardless of whether the object of attention arises within the mind's eye or through exteroception (Basar *et al.* 2000, Howard *et al.* 2003, Raghavachari *et al.* 2001). So, whether or not there exists a single "clock" function in the brain, it seems very likely that the inherent organization of the perceptual system provides the NCC mediating the perceptual epoch. As far as we know, there is no way to bring introspection to bear in deciding among competing theories of temporal processing in the brain. What introspection does tell us is that there must be some such mechanism whether it be central or distributed to account for the experiential reports of mature contemplatives. In short, the final correlation of epochs and frames is an empirical task yet to be completed.

TEMPORAL PROCESSING ACROSS PERCEPTUAL EPOCHS

There is much more to the experience of time, of course, than the perceptual epoch. Concentrating upon the perceptual epoch is limiting ourselves to sub-second phenomena. The epoch does provide the most molecular sensory and sensible ground for all more molar temporal processes within which the epoch is nested. The common notion of *living through* is precisely the experience of an endless reiteration or flow of epochs. This is the case for all human beings, regardless of ethnicity, as well as for human babies (Brannon *et al.* 2004, Droit-Volet 2002, Van Manen 2018) and non-human mammals (Gibbon, Church and Meck 1984). We have seen that no temporal discrimination is possible within a single epoch. Sensations arising in a single epoch are perceived to be simultaneous. Thus, all temporal discriminations operate across epochs, be they the simple superimposition of iconic memories and other rememorations across a short, sub-second duration of epochs

(Husserl's retention), or more complex, multi-second-plus processes like the sequencing and coordination of behavior and experience in bringing about a desired event in perception (e.g., lifting the cup to the mouth and sipping to experience the taste of coffee). This is the central essence of "living through."

It is accurate to say that the more molar the temporal operation, the more complex, distributed, and cognitive will be the NCC underlying temporal experience—and the more likely to be the focus of awareness. There are many situations in which, due to the obduracy and affordancy of the environing world, we must experience, make judgments and act within an allotted duration (e.g., taking a timed test, catching a bus, drinking the milk before it spoils). Obviously, lengthy durations of experience and activity involve widespread areas of the brain in addition to those mediating perceptual epochs. Depending upon the type of temporal integration, areas as diverse as the prefrontal cortex, the basal ganglia (a system of nuclei buried deeper in the forebrain), the inferior parietal lobule (a region of cortex on the side of the head above our ears), and the cerebellum (located low in the back of the head) may be involved (Pastor *et al.* 2004). The role of prefrontal cortical processes in selecting, exciting, and ordering sensory activity into a temporally meaningful organization or "plan" is of primary importance in understanding the relations between inherent temporal processing and the influence of culture (Laughlin 1988a, 1992a; see also Miller, Galanter, and Pribram 1960, Pribram 1971, TenHouten 2005: 109). Elsewhere I have suggested that our sensory experience is constituted by a dialogue between order imposed by the prefrontal cortex ("intentional meaning" or "intentionality") and the sensory order imposed in secondary association cortex, which is fed by both the stream of afferent data from the senses and rememoration (together producing "perceptual meaning;" see Laughlin 1988a, Laughlin, McManus, and d'Aquili 1990; see also TenHouten 2005: 111–12). It is this on-going dialogue between the prefrontal cortex and secondary sensory cortex that probably produces what Damasio (1999b: 160) calls the "single Cartesian theater" of conscious experience.

In any event, it is important to understand that the imposition of meaning (via rememoration) upon perceptual epochs is a higher-order cognitive act, one that occurs in the cortex, and one that may be significantly influenced by the way that time is encoded grammatically and narratively in particular languages. For example, visual rememoration arises neither in the retinae of the eyes, nor in the geniculate body on the way to the cortex, but within the cortex itself (Koch 2004: 273–81, Fuster 2003). Again, the recognition of novel stimuli takes time, and cannot occur within the same epoch within which the stimuli are initiated—hence the lag (or "latency;" see Grossberg and Grunewald 1997) between presentation and recognition (literally an act of "*re*-cognition").

Part of the dialogue between the executive regions of the prefrontal cortex and the sensorium seems to involve septal-hippocampal centers in the midbrain. Orbitofrontal nerve tracts from the prefrontal cortex richly reciprocally connect with the hippocampus, and dorsolateral prefrontal tracts reciprocally connect with the lateral septal area. These areas are also connected to secondary sensory cortical areas and seem to receive sensory information that is already abstracted from the initial processing in primary sensory cortex. That is, in the phenomenological sense, the sensory information arriving at septal-hippocampal sites appear to be highly sensible. This accounts for why natural perception is primarily focused on meaning, rather than on the sensations instantiating and fulfilling the meaning—this being, as we shall see, a crucial element in adaptation to the affordancy and obduracy of extramental reality.

It was once thought that the hippocampus was a memory storage center. It is now suspected that the septal-hippocampal system does not actually store memories, but rather is an area that anticipates what will be found in the next perceptual epochs and attempts to match what does arise to an order predicated upon memories arising elsewhere in the brain. The septal-hippocampal system is, in Husserlian terms, an area (perhaps *the* area) of the brain specialized to blend "retention," "now-points," and "protention" into an apparently smooth and integrated stream of meaningful experience. EEG recordings from sites in both prefrontal cortex and hippocampus indicate significant slow wave negative activity correlated with attention to sensory events. Prefrontal theta waves seem to be associated with concentration upon sensory objects, and slow wave, low amplitude prefrontal waves (so-called "contingent negative variation") with anticipation of delayed motor response to sensory events—as when one sees an opportunity in the near future to do something and must wait a while to do it (see Fuster 2003: 169, 2013, 2015, Fuster and Bressler 2012, 2015, Stuss and Benson 1986: 70). Hippocampal theta seems to be an artifact of a general pacemaker function. The relations among these various slow wave forms on the one hand and perceptual epochs on the other hand is not known, but they almost certainly involve the temporal organization of cognitive and perceptual functions grounded upon the flow of perceptual epochs.

It not only takes time to perceive something, it also takes time to do something. Sequences of motor activity can be as simple as a reflex or as complex as playing a Chopin étude or running a marathon. Complex sequences of behavior take time and involve the kind of feedforward perceptual processing we have seen above, as well as sequential ordering of motor activities (Harrington *et al.* 1999, Rosen 1985, Soltani and Koechlin 2022). When we wish to accomplish a goal, what we are actually doing is behaving now such that we achieve a certain perceptual outcome in the future, and we organize our behavior to both control our body and sensory orientation toward the world, and launch action designed to accomplish the goal. This temporal integration of behavior is mediated by cognits in the premotor cortex (on the side of the head above and forward of our ears), as well as inferior parietal cortex and the cerebellum (Harrington *et al.* 1999). In Joaquín Fuster's (2003: 77) sense, this constitutes a more abstract level of coordination than is the case with a simple stimulus-response event: "Note that we have entered a higher level of abstraction, executive abstraction in the time domain. The representations are no longer defined solely by spatial coordinates but also by the temporal coordinate" (Fuster 2003: 77).

Complex sequences of behavior must be learned, and the area of the brain responsible for supervising premotor sequencing is the prefrontal cortex. The prefrontal cortex is the home of the brain's so-called "executive functions" (Dehaene 2018, Dehaene and Changeux 2011, Kolk and Rakic 2022, Koch 2004: 129–30, 2019, Fuster 2003, 2015, Stuss and Benson 1986; Changeux 2002). This area is, among many other things, interested in and oversees the development of motor networks that mediate the temporal sequencing of behavior (i.e., move this, then move that, then move this; see Soltani and Koechlin

2022). When one learns to tie one's shoelace or necktie, prefrontal areas supervise the sequence of motor skills necessary to accomplish the task. But once learned the premotor networks become autonomous and the prefrontal cortex loses interest in, and awareness of, the constituent elements of the process.

Of primary importance to our understanding of time-consciousness is the ability of the prefrontal cortex to enact plans—a plan being defined as "any hierarchical process in the organism that can control the order in which a sequence of operations is to be performed" (Miller, Galanter, and Prebram 1960: 16; see also Pribram 1971). The prefrontal cortex is the planning center of our brain par excellence (Fuster 2014, 2017, Fuster and Bressler 2015). Our prefrontal lobes are responsible for lengthy time-binding operations that may take many minutes, hours, and even days and years to unfold. Our nearest primate relatives, the chimpanzees, have evolved fairly advanced prefrontal cortical areas and are able to mount elaborate and lengthy plans (Zoh, Chang and Crockett 2022), such as complex social hunting strategies (Stanford 1999), which lower primates like the baboon are incapable of organizing. Our human prefrontal cortex is far more evolutionarily advanced even than that of the chimp's (Kolk and Rakic 2022). Indeed, the increased size of our prefrontal area is the single most dramatic evolutionary advance in hominid physiology (Fuster 2014, Jerison 1973, 1985).

Our vastly increased capacity to design plans, integrate behavior and experience in lengthy temporal sequences, and communicate these plans to others, is what allows us to think in historical terms and set goals in the distant future. It is important, however, to keep in mind that the process of *time-binding* (Korzybski 1921)—of organizing plans that require lengthy durations to complete—is a hierarchical process in which lower-level, more molecular processes like those mediating the perceptual epoch and individual behaviors become integrated into, and nested within higher-level, more molar operational strategies (Fuster 2003, 2014, Fuster and Bressler 2015). The failure of social scientists to understand the nested nature of the structure of time-consciousness has led many of them to the erroneous conclusion that time is solely a cultural construct—but more on this issue below. The point to remember is that temporal consciousness is not only cultural but also a thoroughly physical, embodied process with millions of years of natural selection behind it. Although one's upbringing influences the way we think about, symbolize, and experience time, all time-consciousness is also grounded in the neurophysiology of temporal processing. What we are terming sensory and sensible time-consciousness is thus universal, not only to our species but with respect to more molecular processes like the epoch, to all large-brained primates and other mammals (see Richelle *et al.* 2015, Choe, Kwon and Chung 2012).

CONTINUITY, CYCLICITY, AND CAUSATION

As for other animals, time-binding is immanent in our understanding of the world. As we have seen, the hierarchy of perceptual-cognitive processes that result in our sense of time range in duration from rememorative acts across perceptual epochs (time within the sub-second to a few seconds' duration) to full-blown plans and historical memories (time durations lasting from minutes or hours to years and generations). The mammalian neurocognitive system is designed to time-bind and abstract from the stream of perceptual epochs information pertaining to the following three fundamental pattern cognits.

1. Continuity of objects and processes

Awareness and behavior combine to maintain the continuity of an object over epochs. Rememoration is projected onto the stream of momentary sensations, and the sensory field is stabilized over epochs to fulfill the anticipated iterations of the object. This produces a coherent perception for the duration of sensory awareness. In this way we may gaze at an object or event in the world for as long as we wish, or until the object or process is gone from view or drops out of notice.

2. Cyclicity of process

Our mammalian nervous system is especially designed to detect recurrent patterns from the dynamic flow of sensations, and it is these patterns that we tend to become aware of and act upon. Recognition, of course, is based upon the recurrence of patterns discernible in the stream of epochs. We recognize a Boston Terrier or an ocean wave because we have encountered it before. (Incidentally, it is interesting that "time" and "tide" are related words in Old English.) In the same way we recognize cyclically occurring events—eating follows hunger, night follows day, the race cars lap the field, the anthem is sung before the first pitch, and so forth. Recognition of cycles allows us to anticipate and prepare for events before they arise in the sensory field. These cycles may be as short as the beginning of the next sentence, and as long as the number of shopping days until Christmas—or longer.

3. Causation

Our mammalian brain is also designed to cognize causal sequences and causality within events. We know causation through the recognition of the interweaving of movements among objects within a single process—the arm pushes the cue, the cue strikes the cue ball, the cue ball hits the seven ball and the seven ball (with any luck) rolls into the pocket (see Michotte 1963, Rolfs, Dambacher and Cavanagh 2013). We can become aware of both objects (arm, cue, balls, pocket) and their interrelated movements within a single process ("making a shot").

All mammalian brains operate to structure experience in each of these three ways. An animal may be aware of all three, or any combination of them at any given time. What differs among mammalian species are, among other things, the complexity and length of durations bound into temporal-cognitive units by species-specific cognits. Humans, of course, excel at modelling the world using these three pattern cognits (Goody 1968). These operators remain for humans as potently adaptive as they do for all other mammals, for they tend on the whole to model the environing world in a veridical way. More than any other mammal, the importance of learning, utilizing these primordial essential structures of time-consciousness, becomes paramount, and each society teaches its own variations in interpreting time and change, and organizes its social relations in accordance with temporal interpretations.

It is our contention that higher order temporal categories, plans, and interpretations are extensions of these fundamental pattern cognits—i.e., are reproductions of these structures up through the nested networks that bind experience into temporal units, and these units are projected out upon the world in the natural attitude as "real." Chronology (that is, the temporal, causal, or a-causal ordering of events) is grounded experientially in both the continuity and cyclicity cognits. Indeed, the early Old English meaning of "time" implied the measurement of segments of duration. All known chronological systems involve both historical sequences pegged both to landmark events, and to lunar, solar, or astronomical cycles. Often a chronology (or "history") implies the causal cognit as well, as when one event is preceded or succeeded by another event with which it is causally linked—i.e., event A (say, a revolution) is considered by people to have been a sufficient and perhaps even necessary condition for event B (formation of a new government). In traditional societies such chronologies often begin in mythological time in which stories account for the origins of causal chains of events leading to the present and beyond.

CULTURE AND TIME-CONSCIOUSNESS

Culture is the word we sometimes use for the *pool of information* we all draw upon as members of our social group (Goodenough 1971, Wallace 1970). We are all conditioned (or "enculturated") during childhood by our parents and others of our group, and this conditioning influences the ways we perceive, cognize, imagine, interpret, emote, communicate, and behave. This conditioning also influences the formation of material objects, which we call "cultural artifacts," or what the philosopher Wilhelm Dilthey called "objectified mind" (see Throop 2002, 2009). These artifacts are the product of culturally informed inter-subjective acts upon the material world (buildings, tools and utensils, iconic art, clothing, containers, written texts, and so forth), and as such these artifacts, to some extent at least, provide archaeologists with access to the ways of life of long dead peoples.

Of course, the other members of our social group are each and severally part of our environing world and provide the social aspect of obduracy and affordancy to which each of us must learn to adapt, especially during our formative years. Because of this interpersonal adaptation, we grow up somewhat similar to other group members and different from outsiders. This very flexibility to create different ways of knowing and acting in the world is our greatest adaptational asset (Fuster 2014, 2017). One group of people may learn all about planting maize and anticipating the seasons, while another group learns about working in factories and offices and keeping to clock-and-calendar schedules (Postill 2002). One group learns to hunt and anticipate the movement of animals, another learns to fish and predict where the fish are likely to be at any given time. We may learn at our parent's knee stories which are rife with information about our heritage and how our ancestors learned to wrest a living from the land or from industry, and to react effectively to hailstorms, tsunamis, economic depressions, and other untoward changes (Laughlin and Brady 1978). Virtually all learning involves time-binding at the higher cognitive levels. Indeed, it is nearly impossible to imagine learning anything that does not involve time in some way—time to apprehend, identify, and interpret, and time to take appropriate actions and to build artifacts.

INTEGRATING THE UNIVERSAL AND THE CULTURAL

Yet, despite the importance of cultural differences among societies, we humans are as much alike as we are different. We all speak a language, walk on our hind legs, eat cooked foods, procreate, form some kind of family unit, make music and art, carry out rituals, play games, create and pass on stories about how things came to be. We also base our understanding and behavior upon the same "wired-in," nested temporal processing and pattern cognits. We all experience linear and cyclical processes. We all recognize causal relations among objects and events. At the level of cognition, language, and imagery, however, there are often significant variations in time-consciousness. And for very good reasons. The documentation of such variations has been the prime focus of anthropologists in their studies of social groups (see Bender and Wellbery 1991, Gell 1992, Goody 1968, Hodges 2008, Hughes and Trautmann 1995, James and Mills 2020, and Munn 1992 for relevant reviews of the anthropology of time). As Peter Rigby (1995) notes, most of the material analyzed by anthropologists relative to time are language categories, which are of course the most culturally variant aspects of time-reckoning (e.g., Whorf 1956). Yet, even within these apparent variations we can find universal elements that are present in perceptual and cognitive operations grounded in the perceptual epoch and informed by pattern cognits (see also TenHouten 2005: 2).

Each society exhibits a more or less complex set of beliefs about duration—beliefs that are really elements of the society's more general model of the world that incorporates what Alfred Gell (1992: 235) called a "time-map." A time-map is a society's most general, most conscious, metaphysical, perhaps even cosmological model of time. Time-maps are never delimited solely by a society's ideology, although an individual's sense of time may be influenced by that ideology. Culture, in fact, is rarely determinate, but rather tends to be informative in the everyday temporal judgements and interpersonal interactions of people (see Bourdieu 1977). Put another way, one's culture never provides more than a portion of the information one incorporates into normal experience. While all peoples experience time via all three pattern cognits, some groups may emphasize one pattern over the others in their cosmological and mythological orientation, just as different grammatical categories will emphasize some patterns over others. Ethnographers have clearly shown how a people's time-map facilitates social relations and economic activity within the context of their particular local geographical conditions.

In past generations, much was made in anthropology about how the time maps of traditional peoples differ from those of modern technocratic societies. Traditional (sometimes erroneously called "primitive") peoples, according to this view, have a fundamentally different mentality than so-called civilized folk, and thus live more in the present, and cognize time as a system of recurrent cycles, while Westerners live with their minds riveted on the future and cognize time in a lineal series of episodes (see e.g., Lévy-Bruhl 1966[1923], Evans-Pritchard 1939). The latter time-map was assumed to be the product of industrialization and facilitated by the invention of clocks. Such dualistic accounts of cultures and their time-maps have more recently come into disrepute as being both over-simplistic and empirically inaccurate (Adam 1990: 16–19, TenHouten 2005: 2–3, Gell 1992: 34). A moment's reflection about our own Western, supposedly linear, time-map will reveal the over-simplification: If we are limited to linear time-cognition, then how is it we live out our lives in a welter of recognized, recurring cycles—day and night, a weekly round of days ("TGIF"), annual seasons, recurring holidays like Christmas, Easter, Veterans' Day, birthdays, vacations, a daily cycle of more or less ritualized meals (breakfast, lunch, high tea, dinner, nighttime snack), annual round of sports seasons, on-and-on? Consider my supermarket clerk who in a single exchange expressed awareness of both clock time (minutes to the end of his shift) and cyclical time (alternation of work and leisure periods). By the same token, as Gell (1992: 34) points out, if traditional peoples are only aware of cycles of recurring events, how is it possible that they can distinguish last year's event from other different events of the same kind in previous years—an ability they obviously have, or they could have no sense of history.

Culture thus influences the way we orient ourselves to duration—usually lengthy durations over hours to years (although when we think of the moment-by-moment coordination of talk and interaction as inflected by cultural and linguistically encoded temporalities, the effects of culture may be understood to occur on a significantly more molecular level). As with other aspects of experience, we become conditioned to integrate our everyday experiences within a worldview that emphasizes a particular standpoint pertaining to group values, beliefs, social strategies, relationships, and history. We all experience sensory time-consciousness in the same way, but just which objects and events receive our awareness will vary from person to person and from group to group. And how we integrate our sense of continuity, causation, and cyclicity will be informed from our personal history and our society's pool of information. The most dramatic and forceful of influences will be our group's cosmology, including its stock of lore and mythic stories, its cycle of ritual enactments and the teachings of its purveyors (shamans, healers, parents, instructors, teachers, leaders, and so forth). But also, we find that contingencies in the environing world can produce distortions in our experience of time, regardless of our cultural knowledge of time (Knight 2021). Talk of cosmology, lore, and myth most certainly brings us to the problem of narrative and time. It will be productive to turn to such matters, however, only after first attending to the place of temporality in the actual, everyday articulation of subjectivity.

SCHUTZ'S PHENOMENOLOGY OF SOCIAL ACTION AND THE ARTICULATION OF EXPERIENCE

Drawing directly from the work of Henri Bergson (1910[1889]) and Edmund Husserl (1982[1913], 1993[1931]) in the context of a critique of Max Weber's (1978) theory of meaning and social action, Alfred Schutz (1967[1932]) provides us with a means to extend our insights still further to an understanding of temporality within the context of social action. Keep in mind that we are inherently social beings, and this evolution affords us with adaptational strategies involving socially coordinated action. A central insight of Schutz's is his recognition that there is an ever-present tension between "living experience within the flow of duration and reflection on the experience thus lived through" (Schutz 1967[1932]: 70, see also Throop 2003b, Throop and Murphy 2002). Accordingly, he suggests that "the meaning of an action is different depending on the point in time from which it is observed" (1967: 65). This is a crucial point that is often overlooked by social theorists. As C. Jason Throop (2003b) has argued, it is important for social theorists who are engaged in analyzing any given stretch of social action to distinguish between the retrospective "ends" that partially structure the field of recollected past lived experience and the projected "ends" that arise in the immediacy of the present moment of duration. In this respect, it is possible to discern at least four different temporal orientations to which a subject's modes of attention may be directed in the flux of social action. Each of these orientations may differentially structure the experience of self and world. These include:

1. Orientation toward the present. An orientation to the present epoch that consists of unfulfilled protentions as open anticipations toward an indeterminate future.

2. Orientation toward the future. An explicit future orientation that consists of imagined anticipations of a determinate future that are predicated upon residues of past experience that emerge, as Mattingly points out, "even in the midst of action" (1998: 155).

3. Orientation toward retrospection. A retrospective glance that entails the plotting of beginnings, middles, and ends over the already elapsed span of a delimited field of experience.

4. Orientation toward possibilities. The subjunctive casting of possible futures, and even possible pasts, across the "fluid space between a past and a future" (Mattingly 1998: 96; see also Bruner 1986, 1990, Good 1994, Ricoeur 1980, 1984).

Again, social actors may shift their orientations between these differing temporalities within the context of any given stretch of social action. Such shifts in temporal orientation may significantly impact their subjectivity and their interpretation of their own and others' unfolding actions.

Modification in attention to such different temporal orientations serves to change subjectivity in potentially distinctive ways (Leder 1990; see also Berger 1997, 1999, Csordas 1993, 1994c, Throop 2003). Of particular significance for social theorists is, as Michael Jackson notes in his own discussion of William James and Edmund Husserl, the fact that there are "significant differences between the way the world appears to our consciousness when we are fully engaged in activity and the way it appears to us when we subject it to reflection and retrospective analysis" (1996: 42). With regard to the latter, a central way in which retrospection is temporally configured for us humans is by means of narrative.

NARRATIVE, TEMPORALITY, AND EXPERIENCE

Put very succinctly, narrative is the ordering of two or more events in light of some temporal sequence (Labov 1972). As Garro and Mattingly (2010) explain, through narrative mere sequence is transformed into the structure of a plot that imbues sequence with causality, intention, and purpose. By means of emplotment (see Ricoeur 1984: x), events are unified through a narrative "linking of motive, act, and consequence" (Garro and Mattingly 2000: 10; see also Mattingly 1994, 1998, Garro 1992, 1994). And, of course, temporality is manifest in the very structure of narrative itself—a narrative takes time to be told and is thus an articulation of a conceptual plan as discussed above. Accordingly, narrative plays a role in shaping the ways an individual is inclined to reflect on past experience, give meaning to ongoing interaction, while also setting a course for future action (see Garro and Mattingly 2000, Ochs and Capps 2001, Throop 2009). Temporality, according to Ricoeur, is thus "that structure of existence that reaches language in narrativity, and narrativity ... [is] the language structure that has temporality as its ultimate referent" (1980).

Jerome Bruner has noted that there is a "human readiness for narrative" situated in a biologically rooted "predisposition to organize experience into a narrative form, into plot structures and the rest" (1990: 45). As a mode of cognition, narrative thinking and the complex varieties of temporality that are common in narrative are yet a further means through which the experienced temporalities of continuity, cyclicity, and causation are elaborated in culturally and personally meaningful ways.

SUMMARY AND SEGUE

Internal time-consciousness—the ongoing stream of perceptual epochs—may be understood as mediated by a nested hierarchy of neural networks and cognits with the fine structure of the now-moment being the most molecular level of organization, and the complex, narratively configured structure underlying time-maps being the most molar level of organization. We have seen that all people on the planet experience sensory and sensible time-consciousness in the same way because their nervous systems are structured in the same way. Moreover, all people everywhere recognize continuity, cyclicity, and causation within durations of sensible time-consciousness. Where the role of differences attributable to culture enters most prominently is in the interpretation of events unfolding in lengthy episodes of meaningful time-consciousness. And how we understand those events depends a lot on how our group organizes itself socially and politically, how it makes a living and how it is accustomed to speaking about events. Gone are the days when a more naïve anthropology could claim that the minds of so-called "primitive" peoples are somehow fundamentally different from ours. This dualism is not only out of fashion these days, but it is found to be empirically wrong under the scrutiny of modern neuroscience. This is of prime importance to those researchers trying to understand the way of life of long dead societies, for we can now say with good empirical support that they most likely experienced, organized, and talked about time within a range of variation that is very much comparable to the way that humans do so today.

That said, there remains a lag in neuroscience recognition of the iterations apparent to mature contemplation of the primordial hyletic given. This is probably due to the fact that most neuroscientists working on the NCC are not phenomenologists, not mindfulness meditators. They fail to directly perceive the flickering of the hyle as epoch after epoch arise and pass away in their own sensory experience, just as we are not aware of the 24 frames/second iteration of film frames that produce the smooth sense of motion in a TV program or movie. Despite this, we do have information about the refreshing of the hyle. The refresh rate of photoreceptive cells of the retinae is insufficient to track movements effectively faster than about 16 frames per second (e.g., see Gur and Snodderly 1997, Forster 1970). Indeed, we know a great deal about how the senses and brain cobble together information from numerous physical mechanisms about experienced motion, most of which we are not, and cannot be aware (see Møller 2014, West and Howard 2021). We will now turn out attention to operations of the symbolic brain and explore what Husserl's project has to teach us about symbolic processing.

CHAPTER SEVEN

Signs, Symbols, and Communication

Our investigations up to now have shown us how the perceptive world is built as the particular contents that present themselves to consciousness are filled with increasingly richer and more diverse functions of meaning. The farther this process progresses, the broader becomes the sphere that consciousness can encompass and survey in a single moment. Each of its elements is now saturated as it were with such functions. It stands in manifold meaning-groups which in turn are systematically related to one another and which by virtue of this relationship constitute the totality that we call the world of our experience.

– Ernst Cassirer (1957: 191)

Because symbolic reference makes possible much more efficient and complex communication than is possible in its absence, that function alone could explain its evolution. This means that we must at least consider the possibility that during the Paleolithic there was a time when symbolic reference, both in semantics and syntax, played an important part in hominid adaptation, but when symbolism did not fulfil some of the other functions it plays in our lives today.

– Philip G. Chase (1999: 35)

Terrence Deacon (1997) writes that we humans are a "symbolic species" because we are the only animal with a true language. He further argues that the brain and language developed as a single process. It is clear to me that he is correct, as far as it goes, but whereas Deacon begins with daunting questions about why other animals have not evolved language, I choose to begin, as Husserl has, with the "other end" of the process—the innate capacity of the brains of all animals to symbolically process information in adaptation to their environing world (Bekoff 2002, 2007, De Waal 2006). We now know that symbolism is the process by which partial information adumbrated from sensory experience afferently penetrates into other neural structures mediating meaning, including, where relevant, appropriate action. Beginning thus we will be able to answer Deacon's initial question, why do no other animals have language. The answer in short is: Other social animals don't have language because they didn't need language to coordinate social adaptation strategies. A time came during the course of hominin phylogenesis when our ancestors came to need a more complex form of communication to stave off a crisis in social learning and cooperation that might otherwise have led to social chaos. But I am getting ahead of myself. In this chapter I wish to show how Husserl's take on "symbolic intentions" feeds into an account of the evolution of communication among hominins quite naturally.

THE SYMBOLIC PROCESS

The signs and symbols of semiology are grounded in the way perception works in the brains of animals. All brains are symbolic processing systems (Laughlin, McManus and d'Aquili 1990: 163). The primary activity of any animal's brain with respect to adaptation to its environing world is to render sensory objects redundant by entraining the object to higher structures mediating meaning that is stored in memory. Rendering the object meaningful closes a loop in the brain, thus producing a cognitive package we may call a *neural model* (Shore 1988, Laughlin and Loubser 2010). As we have seen, the primordial sensory given as isolated after performing a pure phenomenological reduction is only associated with intuitive insight, not "meaning" in the higher sense of information generated by cognition and stored in memory. What I am saying is that the brain of any animal operates on a universal symbolic process that begins with the sensory given afferently penetrating inwards into a hierarchical system of cognitive structures mediating information we call "meaning." In the inward penetration, the sensory given operates via abstracted patterns as a "key" that unlocks the meaning held in memory. For most people most of the time, this process of *symbolic penetration* is automatic, rapid, and unconscious—what Jody Azzouni (2015: 61) calls "semantic blindness." This process has been thoroughly explored by Husserl with respect to noetic-noematic aspects of intentionality. This exploration continues when Husserl focuses upon the mental operations involved in signs, signaling and communication.

SYMBOLS AND SIGNS

The study of symbolism goes way back to the ancient Greeks in Western philosophy, and hence there is significant confusion and ambiguity about the meaning of terms. To be clear about the terminology I use here, and commensurate with how Husserl uses these terms, when I speak of "symbol" I simply mean something that signifies something else. A *symbol* may be any object like a pointing finger, a stop sign, a costume, a badge, a flag, etc. that stands for an idea, group, belief, social status, place, institution, occupation, or value. As we shall see in the next chapter, conscious images like a tree, the sun, a snake, a mandala, or an ocean can be symbols associated with conscious meaning, and also with unconscious mental operations. According to Husserl, for an object to be a "symbol," it must be paired with its "meaning" in the mind of the individual recipient, *commonly in the form of imagery*—a crucial factor as we will see below.

As to what Husserl means by "meaning" (Ger.: *Sinn*), one must return to his theory of intentionality. Meaning takes its place in the noema as the correlate of the object or event in sensory experience:

> Meaning can be (phenomenologically) defined as the noematic correlate of experience. Meaning is *what* is experienced and consequently *what* we attempt to express in behavior, in gesture, in language. All experience is *experience of something*. Meaning arises only in the noetic-noematic contact with reality which we call *experience of....* . Words, thus, are not meanings; a word or a series of words may *point to* a meaning, but any number of words—including words yet to be invented—can be used to

clarify and define a meaning by designating its various aspects
and thus delineating its structure. A *meaning* is never exhaustively
expressed in any *one word* or even in any combination of words;
meaning always transcends any given attempt at its verbal expression.
(Edie 1976: 158-159; emphasis added)

To reiterate, *meaning is not words*. Meaning is generated by neurocognitive
processes phylogenetically much older than hominins have had language.
Moreover, solitary species (e.g., koalas, bears, moles, wolverines)
operate upon the same neurophysiological intentionality principles as
do more social animals, including primates and hominins. Meaning
may be inherited biogenetically, may be the product of personal and
social learning, or a combination of these processes. When considering
the inheritance of meaning, consider the genetic loading on phobias
(see Beck and Emery 1985, Kendler, Karkowski and Prescott 1999,
Seligman 1971).

The association between symbol and meaning may not be
conventionally shared, being uniquely symbolic for the individual
person. The association between the symbol and the meaning may
arise quite naturally in the direct experience of a person, as for example
when a gray sky and blustery wind indicates a storm is coming, an aura
around the sun portends the coming of snow, the increasing rumble in
the earth may indicate that a herd of buffalo, cows or horses is galloping
nearby, leaves turning yellow signal fall has begun, or a flash of orange
and black in the trees signals a tiger on the prowl. These are associations
that may quickly be shared among group members.

Other associations are learned from others, as when we give a rose
as a symbol of love, or a white lily for death and bereavement. Every
company has its logo, which is some mark or pictograph associated with
its institution. The golden arches indicate the McDonald's franchise.
A stylized GE signifies the corporation called the General Electric
Company. The animal kingdom is rife with examples of species utilizing
discrete sounds and gestures that transmit conventional meaning to
other members of the group, as for example the inherited alarm signals
of vervet monkeys that are keyed to different categories of predators,
and which young monkeys have to refine through learning (Seyfarth
and Cheney 1990).

A *sign* is a subtype of symbol that indicates something else, as when a mark, drawing, gesture, or sound is associated with some other knowledge (imagery, concepts, feelings). Husserl usually speaks of the "sign" because of its connotation of "conventional" signification (see also Dunbar, Knight and Power 1999: 35). That is, Husserl is primarily interested in the symbolic activity of people communicating—a situation wherein everybody in the group more or less knows the same signification of the sign, and thus the sign may be said to be a "language of its own." A sign stands in experience for the object it intends (Husserl 2019[1923/24]: 119). A sign is, in this sense, both "empty" and "inauthentic."

> A *symbolic* or *inauthentic* representation is, as the name already indicates, a representation by means of signs. If a content is not directly given us as that which it is, but rather only indirectly *through signs which univocally characterize it*, then we have a symbolic representation of it instead of an authentic one. ... We have, for example, an authentic representation of the outer appearance of a house when we actually look at the house; and we have a symbolic representation when someone gives us the indirect characterization: the corner house on such and such side of such and such street. Any description of a perceptual...object has the tendency to replace the actual...representation of it by a surrogate sign-representation. (Husserl 2003[1887-1901]: 205-206)

Words and arithmetic/formal logic signs can in this way operate as surrogates for perceptual objects. This is a mental process that Thomas Sebeok (1991: 12) called *semiosis*—the activity of signing. I point to a creature I see and say, "Look at that bird!" You know what I mean, and you turn your head toward where I am pointing and sure enough you see a Northern Goshawk circling in the sky. Your perception of the Goshawk is authentic. My words to you are not. Nor is any image you may have formed in your mind before actually perceiving the Goshawk. Had you turned your head and found no bird whatever, you still would have understood my reference to a bird, but the sign would remain empty of the intuitive, hyle-filled form that would equate to the sign.

This is surrogate signification at its most primitive level (see Byrne 2017). But signs can also stand as surrogates for concepts and abstract ideas. If I say to you, "It is impossible to square a circle," you may think a moment and nod your head in agreement. A "square" signifies an abstract figure with four equal sides and four equal angles. "Square" is an idea, not a thing. So too with a "circle." I can think about circles and squares and other geometric figures for hours, if I am bored enough, yet never actually perceive a circle. Of anthropological interest (see Chapter 10) is that in many traditional societies people may use a sign in one state of consciousness that indicates an authentic perception in another state of consciousness, as for instance when I refer to "my late Uncle Jim" who spoke with me last night in a dream.

Expressive and signitive acts occur so smoothly and automatically because our brains are wired to associate noetic and noematic elements as a package. Linking thing and meaning is one of the fundamental processes facilitating mental adaptations to the environing world.

> And so perfectly and assuredly do [signs] surrogate for the concepts really intended, that in the majority of cases we do not notice the distinction between the two at all, in spite of the huge gulf separating them. The signs and fragments of experiences stand in place of the genuine concepts, but *that* they do so is unnoticed by us. (Husserl 1994: 31)

I like to think of signs as wee magnets that attract meanings like patterns of iron filings. Move the magnet around and it automatically drags the "meaning" filings along with it. If I present to you the complex sign:

hamburger

I suspect every one of you will interpret the sign in nearly the same way. Indeed, you may even imagine a hamburger, fantasize about it. We all know what I am talking about. I am talking about a juicy sandwich invented a century or two ago and usually built around a ground beef patty between slices of bread. The meaning is conventional. There is nothing about the sign "hamburger" that resembles a sandwich in any way. I could replace the sign "hamburger" with:

gobledigot

And if we all agreed that this is the new sign for the sandwich we are discussing, I could go on and on talking about gobledigots and we would all know what I am talking about. Indeed, this book is full of signs the meanings of which we once learned as children and have available in our memory banks. As philosopher Filip Mattens describes:

> Coming across an illegible scribble in the margin of a book, one may spend a while trying to "see" what is actually written there. But then, all at once, the words become clear; the word-types are recognized. It says "*indocilis.*"[42] Now, obviously, it could be that my reading ends here, with the act of deciphering, if I don't know what the word means. For the most part, however, *my intention instantaneously pushes through to the meaning of the word*, unnoticed, as if there were no shift between the inscription that I see and its being significant. The meaning-intention, which is triggered in this way, then *tries to find fulfillment in an intuitive givenness of what is meant.* (Mattens 2008b: xiii; emphasis added)

The mental process of "pushing through" from the form of the sign to its full significance is automatic. That is why we can speak of a symbolic brain. In most cases, the signs we use are arbitrary in that they bear no resemblance to the signified, and yet the "pushing through" to the correct meaning flows quite smoothly, once the deciphering occurs.

Notice that I referred to the above as a *complex* sign. This is because it is made up of constituent signs we call "letters" that by cultural convention we associate with individual sounds that make up our speech. "Hamburger" is made up of sounds like "h" which signals a hissing sound made in the back of my throat, which is followed by an "a" which signals an "aaa" sound, and so on. Again, these are all arbitrary. Neither the letters nor the whole word "hamburger" resembles the speech sounds or the sandwich under discussion.

Suppose now I present to you another complex sign:

---

[42] *Indocilis* means "unteachable." I had to look it up.

Does this sign mean anything to you? Perhaps you recognize it only as an Egyptian hieroglyph, and it means little more than that to you. If you are familiar with hieroglyphs, you might recognize that this is a *cartouche*, a sign representing a rolled-up scroll with certain sub-signs associated with a specific Pharaoh, in this case Nefertiti. If you had lived in ancient Egypt during those long-ago days and were literate, you would have known the meaning of the sign immediately—its meaning would be conventional and would, taken as a whole, have had religious significance as a sigil. But in this case the sign utilizes stylized pictures of things associated with Queen Nefertiti, rather than totally arbitrary marks like an "h", a "ﺏ", or a "¥". Indeed, many languages that were once written pictographically gradually became less pictographic and eventually became ideographic as the signs became more and more abstract in design and meanings become more conventional.

HUSSERL ON SIGNITIVE ACTS

For Husserl, *signitive acts* (Sebeok's "semiosis") are "empty." Perceptual acts are "full." Let us explore what he means by this distinction. As we have seen, most signs we use in communicating information to each other by speech, gesture, writing, drawing, or acting are both arbitrary and conventional. If I mention "hamburger" to you, you know what I mean, but there is no hamburger present, except perhaps in your imagination. The sign "hamburger" is *empty* of hyletic fulfillment, and is thus experientially "empty." In general all ideas are "empty" until fulfilled in perception by instantiating sensuous hyle filling forms and above all, intuition. Please keep in mind that Husserl is not defining signs here, but rather describing how we experience signitive acts.

> Between perception on the one hand and, on the other, the
> presentation of a symbol in the form of an image or meaning
> there is an unbridgeable and essential difference. With these types
> of presentation, we intuit something, in the consciousness that it
> copies something else or indicates its meaning; and though we
> already have the one in the field of intuition, we are not directed
> towards it, but through the medium of a secondary apprehension
> are directed towards the other, that which is copied or indicated.
> There is nothing of all this in perception, as little as in plain
> recollection or fancy. (Husserl 1982[1913]: 136)

We do not have to reason-out the difference between pure perception
and symbolic expression. We intuit the "going beyond" immediately
if the object is known to us as a symbol (flag, road sign, word,
pointing finger, etc.). As Husserl would say, the sign is "animated"
by its meaning. Indeed, we often are barely aware of the symbol-as-
sign because our awareness is engrossed in the meaning. We are not
really aware of the word-signs following one upon the other as we read.
Rather, there is a flow of meaning automatically unfolding serially as
our eyes scan the page. "The felt surface of language does not in itself
typically engage our attention; what is presented to us phonically or in
print—the 'vehicle'—is normally surpassed and even suppressed as we
attend to the specific meaning conveyed by this vehicle. Contrastingly,
in mythic, gestural, and aesthetic phenomena our attention is riveted
directly onto the phenomenal surface; what we are looking for happens
at or on this surface, not beyond or behind it" (Casey 1971: 198).

In his early career Husserl was interested in mathematics and logic
(see Husserl 1970 [1900-01], 1994, 2003[1887-1901], 2008[1906-1907]).
Within this context he first developed his understanding of symbolism
and signs.

> Thus, as the sign for something (for a content in general) any
> and everything can serve which marks it out—which is suited to
> distinguish it from other things, and by which we then are in a
> position to re-identify it. But for us this re-identification comes
> into consideration not merely as a psychological mechanism that
> functions without our needing to be aware of it—one which,

upon the occasion of the one representation, calls the other back into consciousness without our having, even in some general sense, to be conscious of the fact that it is precisely the former which has recalled the latter and mediated its re-identification. In order for the concept of *sign* to be possible, and in order for us to be able purposively to invent and use signs, the relationship between the sign and what is designated must be specifically noticed. (Husserl 1994: 21)

If I, as a working stiff, mention that the "suits" are on the factory floor, everyone knows this reference to clothing signals the presence of management. If the news anchor reports that more people are dying in "red" states than "blue" states, I know that she is referring to states that voted predominantly one way or the other during an American election. And if a policeman refers to one of his suspects as a "wiseguy," he is telling us the suspect is a member of an American crime family. Husserl went on to suggest non-exclusive distinctions that can be experientially made between different types and usages of signs (Husserl 1994: 21-51). These get needlessly complicated and tedious, reminding me of the 20-odd types of causation described in the last book of the Buddhist Abhidharma I encountered in the course of my Buddhist studies. But Husserl's conclusions are important:

Our investigations up to now concerned symbols and symbolic processes of the lowest level. In the course of natural unreflective thought, these stand in as surrogates for authentic representations, judgments, and inferential processes. They do so in virtue of the lawlike tendency of our nature, without there being present any specific consciousness of this their function—and much less, then, their employment being governed by logical motives (whether previous or accompanying). But besides these *natural* surrogates (as we may concisely designate them) we use, and to the widest of extents, *conventional* surrogates. We invent symbols and symbolic processes, or use those invented by others, as supports and surrogates for representations and judgment processes. And in this we proceed purposively, fully aware that we are dealing in the symbolical. (Husserl 1994: 43)

Husserl recognized within the context of his phenomenological investigations that at its lowest level of processing of symbolic relations, our brainmind is little different than the same processes operating in infrahuman animals (Husserl 1994: 25; see also Stegmann 2013, Scarantino 2013). We symbolize because it is our nature to do so—it is how our brains are "wired" such that patterns adumbrated from the primordial sensory given in experience can quickly and efficiently penetrate to cognits mediating a full bundle of meaning which becomes the signification of the patterns-as-symbols. As we shall see below, this finding dovetails with my theoretical explanation for the evolution of language.

During the course of his meditations, Husserl also came upon something very interesting about numerical signs. He discovered that cardinal numbers are signs indicating quantities, yes, but also that experiencing three dogs is fundamentally different than experiencing fifty dogs. Direct experience of small quantities is both hyletically filled and intuitive—they are "genuine." We do not have to count the dogs to know there are three of them. In other words, the quantity three is given intuitively in perception. The intuitive experience of three is an essence, as is the experience of two or four. But there is an upper limit to the quantity one can intuit in the perceptual act before one has to revert to counting, which is a different state. Husserl guessed the watershed to be about twelve. Psychologists have since come up with different watershed quantities, most famously George Miller (1956) and his seven plus or minus two approximation. And we now have evidence that non-human animals, including birds, have something like an essential numeric essence (Gelman and Cordes 2001). Thus, when we speak of "a couple" we are referring to an "authentic" intuitively present experience, whereas if we speak of "a gross" of eggs, we know what we mean—"gross" is a sign—but we cannot directly experience that quantity intuitively. When one imagines animals, including humans, interacting with the environing world, an authentic numerical sense would come in quite handy—one water buffalo might be adaptationally different than five water buffalo.

> Concepts, or contents in general, can be given to us in a twofold manner. First, in the *authentic* manner, namely, as that

which they are. Second, in the *inauthentic* or *symbolic* manner; namely, through the mediation of *signs*—signs which are themselves authentically represented. Thus, for example, any intuitive representation in sensation or fantasy is an authentic representation, provided it does not serve us as a sign for something else. But if it does so serve, then in relation to this latter it is a symbolic representation. (Husserl 1994: 20)

In the strictest sense, proper names of people are signs. If I speak of my daughter Kate, my friends and family know that I am indicating a specific real person, a "general representation" of Kate-the-being. Indeed, any object of consciousness is a sign in the sense of being indicative of the meaning of the object. When the primordially given sensory object is intended as an indication of something else, it is a sign, and the intentional act is a signitive act that is "empty" if that which is intended is not present in the act.

Husserl used the distinction between the indicative and expressive functions of signs. A sign is *indicative* when it points to something else. If you wave an American flag at me, it may indicate to me that you are a patriot, that you are a right-wing zealot, or that you want me to gather round with a group, depending upon the situation ("state of affairs" in philosophy jargon) in which the flag waving is embedded. You might ask me where the nearest lavatory may be found, and I respond "there" while pointing my finger, my utterance and my gesture both being indicator signs (Husserl 1970 [1900-01], Vol 1: 183-184). If I am out hunting and find some fresh scat, it indicates to my mind that a deer or bear has passed this way. If I come up to a red sign at an intersection, it indicates to me my appropriate action, which is to stop before proceeding. In short, *a sign is an indicator if it is paired with something else in the mind of a perceiver.* A wide range of animals exhibit indicative communication (Smith 1981; see also Bradbury and Vehrencamp 2011). An animal may use body posture, ritualized movements, or an utterance to indicate to conspecifics the direction of a potential danger, or its intentions to do something. Honeybees famously use their "waggle dance" movements to indicate the direction, nature, and quantity of a food source they have discovered in their wanderings.

A sensory object perceived in its primordial sensory given may or may not be a sign, depending upon the intuition accompanying the hyle and form constituting the object:

> On no account should we fall into the fundamentally perverse copy-and-sign-theories which, without taking the physical thing specially into account, we considered at an early stage and likewise disposed of in the most general form. *An image or sign points to something that lies beyond it, which, could it but pass over into another form of presentation, into that of dator intuition, might "itself" be apprehended.* A sign and copy do not "announce" in its self the self that is signified (or copied). (Husserl 1982[1913]: 160; emphasis added)

The sign-ness function of the sensory object depends upon the Watcher apprehending it intuitively as a sign. For some Christians and Moslems, the increased turbulence of hurricanes we are experiencing as I write this and that appear to be due to climate change may be taken as signs of the End Times. There is nothing in the occurrence of a devastating hurricane that "announces" anything about End Times. The minds of individual religious ideologues add this "pointing to something beyond" to the experience of the storm. The connection between primordial event and scripture is a strictly mental link that most of the rest of us do not make. For Husserl, that link between primordial given and the "pointing to something beyond" is a noematic act that accompanies the noetic presentation of the object-as-sign (see e.g., Husserl 1982[1913]: 291-292).

As we will see in the next chapter, images and fantasies are authentic presentations, just as are direct sensuous experiences in perception, for no matter how obscure or clear the images, they are chockablock with hyle. But if those same images and fantasies are interpreted as representing unconscious processes which cannot, in principle, be perceived, then the images and fantasies are signs pointing toward the invisible content of the mind—more a Jungian process than one of Husserl's concerns (see Brooke 1991). It is the orientation of consciousness toward the object—its intention—that makes the difference. Generalizing, Husserl would distinguish *image consciousness* or *picture consciousness* (Ger.: *Bildbewusstsein*) from ordinary sensuous consciousness as the state within which the object of our consciousness is an image, as when I imagine my mother's face before my mind's eye, or I see my mother's face in a photograph. In the latter case I am perceiving a photograph as the primordial sensory given within the context of which I recognize my mother's face. "*[T]he intentional object of a presentation is the same as its actual object, and on occasion as its external object, and that it is absurd to distinguish between them*"(Husserl 1970 [1900-01], II: 127). I am seeing a genuine object, the photograph, and I am seeing the *image* of my mother. In this sense, the image of my mother is a symbol, and in Ernst Cassirer's sense (see epigraph at the start of this chapter) a symbol very *pregnant* with meaning (Husserl 2005[1898-1925]: 19-22).

Husserl noticed that signs often have overlapping meanings, thus causing natural signs to be "ambiguous" in signification. Many years later, Eleanor Rosch and her colleagues highlighted the same feature of natural categories like birds, rocks, trees and so forth (Rosch 1977, 1978, Rosch *et al.* 1976). In discussing this problem for the development of the sciences, Husserl suggests that each discipline must be cautious about their definitions, a process by which the scientist can "control this nuisance of 'ambiguity'" (Husserl 2008[1906-1907]: 25). In today's fuzzy category theory, this is called "crispifying" the categories. Husserl's concern for the necessity of crispification of categorical boundaries not only eliminates ambiguity but makes mathematics and logic possible (see Hartimo 2017).

Natural language

There are a number of universal characteristics that define our species, e.g., the family, ceremonial ritual, storytelling, tool-making and retention, gender and age-based roles, and music, natural categories, to name but a few. While every known human society is organized around the family, the exact form of the family will vary greatly across cultures (Flinn 2011). All societies recognize and make music which is an activity mediated in part by inherent neural structures (Masataka 2009, Morrison and Demorest 2009, Patel 2008). Humans everywhere love to tell and hear stories under circumstances ranging from informal conversations and singing to formal oratory, drama, recitation, mystery plays and so on

(Mellmann 2012). All human societies categorize features of nature in much the same way that science does, recognizing "species" of plants and animals that interbreed as belonging to the same category (Atran 1998, Atran and Medin 2008). One of the most obvious and important of cross-cultural universals is spoken language. And like all the other universals, there are both variations in the details we find in different languages, and essential structures that we inherit biogenetically and thus are universal. One excellent example is the cross-cultural invariance in parent-infant communication by speech and song (Hilton et al. 2022).

It is an error of the first water to speak of the evolution of language as distinct from other forms of communication, leading to such silly debates as to which came first in phylogenesis, speech or gesture (see McNeill 2012: 11-14, Chap. 3). Our best guesstimate is that our ancestors living 5 to 10 million years ago used vocal utterances, conventional movements, ritualized forms combining dance, vocalization, rhythm and melody, body postures, and gestures to communicate among conspecifics, much as monkeys and apes do today. Indeed, utterances and ritualized movements ("displays") are common among birds (Wheatcroft and Price 2013; also see Sturdy and Mooney 2000 on emperor penguins) and mammals (Seyfarth and Cheney 2003, Smith 1981, Searcy and Nowicki 2010) for expressing both their intentions and to influence the behavior of conspecifics.

There are numerous theories out there about how language first came to be and how it evolved. I have neither the space nor the inclination to review the various theories, for that has been done by others (see e.g., Bouchard 2013, Christiansen and Kirby 2003, Hoffmeyer 2008: 290-301, Hurford 1999, McNeill 2012). As far as I know, none of these theories are informed from the phenomenology of language (but see Azzouni 2015, Inkpin 2016, Ruthrof 2021).

HUSSERL ON LANGUAGE

It is curious that, as central to human adaptation as language proved to be, the phenomenology of language is a fairly neglected subject (for exceptions, see Azzouni 2013, Bundgaard 2010, Derrida 1973, Inkpin 2016, Kwant 1965, Mattens 2008a, Ruthrof 2021; also see Smith 1997 on the Munich Circle and the phenomenological realism movement's take on language acts, especially the work of Adolf Reinach (1969, Reinach and Crosby 2013)). Yet for Husserl, finding an efficient and flexible means of expressing phenomenological insights is crucial, and as philosopher D. R. Koukal (2008) makes clear, finding that expression facilitates not only communication of insights, but *the actual process of mining for them*. Of course, much of what Husserl writes about signs pertains to their use in natural language.[43] It is critical that we be clear about what Husserl means by "language." Language for Husserl refers to experienced expressive acts—the emphasis here is upon *acts*. He is interested in what we can learn by applying the reduction to expressive acts from within the phenomenological attitude. Hence there is nothing in Husserl's approach that touches upon hidden, black-box, language rule systems *a la* de Saussure's (2011[1916]) *la langue* or Chomsky's "language acquisition device"—neither of which, incidentally, is supported by evidence from today's neurolinguistics (see also Stawarska 2020).[44] Grammar for Husserl refers to the essential structures (or "a priori laws" rendered and reified by certain cultures as "formal conventions") by which individual, irreducible meanings are bound together into a field of meaning over the temporal duration it takes to express an utterance or narrative (Husserl 1970 [1900-01] II: 71-74). As Husserl notes, we can string words together willy-nilly, each of which has a distinct meaning for us, but which when linked together are non-sense:

Bear stump lakeshore quinine.

We have four nouns strung together, each noun having a clear meaning, but the string has nothing to bind the string together. If we rearrange the string to say:

---

[43] If you wish to read more about Husserl's *phenomenology of language*, see Husserl (1970 [1900-01], I: Investigation I, 1970[1936]: 364-365, 1994: 20-51), Aurora and Flack (2016), Bundgaard (2010), Edie (1987: Chap. 2), Inkpin (2016), Mattens (2008a), Ruthrof (2021), Smith (2013: 49-51).

[44] I am particularly indebted to Horst Ruthrof's marvelous *Husserl's Phenomenology of Natural Language: Intersubjectivity and Community in the Nachlass* (2021) for access to as yet untranslated sources in the Nachlass, especially Husserliana XX/1 and XX/2. This is a superb source for Husserl's discussions of *imaginability*.

Lakeshore bear quinine stump.

We have the same four words, all retaining exactly the same meanings and still making no sense linked differently together. This may appear too simplistic to point out, save for the fact that I may be perceiving all four things simultaneously. For Husserl, stringing together component signs in accordance with syntactic rules ("principles of composition;" see Bundgaard 2010) is part of the speaker's expressive act—the part in which the speaker intends to "make sense:"

> These laws of sense, or, normatively put, laws of avoidance of nonsense, direct logic to the abstractly possible forms of meaning, whose objective value it then becomes its first task to determine. This logic does by setting up the wholly different laws which distinguish a formally consistent from a formally inconsistent, i.e. absurd, sense. (Husserl 1970 [1900-01] II: 71)

Husserl made the fundamental distinction between *natural signs* (e.g., a scream denotes fear, a laugh denoted pleasure or amusement, a cringe denotes pain, smoke denotes fire, waving branches denote wind, etc.) which we share with other animals and *natural languages* that, unique and universal to humans, allow us to express meanings in very complex ways.

Language serves at least two functions, as *expression* and as *communication* (Husserl 1970 [1900-01]: 187-190, Casey 1971: 198). We often use language as spoken or written rituals, as acts of communication which do not necessarily intend novel meanings, that are not strictly speaking expressions. Lyrics to songs may or may not be expressive, but in their rhythms and vocalizations may be entertaining and facilitate shared social experiences. Husserl held that these linguistic acts are *empty of expression*. Much of the speaking of politicians at rallies is empty of expression, a state of things that leaves many people frustrated: "All that talk, and nothing said." Of anthropological interest is the fact that traditional spiritual and healing rituals incorporate language utterances in the form of incantations, mantras, and other repetitive kinds of communication that may be devoid of expression (in Husserl's restrictive sense) and yet have *agency* (Gell 1998) or *praxis* (Bourdieu

1977). Language allows the creation of formulaic utterances that are associated with power and causation as with magical incantations.

When we were discussing intersubjectivity back in Chapter 4, we noted that Husserl grounded our experiences of the Other in empathy and to some extent, apperception of the Other as lived body. He made it clear that we can never really get "inside" the Other's head—we can't read minds. But we can via empathy intuit facial expressions and body movements and glean some notion of what the Other is feeling and perhaps intending. He also understood that we had that ability in company with other animals. It is by way of communication that we are able to gain more information about, as well as inform the Other.

Language as expression richly endows communication with the potential of exchange of information in the form of thoughts and meanings, and importantly in creating in the auditor a vicarious sharing of experience via imagination (Ruthrof 2021, Summa 2021). If you and I had a conversation over Zoom, Skype, or some other platform, I could talk your ears off about Husserlian phenomenology and its relevance to anthropology, and you might even learn something, or I learn from you, before you got fed-up and pushed the "quit" button. Or we might have another conversation during which you describe to me your adventures in Thailand or Mexico. Through the magic of your story-telling I would, with the help of my own imagination, share in the experiences you had and that I have not had. This is the power of vicarious experience through the exercise of *image consciousness* (Ger.: *Bildbewusstsein*)—you can literally cause me to experience imaginable scenes, accompanied by feelings, body responses, avid attention, and perhaps for me new knowledge about the world. If you are like me, all I have to do is imagine cutting my finger with a knife to cause my body to react as if the injury were real. I cannot look at a picture of someone standing on the edge of a cliff or roof or mountain ridge without my groin shriveling. I can recall going to see Lon Chaney's 1941 film, *The Wolf Man* when I was ten years old and leaving halfway through the screening in terror. I could not go to sleep without the light on in my bedroom for months afterwards. All of this illustrating the power of image consciousness in producing vicarious experience, a capacity that proved crucial to human adaptation, as we shall see below.

Husserl's post-epoché account of language leads us toward a structuralist view of language and other aspects of communication (Aurora 2018), especially as Husserl's view heavily influenced Roman Jakobson and the Prague Linguistic Circle (Aurora and Flack 2016). For Husserl, language exists naturally in the domain of intersubjectivity and its lifeworld (Chapter 7). Yet despite the importance of language for the enculturation of young members of human groups, early encounters with the environing world by babies mirror the non-linguistic cognitive style common to primates and other animals throughout their lives—a kind of *peramorphosis* that Husserl noticed in human ontogenesis:

> It is easy to see that even in [ordinary] human life, and first of all in every human life from childhood up to maturity, the originally intuitive life which creates its originally self-evident structures through activities on the basis of sense-experience very quickly and in increasing measure falls victim to the *seduction of language*. Greater and greater segments of this life lapse into a kind of talking and reading that is dominated purely by association; and often enough, in respect to the validness arrived at in this way, it is disappointed by subsequent experience. (Husserl 1970[1936]: 362)

Instead of relying upon direct experience of the environing world, children automatically learn the language(s) spoken around them, and through the magic of linking signs to meanings, they increasingly fill their heads with received knowledge, including tales depicting vicarious experiences, much of which bears little relation to their everyday experience. As we have seen earlier, as long as none of the "things" we encounter in doing phenomenology are actually sentient beings, the reduction results in pure insight into how experience of the environing world is essentially structured for the individual perceiver. But when the object of our experience is another sentient being, the reduction takes a *transcendental turn* (see Chapter 4). That is, we encounter an object that is a being with a mind—a being like us in all apparent respects. Husserl held that we intuitively know that another person is like us, and that we share the primordially given sensuous world with others of our kind—our shared lifeworld.

Again, while we can intuitively appreciate our shared lifeworld, *we cannot read each other's minds.* Could we do so, language would be unnecessary and would not have been selected for in phylogenesis. To know what is going on in your mind, apart from the primordial layer of objects, relations, and intuitions in direct experience, requires that we communicate (Noé 1992). And by communicating we reduce the uncertainty with respect to what is going on in each other's minds and lives (Grant 2007).

When we speak or write a word, we are producing an object, a "thing," in the environing world. In the case of a spoken word, we are producing a series of distinct vibrations in the air around us which can be detected by our own auditory sensorium and potentially by the auditory system of another brain, human or otherwise (Husserl 1970 [1900-01]). With respect to speech:

> The verbal sounds have their indications, which, in themselves, refer interdependently to one another and are built one on another. The sounds conjoin to make the unity of a word-formation, which in turn consists of relatively self-contained formations. Each of these is bearer of a unity of indication; and the whole is a self-contained unity, which has noetically the phenomenological characteristic of associative self-containedness and on the parallel side (noematically) the phenomenological characteristic that consists in the self-containedness of an indicated "significational" unity, built correspondingly out of indicative formations. (Husserl 1969[1929]: 57)

Vocal sounds combine to produce spoken words that we recognize as an independent unit of speech. These units indicate meaning, and the auditory unit is paired cognitively with its meaning, its significance.

If we write a word, either by pen strokes or by some tactile system like braille, we are creating a conjoined pattern of lines, dots, or pictograms on paper that we can "read" and others may "read" as well, assuming we both understand the same code. I put "read" in quotes because this is the word we use when we perceive a word on a page. We also use the term metaphorically as when we "read" the spoor of an animal in the bush, "read" someone's horoscope, "read" someone's emotions—i.e., we "read" something when we are presented an object that requires us to interpret it—blind people read braille texts with their fingers and profoundly deaf people read some form of sign language. But calling our interpretive acts that happen to be focused upon an utterance or a written word "hearing," "touching," or "reading" obscures the fact that we are busily interpreting everything in our environment. In normal everyday communication, there is always a "horizon" of multiple objects and possibilities. Taken as a whole, the entire context of experience influences interpretation.

The neuropsychology of interpreting this object as a "coffee cup" and that object as a "word" involves the same processes—processes that are operating in non-human animals as well. Let us repeat: *The primary adaptive function of perception is to detect patterns in the environment and render them meaningful.* This linking of the model with knowing is the act of interpretation—the merging of noesis with noema in Husserlese—and occurs entirely within the brain (see Edie 1987: 28-29). If I utter a word—a string of consonant and vowel sounds—your sensorium will process the string of sounds I make in exactly the same way that you would a clap of thunder, an ambulance siren, and the bark of a dog. In this sense, the entire sensory world of models is *a world of signs* that our brains make meaningful—the symbolic process of neural processing in action. Making sensory patterns meaningful has been one of the most powerful adaptive mechanisms in evolution. This ability, common to all animals with brains, is what led to the evolution of communication. What makes communication possible is that we humans all share the same lifeworld, the entire range of primordially given, sensorial models that constitute the "real" world as we experience it (Husserl 1970 [1936]). An object in the environing world is a sign if its model within my sensorium penetrates to a greater field of meaning held in memory. The object I call "my coffee cup" is not inherently a coffee cup, but rather is interpreted by my brain as a "coffee cup"— the object out in the environing world as I experience it (the *noesis*) is linked via neural connections to the meaning (*noema*) found in a different place in my brain. If I utter the phrase "coffee cup," there is nothing inherently coffee cup-like about the sounds I make, i.e., they are not onomatopoeic. I could as easily utter "Kaffeetasse," "tasse à café, or "kahvikuppi," none of which have anything inherently coffee cupish about them, but which would have been interpreted in the same manner depending upon whether you can understand German, French or Finnish. In common parlance, we would say that the word "coffee cup" *stands for* or *expresses*, not the object in the real world that I am experiencing, *but the idea of coffee cup in my brain*. As you read my words, you have a perfectly good idea of my coffee cup, but you could not describe it *other than in essential terms*.

IDEALITY AND THE PHENOMENOLOGY OF EXPRESSION

Husserl's way of referring to the referent of a sign is its *ideality* (Husserl 1970[1936]: 357). Unlike my uttering "coffee cup" which may both be meaningful and refer to an actual concrete object in my experience, if I utter "hobbit," you will undoubtedly understand I am talking about a fictional species of hominoids found in the pages of J. R. R. Tolkien's novels. There has never existed a species of Tolkien hobbits,[45] and yet we may have an interesting conversation about hobbits, their physiology, their tastes, values and social structures, and their history, all of which exist only as ideas and images in our brains and stories in books and films. So far as I know, humans are the only animals on this planet that can communicate about imaginary objects, events, and worlds—can create a physical, concrete thing (pattern of sound, pattern of lines on a page) in the environing world that evoke sensory patterns that then penetrate to distinct meanings about things *that exist only in the human mind*.

Human communication evolved until we could *express* ideas through signs (Lee 2010)—vocal, gestural, ritualized, and iconographic "tokens" in the real world that are mentally associated with concepts, images, and other forms of meaning.

> For example, when I say, "My hat is gray," (1) my psychic process of judging is manifested and (2) the sense of my judgment is expressed by (3) the sentence, which, in turn, is embodied in (4) the sound that I produce. This sound is also a manifestation of

---

[45] To be clear, an extinct species of hominin, *Homo floresiensis*, was quite small and has been nicknamed "Hobbit" after Tolkien's character.

my judging and of my willing to produce such a sound. Finally, (5) my hat and its color are alleged objects which the sense of my judgment is about. (Cairns 1941: 453)

This does not mean that animals have no ideas in their brain—other animals' brains in fact operate on the construction of ideas just as ours do (see Stegmann 2013). The difference is that there was little to no selection for a complex communication system based upon signs linked to ideas, or for intersubjective communication of ideas. Why, may you well ask? Because up until our unique expansion of consciousness (primarily the evolution of the frontal cortical lobes), intersubjective synching of ideas was sufficiently maintained by the animal's lifeworld. As I have discussed elsewhere (Chapter 4), the biological function of the lifeworld is *to true ideas about the environing world*, both subjectively and intersubjectively. With the expansion of consciousness, ideas among conspecifics could possibly diverge to a maladaptive extent, thus requiring another mechanism (various forms of communication) to maintain adaptive social cohesion in intersubjective view and action.

This evolutionary process among hominins is so fundamental, in my view, that we have to dig deeper into the nature of an "idea"—what is it, how is it constructed, how does it function neurobiologically, and how does the necessity to synch ideas lead to much that we today call "culture."

> The *Eidos*, the *pure essence*, can be exemplified intuitively in the data of experience, data of perception, memory, and so forth, but just as readily *also in the mere data of fancy (Phantasie)*. Hence, with the aim of grasping an essence itself in its *primordial* form, we can set out from corresponding empirical intuitions, *but we can also set out just as well from non-empirical intuitions, intuitions that do not apprehend sensory experience, intuitions rather "of a merely imaginative order."* (Husserl 1982[1913]: 57)

In other worlds, an idea (as Husserl uses the term) exists only in the brain. As such, an idea may be very specific (the "coffee cup" sitting before me now) or extremely general (the class "coffee cup" including coffee cups I have experienced and those I have not). Moreover, I can fantasy about coffee cups I have never seen outside of imagination, and which may in fact have never existed. Language specifically depends upon linking signs and ideas intersubjectively, whether or not those ideas are instantiated in the primordial sensuous given. If in fact an idea is instantiated in experience, Husserl would say that the idea (essence, *Eidos*) is sensuously (hyletically) "fulfilled" by the sensorium. "I spy with my little eye an instantiation of the class 'coffee cup!'" It is my very particular "coffee cup." But of course, it belongs to a set of coffee cups in my kitchen, and I honestly cannot tell one cup from another in the set, nor would that be of any interest to me for one member of the set will instantiate my idea of a cup as well as any other. Indeed, my "coffee cup" sitting right in front of me would not be a coffee cup at all if I had no idea of what constitutes a "coffee cup." That does not mean I might not have a favorite coffee cup and no other cup will do. However, that would mean that the idea of the cup in my head would simply be more specific in its characteristics.

Husserl distinguishes ideas from facts (Husserl 1982[1913]: 52-54). I can describe for you all sorts of "factual" (empirically confirmable) information about my coffee cup sitting before me right here, right now. But the *idea* of the coffee cup is at the other end of a continuum of generality. We have ideas about all sorts of things *in general*—physical things, relations and properties, mental operations like seeing and hearing, imagining, feeling, conceptualizing, etc. We even have ideas about theorizing, hypothesizing, thinking, experimenting, etc. Indeed, we have in our brains an idea(s) about anything we can experience. More than that, we can and do have ideas about things that may have never existed, like blue fairies, black holes, dilithium crystals, the grim reaper, Noah's ark, Shangri La, and on and on.

The brain in all animals is very interested in "ideas-in-general," and among humans, even ideas that are "empty" of content, thus purely logical (e.g., numbers, syllogisms). "Meaning in general" is for Husserl (1982[1913]: 71) the highest form of genus, relative to species. We are speaking here of ideas within ideas, within ideas, and so forth. My specific coffee cup is one of a "set of coffee cups," a member of the general class "coffee cup," which is a subclass of the class "cup," which is in turn a subclass of the class "tableware," "container," or "dish." You can see by reflecting upon this and other idea-chains within your head that having ideas-in-general is what cognitions about objects of experience are all about—general applicability with instantiations in sensory experience now and again to keep them linked to reality. Were languages limited to signs having specific, concrete objects as their reference, communication would be bogged down into a quagmire of specificity and rampant, overwhelming novelty. Knowing how to drink coffee out of my specific coffee cup could not be generalized to having coffee out of a cup you provide for me. General knowledge about classes of objects is far more efficient and can feed forward to objects I have not yet encountered. Methodologically speaking, we phenomenologically come to know the essential nature of the idea by "free variation" of objects and classes included within the idea as it is transformed in imagination and cogitation (Husserl 1982[1913]: 57-58; see Chapter 3).

Parenthetically, as psychologist Eleanor Rosch and her colleagues have shown, natural categories (read "classes" or "ideas") have fuzzy boundaries (Rosch 1977, 1978, Rosch *et al.* 1976). That means that things in experience tend to be more or less instances of the category—of the idea in general. Robins and chickadees are more bird-like than emus and chickens. There are coffee cups that can only be experienced as coffee cups (the "classic" coffee cup). Others, like my present coffee cup, can as easily be classed as a "coffee mug." Still other coffee cups may blend seamlessly into the category "tea cup." The classic example of this fuzziness is to be found in basic color categories which have been found to be primordial (i.e., neurobiological, and culturally universal; see Berlin and Kay 1969, Kay and Maffi 1999) and pre-linguistic in nature (Ozturk, Shayan, Liszkowski and Majid 2013). The closer an exemplar gets to a boundary between basic color terms, the more ambiguity occurs in classification judgements about which basic color term a specific color belongs.

Husserl notes that as necessary as language is to our everyday way of life, natural language is "imperfect" and thus must be "fixed" by crispification of terms in the service of logic and science (Husserl 1970 [1900-01], I: 23). What makes language imperfect is the ambiguity of meaning connoted by words, including overlapping fields of meaning and multiple meanings. Again, natural ideas, concepts and categories tend to be fuzzy and indeterminate. This serves natural language well, for the ambiguity of meanings of individual words allows flexibility in adjusting meanings at the level of sentences and texts (see Kahane

2001) which are the levels most common in everyday conversing, story-telling, explaining, reporting, and so forth. But for Husserl, this is insufficient for the purposes of philosophy, logic, and science which all require crucial concepts and categories to be clear in both inclusivity and exclusivity of membership (Edie 1987: 29).

Neurophysiologically speaking, what constitutes an "idea" as Husserl uses the term? An idea is a bundle of associated information that is mediated by a neural network, and which is activated either by itself (after all, an idea is mediated by living cells in intimate interaction with each other), or by another neural network. For instance, a given primordial pattern in sensory experience may operate as a key penetrating to and activating the neural network(s) in episodic memory mediating the idea(s). An idea generally contains more information than any particular, concrete instantiation or "fulfillment" of the idea in sensory experience. Husserl particularly pointed to the importance of nesting "simpler" meanings within "more complex" meanings, and the ability of language to express hierarchies of meaning within utterances or texts (Husserl 1970 [1900-01], Vol 2: 50-53, Bundgaard 2004).

> The function of concepts, it is said, is to enable the thinking mind to transcend the limits set by the unsurveyable multiplicity of individual singulars; their economizations of thinking enable the mind to reach its goal of knowledge indirectly, as it could never have reached it directly. General concepts make it possible for us to treat things in bundles as it were, to make assertions about whole classes of objects at a single 'go'; we can therefore talk about countless objects, instead of conceiving and judging each object 'on its own'. (Husserl 1970 [1900-01]: 277)

And as we have seen, that is the whole point in brains constructing ideas-in-general, which in turn can interact at a very abstract and generalized level of processing by structures most likely located over wide areas of cortex (Fink and Benedek 2013). Evidence suggests that novel ideas are constructed in the area of the cortex called the left hemisphere's supramarginal gyrus and are formed in relation with other ideas, perhaps of long standing (Benedek et al. 2018).

Another way of making sense of the domain of ideas is to simplify our view somewhat and think in terms of ideas within ideas in a continuum from primordial (universal) things, relations, and intuitions at one extreme of experience to highly variant and socioculturally constructed general ideas.

> [T]he determinations of things as familiar or strange, useful or useless, finished, half-finished, or spoiled—their determinations as tools or monuments, as slaves or pets or kings—all such determinations are intrinsically relative to psychic activities and *belong to the cultural stratum of the world*. A stone is naturally a real thing with a particular shape, size, rigidity, and color. It may also be a real paperweight or a real hammer, but only culturally, i.e., in relation to someone who uses (or might use) it to some intended end. Thus, the realm of individual reality contains cultural as well as natural determinations. At the same time, the objective cultural stratum of the world contains more than just the *real* cultural determinations of real objects. It also contains non-real, ideal objects; among them, verbal expressions. (Cairns 1941: 454-455)

All communicative expressions are broadcast via the environing world and involve both essential and cultural aspects. A communicative act—whether it be a reenactment, a speech, a piece of art, a ritual, a written document, a signal, a poem, or lyric—involves a technical change in the environing world that in turn is perceived as primordially given in the experience of someone else (the auditor). This primordial given operates as a key to the layers of ideas, within ideas leading to culturally conditioned interpretations and responses. If I speak to you, I change my behavior in such a way that I cause vibrations in the air that you pick up and interpret. If I write to you, I change my behavior leading to creating a series of notations on paper that you perceive and interpret. In every case my actions are intentional. In Husserlian terms, the meaning in my head (*noema*) is transposed into commands to my speech center to physically perturb the environment (*noesis*) so as to express my meaning so that I can share it with you. Short of direct mind-to-mind (parapsychological) communication, all communication has a technical phase, and in the case of writing, or speaking via radio or telephone, a technological phase (Ihde 1991, 2016).

INTERPRETATION

In communicating, there is commonly a difference between the meaning intention of the speaker and the interpretation of the speaker's utterances by the auditor(s).

> The hearer perceives the speaker as manifesting certain inner experiences, and to that extent he also perceives these experiences themselves: he does not, however, himself experience them, he has not an "inner" but an "outer" percept of them. Here we have the big difference between the real grasp of what is in adequate intuition, and the putative grasp of that which is based on an inadequate, though intuitive, presentation. In the former case we have to do with an experienced being, in the latter case with a presumed being, to which no truth corresponds at all. Mutual understanding demands a certain correlation among the mental acts mutually unfolded in intimation and in the receipt of such intimation, but not at all their exact resemblance. (Husserl 1970 [1900-01], Vol 1: 190).

The correlation among mental acts depends first and foremost on the ideality of the structure of speech acts (Wilshire 1978). At its most basic primordial level, a speech act is a string of *sound images* (De Saussure 2011[1916]). A spoken word enters the environing world as vibrations in the air that are tracked by the auditor's sensory system. The primordial given of the world object is not a perfectly veridical representation of the vibrations, but rather the detection of a pattern within the vibrations. This pattern is the sound image ("mental impression;" see Derrida 1973: 46-47) which is redundantly associated with a concept(s). Even the phonemes themselves are ideas, for they remain the same regardless of how many times they are repeated, the frequency range of the speaker's voice, or the position of the allophone in the vocal series. The phoneme /d/ in "dream" is the same phoneme regardless of whether spoken by a child or an adult, in a poem, song or narrative, or repeated to oneself sub-vocally. The /d/ phoneme, as well as the word "dream" are sound images. They are redundant to both speaker and auditor. Indeed, they operate below the level of awareness in everyday natural discourse, for, while speaking, *we are aware of expressing ideas*, and while listening, *we are aware of meaning*. The apperception of the auditory sound images and evoked meanings occurs so rapidly that they appear to the "natural" (pre-phenomenological) mind as simultaneous. We do not have to spend any time figuring out what the words mean—the meaning is just there, sound imagery and concepts melding seamlessly and automatically.

Yet in most communications the distinct words are not islands, but steppingstones that when taken together lead to more complex meanings—the meanings encoded by sentences and texts. Just as the significance of a given object of normal sensory experience is influenced by the object's surround, relations, and horizon (see Chapter 3), so too is the meaning evoked by each word in an utterance influenced by all the other words in, say, a sentence—evoking idea within idea and so forth eventually communicating a narrative. Within the narrative there are clumps of meaning that, when written down, may result in distinct paragraphs, each with its own essential idea. Thus, language in both written and spoken mode depends upon many of the selfsame essential structures as does my experience of my coffee cup.

THE CRISIS OF EXPANDING CONSCIOUSNESS

All of which brings us back to Deacon's intriguing question, why don't other animals have language (see Bouchard 2013: 7 on the same question)? As we have seen, animals very likely do not communicate to change each other's minds, but rather to manipulate and inform other group member's experiences and behaviors (see Dawkins and Krebs 1978; but cf. Scarantino 2013). The possibility of changing other's minds most likely had to await the evolution of hominin communication in service to a very palpable crisis that arose along the phylogenetic path to hominization. That crisis—let us call it *the crisis of expanding consciousness* (or henceforth *the crisis*)—emerged when the hominin brain, especially the prefrontal cortex, first showed the capacity for modeling the environing world in spacetime beyond the limits of any one individual's perceptual field.[46] As psycholinguist Brian MacWhinney (2002: 233) notes: "Language is a unique hallmark of the human species. Although many species can communicate about things that are physically present, only humans can use communication to construct a full narrative characterization of events occurring outside the here and now." But, as MacWhinney also argues, how and when the watershed occurred is nearly impossible to determine, and, considering we are speaking about 6 million years of hominin evolution, the watershed era may well have spanned hundreds of thousands of years, and perhaps was subject to fits and starts. In a very real sense, it is wrongheaded to think about this issue as simply being a before and after the emergence of full-blown human language. There no doubt occurred many kinds of language competence in the interim between pre-crisis times and modern human systems of communication.

My own suspicion, shared with Merlin Donald (1991, 2003), is that the emergence of language occurred gradually until it accelerated during the era of *Homo erectus* variations. Keep in mind that populations of *Homo erectus* were alive as recently as 108,000 years ago—contemporaneous with Neanderthal, archaic and early modern humans, *with whom they interbred*. The fossil record suggests that the rapid allometric increase in brain to body size in hominin phylogenesis became evident after about 2 million years ago to something like 200,000 years ago with early modern humans (Dunbar 2016: 20-22).

I have never been persuaded that fossil remains tell us very much directly about the evolution of language, or anything whatever about the complexification of physiological properties of human neurons, or modified, more complex synaptic development so crucial to human cognition and communication (Kolk and Rakic 2022).[47] Many distinctions linked to the presence of speech (but not necessarily language) are tenuous at best (e.g., evidence of "control" of vocalizations), and downright silly at worst. One of the silliest ideas that have been floated, and still pops up from time to time, was linking the structure of the voice box to the presence or absence of language, especially with regards

---

[46] Gene d'Aquili and I originally called this crisis (very clumsily I confess) the "cognitive extension of prehension" (Laughlin and d'Aquili 1974: Chap. 4).

[47] For the difficulties in this regard, see Dunbar (2016: 235-244).

to Neanderthals. No one has ever argued that the range of vocal sounds that a hominin could produce had anything to do with the ability to express ideas via vocalizations, much less gestures. No one believes that if *Homo erectus*, or even *Homo habilis* for that matter, had some form of spoken language it would sound the same as human speech today, or have anything like the range of vocal sounds. Derek Bickerton (1990) suggests that we call the language that *Homo erectus* might have spoken a *protolanguage*. This has value to us if only to emphasize that early hominin speech would have been different than that spoken by humans today. Meanwhile, what is continually missed in the myriad discussions of the evolution of language is what happened in human phylogenesis that was so unique and that necessitated the expression of ideas and images among members of a hominin social group.

Many authorities have argued that language is a biproduct of cultural invention (see Bouchard 2013: Chap. 1 for a summary). I reject these theories for several reasons. One reason is that the notion that we are the only animal with "culture" (read social learning) is false. Many animals exhibit culturally transmitted traits (see Hill 2009, Laland and Galef 2009, McGrew 2010). Another reason is that neither "culture" nor language is a necessary or sufficient condition for the other. As Pinker (1994, 1995), Pinker and Bloom (1990) and Pinker and Jackendoff (2005) have shown, single feature explanations for the emergence of language—for instance, "recursion," the ability to embed ideas within ideas—will not wash in light of neuroscientific evidence for the complex functions involved in mediating language, especially the universal regularities of grammar. I would argue, along with Steven Pinker *et al.*, that evolution of language took a very long time to evolve, including the time it took to build requisite cognits and to extensively lateralize hemispheric functions with respect to concept/ grammar construction and the speech faculty. In other words, both social learning and social communication co-evolved in our species because of the crisis, both imposing strictures on how divergent group member cognized worlds could become while still allowing sociality, social cohesion, and social adaptive strategies. Keep in mind however, just as with different media of communication, prelinguistic hominin brains were already lateralized with respect to functions to some extent, and during the course of enhanced encephalization, hemispheric functional asymmetries continued to accelerate (Cozolino 2014: 18-21, Holloway and De La Costelareymondie 1982, Rilling and Insel 1999).

What the endocast data do tell us a lot about is the profoundly crucial development of the prefrontal cortex of the hominin brain, for this unique change is so completely linked to what it is to be human, particularly the potentially catastrophic changes that brought about the crisis (Schmidt and Polleux 2022). The emergence of a large prefrontal cortex is the single greatest morphological change marking human evolution. The prefrontal lobes constitute something like 29% of the total cortex in modern humans, compared with 17% for Chimps, 11.5% in gibbons and macaques, 8.5% for lemurs, 7% for dogs and 3.5% for cats (Fuster 2015: 9-10). Alas, we cannot determine an exact percentage of prefrontal cortical processes from studying the fossil remains of extinct hominins. As you probably know, the only evidence we have with respect to hominin neurophysiological evolution comes from natural and experimental endocasts of the inside of fossil skulls. Over time, the picture of early hominin evolution has just gotten more complex and uncertain as one fossil discovery after the other is published (see Li 2002). Endocasts are not molds of the brain, but rather only give us information about the inner surface of the skulls, and very little about the reorganization of neural structures below the surface of the cortex over the course of phylogenesis. Yet endocasts do tell us something about the cortical surface structures, especially with respect to speech (Holloway 1981, 1983a, 1983b, 2015).

In any event, the crisis of expanding consciousness arose during some as yet undatable watershed era when hominin brains with rapidly expanding prefrontal lobes and auxiliary structures became capable of constructing cognized worlds that significantly exceeded any one individual's perceptual field, both in time and space, thus creating the conditions for potential discontinuity among the cognized worlds of group members and jeopardizing the powerful adaptive advantages of sociality and social action. Why? Because the maintenance of social cohesion and strategies—including the synergistic effects of diverse personality types among social animals (Page 2007)—depends upon members of the group operating from more or less the same mental script, more or less the same worldview, more or less the same interpretation of events and contingencies (see especially Patočka 2016: 94, Tomasello

2008). The crisis would have increased the desynchronization among member's cognized worlds—knowledge about extended spatial mapping and knowledge about future happenings (plans, goals, anticipations).

Husserl anticipated the evolutionary impact of the crisis when he wrote:

> Without the possibility of external, enduring marks of reference …as supports for our memory, without the possibility of symbolic representations serving in the place of authentic representations that are more abstract or too difficult to keep distinct and to operate with (or, indeed, serving in place of representations that *as* authentic are altogether denied to us), there would simply be no higher mental life—much less, then, science. *Symbols are the great natural instrument by which the limits of our psychical life, originally so narrow, are broken through, and by which the essential imperfections of our intellect are, at least to a certain degree, rendered harmless.* Through characteristic detours, sparing of higher thought, they enable the human mind to accomplish things which directly, in the workings of authentic knowing, it could never bring about. *Symbols serve the economy of mental achievement as tools and machines do the economy of mechanical achievement.* (Husserl 1994: 29; emphasis added)

As desynchronization of views increased, there would have been a concomitant increase in the selection in favor of groups whose members' brains were capable of intersubjective synchronization via some kind of information sharing (by way of gestures, mimicry, enactment, rituals, iconography, vocalizations). By "information" I do not refer to the modern technological sense of the term.[48] When I refer to "information" it is in the older commonsense meaning of the term: To inform something is to literally *in*-form it—change its internal

---

[48] The confusion in science about what "information" means arose in part because a renowned scientist usurped the commonsense notion of information for very specific technological purposes. In his now famous 1948 article, "The Mathematical Theory of Communication" (reprinted in Shannon and Weaver 1963), Claude E. Shannon, then a Bell Laboratories scientist, defined information in a very special mathematical way and thereby changed the use of the term in many scientific circles from a biological interpretation to a mathematical and technical meaning.

organization. When that something is a brain, then to inform the brain means to change its internal neural organization:

> [...]I would like to use the word information, but in its more original etymological sense of *in-formare*, to form within [...]. We can define in-formation as the admissible symbolic descriptions of the cognitive domains of an autonomous system. We shall always write it with the hyphen to convey the differences of this view from that of information in the computer gestalt. (Varela 1979: 266)

In the old sense of the term, a signal or sign need not "contain" any information. It need only in-form the receiving brain—the sign literally *in*-forms the recipient. For one brain to intentionally inform another brain, the informing brain must be able to communicate with the informed brain, and the informed brain must change the organization of its own specific neural networks, however slightly or dramatically (Laughlin and Throop 2003). While social learning is commonplace among social animals, human social learning *evolved to produce systems of teaching*, or as Csibra and Gergely (2006, 2011) term them, systems of *natural pedagogy*—social learning in which the "teacher" is concerned with and gives feedback for the "pupil's" responses. Such institutions seem to be an adaptation in those cases where knowledge is "obscure," as in tool-using skills and hunting strategies. Ethnographically speaking, it would seem that the simpler the society, the less pedagogical learning occurs (Hewlett *et al.* 2011).

In the special case of one brain "teaching" or "training" (neurophysiologically *en*-training) another brain, significant changes will occur in the recipient's neural structures influencing their viewpoint on things. Among modern humans, training for skills and techniques, change in social status, knowledge, understanding, behaviors, etc., is fundamental to conditioning for "professionalism" in myriad institutions like the military, police, scouting, accounting, plumbing, nursing, and what have you. Our K-12 schools are institutions for in-forming the brains of future adults in a technocratic situation where extreme control over perception and learning is required. Traditional societies have for centuries ritualized life-crisis events to radically transform the brains of their youth, e.g., African "bush schools" (Murphy 1980).

The social bonding and intersubjective informing of communication was clear to Husserl. In *Ideas II* he wrote:

> Now, however, the task is to gather up into unity all the social Objectivities (with the limit case of the ideally possible isolated individual [e.g., a hermit, survivor cast alone upon an island]) that are in communication with one another. It should be noted here that the *idea of communication* obviously extends from the single personal subject *even to the social* associations of subjects, which, for their part, present personal unities of a higher level. All such unities, as far as their communication extends, a communication produced factually or one yet to be produced in accord with their own indeterminate open horizon, do not constitute merely a *collection* of social subjectivities, but instead they coalesce into a social subjectivity inwardly organized to a greater or lesser degree, which has its common opposite pole in a surrounding world, or an external world, i.e., in a world which is *for* it. (Husserl 1989[1952]:206)

Thus, for Husserl, human beings require communication as a necessary condition for establishing and maintaining the social cohesion requisite for group adaptation to the environing world. The increasing need for communication of sufficient complexity to maintain social solidarity during crisis times would have been significantly threatening enough to alter natural selection within the niches occupied by hunting and foraging hominins. Selection for increased intersubjective sharing of information would have been in favor of those symbolic mechanisms that already performed informative functions, including mimicry in social learning, enforcing status differences, ritual enactments, vocal utterances, facial and body language, music and dance, and gestural systems—what some authorities like to bundle under the extremely fuzzy umbrella term *pre-language* (Givón and Malle 2002). On my account, the hominin stages prior to accelerated selection for more complex communication, including language, was not a "pre-language" period in which neural and other physical structures were incapable of communication, but rather there simply was no selective pressure to do so despite the fact that those early hominins were cognitively advanced animals (see Gillespie-Lynch *et al.* 2014).

In my opinion, after the point at which the crisis began to threaten sociality in hominin species (whatever species they may have been), Terrence Deacon (1997) is correct in suggesting that brain and language came to evolve in tandem. It is important to emphasize that the expansion and complexification of the prefrontal lobes produced the crisis, but it also participated in a very central way in the solution to the evolutionary conundrum, for the dorsolateral prefrontal cortex took up the task of mediating complex issues involving language and speech. The dorsolateral prefrontal cortex:

> … seems to be engaged in those aspects of language processing that exceed simple, rule-based, and highly automatized mechanisms of phonological, syntactic, and lexical–semantic processing. Such aspects come into play in case of certain stylistic features and in complex situations when language processing approaches its limits, for example, in case of ambiguity, novel, or nonliteral meanings, or garden path structures, when extra-linguistic cues have to be integrated, or when a speaker has to change into a different language. Thereby, the DLPFC seems to be important for controlling temporary functional connectivity patterns, for cognitive switching, and also for acting as part of an emergency brake if the ongoing process of language communication approaches a "dead end." (Hertrich *et al.* 2021: 1)

Furthermore, areas of the prefrontal cortex are linked to social cooperation and establishing group norms. Research has revealed:

> …a medial prefrontal network common to nonhuman primates and humans supporting a foundational process in cooperative decision-making: valuing outcomes for oneself and others. This medial prefrontal network interacts with lateral prefrontal areas that are thought to represent cooperative norms and modulate value representations to guide behavior appropriate to the local social context. …[W]e propose that more recently evolved anterior regions of prefrontal cortex play a role in arbitrating

between cooperative norms across social contexts... . (Zoh, Chang and Crockett 2022: 1)

In addition, as neuroscientist Michael Arbib (2012) has shown, multiple features of brain organization would have come into play, including those intersubjective cognits containing mirror neuron systems (see Chapter 4) that mediate imitation, pantomime, and other uses of motility to reflect the behavior of others. Arbib argues that the pressures propelling selection for complex communication were built "atop" the systems already in place, especially those processes incorporating mirror neurons (Arbib 2012: 173; see also Cozolino 2014: 208-210). In other words, the existence among primates of mirror neuron systems might be a necessary condition for the evolution of language—as they certainly are for empathy (see Chapter 4)—but the presence of these systems certainly is not a sufficient condition for language (monkeys and apes also have mirror neuron systems). I am suggesting that both the necessary and sufficient condition for intense selective pressure is the crisis of expanding consciousness caused by the evolution of the cortex, especially the prefrontal cortex and its modelling and executive/planning/time-binding functions.

Hominins at the time of the crisis did not have to "invent" a new system of perception at the essential level to communicate, for it was already onboard and functioning in everyday perception. Take for example the "alarm call" utterances made by Vervet monkeys mentioned before which we know are predator-specific (Seyfarth, Cheney and Marler 1990, 2003). One vocalization signifies a leopard is in the area, another signifies an eagle, and a third signifies a python. The monkeys are conditioned to respond to each call differently. For adults, the meaning of each call is clear, but infants are very fuzzy in their use of the calls, giving the leopard call for other mammals, the eagle call for different kinds of bird, and the python call for other snake-like objects. As the infant grows, it learns to be specific with its utterances. Each utterance is an idea communicated by way of biogenetically inherited essential structures, sound images penetrating to the appropriate idea and response pattern in all adult members of the troop.

It is crucial for us to realize that "syntax" is a word we generally reserve to refer to the formal temporal structure of spoken and written language, but something like syntax is the case with all intentional acts, whether involving communication or not. Indeed, I concur with Thomas Schoenemann (1999) who argues that what most of us call "syntax" is an emergent property of extremely complex semantics. In other words, the complexity of expression increased to compensate for the desynchronization of worldviews, and as more and more complexity in the expression of ideas became selected for, logical relations already present in cognition began to apply in constituting expressions of reason, goals, and purpose. These structures of relationship even obtain for objects in pure perception which are embedded in relationships with other objects, relations, and intuitive meanings (see Chapter 3). What the hominin communication revolution eventually evolved to do is to create very complex ideas that were communicable among conspecifics through temporally structured communicative acts (McNeill 2012: 76-95). Here we encounter one of those apparent paradoxes that inhabits every form of communication: While a complex idea may occur spontaneously and in toto in the mind (a piece of music, a story, an explanation, a command, a judgement, a plan, etc.), it takes time to communicate the complex idea to others. As Levi-Strauss pointed out somewhere, myths, like symphonies, are *essentially atemporal in their essential structure, but take time to unfold in action.*

We evolved to create for Others an imaginary world made up of empty ideas. Selective pressure would be towards communication that allowed one group member to "give an account" and "make sense" of adventures and explorations for which their auditors had not been present.

> When we say that a person is able to "give an account" of his mental processes we mean by this that he is able to communicate them to other people by means of "symbols," that is by actions which, when perceived by other people, will occupy in their mental order a position analogous to that which they occupy in his own; and which, in consequence, will have for those other persons a meaning similar to that which it possesses for him. (Hayek 2014[1952]: 135)

I may have been someplace you have not been and communicate sufficient information about that place that it becomes part of your cognized world. If I were a traditional hunter-gatherer, freshly returned with my fellow hunters bearing meat, I may well be called upon with my fellows to enact the hunt in celebration of our success. Thus, we are able to share aspects of the hunt with the non-hunters and children of the group so that to a very significant degree we all share the experience vicariously. Or in another context I may create a poem or song commemorating our great hunt, again sharing information with those who have not been there. My auditors now have within their store of lore ideal events replete with animals and places and conditions they did not share in the reality of direct sensuous perception. It is not clear whether there are any other animals that can do this, and almost certainly no primates do so in the wild.

During some period over the duration of the crisis, our ancestors began to communicate ideas that did not depend upon simultaneous subjective perception—ideas that transcended immediate experience and operated as correctives to other group members' experiences, views, interpretations, and actions. Husserl was remarkably tuned-in to the importance of this evolutionary complexification of consciousness:

> Man's superiority lies in his intelligence. He is not solely a being who brings perception and experience to bear on external situations: *he also thinks, employs concepts, to overcome the narrow limits of his intuition.* Through conceptual knowledge he penetrates to rigorous causal laws, which permit him to foresee the course of future phenomena, to reconstruct the course of past phenomena, to calculate the possible reactions of environing things in advance, and to dominate them practically, and all this to a vastly greater extent, and with vastly more confidence, than could otherwise be possible. (Husserl 1970 [1900-01] I: 125; emphasis added)[49]

Another way to say this is that the watershed was passed when one group member could share experiences vicariously by whatever communicative medium.

---

[49] Husserl is describing here what Jean Piaget termed "concrete operational thought" (see Piaget and Inhelder 2013).

Basically, from a phenomenological perspective, what is being sought in psychological research is the phenomenal world or the experiential world of the participant. Unfortunately, there is no direct access to this world, so it has to be accessed indirectly through some form of expression. There are many forms of expression, from concrete behavior to artistic, and each has its own set of peculiar difficulties with respect to the assessment of the participant's experiential world. Of course, one of the major forms of expression is language, and it holds a privileged, but not exclusive, place with respect to the determination of the world of the other. We often listen to the stories people tell us when they have had experiences that we have not. We often read travelogues or other accounts of travel in order to get a sense of places to which we have not been. These narratives extend our own experience by giving us insight into what others have experienced or, in other words, we learn something about the experiential world of the other as well as something about the world that was experienced by the other. (Giorgi 2009: 107)

Remember what we have learned from Husserl: *Ideas are empty*. Moreover, ideas are as empty for a macaque monkey or a dolphin as for a human. The hominin brain was already wired to operate on empty ideas instantiated here and there in experience long before natural language emerged. We still do this all the time and think nothing of it. We can have enjoyable conversations about hobbits, unicorns, xenomorphs, hyperdrives, superheroes, and nanobot swarms even though we have never encountered these classes of "objects" in direct experience. And of course—of crucial importance—*we can communicate about ideas that have no adaptive significance to us, our group, or species at all.* This was not the case among earlier hominins who gradually learned to communicate more complexly about ideas, but those ideas derived originally from direct experience of their environing world. These communicating hominins were simultaneously able to remain rooted in the perceptual world—their niche-relevant experiences—and maintain the affordability of social action in respect to that world. Much later, members of the *Homo* genus could formulate and communicate ideas, imaginary experiences, dreams, plans, etc. that had neutral impact on fitness. They could reason as individuals and as groups and the results of their reasonings could be dead wrong, and still not effect adaptational relations with the real world (Husserl 1989[1952]: 233). Individuals and groups can be motivated by all sorts of concerns, drives, desires, motivations, and so forth without necessarily hampering group fitness.

PRAGMATICS AND AGENCY

Thus, placing language within the context of evolutionary processes and selective pressures, it is necessary to focus upon the pragmatic aspects of communication, and especially speech acts. As John L. Austin (1975, 1979) shows in his analysis of how language is actually used by people, speech acts are a form of praxis. *Language gets things done.* Remember, what brought about the crisis in the first place was the rapid evolution of the prefrontal lobes of the brain. Among other things, the prefrontal lobes as they became larger and more complex mediated planning ever further out into the future, and further away from immediate sensory experience. Potentially, this development made possible desynchronization of the plans of individual group members, and of the comprehension of the environing world among them. As we have mentioned above, babies today spend their early life engaged with what arises and passes away in their sensoria, and only later begin to focus their attention on the guidance of peers and adults. This shift in ontogenesis brings language more fully into the process of social learning. As Alessandro Duranti (2009) notes, Husserl demonstrated the role of speech in *modifying* the attention, intention, and social salience of interpretation in intersubjective encounters (Husserl 1982[1913]: 219). By underscoring the pragmatic functions of speech, Husserl influenced Pierre Bourdieu for whom speech as praxis became vital for his theory of habitus (Atkinson 2018, Bourdieu 1977, Throop and Murphy 2002).

Back in the era of the crisis and the on-going selection in favor of more complex cortical structures, the impact of more complex communication upon sociality would have been profound. Communication carried with it the potential for modification of individual natural attitudes (including "cultural" knowledge) toward a shared worldview. The sharing was not limited to the truing functions of the primordial sensory given—a function operating in all social animals—but also included the products of higher cortical processes mediating ideas, maps, meanings, plans, beliefs, and feedback loops reinforcing patterns of habitus.

> We speak of modifications here just in so far as every reflexion has its essential origin in changes of standpoint, whereby a given experience or unreflective experience-datum undergoes a certain transformation—into the mode, that is, of reflective consciousness (consciousness of which we are aware). The given experience can itself already possess the character of a reflective consciousness of something, in which case the modification is of a higher grade; but we are thrown back at last on absolutely irreflective experiences and the real (*reellen*) or intentional data implicit in them (*Dabilien*). *Every* experience can now be translated in accordance with essential laws into reflective modifications, and along different directions which we shall learn to know more accurately still. (Husserl 1982[1913]: 219)

All you need do to exemplify the change that can occur in experience with reflection is to become aware of your awareness of an object. You "wake-up" to the process of experiencing the object, and in so doing, you alter the organization of noetic-noematic interplay. The act of being aware of the object becomes the object. And the fact that I, with the use of linguistic signs laboriously typed by me upon this page, can alter your experience in a direction I intend illustrates the power of signs, and especially linguistic signs, to influence your view, if only for a moment. It is this power through the use of language and other forms of communication to modify your view that made all the difference back in crisis times. Imagine if you will, we are sitting around the campfire (as far as we know now, *Homo erectus* domesticated fire) munching upon skewers of smoked mammoth haunch and I suggest that our best bet tomorrow is to hunt inland again for game where we found them last week. In response, you describe seeing turtles aplenty on the beach just this morning. So, we all decide to go turtle hunting tomorrow. This scene is reminiscent of a worker bee doing a waggle dance in the hive letting everybody know where to fly for pollen. Same function, different social creature.

The power of signs to modify consciousness in a social setting cannot be overstressed (see Duranti 2009). With but a simple utterance, one group member can bring the certainty of another's belief into question by reporting anomalous experiences heretofore not shared with the Other or the group. Not only are all group members' views trued by the lifeworld they all share and inhabit, but experiences vicariously shared with someone may modify their judgment as to the veridicality of their belief (Husserl 1982[1913]: 304-306). Back in crisis times, this synchronization of group members' views (concepts, ideas, feelings, attitudes, etc.) through communication gradually evolved into "culture" of the complex sort that has proven advantageous to humans over the past 200,000 years or more. It is doubtful for instance that at the time of the crisis hominins could not be said to hold "cultural belief systems" or worldviews in the sense of a socially learned system of ideas about the environing world divorced from perception. Certainly, the anthropoid apes of today do not exhibit belief systems, although there are data suggesting apes operate upon a rudimentary intersubjective understanding of true and false views (Andrews 2018, Buttelmann *et al.* 2017). As with most animals, knowledge is tied closely to immediate perceptual experience and the lifeworld.

ON ADAPTIVELY EXTRANEOUS BELIEFS

Eventually, over thousands of generations, hominins evolved a communication system so rich in information sharing that they could individually entertain a worldview partially divorced from direct experience, and the truing influence of the lifeworld. Today we can play with ideas so distant from everyday moment-by-moment direct experience that the ideas form a world of their own, existing solely in the minds of believers. We can contemplate mathematical constants like π, geometric concepts like the "perfect circle," invisible cosmic categories like "dark matter," the expanding universe, the Big Bang, possible historical developments like the Mother Tongue, the "bicameral mind," and ancient Atlantis, imagined creatures like sandworms, orcs, xenomorphs, and dragons, and eschatological possibilities like eugenics, Dyson Spheres, End Times, and happy hunting grounds of various configurations. During a crucial period of time, sometime after the crisis began, hominins became able to conceive of, and believe in the reality of, objects, events, scenarios, domains, otherworlds, etc. that are barely, if at all, instantiated in experience. Yet as outlandish and "unrealistic" as such belief systems might have become in ages past, *as long as they did not interfere with physical adaptation, no selective pressures would have come into play to alter the course of brainmind evolution* (Laughlin and d'Aquili 1974: 90-98). Henceforth when I wish to refer to this advanced cognitive capacity of hominins, I will refer to *adaptively extraneous beliefs* (AEB).

AEB include the various kinds of unreal notions and objects I just listed above. Indeed, Husserl's method of eidetic free variation is really an exercise in playing within the domain of AEB. As we saw earlier, free variation releases the inherent limitations imposed by the lifeworld on the kinds of things we can imagine and which either fall within intuited classes in principle, or range outside those categories (as with our playing with the paperclip). Although technically free variation is a method for exploring the limits of universality and invariance of essential structures and ideas, the method also invites creativity and new possibilities, and can potentially result in discoveries that prove advantageous or aesthetically pleasing.

The capacity to formulate ideas evolved to render patterns in the sensuous given as meaningful. But one of the consequences of this neural faculty was that ideas, whether associated with sensuousness or simply empty can become the grounds for beliefs within the natural attitude of the individual and even elements in the group's worldview (Deeley 2004). Peer group pressures can reinforce beliefs that are actually contrary to reality as potentially trued by sensuous intuition. Not only that, but social forces can cause individuals to attend only those sensuous experiences that instantiate the belief, and disattend those that are anomalous. As any student of political science knows, the most common exercise of political power is the control of perception (see Powers 2005). The social mechanisms for this kind of control are to be found in the political application of rituals such as ancestor worship, political rallies, church services, and military ceremonies.

Beliefs that are contrary to reality can infect masses of people. Marxists have emphasized this power of political movements and ideologies over the minds of the masses, a phenomenon Friedrich Engles called *false consciousness* (Lukács 1967). False consciousness refers to beliefs held by people which in fact cause them to lose political power and influence—attitudes that work against their own self-interest. This is the role of propaganda in which a political figure or group spins information about events that is both false and held to be true by the masses. As I am writing this, millions of people have been persuaded that Donald Trump won the 2020 presidential election in the United States when all the empirical evidence proves that he lost. This is false consciousness in action and is contrary, according to Husserl, to the values and processes that orient science toward truth grounded solely in the primordial sensuous given (see Husserl 1970[1936]: 190, 2002[1910]). Husserl's understanding of "culture" in the form of different worldviews is antithetical to extreme relativist accounts that treat scientific theories as just another form of worldview. For Husserl, worldviews are a kind of religious faith held by individuals that orient them within their personal streams of consciousness and social conditions (Husserl 1970[1936]: Appendix IX). As such worldviews are incommensurable while science and its theories are applicable by all people. Hindus and Christians, Māori and Bantus may hold different worldviews, but are equally capable of producing commensurate science. As Husserl showed, however, knowledge from the primordial sensuous given is *apodictic*; that is, cannot be false (Husserl 1982[1913]: §6).

SUMMARY AND SEGUE

Husserl phenomenologically distinguished between the indicative function and the expressive function of signs. The finger pointing at the moon is indicative while the finger twirling in circles as ones temple expresses mental derangement. Language is a system of signs strung into packages of meaning that express ideas. His concern was entirely about natural language as an expressive act that can be studied from within the phenomenological attitude just as can any other object of consciousness. Words are subsumed within longer expressions in an organic fashion which, while taking time to unfold in reality, is essentially atemporal in structure and monadic as narrative.

Using Husserl's methods, we unearthed the possible mechanisms by which we can answer Terrence Deacon's question, why language in humans and no other animals. We saw that as the human brain became cortically more complex, it became able to develop ideas and systems of ideas in the individual brain that exceeded reality as sensually perceived. This ability set the stage for a crisis of expanding consciousness leading to deficits in sociality and resulting in selection for more and more complex communication. This probably occurred during *Homo erectus'* era, but there is yet no way to know for sure. But clearly, whenever the crisis arose, it would have increased the sharing of experiences and knowledge which would have led to a more *Homo* kind of "cultural" efflorescence, characterized by a greater adaptive reliance upon socially controlled learning and reinforcement of pro-social attitudes and the learning of social strategies. The significance of this shift cannot be over-emphasized. Nor can the emphasis Husserl placed upon how knowing and knowledge works.

CHAPTER EIGHT

Knowing

*If we may trust our arguments, we must not only draw a general
distinction between the perceptual and the significant element in the
statement of perception; we must also locate no part of the meaning in the
percept itself. The percept, which presents the object, and the statement
which, by way of the judgement (or by the thought-act inwoven into the
unity of the judgement) thinks and expresses it, must be rigorously kept
apart, even though, in the case of the perceptual judgment now being
considered [proper names], they stand to each other in the most intimate
relation of mutual coincidence, or in the unity of fulfillment.*

– Husserl (1970 [1900-01], II: 199)

*Suppose an individual actually knew in detail how his or her brain
works. Would we expect that person to abandon his or her reactions to
others in terms of propositional attitudes—beliefs, desires, and intentions?
I think not. But knowledge of the workings of the brain might at least give
that person the ability to reject preposterous assumptions and cant.*

– Gerald M. Edelman (2006: 151-152)

There exists a natural compatibility between Husserlian phenomenology and the anthropology of knowledge. Anthropology has
been interested in what the planet's peoples know and how they
come to know since the initial work of Bastian whose methodology was
to collect as much data about how different peoples make sense of the
world, and then deduce patterns of similarity between them to get at
species-wide *Elementargedanken* or "elementary ideas" (see Chapter 1).
Although Bastian's program was not followed for reasons I have already
outlined, ethnological concern for what and how peoples know has
continued to the present day (see Barth 2002, Cohen 2010, Crick 1982,
Harris 2007). A typical anthropological analysis of a culture's knowl-

edge system delves into its system(s) of belief (what the people know, their worldview, or their *ethno-ontology*) and their *ethno-epistemology* (how a people come to know; see Laughlin 2013a, Maffie 1995, 2005, Mizumoto, Ganeri and Goddard 2020). Anthropology thus mirrors a classic distinction used in philosophy between ontology and epistemology. But as ethnography shows us, the crispness of logical categories like these tend to offer poor models of *ethno-logic* on the ground among different peoples (Laughlin 1993, Hamill 1990).

I have discussed Husserl's approach to knowledge, especially intuitive knowledge, in previous chapters, but given that his program was always about laying the foundations of knowledge in the primordial intuitive sense, it would behoove us to explore his discoveries about knowing, layering of meaning, and systems of knowledge in more detail.[50] As Husserl set down in *Logical Investigations I*:

> Pure phenomenology represents a field of neutral researches, in which several sciences have their roots. It is, on the one hand, ancillary to psychology conceived as an empirical science. Proceeding in purely intuitive fashion, it analyses and describes in their essential generality—in the specific guise of a phenomenology of thought and knowledge—the experiences of presentation, judgement and knowledge, experiences which, treated as classes of real events in the natural context of zoological reality, receive a scientific probing at the hands of empirical psychology. *Phenomenology, on the other hand, lays bare the "sources" from which the basic concepts and ideal laws of pure logic "flow,"* and back to which they must once more be traced, so as to give them all the "clearness and distinctness" needed for an understanding, and for an epistemological critique, of pure logic. (Husserl 1970 [1900-01], I: 166; emphasis added)

In short, Husserl wished to track the roots of knowing back to "the things themselves"—as we saw in Chapter 3, pure phenomenology

---

[50] If you wish to read more about Husserl's phenomenology of *knowledge*, see Husserl 1970 [1900-01] II, 1982[1913]: Section 4, 1999, 1970 [1900-01] II: 226-249, 2008[1906-1907], 2019[1917/18]; see also Kohak 1978: Chap. 5, Levinas 1995, Moran 2000, 2005.

involves a disciplined meditation upon what presents before our eyes in the intentional act. "Logical concepts, as valid thought-unities, must have their origin in intuition: they must arise out of an ideational intuition founded in certain experiences, and must admit of indefinite reconfirmation, and of recognition of their self-identity, on the reperformance of such abstraction" (Husserl 1970 [1900-01], I: 168).

Thus understood, combining the pure phenomenology of knowing with neurocognitive research should be fundamental to an ethnological comprehension of the role played by knowing (including logic, reason, thinking, and communication of knowledge, as well as intuition) grounded within the lifeworld and in constructing personal and cultural knowledge systems. Simply put, Husserl notes, koan-like, "If I call this intuited object a 'watch', I complete, in naming it, an act of thought and knowledge, but I know my watch, and not my knowledge" (Husserl 1970 [1900-01], II: 323). If you grasp this distinction in your experience, you have gone a long way toward understanding Husserl's view of knowing.

HUSSERL'S PHENOMENOLOGY OF KNOWING

For Husserl, *knowing* (Ger.: *Erkennen*) is a subjective process, and all forms of knowing have their roots in subjectivity, in individual lived experience. Knowledge obtained in direct experience comes before higher forms of knowing, levels he termed "objective" and "theoretical." Knowledge in the common objective sense is a product of subjective knowing—an "achievement" of subjectivity (Husserl 1970 [1900-01], I, Prol.: §62). In short, perception itself is the primal way of knowing both self and environing world. Higher level theoretical knowledge derives from a turning in the seat of consciousness towards the objective or theoretical attitude, a shift in awareness that one can sense, recognize, and describe.

> The remaining lived experiences, e.g., feeling-experiences, lived experiences of this or that special kind, are indeed lived; as intentional lived experiences they also are constituting; they constitute new *objective strata* for the object in question, but ones

in relation to which the subject is not in the theoretical attitude, and thus they do not constitute the respective theoretically meant and judgmentally determined object as such (or help determine this object in a theoretical function). It is only by means of a *shift* of the theoretical regard, a change of theoretical interest, that they emerge out of the phase of *pre*-theoretical constitution into the theoretical; the new strata of sense enter into the framework of theoretical sense, and a new object, i.e., one intended in a new and more proper sense, is the Object of the grasping and theoretical determination in new theoretical acts. The total intention of consciousness is there with an essentially changed one, and the acts responsible for the giving of *other* meanings have also experienced a phenomenological modification. To what extent this is a necessary state of affairs is evident from the fact that *even the theoretical acts*, by means of which the pure subject relates to a given Object delimited by a constitutive sense (e.g., an Object of nature), no matter how they occur as subjectivating, attributing, collecting, relativizing, and other acts, *at once also exercise a constituting function*. "Categorical" objectivities thus are constituted (in a quite definite sense; objectivities of thought), which, however, for their part, first become *theoretical Objects* precisely when the theoretical subject intentionally focuses on these new objectives (i.e., above all, on states of affairs, collections, etc.) and so performs new acts which grasp them in their being and determine them theoretically; thus, these acts are subject-acts, predicate-acts, etc., of a higher level. (Husserl 1989[1952]: 6-7)

Recognizing that all knowledge is either presented a priori within the structure of the intentional act, or is "constituted" (i.e., cognitively constructed) within the noema by way of this shift in attitude.

Knowledge, as [Husserl] always insists [...] is an accomplishment of subjectivity; or, to put it another way, objectivity is an accomplishment of subjectivity. His unique insight is that science comprises not just a set of true   propositions about a domain of objects; it is also a set of *achievements, accomplishments*, or *performances* [...] of knowing subjects, "a unity of acts of thinking, of thought-dispositions" [...]. Every item of knowledge is gained, achieved, and preserved in specific acts of judgmental contribution of subjectivity without "psychologizing" it. (Moran 2005: 105)

Within the intentional act a modification occurs in the intentions of the pure ego from mere perception of the primordial object accompanied by intuitive insights to an attitude of theoretical interest. Let us suppose that you are in a museum and are standing in front of a painting by Jackson Pollock. You experience pleasure at the flow of colors, curving lines, and 3D textures as well as the overall composition. Then you become interested in just how and which order the artist went about depositing layers of paint splashes and rivulets and perhaps stubbed-out cigarette butts, bits of paper, etc., and then you begin to analyze how Pollock's approach to abstraction differs or is similar to other abstract expressionists like de Kooning, Rothko, and Motherwell. Then perhaps you think about where Pollock's "action" painting fits in with the overall abstract expressionist movement.

What I have just described is how your stream of consciousness is modified by the interest of the subject and additions to the noemata— you as pure ego and your intentions—shifting from appreciation of, say, the aesthetic moment to theoretical interests related to the object. You experience a change from what Husserl would call the aesthetic attitude to a theoretical one. This is the basic process by which the primordial sensory given participates as an Object (capital "O" object in Husserl's texts) within theoretical judgments and formulations at a higher cognitive level. Mind you, the process is reversable. We might have been motivated out of theoretical questions and uncertainties to visit the museum to see this particular Pollock masterpiece, and while observing the piece we may experience rapture even while seeking information relevant to our theoretical interests (Husserl 1989[1952]: 9).

If you happen to be a Sherlock Holmes fan, you will instantly recognize the master's dictum, "you see, but you do not observe. The distinction is clear."[51] It is this kind of distinction that Husserl uses to show how perception can become data (Ger.: *Evidenz*) for higher order knowledge systems, especially when we intensify our awareness (Kohak

---

[51] From the short story "A Scandal in Bohemia."

1978: 119). As William James taught, there is no level of knowing more fundamental than direct experience, and experience is the ground of all empirical sciences. Moreover, as we have already said, the intentional act is about instantiating ideas—*eidos* (categories of things, relations and events). Sensory stimuli cause sensory input, which is automatically and eidetically identified, or alternatively the intentional act goes in search of a sensory object that instantiates the idea in form and hyle (Chapter 5; Husserl 1982[1913]:158-164).

Almost instantaneously we know the object.[52] Back in Chapter 3, I asked you to gaze around your surroundings and notice that there is probably no object that you do not recognize (know, identify). The process within experience and intentional acts that links the form/hyle of the objects and the knowing is automatic. You do not have to think about it. Husserl describes this process of perceiving and knowing clearly in *Logical Investigations I*:

> [...] I must expressly emphasize the fact that I use the words "objectivity," "object," "thing," etc., always in the widest sense, in accordance, therefore, with my preferred sense of the term "knowledge." An object of knowledge may as readily be what is real as what is ideal, a thing or an event or a species of a mathematical relation, a case of being of what ought to be. This applies automatically to expressions like "unified objectivity," "interconnection of things," etc. [...] Both sorts of unity are given to us, and can only by abstraction be thought apart, in judgement or, more precisely, in *knowledge*—the unity of objectivity, on the one hand, and of truth, on the other. The expression "knowledge" is wide enough to cover both simple acts of knowing, as well as logically unified interconnections of knowledge, however complicated: either of these, considered as a whole, is a cognitive act. If now we perform an act of cognition, or, as I prefer to express it, live in one, we are "concerned with the object" that it, in its cognitive fashion, means and postulates. If this act is one of knowing in the strictest sense, i.e., if our judgment is inwardly

---

[52] Mature contemplatives experience arising images that take a tiny amount of time before they are recognized. In normal perception the object and its categorical intuition would seem to appear simultaneously.

evident, then its object is *given* in primal fashion (*originär*). The state of affairs comes before us, not merely putatively, but as actually before our eyes, and in it the object itself, *as* the object is, i.e., just as it is intended in this act of knowing and not otherwise, as bearer of such and such properties, as the term of such relations, etc. It is not merely putatively, but actually thus, and *as* actually thus it is given to our knowledge, which means that it is not merely thought (judged) but known to be such. Otherwise put, its being thus is a truth actually realized, individualized in the experience of the inwardly evident judgment. If we reflect on this individualization, we perform an ideational abstraction, and the truth itself, instead of our former object, becomes our apprehended object. We hereby apprehend the truth as the ideal correlate of the transient subjective act of knowledge, as standing opposed in its unity of the unlimited multitude of possible acts of knowing, and of knowing individuals. (Husserl 1970 [1900-01], I: 145)

If you can read Husserl-speak, then you will find no clearer explication of seeing and knowing in all of his translated writings. If you cannot read Husserl with ease, then let me parse out some of what he is saying in plain English:

1. Broad connotations. Husserl prefers to use analytical terms in their broadest connotations so as to clarify the essence he is describing. He depends upon the narrative context to clarify terms.

2. Real or idea. An object (coffee cup) that you know about can be either real or an idea (we discussed this in Chapter 3). Remember, percepts are actual instantiations of *eidos* with which they are mentally correlated.

3. Perceptual context. An object within your perceptual field appears in a context of other objects and relations (coffee cup on desk with laptop, keyboard, stapler, pens, etc.). Only by focusing on the intended object and thinking about it can it be abstracted from its real context. The context does not vanish. It is still there. But when we focus on one object to the exclusion of other objects, we have abstracted it in our thoughts.

4. Simple and complex. Knowing can be simple or complex. I see the coffee cup and know it to be my favorite. I recognize it. Or I can connect my knowing of the cup with other knowledge I may store in memory about other coffee cups, the history of ceramic cups, the difference between factory produced and hand-thrown cups, etc., etc. Or, I have the fervent belief that all sheep are white. I suddenly perceive a sheep with brown wool. I connect my firsthand observation of the brown sheep with my belief that all sheep are white. Perhaps I decide that my belief is wrong, and the brown sheep proves the point. Or perhaps I wonder if someone has dyed this previously white sheep's wool brown. The simple knowing that I am seeing a brown sheep branches out in my mind, broadening into more and more interconnections between knowings (judgements, decisions, cognitive associations, anticipations, etc.) until the perception of the brown sheep stands as a nexus within a complex web of knowing.

5. Structured thought. If my thinking is rational (logical) then the interconnections will not be mere lateral thinking or reverie, but will follow more or less formal, structured thought. If expressed, say, in speech, the auditor will presumably understand both the worlds and the structural elements.

6. Intentionality. Keep in mind that Husserl is referring to knowledge as it occurs within the intentional act, *not* knowledge stored in a book or computer somewhere removed from our unfolding stream of consciousness and lived experience. Parenthetically, and of interest to anthropologists, the fact is that prior to the invention of writing, virtually all knowing was of this lived sort—natural knowing. Knowledge was mostly lived experiential knowing. The kind of knowing experienced by all non-human animals. And in natural lived experience I am "concerned" with the meaning of the object and its "postulates;" i.e., what the object suggests to me, or what questions arise about its truth or its implications as a basis for believing something, thinking about something, or communicating with others about something.

7. The real. The object of perception is not "putative" (that is, not thought to be real) but is *really there* primordially. It is "original," "real," "concrete," "actual." The object and all its properties of form and hyle are actually "before my eyes." The relations both within the object as properties and between the object and other objects and relations are real, and I simultaneously know them to be real. This sense of truth about direct experience ranges from merely adequate evidence to complete apodicticity (Husserl 1993[1931]: 14-16). It is the role of phenomenology to return to those experiences that optimize apodictic knowledge, and thenceforth lead a life in tune with the real, and speaking intersubjectively, in tune with the lifeworld (Husserl 1970[1936]: 340).

8. Object as individualized. Finally—and this is crucial—when we perceive the actual object, it is "individualized" before us. This coffee cup is *this* coffee cup and no other. This is knowing apodictically (see Laughlin 1994b). We *perceive* the coffee cup. At the same time, this individual perceived coffee cup instantiates *the idea* of coffee cup. When we shift from the individual to the idea, "we perform an ideational abstraction," we abstract (separate, mentally remove, dissociate) the idea from the real thing and the "truth" of the coffee cup blends with other knowledge and becomes for us in that moment an apprehended (*apperceived*) coffee cup, an object now more pregnant with significance, more idea than thing. The truth of the coffee cup has been elevated to a transcendent cognitive level independent of "the transient subjective act of knowledge."

WHAT IS THOUGHT?

This is primordial knowing. If so, then what is thought? For Husserl, *thought* refers to cognitive operations based upon ideas (*eidos*).[53] In other words, sensory objects (or states of affairs) cannot be thought until they are paired with their respective categorical intuition. We cannot think about something until we know what it is, and of course within an evolutionary neurocognitive context the function of thought, grounded in categorical intuition, is to optimize adaptation to contingencies in the environing world. I cannot imagine that a bobcat skulking under a bush is ruminating upon the exact value of π, but I can imagine it ruminating whether or not he can capture the rabbit it sees without taking too great a risk. The bobcat will make a judgment based upon its recognition of the object as a specific kind of food source. Thus, we can see why Husserl's description of thought and judgement are the

---

[53] If you wish to read more about Husserl's understanding of *thought* and *thinking*, see Husserl 1982[1913]: § 7, 71, 125, 1969[1929], 2019[1917/18]; see also Edie 1976: 17ff, Welton 2000: Chap. 2.

same. Often judgment is the precursor thought to action. Both, by the way, are mediated by the ventrodorsal axis within the medial prefrontal cortex of the brain (Maisson *et al.* 2021).

For Husserl, the experience of thought is an attitude within an intentional act. "I" (as subject or "ego") enter an attitude of thought ("*cogito*") in which "I" think about idea(s) (*cogitatum*), some of which pertain to the sensory object and some of which do not (the "*cogitation;*" Edie 1976, Welton 2000). There are philosophers and social scientists who mistakenly presume that thinking requires language—e.g., see Edie (1976: 17) who claims Husserl held that thinking always involves language and speech. Husserl in fact never made such a claim but was referring to thinking as it is *communicated intersubjectively*, as in scientific discourse, statements, judgements, propositions, and texts (Husserl 1970[1936]: 166). Apart from the use of language to express thought, however, individual thoughts may be "bare acts of thinking and bare thoughts" (Husserl 1969[1929]: 19) which may involve categories of objects and relations, intermodal concepts (Burge 2010a), intuitive insights, imagination, cognization without words (Weiskrantz 1988), and so on.

Anthropologists in the past have made the same anthropocentric claim about thought and language[54] which of course implied that animals cannot think, and even early hominins could not think before the "invention" of language. This implication is absurd of course. Humans did not "invent" thinking (Hamill 1990). Animals with brains, and especially animals with cortical brains, do think in Husserl's sense of "bare thoughts" which can be more complex than primordial insights and probably abstract without becoming propositional.

Even if phenomenological analysis of concrete thought-experiences does not fall within the true home-ground of pure logic, it nonetheless is indispensable to the advance of purely logical research. For all that is logical must be given in fully concrete fashion, if, as an object of research, it is to be made our own, and if we are to be able to bring to self-evidence the a priori laws which have their roots in it. What is logical is first given us in imperfect concepts, as a more or less wavering

---

[54] Leading of course to the perennial debate over the influence language has upon perception, thought, and emotion—the so-called "Sapir-Whorf Hypothesis" (see Hussein 2012).

assertion. We do not therefore lack logical insights, but grasp the pure law with self-evidence, and see how it has its base in the pure forms of thought. (Husserl 1970 [1900-01]: 167)

Pure logic is a socially-shared, institutional model of the laws of reason—i.e., normative (Husserl 2019[1917/18]: 6). Our knowledge of the "pure laws" of reason derive from adumbrated, primordially a priori patterns in concept formation, evaluation, and formalization. For Husserl, if pure logic does not account for actual concrete apperception and conception, then that logic is empty and experientially useless. Logic, in other words, is our socially shared model of how the brain makes associations (genetic, causal, systemic, etc.) in experience. Human logic as it presents in primordial fashion in everyday experience is a type of animal logos.

Animal *logos* is an ethological reality while whether some animals are capable of non-linguistic pre-propositional thought remains an empirical question (Burge 2010b). We now know a lot more about animal cognitive abilities than before (Tomasello 2014, Wild 2020), and it is now clear anthropologists and others have routinely mangled individual thought and social thinking/expression and cultural conditioning of thought and belief. Among animals, even highly social animals, the adaptational value of cognition is primarily loaded upon individual thought, while among humans an evolutionary shift occurred to selection for cooperative thought dependent upon complex communication and standardization of intentional acts (see Chapter 7 where we discussed the "crisis of expanding consciousness").

Objective knowing of the kind that appeals narrowly to science and more broadly to socially shared knowledge has its basis in intersubjectivity and the sharing of a lifeworld. For Husserl there are two types of interconnectivity, or "unity," of reality: the *interconnection of things* and the *interconnection of truths* (1970 [1900-01]: 144). At the primordial level, we know within our own stream of consciousness, and we know that we share that knowing with the Other. But it is through acts of interconnectedness and communication that higher levels of objective knowledge are constituted and become recognized as "objective" and socially shared in both kinds of interconnectedness. Within the unity of things, you and I can agree that we each have in our homes different types of liquid containers. Within the unity of truth, we can visit each other's homes and ascertain that we do indeed both have exemplars of those different types of containers.

CONCEPTUALIZATION

Thought is based upon our ability to conceive. A *conception*, or simply a *concept*[55] is an idea that clumps events and things together by similarities. Natural conceptions and categories tend to be inherently fuzzy (Rosch 1977, 1978, Rosch *et al.* 1976). That is, natural concepts are characterized by fuzzy meaning boundaries. We tend to think of birds as feathered flying creatures, but there are flightless birds, and some people think that bats (actually mammals) are birds. Fuzziness is anathema to good science and formal logic which demand concepts that are crisply inclusive and exclusive. For Husserl, concepts are ideas and can be manipulated and modified in consciousness and without reference to what is going on perceptually:

> [T]o every concept belongs *an infinite extension of purely possible particulars*, of purely possible conceptual objects. It I imagine things, I apprehend in them as pure possibilities the concept of the thing. I can find the same concept in actual things; stated more precisely, in intended things which I posit as actualities on the basis of actual experience, these give themselves as particulars realizing the same universal which, in imagination, is not truly realized but only quasi-realized in the possibilities discerned.
>
> Consequently, *the possibility of the formation of general objectivities*, of "concepts," extends *as far as there are associative syntheses of likeness*. On this rests the *universality of the operation of the formation of concepts*; everything which, in some way or other, is objectively constituted in actuality or possibility, as an object of actual experience or of imagination, can occur as a term of

---

[55] If you wish to read more about Husserl's notion of *concept*, see Husserl 1973[1939], 1970 [1900-01], I and II, 1982[1913], 1973[1939], 2019[1917/18]; see also Färber 1943.

relations of comparison and be conceived through the activity of eidetic identification and subsumption under a universal.

> [...] Naturally, concepts as *pure* concepts can, from the first, originate *outside of all relation to current actuality*, namely, by the comparison of pure possibilities of the imagination. It is clear thereby that every actual likeness, acquired in this way, of possibilities given as existing (as existing, not in the sense of a reality of experience, but precisely *as* a possibility) intentionally includes in itself a possible likeness of possible actualities and a possible universal in which they can possibly participate. On the other hand, even if they were formed originally on the basis of experience as actual generalities, concepts can always be apprehended as pure concepts. (Husserl 1973[1939]: 329-330)

If I begin thinking about "bird" as a concept, I can imagine birds that I really have seen, or have seen in pictures, heard others describe, read about in stories. But I can also imagine birds that have never existed outside human imagination. There is no practical limit to the new forms of bird that I can create in my mind. I can imagine flamingo-like birds who land on water with skis in the place of feet. I can imagine raptors with four wings, with three heads, or as big as an elephant. Herein lies the connection between conceptualization and creativity. If you take a Jungian point of view (which I do), then we are born with a head-full of contentless concepts (archetypal concepts) that become triggered by instantiation in experience (Jung 1968a, Stevens 1982).

Natural concepts have their basis in the "sensuous founding acts" of pure intuition:

> Acts of straightforward intuitions we called "sensuous," founded acts, whether leading back immediately or mediately to sense, we called "categorical." But it is worth our while to draw a distinction, within the sphere of categorical acts, between those acts that are *purely categorical*, acts of "pure understanding," and *mixed acts of understanding that are blended with sense*. It lies in the nature of the case that everything categorical ultimately rests upon sensuous intuition, that a "categorical intuition,"

an intellectual insight, a case of thought in the highest sense, without any foundation of sense, is a piece of nonsense. (Husserl 1970 [1900-01], II: 306-307)

A natural category may form a concept. The concept is real if it is at least a mixed form of category and relates in part to founding intuition. If not, the category and concept are literally nonsensical and empty with respect to sensuous content.

This issue underscores the genius of Husserl's meditations, and his ability to make distinctions that when placed in neuropsychological and evolutionary context allows a phenomenological opening of great relevance to anthropology, as well as the other human sciences. Natural concepts, grounded in sensuous experience are open because they are formed *in time* (i.e., they have history).

We can now also go beyond experience, and the comparison of objects actually given in experience, and pass over to free imagination. We imagine similar particulars—similar to actualities which have been actually experienced to begin with—and thereupon as many as we choose, that is, always new, individually different from one another, as similar particulars, and such that, if the experience had continued, they could actually have been given to us. Thus, to every concept belongs *an infinite extension of purely possible particulars*, of purely possible conceptual objects. If I imagine things, I apprehend in them as pure possibilities the concept of a thing. I can find this same concept in actual things; stated more precisely, in intended things which I posit as actualities on the basis of actual experience. (Husserl 1973[1939]: 329)

Concepts, at least those produced in human brainminds are never limited in everyday life to the sensuous present. Concepts by their nature are genetic productions—they order and are applied to experiences had over the course of time. Concepts remain open, organic structures that change over the course of one's life, and, like iron filings drawn to a magnet, they incorporate new material, some actual and some imaginary, over years.

REASON AND RATIONALITY

Reasoning is the creation of new knowledge from old knowledge (Fuster 2003: 224). Reason (Ger.: *Vernunft*) connotes for Husserl a far broader scope within thought than is usually the case among mathematicians, logicians, philosophers, and many scientists. Reason is not limited to the confines of formal math, logic, or rules of empiricist epistemology. Rather, reason begins and is grounded in direct primordial seeing (Kohak 1978:119-120):

> *Immediate "seeing" (Sehen)*, not merely the sensory seeing of experience, but *seeing in general as primordial dator consciousness of any kind whatsoever*, is the ultimate source of justification for all rational statements. It has this right-conferring function only because and insofar as its object-giving is primordial. If we see an object standing out in complete clearness, if purely on the basis of the seeing, and within the limits of what we grasp through really seeing, we have carried out processes of discrimination and conceptual comprehension, if then we see (as a new way of "seeing") how the object is constituted, the statement faithfully expressing this has then its justification. If we ask why the statement is justified, and ascribe no value to the reply "I see that it is so," we fall into absurdity [...]. (Husserl 1982[1913]: 84)

Both reason and the effort after truth are universal characteristics of mankind (Husserl 1970[1936]: 338) and are biogenetically bound to primordial seeing, and because our consciousness is always operating within space-time, involve also our plans, anticipations, expectations, and so forth. Reason is not limited to cognitive acts, but also includes evaluative judgments and thoughtful praxis (Husserl 1982[1913]: 406). We know truth, we know our statements are correct, solely by reference to our direct primordial seeing. We know our acts are right because we see that they are right. For Husserl, the life of reason is the life of responsibility to bring our values and actions into accord with the epistemic evidence of our senses. It is not uncommon in philosophy to speak as though "logic" and "content" are independent mental factors. While the two may be treated this way in formal settings like mathematics and symbolic logic, in everyday, natural exercise of reasoning, logic and content are two sides of the same coin (Hamill 1990: 6). Nor would it make sense evolutionarily if they were independent for adaptation requires judgments about actual events and things in the environing world where reason and praxis are united (Edelman 1992). Naturalizing epistemology so that rational faculties are seen as evolutionary factors makes it far easier to integrate what we know about consciousness and how we know the brain works (see Bishop and Trout 2005, Edelman 2006).

Husserl began his phenomenological explorations of knowing with the intent to discover a primordial intuitive basis underlying the more formal "laws" of logic and mathematics (Husserl 1994a, 2003[1887-1901]). Later in his career he shifted to describing reason in its everyday lived sense. I focus on my coffee cup which presents within my perceptual field and its inherent horizon within which relations and changes and intuitive insights arise, all before my senses. Because I am an anthropologist, I am more aware than most folks of the evolution of containers and how crucial their invention proved for human adaptation, especially with regard to storage and preparing of food resources. These connections just spontaneously pop into my mind as I gaze at the coffee cup. I am then aware of how fuzzy the concept of "coffee cup" is. Is it a coffee cup simply because I use it to drink coffee? Not really. I do not have to think about the cup before I recognize it as a "coffee cup." And indeed, I have seen very abstract and artistic renderings of coffee cups from which no one would even think of drinking. As we have seen, "coffee cup" is a percept and a concept, an idea in my head.

We humans reveal rational thought in communication and cooperation with group members (Tomasello 2014: 109). Collective decisions, reasons, judgments, and evaluations may or may not be grounded in direct seeing. Humans across cultures may make judgments derived from biogenetic proclivities such as how we conceive of space as quartered by the cardinal directions (Brown 1983). The reasons for proposed actions may derive from a cultural belief that something is so or may be an expression of an ideology perhaps miles from anybody's direct seeing, or even in complete contradiction to direct seeing. All of this is possible in the natural attitude, and may be the cause of maladaptive judgements, decisions and plans that in hindsight we may conclude were "unrealistic" and even totally fabricated with little or no reference to reality (Schnider 2018). For Husserl, this kind of thought may under certain circumstances produce evil, in which case the reasoning is likely to be mere rationalization and is based upon "empty" reasons, "empty" rationality (see Husserl 2010[1907]: 45-46, 1970[1936]:291).

Our rational attitude must ever seek roots in reality:

> In principle our task remains everywhere the same: we have to bring to knowledge the complete system of conscious formulations, covering all levels and strata, which constitute the primordial givenness of all such objective entities, and therewith make intelligible the equivalent, in terms of consciousness, of the relevant type of 'reality.' Everything also which we should say in truth so as to exclude the many misunderstandings into which we so easily fall concerning the correlation of Being and Consciousness (as, for instance, that all reality "resolves itself into psychic factors") can be stated only on the ground of the essential connexions of the constitutive groups, as apprehended from the phenomenological standpoint and in the light of intuition. (Husserl 1982[1913]: 422)

What Husserl is driving at is to privilege the effort after truth over the effort after meaning, a distinction I introduced back in Chapter 5 when we were discussing the hyle. Husserl realized that a phenomenology of knowing, a phenomenology of reason, returns us to the inherent dialog between primordial knowing via the senses and intuition, and the body of knowledge of the environing world we require to adapt. This is no different for other animals with brains and cognitive systems (Husserl 1970[1936]: 187).

The proportion of any society's population that become skilled at higher level cognitive processing is in part a genetic factor and in part a cultural trait. All normal humans are born with the ability to think (Hamill 1990: 2). How complexly and skillfully people think is partially determined by the value placed upon rationality of various kinds by the culture (see Edelman 1992: 174; Hamill 1990). But the rational faculties of people going about their daily lives will almost inevitably be linked to experience and praxis, thus forming (in Husserl's words following Kant) *practical reason* (Funke 1984). Practical reason automatically and primordially links willing, axiological evaluations including emotions and praxis. The complexity of thought of which any individual is capable in any society involves development and conditioning (Laughlin 2017a).

Metaphor and analogical reasoning

Anthropology is particularly interested in metaphor, because the concept is useful in accounting for cross-culturally common phenomena like myth, totemism, ritual, iconography and so forth (Fernandez 1991, Turner 1974, Winkelman 1996). As we have seen, Husserl had some interesting things to say about metaphor. Arbib and Hesse (1986: Chap. 8) underscore how the brain inherently mediates a lot of meaning by way of *metaphorical thought*—taking an utterance out of its literal context and using it in an analogous context, e.g., "tax-time poses a heavy burden on the poor," "my buddy Pete is an ass," the Christmas tree is a kind of "tree of life," etc. As phenomenologist James Edie notes with respect to body metaphors:

> Since language is intrinsically appresentational of experience and therefore "anthropocentric," it is hardly surprising that it should be largely "anthropomorphic" as well. From the beginnings of language men have invested objects of thought with the familiar aspects of the lived human body and its processes. If we attempt to resolve thought (in the form of language) into its primitive elements, we do not discover timeless, logical structures but experienced lifeworld events in terms of which historical man has oriented himself in concrete existence. (Edie 1963: 546; see also Edie 1976: Chap. 5)

Metaphorical thought expressed by language makes sense to us, regardless of our mother tongue or culture, because it reflects at the level of communication the pre-given, primordial extension of intuition into the realm of ideas. Husserl does not make an issue of "metaphor" per se, as does say Levi-Strauss (2021[1962]), but he implies that the roots of metaphorical meaning can be found in the free variation of *eidos* which may range from the literal apperception of ideas bound to the object in intentionality to the free association of empty ideas only indirectly related to sensory and embodied perception. What he does emphasize is the importance of the congruence between the intentional meaning of metaphorical utterances and the interpretive acts on the part of the auditor.

Metaphors and metaphorical thought may constitute central themes in societies. The profound importance of metaphorical thought was underscored in one of anthropology's preeminent texts, Mary Douglas' *Purity and Danger* (1966), in which she shows that the notion of "dirt" carries the metaphorical range of meanings pertaining to disorder and in many societies is the raison d'être for rituals of purity. If rituals of purification fail to be carried out, the consequences would be a fall into chaos and evil. Not that the people themselves understand this distinction. It is clear that humans are hard-wired to make up stories. Stories seek out causal sequences, even when the actual causation is invisible or unknown. This processing of historical events into stories is produced primarily by what neuroscientists call the *left-hemisphere interpreter* (Gazzaniga 1985, 1995, Gazzaniga *et al.* 1985, Phelps and Gazzaniga 1992). "The interpreter is a system unique to the human that elaborates on data presented to it and makes inferences about the meaning of the data" (Phelps and Gazzaniga 1992: 293). So far as we know, humans are the only big brain social animal that tells stories to present (Husserl would say "appresentation;" see Chapter 8) a coherent public account of events in which causal factors are inferred (see Dunbar 2016)—of profound importance to hominin adaptation to what I call the "crisis of expanding consciousness" (see Chapter 7).

With respect to neuropsychology, reason and intelligence are highly correlated (see Haier 2017: 124). Intelligence is one of those universal factors that anthropologists generally ignore, despite ample evidence that intelligence impacts a myriad of cultural elements (see Laughlin 2017a). For Husserl, the primal function of intentional acts is to make reality "intelligible" (Husserl 1970[1936]: 169). The stream of consciousness is, as we have seen in Chapter 6, a series of temporal epochs, a reiteration of epochs which sink into memory behind us and that we anticipate before us. Through reason we are able to unite the memories of these epochs into a narrative the complexity of which may range in intelligence from children's "just-so" stories to elaborate and highly intelligent mythologies that may take days to recount (see e.g., Jorgensen 1980 on story-telling among the Telefolmin people of the Pacific).

There are of course different kinds of reasoning. With respect to metaphorical thought, the ability of the brain to compare objects and detect similarities of form, hyle, relations and patterns is called *analogical reasoning* in neuroscience—reasoning based upon commonalities between events, objects, and relations. For Husserl, this kind of reasoning arises primordially in intuition ("analogizing apperception;" Husserl 1993[1931]: 108-111) and then recurs in higher and more abstract cognitive processes. Indeed, it is by way of primordial analogizing apperception that we come to the Other in intersubjectivity (Chapter 4)—we automatically recognize the Other as being "like me." It is analogical reasoning that produces cross-culturally universal metaphorical thought and use in communication.

Analogical reasoning is one form of *inductive reasoning*—problem-solving reasoning by which we make general conclusions from patterns adumbrated from specific perceptions or observations. We know that analogical reasoning (along with other kinds of reasoning) at the cognitive level is mediated by prefrontal cortical areas (Fuster 2003: 232, Hammer *et al.* 2019, Hobeika *et al.* 2016). The precise area mediating analogy depends upon the domain (e.g., visuospatial, semantic, multimodal) wherein the abstraction is made. Analogical reasoning is a kind of abstract cognition mediated in domain appropriate regions of the part of your brain's cortex that lies above and forward of your temple, variously ranging over the middle and inferior frontal gyri and the rostrolateral prefrontal cortex. Generally speaking, the more abstract the reasoning, the more forward of the cortex the activity.

We are most often aware of metaphor and analogical associations in our use of language, but analogical and other forms of inductive reasoning are ancient and evolved prior to selection for language and other complex forms of communication among hominins (Hamill 1990). "Inductive reasoning is present in many different animals, and the multiple ways in which it is expressed show continuities in nature:

to different degrees and levels of competence, animals seem to be able to perform causal inference, probabilistic inference, optimizations of strategies based on observation, categorization, etc. Thus, animals are crucial behavioral ambassadors to the study of inductive reasoning in humans" (Sauce and Matzel 2017: 6-7). Indeed, I suspect that analogical reasoning was one of the first forms of abstract thought to evolve. At some point in the vastly distant past, animals first became capable of growing new cognits that reduced or replaced older cognits. We know that the adaptive function of perception is the detection of recognizable patterns in the environing world. The selective advantage for brains capable of extending cognitive associations based upon similarity of patterns seems obvious, especially as this ability is fundamental to creativity. And it is clear that human children are capable of this kind of reasoning quite early on in their development (Goswami 2013). Analogical reasoning was one of the first forms of logic that allowed animals to distance themselves from dependence upon raw perception.

EVIDENCE

Imagine that I say to you, "Russia just attacked its neighbor Ukraine." You ask, "Is that true?" and I reply, "Evidently." What do you mean by "is that true?" and what do I mean by "evidently?" You are asking how I know that Russia has attacked Ukraine—i.e., what is my evidence? I am asserting that there is evidence known to me that Russia has indeed attacked Ukraine. I may have directly witnessed the Russian tanks rolling into Ukraine, I may have read reports in news broadcasts or newspapers, or I may just be repeating what I heard from a third party while chatting with them over coffee or emailing on the Internet. Whatever my evidence, this is an example to the appeal to reality for the truth of things. We quite naturally and automatically refer to sensory data to true our knowledge.

Anthropology has long been interested in how narratives relate to reality. The great British ethnographer, E. E. Evans-Pritchard, is credited with raising the issue of epistemological variations among peoples when he famously explored the reasoning used by the Azande people of Africa to explain untoward events by recourse to witchcraft

(Evans-Pritchard 1937). He showed that whereas we might explain why a person fell down and injured themselves on a path they have walked along every day for years by applying a probability model (sooner or later someone is going to fall down on this path, it's a matter of probabilities), Zande folk want to know why this particular person fell and hurt themselves at this particular place and time today. One answer is that this person was cursed by a witch. Our explanation is that this person tripped over a root and that caused the fall and injury. A Zande might reply, he has been stepping over that same root for years without tripping. Why him today?

Husserl was concerned with experience and evidence throughout his writings. Evidence[56] (Ger.: *Evidenz*) ranges from the *absolute givenness* (Ger.: absolute *Gegebenheit*) of primordial sensuousness to the less certain and downright inadequate form of beliefs and opinions (Husserl 1999: 24-25). The only evidence that reaches total certainty, devoid of any doubt, is the evidence of our senses—that is, the absolute givenness of our primordial sensory experience:

> Evidence is, in an *extremely broad sense*, an "experiencing" of something that is, and is thus; it is precisely a mental seeing of something itself. Conflict with what evidence shows, with what "experience" shows, yields the negative of evidence (or negative evidence)—put in form of a judgment: positive evidence of the affair's non-being. In other words, negative evidence has as its content evident falsity. Evidence, which in fact includes all experiencing in the usual and narrower sense, can be more or less perfect. *Perfect evidence* and its correlate, *pure and genuine truth*, are given as ideas lodged in the striving for knowledge, for fulfilment of one's meaning intention. By immersing ourselves in such a striving, we can extract those ideas from it. Truth and falsity, criticism and critical comparison with evident data, are an everyday theme, playing their incessant part even in pre-scientific life. (Husserl 1993[1931]: 12)

---

[56] If you wish to read more about Husserl's notion of *evidence*, see Husserl 2008[1906-1907], 1993[1931], 1999, 1969[1929]; see also Bachelard 1968, Farber 1943, Ferrarello 2016, Held 2003b, Levinas 1995, Moran 2000, 2005, Sokolowski 1964, Staiti 2017, Steinbock 2021.

As we know from neuropsychological research, the brainmind operates by feeding forward into reality as an "incessant" test of our knowledge. Each step I take on the floor or in the yard acts as feedback into my apperceptions about there being a solid ground for my step. This is as much the case for other animals, as it is for humans. Each temporal epoch operates to true-up our knowledge. Each moment of experience is evidence related to our "meaning intentions."

> [T]here is *another sense of transcendence*, whose counterpart is an entirely different kind of immanence, namely, *absolute* and *clear givenness, self-givenness in the absolute sense.* This givenness, which excludes any meaningful doubt, consists of an immediate act of seeing and apprehending the meant objectivity itself as it is. It constitutes the precise concept of evidence, understood as immediate evidence. All knowledge that is not evident, that refers to or posits what is objective, but *does not see it for itself,* is transcendence in this second sense. In such knowledge we go beyond what is *given in the genuine sense,* beyond *what can be directly seen* and *apprehended.* Here the question is how can knowledge posit something as existing that is not directly and genuinely given in it? (Husserl 1999:27-28)

This is one of the fundamental problems that animal brainminds must solve in an adaptational sense. It is the case that most causation involved in experienced reality is invisible. Indeed, the sensory pixels that make up the hyle of sensuous things are invisible to those who have yet to reduce them. What happens on a moment-by-moment basis is that the meaning of things fills in the gaps within the perceptual field as intuition.

We need to use caution here, because most of us without phenomenological training—unable to reduce experience to the primordial given at a moment's notice—cannot easily distinguish between what is self-evident in experience and what is apperception (information added to the experience by meaning functions). *Self-evident* means that everything that is necessary for evaluating the truth of something is given in the perception of the object or event (Husserl 1969[1929]: 156-157). While operating within the natural attitude, it is very easy to misconstrue the value of our evidence in support of our beliefs and theories about the world (Husserl 1969[1929]: 277-279). As I have said before, getting to the truth of things requires effort. When we do learn to enter the epoché and focus upon the primordial sensory given to the exclusion of all else, then we have in effect encountered the truth itself. That is, when our meaning perfectly matches the self-evident fulfilment of our intention, then the meaning is true (Husserl 1970 [1900-01], II: 259-267).

During the course of teaching anthropological methods, I have emphasized what I call the *rule of multiple interpretations*, to wit, "there is no such thing as an experience that admits of one and only one interpretation." What this means in terms of ethnographic fieldwork is that we need to distinguish between what our hosts are experiencing and what those experiences mean to them. We should as clearly as we can record the host's account of their experiences—what they actually saw—but we are never required to believe their explanations or interpretations of what they have experienced, especially when those interpretations appear to us to be irrational (see Horton 1967, Sperber 1985: Chap. 2). Also, in our everyday lives, we should (if we aspire to phenomenological proficiency, we *must*) be clear in our own minds just how good a match there is between our reduced experiences and our interpretations (beliefs, ideas, ideals, plans, etc.). In a very direct way, *reality trues out beliefs*. Ideally, and from a Husserlian vantage point, our beliefs and our experiences should always match perfectly. But, of course, they never do.

SUMMARY AND SEGUE

Anthropology at its core is the cross-cultural study of peoples' knowledge, and the Husserlian approach to knowing is supportive and compatible with that orientation, for the latter is the study of how the human brainmind comes to know what it knows, regardless of enculturative background. Husserl's methods track the roots of knowing back to "the things themselves." Pure phenomenology involves a disciplined meditation upon what presents before our eyes in the intentional act. It is also within the intentional act that percept meets meaning—as Husserl says above, percept and meaning are intimately coincidental.

Knowledge is fundamentally subjective with its roots buried deeply in the ongoing flow of lived experience. Any claim to "objective" knowing derives solely from intersubjective communication and of course the lifeworld. Meaning and theory are constituted as part of the noema, a common ingredient of the intentional act. Consciousness may be bivalent in the sense that in one attitude in which the focus is upon the percept (the primordial sensuous flow) or in another attitude upon the meaning, judgment, description or theory coincidental with the percept. These are, as you can easily demonstrate to yourself, two states of consciousness. All of these operations depend upon ideas, including thought. We cannot think about something we know nothing about. Thought takes place within the context of an intentional act, even if no percept is presenting itself. The Watcher can focus on the idea of e $= mc^2$ and cogitate about other ideas and meaning associations within ruminations, but the ideas must contain knowledge. These intentional acts are higher cognitions, carried out in the cortex of the brain, with no direct presentation of percepts. Reason, on the other hand, is not limited to the confines of formal logic, but rather begins and is grounded in direct primordial seeing. Reason makes new knowledge out of old knowledge. Reason and the effort after truth are universals associated as they are with primordial seeing. Reason occurs in space-time, and thus is intimately involved in forming plans, expectations, and so on. Broadly speaking, reason is not limited to cognitive acts, but also includes evaluative judgments and thoughtful praxis.

Husserlian phenomenology is not limited to knowledge derived from or grounded in sensuous experiences stimulated by the "external" environing world. We must remember that our bodies are part of the environing world, and that includes our brains. We are literally transcendental beings relative to our knowledge of ourselves. And just as we can reduce and study a coffee cup "out there," we can also reduce and study experiences emanating from within our being. At the lowest level of sensuousness, we are aware of our bodies through interoception, an umbrella term for our myriad experiences like headache, hunger, thirst, pain, arousal, anxiety, bliss, etc.—all are forms of knowledge in service of *allostasis*, the mechanism that keeps us behaving in ways that maintain our body in homeorhetic well-being. At higher levels of awareness, we obtain knowledge of the inner life of our psyche in ways that were also of great interest to Husserl, and of relevance to a broader picture of Husserlian neurophenomenology.

CHAPTER NINE

Husserl and the Unconscious

In accordance with Husserl's phenomenology, we have found an answer by providing a definition of the unconscious in terms of passive intentionality, which belongs to consciousness in the mode of inactivity but still has the possibility of being awakened again in the context of passive syntheses. In this sense the unconscious has been characterized as something that is sunk but not unreachable, and the transcendental-phenomenological reduction appeared as the only viable way to reach this deep dimension, to bring light into this "night," to reactivate this inert level of consciousness by disclosing its intentionality.

– Alice Togni (2018: 83)

In this chapter I will suggest how we may compare Husserlian neurophenomenology with a Jungian perspective on the dynamics of the psyche to expand upon Husserl's approach to the unconscious. As we saw earlier (Chapter 1), recourse to phenomenology followed the increased interest in the study of embodiment, sensory experience, and the self in sociology and anthropology (Csordas 1994b, Good *et al.* 1992, Hickey and Smith 2020, Thanem and Knights 2019). In addition, over the last several decades, the influence of Carl Jung's depth psychology has increased among those approaches concerned with sociocultural productions mediated by biopsychological structures, or *archetypes*, as they relate to dream imagery, mythology, and spiritual iconography across cultures. Of particular interest has been Jung's more complex, organic, and biogenetic view of unconscious activities within the human psyche, overshadowing Freud's more mechanical conception that dominated social science in the first three quarters of the last century (see Hunt 2012, Hillman 2021, Krieger 2014: Chap. 7, Walker 2012). Combining these perspectives will allow us to explore those so-called "limit-problems" ("limit-phenomena") that involve experiences of the inner world of the psyche. As we shall see, the Husserlian and Jungian views of the phenomenology of the unconscious are quite compatible, as are each with corresponding neuroscience (Brooke 1991: Chap. 7, Jansen 2005).

As we have seen in previous chapters, the normal orientation of Husserlian methods, even as applied by Husserl himself, reveals an ethnocentric bias towards sensory experiences of the external environing world while awake, including intersubjective experiences of the Other. This is quite understandable given his project was oriented from the get-go toward providing a phenomenological foundation for natural science (Nenon 2013b). But this orientation toward experiencing the physical world should not blind us to the fact that Husserl also explored other domains of the psyche, including the unconscious.

HUSSERL ON THE UNCONSCIOUS

Husserl's notion of the unconscious and universal, inherent "drives" was influenced by the Freudian psychology of his day (Bernet 2002, Tougas 2013: 30-32).[57] In fact, Husserl and Freud were contemporaries and were influenced from the same history of thought:

> The work of Husserl and Freud had common sources in the philosophy, psychology, and physiology of the nineteenth century. Herbart, Brentano, Helmholtz, Fechner, Wundt and Mach were among the towering figures in their common background who had influence on their respective work. Although contemporaries who had little concern for the other's professional interest, Husserl and Freud nevertheless struggled with some common problems. One of these is the relationship of sensation to memory and to the experience of time. The concepts of sensation, memory and time were, in fact, artifacts which the empirical methods of nerve-physiology, the psychophysical testing of sensory thresholds, as

---

[57] If you wish to read more about Husserl's phenomenology of the *unconscious*, see Husserl 1969[1929]: Appendix II, 1973[1939]: 279, 1970[1937]: 188, 237, Appendix VIII by Eugen Fink; see also Bachelard 1968: 187-188, Bernet 2002, Johnson 1980, Kohak 1980, Sieroka 2015, Tougas 2013: Chap. 7.

well as the metaphysics and positivism of the late nineteenth century had left them. (Mishara 1990: 29)

As Husserl noted in *The Crisis of European Sciences and Transcendental Phenomenology*:

> [C]oncerning the problem of the "unconscious" that is so much discussed today—dreamless sleep, loss of consciousness, and whatever else of the same and similar nature may be included under this title—this is in any case a matter of occurrences in the pregiven world, and they naturally come under the transcendental problem of constitution, as do birth and death. As something existing in the world common to all, this sort of thing has its manners of ontic verification, of "self-giving" which are quite particular, but which originally create ontic meaning for beings of such particularity. (Husserl, 1970[1937]: 188)

Part of that "self-giving" is awareness of we ourselves as embodied beings with a psyche far greater than the ego (Husserl speaks of the psyche as *die Seele* or "soul," implying the spiritual aspect of the embodied mind; see e.g., Husserl 1993[1931]: 117-120, Fink 1988: Appendix II). The unconscious is in part due to our ability to systematically disattend potential objects of awareness. Thus, unconsciousness, "...is no mere privation, but itself a quality of consciousness" (Husserl 2008[1906-1907]: 249; see also Sieroka 2015).

We also intuit all of this about the Other in intersubjective operations (Husserl 1993[1931]: 108-116). In addition, we know the unconscious because we are capable of consciousness, and it is common to be aware that we are unaware of something, that something is "dimly apparent" or absent from our stream of consciousness (see Fink's 1936 note appended to Husserl 1970[1937]: Appendix VIII). In other words, engagements with unconscious processes are primordially intuited and constructed (Husserl uses the term "constituted") by way of a subjective act of intentionality—e.g., we are aware while conscious that we have lost, may lose, and will lose consciousness of something, or have regained awareness of something that was previously lost. We can be and often are aware of the *absence* of something, though that something remains unconscious (Bernet 2002).

In addition, experiences of any kind are structured (constituted, assembled, entrained) by the nervous system and this structuration includes experiences originating in unconscious processes. For instance, from within the scope of an intentional act we may form a judgement (assessment, evaluation, decision, question) about the object of consciousness, lose track of the judgement, and then retrieve the judgment later on. Where does the judgment go in the interim? Husserl often seems to be thinking metaphorically when he describes the unconscious as, "...the hidden and stratified *underground of consciousness*: this is a deep realm of sunken thoughts, volitions, and values within the life of the soul. Precisely because of its stratification, Husserl often speaks [metaphorically] of "sedimentation" [or "precipitation"] and identifies this multi-layered underground of consciousness with what is below the zero, but it isn't zero itself" (Togni 2018: 79; emphasis added). For Husserl, the judgment just "sinks" into an underground of unconsciousness:

> It then sinks ever further into the background and at the same time becomes ever more indistinct; the degree of its prominence gradually lessens until it finally disappears from the field of immediate consciousness, is "forgotten." It is henceforth incorporated into the passive background, *into the "unconscious,"* which is not a dead nothingness but a limiting mode of consciousness and accordingly can affect us anew like another passivity in the form of whims, free-floating ideas, and so on. In this modification, however, the judgment is not an original but a secondary passivity, which essentially refers to its origin in an actual spontaneous production. In this passive modification it therefore represents, like every other passivity which has arisen through the modification of what is originally constituted as a source, a habituality of the ego, a permanent possession, ready for a new associative awakening. We can turn again toward what is awakened in the form of a whim, a free-floating idea, we can bring it nearer, make it more distinct; and, finally, by renewing its articulated accomplishment under certain circumstances, we can restore the judgment to self-givenness. (Husserl 1973[1939]: 279; emphasis added)

Husserl refers to this common loss of awareness of something that later pops up again, *retention* (Husserl 2001[1920/24]).[58] Although he usually did not use the term, the "unconscious" is the place where these memories live when not being objects of awareness. He is speaking here, of course, of the Freudian *personal unconscious*, with which Jung agreed as far as it went. For Husserl, the distinction between conscious and unconscious is not simply one akin to an on-off switch. Rather, awareness forms a gradient, there being intense awareness of the object within a field of perception that grades-off to bare awareness at the periphery: "What is actually perceived, and what is more or less clearly co-present and determinate (to some extent at least), is partly pervaded, partly girt about with a *dimly apprehended depth or fringe of indeterminate reality*" (Husserl 1982[1913]: 102). Husserl's description of gradience is now partially confirmed by neuropsychology, suggesting that the degree of awareness is mediated by lesser to greater processing at the cortical level (see e.g., Anzulewicz *et al.* 2015, Bayne, Hohwy and Owen 2016). Beyond the fringe is the rest of reality (both external and internal) which is at the moment indeterminate and unavailable for awareness (see Bachelard 1968: 187). This world beyond the fringe includes our own embodied psyche or brainmind which may be beyond our neural capacities to experience.

> Not only do the fringes of the past and future, the just-past and the just-about-to-be, influence the constitution of objects and the self, so does the past in the form of ego-attitudes and habitualities sedimented in memory. Husserl goes so far as to introduce the idea of "unconscious" to explain how our past experiences continue to influence us even when they have been forgotten [...]. Unconscious for Husserl is only derivative from individual memory; it does

---

[58] Some unfortunate people suffer from what is called anterograde amnesia that may follow an injury of some kind. This syndrome is one in which the person cannot form short-term memories but can remember experiences before the injury (Aggleton 2008). In Husserlian terms, the awareness of something "sinks" into oblivion (not the unconscious) and is irretrievable—clearly it cannot be *retained*. The effects of the syndrome are hard for most of us to imagine but it plays a central role in the 2000 movie *Memento*, which can give you a taste of what the malady must be like with which to live.

not designate a realm of pregiven but repressed basic instincts that are the basis of personality. In *Formal and Transcendental Logic,* Husserl says that when experiences sink down into "… the universal substratum—the so-called *'unconscious,'* which, far from being a phenomenological nothing, is itself a limit-mode of consciousness" [Husserl 1969[1929]: 319] they can continue to exert an effect on present experiences. For, he continues, this sedimentation of past experiences is a horizon that "… accompanies every living present and shows its own continuously changing sense when it becomes 'awakened'." The only barrier to the awakening of these sedimented ego-habitualities and attitudes is the lapse in time since the original experiences occurred and an associative springboard in the ongoing present, a new experience similar to the past one. (Johnson 1980: 319)

However, though influenced by the Freudian notion of the unconscious, Husserl dealt with aspects of experience that are better fitted into a Jungian view of the unconscious (Tougas 2013: Chap. 7). For instance, Husserl realized that there can be an awareness of unconscious processes that lie behind sensory experiences, but of which we may never become directly aware. This is an apt description of how archetypes mediate experiences. Speaking neurophysiologically, Soon *et al.* (2008) have shown that when we make decisions, neural processes have already begun processing information up to 10 seconds before we are aware of the decision. Moreover, there is ample evidence that many of the operations carried out by the right hemisphere of the brain in most people occur with minimal or no awareness (Joseph 2013, Schore 2004). Indeed, it is hard to find any activity of consciousness, regardless of intensity of awareness, that does not involve the entrainment of unconscious mental processes (Nunez 2010: 43-44, Vedantam 2010). In fact, conscious and unconscious processes may conflict with each other (Ginot 2015: Chap. 10). Indeed, Husserl is also pointing to the role of emotion-toned complexes (neural networks resulting from trauma) that tend to operate unconsciously to motivate sensuous experiences (Escamilla 2020, Krieger 2014: Chap. 3).

Jung's theory of the unconscious was more elaborate in scope than Freud's (Husserl was not wedded to a Freudian theory of the unconscious) and has certain advantages for us as both phenomenological and theoretical anthropologists—in particular Jung's conception of the *collective unconscious*, which, like the lifeworld, is thought to be universal, species specific, and hence biogenetically derived (Joseph 2013: 17-19, Jung 1968a). I realize that Jung's conception of the collective unconscious is controversial, especially for certain diehard, anti-essentialist psychologists and social scientists, but this is not the place for me to argue for its scientific advantages over other conceptions, for I and my colleague, psychologist Vincenza Tiberia, have done so elsewhere for the benefit of our anthropological colleagues (see Laughlin and Tiberia 2012). I will only add that Jung, unlike Freud, was a contemplative phenomenologist in his own right (see Brooke 1991, Carafides 1974), and his views about the collective unconscious derive from his own direct experience of imagery arising in dreams, visions, and fantasies, coupled with insights he had from comparing the delusional imagery of psychotic patients and the imagery described in mythology (Jung 1965). For Jung, the foundations of the psyche are the innumerable archetypes we inherit by virtue of being human, and once potentiated, develop like other processes in the psyche.

In modern parlance, the archetypes are inherent neural circuits that are genetically organized during the neurogenesis of the young brain (see Escamilla 2020 and Krieger 2014: Chap 7 for discussions of this issue). The total of the inherited archetypes in each individual brain constitutes one's collective unconscious, structures that mediate all we psychologically share as members of the human species (Jung 1968a, Kluger 1975, Hobson 2018, Laughlin and Tiberia 2012, 2016). Depending upon adaptation to the physical and social environment, some archetypes develop while others languish in a relatively undeveloped state. Experience with the archetypes will lead to the coalescence or "agglomeration" of associations related to the archetype. Thoughts, memories, emotions, imagery, and reactions may all become clustered about the developing archetype. Hence, the roles of the physical and sociocultural environment are primary in the development of complexes, and thus the entire psyche (the total of all archetypes and complexes, whether conscious or unconscious) is the product of both genetic inheritance, development, and enculturation.

For Jung, as for Husserl, *conscious experience is embodied*. The ego [for Husserl, the ego-pole or 'I-pole' (Ger.: *Ichpol*); see Husserl (1977[1931]: 67-68)] is one complex (Husserl would say "monad") among many which becomes the presiding structure, or the "ego-complex" (i.e., the "I"). One function of consciousness is to maintain the relationship between the ego with its purview of perceptual field and horizon, and the unconscious (Jung 1970 [1955/56]: 371n). The development of the ego and consciousness unfold in tandem. Metaphorically speaking, "the conscious rises out of the unconscious like an island newly risen from the sea" (Jung 1954: 52). The psyche is full of structures that mediate aspects of perception, intuition, cognition, imagination, emotion, and action that may or may not be conscious to the ego—some in fact never are. Above all, consciousness for Jung is not a thing, not an entity. Jung saw consciousness in a very Jamesian way as a dynamic flow of experienced moments in which first this and then that archetype or complex entered ego awareness by way of their productions. For Jung, consciousness arises with the ego at its center, for Husserl as the "I-pole" of all intentional acts.

PURE EGO

I have touched upon the issue of the ego in previous chapters. It is about time I clarify what Husserl means by the concept.[59] From before birth and onwards into childhood, we humans develop an *empirical ego* (or "personal ego") as a presiding "complex" in the ongoing dialog with the vast background of the environing world and the Self (see Rochat 2001: 44). The empirical ego is the "I" of everyday life, of the natural attitude, built up of lifelong habits, techniques, and strategies for dealing with environmental and social contingencies that constitute a personal history, and that gives each of us a sense that when something happens in our stream of consciousness, it is "me" that is always there. The naïve egoistic view within the natural attitude is replete with beliefs,

---

[59] If you wish to read more about Husserl's description and understanding of the *ego*, see Husserl 1989[1952]: Sec. 2, Chap. 1, and Sup. II, 1993[1931]: 25-26, Fourth Meditation, 1982[1913]: Chap. 4, 232-234, 2019[1923/24]: 242-247, 555-558, 562-565; see also Costello 2012, Held 2003a: 47-48, Kern 2019, Luft 2015: 139-141.

assumptions, attributions, etc. about the Self, patterned responses to events and people, an entire library of concepts in our head about our self, we routinely use to get through life in pursuit of our desires and instinctual urges (Husserl 1989[1952]: 223-231).

But this version of the ego is a complex product of development, a layering of memories of experiences, habitual praxis, thoughts, images, and feelings. It does not "survive" a phenomenological reduction during which, taking the ego itself as an object, one element we believe defines the "I" after another becomes an object of scrutiny and subsequent bracketing eventually leaving nothing left of the "I" except the irreducible subject, the pure ego, the "transcendental" ego—"namely, the I that I, the philosophizing person, by questioning back after the subject of performance... according to the method of the phenomenological reduction of all my world—and my self—apperceptions, find as my ultimate I" (Husserl 2008: 5n).

Reducing the ego to the pure subject around which the noema clusters is far harder for some than the immeasurably easier task of reducing a coffee cup, the pure sensory given around which the noesis forms. Using our imagination, we can imagine that both the noesis and noema are mandalas with the object and subject forming the center of each respectively. The pure ego is simply the Watcher which is: (1) irreducible and thus is an essence, (2) the structure within the constituting structures of consciousness that unites the temporal "I" (it is the same "I" writing this sentence as wrote the previous sentences) over the epochs of "now points," (3) inseparable from the real immanent Body, and (4) the subject that intends every object of experience. When Husserl terms the Watcher the pure ego, he is noting that it is the essential, a priori subject of the intentional act.

> I take myself as the pure ego insofar as I take myself purely as that which, in perception, is directed to the perceived, in knowing to the known, in phantasizing to the phantasized, in logical thinking to the thought, in valuing to the valued, in willing to the willed. In the accomplishment of each act there lies a ray of directedness I cannot describe otherwise than by saying it takes its point of departure in the "Ego," [...]. (Husserl 1989[1952]: 103-104)

When Husserl speaks of the "transcendental" ego, he is referring to the Watcher's concreteness and originariness, to its reality as a function within the Body. It is the pure, transcendental ego that does the phenomenologizing, all the rest of the natural attitude "soul" having been reduced to a subjective point of view upon the object (Husserl 1993[1931]: 89). Within the context of intersubjective phenomenologizing, the Watcher realizes that she is not alone in an idealistic, solipsistic universe, but is one among many other Watchers intending objects in the self-same environing lifeworld:

> The (phenomenologizing) methodological demonstration of primordiality in my ego, as that in which an alien ego constitutes itself and thus an open totality of alien egos is temporalized, shows that every alien Other has his primordial environing world, and that right through all these givens of presentification [...] there necessarily runs an identity of acceptedness, the same nature for all, for my proto-modal primordial environing world and for every empathically presentified. Therein for any ego its organic body—"monads," subjects have their bodies, their localization in the one all-inclusive nature for every one of these subjects. (Husserl in Fink 1995: 165-166)

What makes the reduction of the ego far harder than the reduction of the object of consciousness is that the act of phenomenologizing the ego transforms the ego—it is literally Self-transformation. As Eugen Fink writes:

> We wish simply to indicate and emphasize that the reducing I is the phenomenological onlooker [read "Watcher"]. This means he is, first, the one practicing the epoché and then the one who reduces, in the strict sense. In the universal epoché, in the disconnection of all belief-positings, *the phenomenological onlooker produces himself.* The transcendental tendency that awakens in man and drives him to inhibit all acceptedness nullifies man himself, man *un-humanizes* [...] himself in performing the epoché, that is, he lays bare the transcendental onlooker in himself, he passes into him. This onlooker, however,

does not first come to be by the epoché, but is only *freed* of the shrouding cover of human being [...]. (Fink 1995: 39-40; emphasis added)

The Watcher or "onlooker" is nothing new, for the Watcher is the essential subject that has performed intentional acts all along the way. It is only by coming to *realize* the impermanence of anything with which I previously identified, other than the Watcher, that true transpersonal reorganization of the ego occurs (see next chapter). What Fink means by "un-humanizing" is the bracketing of all the enculturated self-identity information that paved my way into my community as a "culture-bearer" (see also Laughlin 2020a: 221-222, Roberts 1993 on the realization of "no-self").

INTRODUCING LIMIT-PROBLEMS

In performing a reduction within any experience, whether of the outer environing world or the inner world of the psyche, one becomes aware that there is a horizon that limits what can and cannot be experienced directly, what intuitive information can and cannot be acquired, and that effectively restricts the normal course of a phenomenological epoché (Fazakas and Gozé 2020, Fink 1995, Steinbock 2017). We played with doing simple pure phenomenological reductions of sensory experiences in Chapter 3. We saw that even the object provides perspectives, some of which are *perceived* or "presentified" (the side of the coffee cup I can see) and some of which are *apperceived* or "appresentified" (the side of the cup I cannot see but intuitively know is there)—we intuit the apperceived aspects as part of the primordial given without recourse to higher cortical processing, reason, or inference (Husserl 1982[1913]: 109). Clearly then, the brain is interested in making wholes out of parts, whole things out of glimpses of aspects, and rendering whole objects meaningful.

Of particular interest for us is that our sense of identity as both object and subject of intentional acts—our "givenness" of Self, of "I," or ipseity—presents us with limitations at every turn (Fricke 2018), and in some cases there have occurred memory constructions (e.g., traumatic events, visions, numinous "culture pattern" or "big" dreams) during our childhood development that are not given in our everyday experience as adults, but which nonetheless may mediate our adult stream of self-awareness. For instance, if, like me, you are a neurotic, there is a background of anxiety that can pervade even the least threatening intentional act. This usually unconscious element may nonetheless influence judgments you make about what you are perceiving, and indeed may well color a priori intuitions associated with the object. Fink (1995: 70-71) suggests that at this juncture in our phenomenologizing the integration of theoretical material may help us in deepening the intuitive grasp of the experience. Husserl says as much in some of his writings, especially in the so-called C-Manuscripts (Marosan 2020), where he suggests a method of *constructive phenomenology* in which the given information within the epoché is augmented by theoretical material grounded in solid empirical science and at the same time is intuited with absolute certainty to be implicated in the experience:

> The essential point of constructive phenomenology or phenom-enological construction is *to unfold the principally invisible in a phenomenologically legitimate way*, which cannot be brought to an intuitive givenness for theoretical reasons. At a certain point we reach the boundaries of possible intuitive grasp of things, but we can discover a set of apodictical implications, which motivate us in an apodictic way to perform phenomenological constructions, and thus thematize phenomena which cannot be presented in an intuitively completed or filled manner. (Marosan 2020: 7; emphasis added)

Fink elaborated this constructive extension of the reduction in his *Sixth Cartesian Meditation* (1995) so as to clarify and perhaps even transcend ipseity and other limit-problems.[60] Limiting factors include the culture and history (development) of a person (Husserl, 1970[1937]: 6-7), a person's birth, death, "dreamless sleep," "loss of consciousness," and of course the unconscious (Husserl, 1970[1937]: 188-189). This is reminiscent of Marcel Proust's famous encounter with tea, madeleine

---

[60] It is important to note that Eugen Fink was Husserl's assistant and collaborator, as well as a contemplative phenomenologist in his own right. Fink's *Sixth Cartesian Meditation* was read and approved by Husserl before his death (see Geniusas 2020).

cakes and involuntary memories: "No sooner had the warm liquid, and the crumbs with it, touched my palate, a shudder ran through my whole body, and I stopped, intent upon the extraordinary changes that were taking place. An exquisite pleasure had invaded my senses, but individual, detached, with no suggestion of its origin" (Proust 2020[1913]: 13). Involuntary memories that arise in sensory experiences may be due to the loss of awareness of originary experiences, ideas, images, and other psychological acts to the unconscious:

> But [a] judgment can also be abandoned in its retentional reverberation. It then sinks ever further into the background and at the same time becomes ever more indistinct; the degree of its prominence gradually lessens until it finally disappears from the field of immediate consciousness, is 'forgotten.' *It is henceforth incorporated into the passive background, into the 'unconscious,' which is not a dead nothingness but a limiting mode of consciousness* and accordingly can affect us anew like another passivity in the form of whims, free-floating ideas, and so on. In this modification, however, the judgment is not an original but a secondary passivity, which essentially refers to its origin in an actual spontaneous production. (Husserl 1973[1939]: 279)

Within the "passive background" may lie unconscious memory formations such as that which can form around early childhood trauma, perhaps even due to a traumatic birth (see Steinbock 2017: 5-10). A "bad" birth may leave a record in deep memory that continues to influence experiences for a lifetime. Birthing trauma may be re-experienced as feelings, images, and body postures/movements later in life, perhaps as a consequence of therapeutic treatments leading to so-called abreaction "primal-scream" or "re-birthing" experiences (Lilienfeld 2007). Any contemplative who knows the roots of their neurosis by way of meditation experiences can attest to the power of early trauma upon their daily lives (e.g., Williams, Francis and Durham 1976). Most of us have not experienced death, and yet the inevitability of our dying influences our experiences in life (see especially Becker 1973, Laughlin 2020: Chap. 12), perhaps underlying the anxiety states mentioned above.

Moreover, and in very Freudian-like reasoning, Husserl notes our ability to repress mental processes that we do not wish to acknowledge—repressions that make up what Jung called the "shadow" layer of the psyche—all the nasty bits of ourselves we wish to deny. In *The Crisis of European Sciences and Transcendental Phenomenology*, Husserl notes that with respect to unconscious intentionalities, "...this would be the place for those repressed emotions of love, of humiliation, of ressentiments, and the kinds of behavior unconsciously motivated by them which have been disclosed by recent depth-psychology" (Husserl, 1970[1937]: 237). Of equal importance, there are the activities of the psyche that remain forever beyond awareness, but which nonetheless influence experience. The classic examples are the archetypes which, on Jung's account, are never directly perceived (Jung 1968a: 42, 1969a: 210). When active, the archetypes may mediate instinctual acts, intuitive knowledge, and imagery/fantasy objects that may burble up into consciousness. Indeed, archetypal structures underlie and produce the symbolism that is so fundamental to all mythological and cosmological systems and that are responsible for the patterned similarities among these systems across cultures (Jung 1969a: 206, Edinger 1972: 4, Laughlin and Throop 2001).

Digging deeper into what Husserl learned from his meditations, there is always the object of perception, be it an object surrounded by apprehended objects, relations, and intuitions, or be it the "misty horizon" (Husserl 1982[1913]: 102) beyond which the world opens out into infinity. The horizon of each moment of awareness forms a "continuous ring" around the object of perception that marks the fuzzy boundary beyond which awareness fades toward non-awareness. Yet much that is going on beyond the horizon impacts the field of primordial sensory given, its relations and intuitive associations, as well as how the ego stands relative to the object (see Tougas 2013: Chap. 7). Moreover—and of great importance to ethnography—several limit-phenomena are precisely the experiences of great utility to peoples raised in those cultures that treat experiences had in dreams, visions, fantasies, possession states, and drug trips as real (Laughlin 2020b, Winkelman and Baker 2015).

> But with the most inner soul level we have a completely different type of problem, that of disclosing its intentionality, of investigating its hidden life, to raise awareness of what is unconscious, to point

out, to fix and to describe—through reflexion—what was and is unreflected experience, flowing life, as something that is sunk, but not unreachable: it cannot be nothing. The intention here is to obtain systematic and methodical experience from the occasional experience of the soul. (Husserl 1925 unpublished quote, Togni 2018: 75)

RECONSTRUCTIVE PHENOMENOLOGY

Thus, Husserl came to realize that there are inherent and situational limits to the application of pure phenomenology. As we saw in Chapter 3, the phenomenological reduction at its very purest occurs in simple, relatively static intentional conditions bracketed away from temporality, causation, history, and encounters with other sentient beings. From the "pure" stance, engagement with the unconscious or any other limit conditions is not possible. Despite this roadblock, we have a sense that there is more happening within the stream of consciousness than can be studied or described using static methods. For instance, Husserl was aware that in any experience there may be present an intuitive awareness that "I" am the same ego that had an experience an hour or a day or years ago, memories of which may be accompanied with imagery and feelings (Husserl 1993[1931]: §33, §44, §47). This continuity of the pure ego as subject of the stream of consciousness operates to, among other functions, facilitate our natural feeding forward into the future streaming by time-binding, not only objects and sequences of objects of perception, but a stable platform of awareness to match that of the continuity of the Body. Just as with my body, I have the automatic sense of myself as subject going back into the dimness of childhood memories. Now my experience is different than five minutes ago, but it is the same Watcher going back billions of epochs until my memory reaches a blank wall built out of bricks of knowledge about my life as described by and learned from others. "I" am not only at the very center of my experiences, but it is the same "I" that has been at the center of all previous experiences, and that will take center stage in all future intentional acts until I die. We do not yet know what systems in the brain mediate this sense of center and continuity of awareness, and the literature is ambiguous on the topic, for it all depends upon how you define "ego." Damasio (1999a: 16) has suggested that networks comprising what he calls *core consciousness* are located in the brain stem and in the cingulate/somatosensory cortex, and which "...provides the organism with a sense of self about one moment—now—and about one place—here." Clearly, the tagging my sense of "I" with my physical being is an ancient component of the pure ego as described by Husserl and may apply equally for other animals with brains.

This awareness of a continuity of subject led Husserl to expand his methods to incorporate awareness of temporality, thus leading to more *genetic* descriptions of experience. This opened the epoché to the effects of historical factors that, although they occurred in the past, leave a residue that continues to influence the current "now" epoch. It also opened the epoché to anticipatory factors present in the "now" epoch that will in time influence future epochs. In addition, it is common for the object of consciousness to remind us of something else. Within the context of the given appears associations with other objects and experiences maintained within our memory (Husserl 1970 [1900-01] I: 186-187).

As Steinbock (1995, 2017) has shown, the genetic expansion led eventually to *generative methods* that extended the phenomenological method further into the realm of efficacious but unconscious causal elements in perception (see Husserl 1993[1931]: 142, 1993[1931]: §38). Husserl's verb "generation" (Ger.: *Generativität*) connotes what anthropologists would call "construction" with respect to socially learned traditions, roles, social relations, meanings, values, and behaviors, perhaps influencing the experiences had by generation after generation of "culture bearers." Much of what we have to bracket in order to phenomenologize our experiences are the product of generativity in Husserl's sense.

Within the boundaries of applying generative methods, Husserl was required to focus upon the role of theorizing about events in the "immemorial past" that might account for objects, relations, associations, etc. in immediate experience (see Bower 2014). Here Husserl was profoundly influenced by the philosopher Paul Natorp (1854-1924) who was concerned with reconstructing the role of subjectivity in psychology (see Luft 2016). The events that impact our immediate experience, as well as our characteristic natural attitude may have their origin beyond the reach of our personal memory.

A method is thus required that is essentially a regression from the immediate given to origins wherever they may lay—including well into our species' past. From the neurophenomenological point of view, the extent of reconstructive phenomenology would include evolutionary, as well as developmental biological factors that cannot be directly experienced, but are accessible to reconstructive theorizing. This methodological extension of generative phenomenology may be used to trace the origins of "cultural" factors impinging upon the lifeworld and is especially useful as we have seen when we peruse the structures of the unconscious, as well as when we enter the domain of moral judgments (see Chapter 11).

Husserl's genetic and generative considerations are parallel to what in Buddhist phenomenology is called *karmic analysis* (Sasaki 1956). The term *kamma* simply means "action," but in the East philosophies do not posit a mind-body duality as we do in the West. That means that activities begin in the mind and may or may not extend outwards into the world by way of behavior. In either case, *kamma* is produced because both mental and physical activities have consequences and feed back into the brainmind. A karmic analysis is a reconstruction of the karmic links that may regress backwards within one's life and may even reach back through multiple lifetimes (as is certainly the case with biogenetic factors conditioning the lifeworld). "We note as a point of interest that for both Husserl and Yogācāra the present moment alone was real, and yet the present *is never anything other than an embodied history*" (Lusthaus 2002: 25; emphasis added).

IMAGINING CONSCIOUSNESS

Perhaps the most commonplace limit-phenomenon experienced by all of us is imagination. It is also one of the faculties of sensory experience Husserl used in his reflections to great effect, both with respect to experiencing imagery and more complexly to fantasy ("fancy," "fantasy;" Husserl 1973[1939]: 340-348, 1977[1925]: 53-65; see also Bernet 2002, Jansen 2005). In everyday acts of intentionality, apperception can invite imagination—not only can I apperceive a whole coffee cup, but I can also imagine what the hidden aspects of the cup look like—I can see any or all the hidden aspects as images before my "mind's eye" without altering my perspective on the real cup. I can direct my lens of imagination inside the cup and explore its fantasied inner surfaces. One is reminded of those cubist paintings in which the artist presents different aspects of an object on the canvas simultaneously. If I elaborate the imaginary exploration of the whole cup, I can fantasize with my mind's eye circumnavigating around the cup, clock, house, or what-have-you. I can continue to fantasize even if the object before my senses is removed. In fact, I do not need a real sensed object to fantasize about the object. I can imagine an airplane that I pilot around and look down at features on the ground. I can get so involved in fantasy role playing that my body and mind "become" my fantasy character. In extreme situations, I can pretend to be something that I am not until eventually I become what I pretended to be. Evidence suggests that identification with a fantasied "playable character" in a role-playing game can be intensely emotional, and the "death" of a character can have real and negative effects on the player, for instance while playing the popular Dungeons and Dragons (Sidhu and Carter 2021). Indeed, the neurobiological functions of role play among animals with brains is fundamental to neural development and identity formation in early life (Bekoff and Allen 1997, Laughlin 1990a). As we shall discuss in the next chapter, ritualized role-playing can have profound effects upon consciousness, a factor widely illustrated in many cultural traditions and spiritual disciplines.

While sensory perception requires an object stimulated by something in the environing world, if we imagine or fantasize about a thing, the images are distinct from the sensory given.[61] If you show me a photo of your dog, the photo in all its aspects is a sensory given, a real thing, but the image of your dog in the photo is not. The photo is real, while the image it depicts is not real in the act of perception (Husserl 1982[1913]): 136, 311, 2001[1900/1901]: 173, 2005[1898-1925]). The same distinction holds between the experience of a real something and the memory of that something. The first is perception and the second

---

[61] Imagination is a fuzzy category and can include imagining things like math problems and concepts that are not images (see Aldea 2013). Here I refer to imagination specifically involving images, as the term implies, and which I read to be Husserl's intention.

is an image or representation of the perception. The critical difference between a primordial sensory given (my visual experience of my coffee cup sitting here next to my keyboard) and image (I close my eyes and imagine my coffee cup sitting next to my keyboard) is that the former is stimulated by the environing world engaging my afferent sensory system placing limits upon experience—if I turn the cup over, the coffee will spill out all over the table and floor—while with the latter neither the environing world nor my afferent sensory systems have any control of my experience—I can imagine turning the cup over and the coffee not spilling out, or spilling up, or spilling sideways.

As Husserl would say, I may derive the image from the phenomenon, but I am free to play with the image in ways I cannot do with the percept because of obduracy. As we have discussed before, the environing world is obdurate relative to all willful acts upon it. I can imagine putting my finger through this table-top, but I cannot accomplish such an act in the real environing world. This distinction led Husserl to the method of eidetic free variation (see Chapter 3) wherein we use the image derived from the percept to explore variations of context and use this exercise to uncover the essences (*eidos*) intuitively present in every act of perception (Husserl 1977[1925]: 54-56, 1982[1913]: 198-201). This method is the "starting point" for exploring essences, for as we freely vary the "fancy-image" derived from primordial sense-data in our fantasy, our intuitive grasp of the limits imposed by the essences emerge. How far and in what respects can I alter the image of my coffee cup until it is no longer "cup-like?" What is essential about the sensory given that I intuit as "cup" (see the exercise with the paper clip in Chapter 3)?

What is perhaps missed by many (see Casey 1976 for an instructive exception) is that Freud, Jung, and Husserl came up with the very same method for accessing "unconscious" and "creative" material by way of imagery. For Freud, the client is encouraged to "free associate" ideas and words, an exercise that can reveal unconscious drives and repressed feelings (e.g., the so-called "Freudian slip"). Jung used a similar method in his "active imagination" exercises that invite dialog not only with personal unconscious material, but with archetypal structures in the collective unconscious. As we saw in Chapter 3, Husserl likewise found that "free fancy" or eidetic free variation can be used to uncover the root *eidos* behind the object of primordial sensory given. What all these methods have in common is the exercise of imagination to seek out hidden structures, or depths of the psyche, but each with his respective project and interpretation in mind.

Cultures often utilize the difference between perception and fantasy to significant effect. There are Buddhist Tantric ("arising yoga") meditations in which a practitioner scans an object in the environing world (bowl of water, mandala, sandpainting, picture, etc.), then turns away and holds the after-image, learning to hold the image with such intensity of concentration that the after-image becomes an eidetic image that can be called-up at will (see Laughlin 2020a: 139-141, Laughlin, McManus and Webber 1984, Chang 2004). Once stabilized, the eidetic image becomes the object of consciousness, rather than the sensory object from which the eidetic image is derived. By removing the obduracy imposed by the environing world upon sensory perception, various changes occur to the eidetic image without the intention of the practitioner. One common change is that the eidetic image perfects itself—geometric distortions, imperfections, blemishes, and the like featured in the sensory given all disappear. The eidetic image becomes (in Husserlian terms) a representation of the inner *eidos* or essential structure—and what Jung would call the archetype.

THE OBDURATE NATURE OF THE UNCONSCIOUS

We see that the environing world (the real world around us) imposes obduracy upon our external senses—if you make up your mind to stick your finger through the tabletop, the real world will thwart your will. Some of the intuitive knowledge accompanying any experience will be about obduracy adumbrated from past experiences. What is less well understood is the fact that the unconscious also imposes obduracy relative to conscious will, but among people unfamiliar with explorations of their unconscious, experiences evoked by unconscious processes are frequently unaccompanied by intuitive knowledge (Laughlin 1997b). The certainty that derives from intuitive grasp of perceptual objects may be absent or diminished when dealing with the unconscious. Max Planck Institute's Wolf Singer (2007) has suggested that selection has been in favor of more concrete, simple, linear object awareness in adapting to the environing world. In other words, getting food while avoiding becoming food did not place selective pressures on the brain to intuit complex non-linear systems:

> This confronts us with a serious problem. Because we lack the intuition to understand nonlinear behavior and therefore focus primarily on linear models, we tend to underestimate the capacity of these systems to self-organize, but at the same time overestimate our ability to control them. As a consequence, we assume that the most effective strategy for stabilizing and controlling these systems is to establish central entities that regulate the distributed processes and steer the system in the desired direction. A glance at the hierarchical structures in our social and economic systems suffices to demonstrate that we are only too willing to follow this intuition and to put it into action. (Singer 2007: S19)

The encounter with the unconscious is a direct inquiry into the dynamics of a nonlinear complex adaptive system. Most people in all cultures are ill-equipped for comprehending their inner neural processes, especially as we humans cannot directly experience the inner workings of the most complex system in the known universe, our own brain.

We commonly speak of the unconscious as a subjective domain, but the embodied Self is in fact comprised of neural and endocrine pathways, themselves being physical structures in the real world within the physical body. We might even say that the unconscious is mediated subjectively by inner "objects" (models, cognits, networks, complexes, schemes) that are part of our *internal* physical world. Our brain is part of the objective physical reality to which our consciousness is designed to adapt, in company with our lungs, heart, intestines, and other organs we rarely ever pay attention to, but know from the functions (breathing, pulse, pains, movements, and sounds) they mediate. You can easily see that this takes us beyond Husserl's strict, self-imposed writ and into a Husserlian neurophenomenology. It leads us to the seeming irony that the brain provides an obdurate nature to its own questing awareness. But there is really no irony there at all, for it is the obduracy of our unconscious processes that allow us to true our knowledge about our Self—our greater psyche. The various forms of unconscious obduracy pop up constantly in clinical settings—for instance, unconscious resistance of the patient towards discussing certain painful memories (Ormont 1986).

Just as most of what goes on in the external environing world is invisible to our perception (Husserl's "misty horizon" above), so too with the unconscious, most processes of which can never be glimpsed directly. In fact, we know the unconscious primarily through imagery and intuitive insights, augmented sometimes by emotions and movements. This nature of the psyche has led to methods for establishing a dialog with the unconscious by way of imagery, for as Jung emphasized, many of the systems mediating the unconscious have a "psychoid" nature— that is, they operate as vital organs with many, but not all the properties of psychological activity (Jung 1969b; see also Addison 2009). Guided visualizations are used to set the stage for this: Perhaps you fantasize you are sitting in a comfortable room with two easy chairs facing each other. You sit in one chair and wait to see who shows up in the other chair. This is an over-simplification, but this kind of active imagination is fundamental to "getting to know" your Self, and is one commonly used in Jungian analytic psychology, as well as in other visualization practices used in therapy.

Just as importantly, Husserl recognized that unconscious processes can "drive" conscious experiences to such an extent that Husserl could speak of *impulsive intentionality* (Ger.: *Triebintentionalität*; see Togni 2018: 77; see also Fink's Appendix VIII in Husserl 1970[1936]). Impulses (drives, urges, instincts) motivate experiences from within our psyche. Husserl does not characterize this type of intentionality as deriving from ego (in the sense of the ego willing the object), but rather from *spirit*, from the unconscious. Impulsive intentionality is "...pre-direct (*aufgewiesene*), non-volitive, and essentially without-ego" (Ghigi 2004). This, for Husserl, was one of the prime sources of insight and creativity (see next chapter). His view is compatible with modern neuroscience understanding of what constitutes unconscious processes (see Barth, Giampieri-Deutsch and Klein 2012: Chap. 14).

What Husserl showed us is that we are at the same time a nexus of subjectivity and a physical object (Ger.: *Leib*) existing in concrete reality (Husserl 1977[1925], 1989[1952]: Chap 3). My body is both the center and source of all perception and a concrete object that may in part or in whole be an object of my (the Watcher's) perception. Any contemplative who has spent time working on body-awareness—Buddhists call this kind of meditation *kayanupassana*, "mindfulness of the body"—will be exquisitely aware of the body as a nexus of environing world obduracy. I can only perceive colors within the narrow range allowed by my retinae and sounds within the range of frequencies that will excite my cochlear hair cells. I cannot swallow an object wider than my esophagus. I cannot fly off the top of a skyscraper without technological aids and survive. I can grasp an object with the palm-side of my hand, but not with the back of my hand. I cannot hold my breath as long as I would like to do while free-diving. My physical being is an object much like any other physical object and is subject to the same laws of physics as a rock, an asteroid, or tree shrew. At the same time, my body is a nexus of affordancy. I can run if I have to, I can eat and digest nutriments, I can communicate using facial expressions, gestures, postures, and other "body language" attributes, in addition to speech.

SUMMARY AND SEGUE

It is useful to keep in mind that most neuropsychological structures comprising the brainmind *operate outside of consciousness all or most of the time*. Structures and processes going on in our brains every day may operate obdurately or may afford us opportunities. Someone gives me a phone number to call and then hangs up. Unless I can write that number down within seconds of hearing it, I cannot remember the number, much as I wish to do so. Yet a friend of mine cannot forget any telephone number she has ever had or used a number of times. Two different bodies, two different sets of obduracy/affordancy.

Husserl has shown us that when it comes to subjective, introspective engagement with unconscious processes, straightforward "pure" and even "transcendental" phenomenological methods are self-limiting. To augment the power of doing phenomenology, expansions have to be added that facilitate grasping what the a priori, post-reduction given can teach us. Genetic material and even generative theoretical knowledge may be required to flesh-out our comprehension of what we are in fact experiencing. Yet even generative phenomenology may be challenged when confronted by reductions occurring within mystical experiences. Husserl occasionally took up such challenges, and his studies of ASC were fruitful.

CHAPTER TEN

Husserl and Transpersonal Experience

*A central feature of shamanism involves the altered state of consciousness
(ASC) central to selection, training and professional activities of divination
and healing. The indication of selection of a Shaman typically begins
with signs manifested in unusual visions, dreams and illness, which are
interpreted as the insistence of spirits that the person undertake arduous
shamanic training that involved deliberate induction of ASC. Training
involved a solitary vision quest in the wilderness imposing diverse austerities:
extensive fasting; sleep, social and sensory deprivation; endurance of pain and
temperature extremes; and various emetic and other substances to facilitate
induction of a visionary experience that gives powers to the Shaman.*

– Michael J. Winkelman (2021)

*Mysticism is characterized by a unique set of factors. The most
important of these are: the attaining of intuitive knowledge or insight
which reaches beyond habitual modes of perception and thought;
the acquisition of certainty about the ultimate nature of reality, an
absolute, or truth; a strong sense of unity and identity concerning both
self and the world; the ineffability of the experience in that attempts to
describe it often result in self-contradictory statements, and; it arrives at
a level or stratum of experience beyond subject-object distinctions [...].*

– Fred J. Hanna (1993a: 42-43)

Many people these days are raised in technocratic societies,
and as such are imbued with materialistic and capitalistic
values (Ellul 2018[1977]). One of the effects of technocratic
value systems is to enculturate people away from interest in any state
of consciousness not oriented toward the external environing world. As
a consequence of their upbringing, these peoples tend to ignore what
happens in their dream lives, as well as other ASC such as visions,

trances, sacred journeys, ritually evoked experiences, and drug trips (Devereux 1992, 2008, Winkelman 1986, 2013b). These alternative experiences are typically considered to be irrelevant in the scheme of things—"calm down daughter, it was only a dream." My colleagues and I have labeled such cultures *monophasic*, referring of course to the single phase of daily awareness we all call "being awake" (Laughlin 1997c, 2011, 2020, Laughlin, McManus and d'Aquili 1990, Laughlin and Rock 2014, Tiberia and Laughlin 2016; see also Cunningham 2022: 116, Lumpkin 2001). While this relative blindness toward alternative states does not affect everybody equally in any one mono-phasic society, the dominant values hold sway in critical processes like identity formation in childhood, communication and sharing of ex-periences, social roles, and the like. This condition may be considered an aberrant product of mass societies, the industrial revolution, and bureaucratic social institutions.

Most traditional cultures, however, are not monophasic, although technocracy is everywhere a constant and powerful acculturative influence. Traditional societies tend to be what we call *polyphasic* in that they pay attention to experiences had in ASC, as well as what we call "being awake" (see Atleo 2006, Lohmann 2019, Saniotis 2010b, Walsh 2018). Take for example how knowledge is evaluated among the *Dene Tha* ("Beaver Indians") of British Columbia. When he began his research with this group, ethnographer Jean-Guy Goulet (1987, 1998) found his hosts were skeptical of knowledge that was not obtained by direct experience in a variety of ASC, especially dreaming. His hosts were reluctant to discuss knowledge obtained during dreaming with anyone, including curious anthropologists, who were not themselves "dreamers." As Goulet put it, "...true knowledge is personal knowledge." The implication is that for the *Dene Tha*, if you have not experienced it, you cannot really know it. It is thus that the anthropology of dreaming inevitably propels us into the transpersonal dimensions of experience. For polyphasic peoples, experiences had in ASC are as real as "waking" experiences are for monophasic peoples (see Lohmann and Goodale 2003).

Anthropology took its lead from psychologists who began seriously studying *transpersonal experiences* back in the 1970s (Cardeña, Lynn and Krippner 2000, Cunningham 2022, MacDonald and Almendro

2021, Walsh 2018). At the time, transpersonal experiences were defined as those considered to transcend normal ego consciousness. Psychologists Roger Walsh and Frances Vaughan used the term to, "... reflect the reports of people practicing various consciousness disciplines who spoke of experiences of an extension of identity beyond both individuality and personality" (1980: 16). They were referring to the empirical ego, of course—the natural attitude ego, not the Husserlian pure ego (the Watcher). More recently, Glenn Hartelius *et al.* (2021) suggests that transpersonal psychology has developed over two "waves" of central issues. The first wave focused upon ASC: "These elements are states of consciousness; often employed in transcendence and typically a transcending of self, ego, ego-based self-concept, or time and space; often toward a cosmic concern or ultimate." The second wave expanded issues of relevance to healthy or advanced life-styles, and personal growth and betterment: "This includes concepts reflecting the present-moment lived experience of embodiment, embeddedness in community and world, engagement with the diversities inherent in community, and enrollment in personal and social transformation" (ibid: 25).

Transpersonal anthropology (Dobkin de Rios and Winkelman 1989, Lahood 2007, Laughlin 1994c, 2012, 2013a, 2013b, Laughlin, McManus and d'Aquili 1990: 18-21, Laughlin, McManus and Shearer 1983, MacDonald 1981, Schroll and Schwartz 2005, Sheppard 2007, Winkelman 2010) has emphasized an interest in societies, techniques, and spiritual knowledge systems grounded in ASC experiences and evoked by people who apply ritual techniques, psychoactive substances, ordeals, and so forth. In studying the cross-cultural use of psychoactive drugs (or "entheogens;" see Ruck *et al.* 1979), Marlene Dobkin de Rios (1984) was forced to conclude that there seems to be an inherent drive among humans everywhere to alter their states of consciousness, often with the aid of drugs, and usually in the interests of accruing self-knowledge, enlightenment, healing power, political power, etc. (see also Saniotis 2010a). This is a pattern that can even be seen among individuals and sub-cultures within technocratic societies, although the dominant value system—the general technocratic worldview—of those societies are rarely informed from ASC. To pay attention to what one learns about the world and oneself from drug trips is considered a hallmark of a "counterculture."

TRANSPERSONALISM AND ETHNOCENTRISM

Transpersonalism as a movement both within science and among people in technocratic societies may be seen as a corrective for unbalanced ego-formation, and transpersonal psychology reflects this effort by accentuating the importance of self-healing, and experiences that inform personal development away from a more materialistic orientation. But many of the techniques, ideologies, and extraordinary experiences evidenced in transpersonal studies are similar to those that are commonplace among traditional peoples. Hence, there is a certain quality of ethnocentrism to be found in the orientation towards development of self-knowledge among those raised in technocratic societies, including those that provide most of the subjects of transpersonal psychological research (Cunningham 2022: 54-55, 86, 114-115). Let me give you an example. Psychology turned its gaze upon a phenomenon known as *lucid dreaming* (Barrett 1991, Green 1968, LaBerge, Levitan and Dement 1986)—that is, dreaming of such vivid, hyper-aware lucidity (Husserl's "vitality") that the dreamer can become aware that they are dreaming while in the dream, and exercise considerable control over what happens in dreaming experiences (e.g., deciding to fly here and there, find one's own body parts, meditate upon dream objects, and so forth).

While lucidity during dreaming is unusual among technocratic peoples, it is common among peoples who consider all experiences as real (Bulkeley 1995, Krippner 1994, Laughlin 2011a: Chaps. 7, 8, 9, 2011b)—or as equally *un*-real or *sur*-real (Bharati 1976). One of the tip-offs to the importance of dreaming among a polyphasic people is if they routinely share their dream experiences. Take for instance dream-sharing among the Mehinaku living along the Xingu River headwaters of Brazil (Grego 1981). The people sleep at night in hammocks hung close together in their long house. As the night progresses, people wake up to add fuel to the fire and reflect upon their dreams. In the morning people share their dreams immediately after waking. These dreams are adventures had by each person's "eye soul" during sleep which detaches from the body and is able to travel around without physical limitations. For the Mehinaku, traveling around as an "eye soul" is just as real as traveling in one's body while "awake." While dream traveling, individuals may pick up important information that, when reported in the morning, may influence what people do during the day. The point here is that just what experiences can be considered "transpersonal" is subject to cross-cultural variation. Despite this, there are universal structures of consciousness and neurophysiological processing that come into play regardless of the society being considered (Laughlin and Rock 2013).

As we have remarked earlier, the causation involved in experienced reality is often invisible to direct perception. We know from ethnographic research that peoples everywhere on the planet are concerned to make causes visible, explicable, and thereby controllable (see Claffert, Baker and Winkelman 2019, Van Leeuwen and Van Elk 2019). Polyphasic peoples routinely consult their experiences had in ASC for information about the causes of events. It makes sense from our neurophenomenological perspective to interpret these fact-finding methods as dialogs with peoples' own unconscious, often tapping into intuitive insights into the way things are (Laughlin 2011). This especially applies to those methods augmented by psychoactive drugs which are known to make engaging archetypal structures easier (Hill 2019).

Husserl handles the cultural variation in knowing, belief, attitude, worldview, and so forth under the concepts of *spirit* (Ger.: *Geist*) and *spiritual world*, thus leaving us with another strange way that he used words (see especially Husserl 1989[1952]: Section 3). He contrasts spirit with *nature*, the former being the domain of *motivational laws* and the latter with *causal laws*. The spiritual world is a world of the mind that is generated by people and perhaps other species in their social interactions, the collective building up of systems of knowledge and praxis. Thus, the "spirituality" in which anthropologists, transpersonal psychologists, and many religious studies scholars are especially interested are included in Husserl's *notion of the spiritual world at the level of belief systems, historicity, and worldview that in part constitute the natural attitude*. As we have discovered together, cultural assumptions, narratives, and beliefs can mangle lifeworld level primordial givenness with cultural constructions such as "city of the dead," "underworld and overworld," "other-than-human-persons" (sprites, demons, ghosts, angels, gods, shape-shifters and were-beings, and so forth), etc. Husserl *did not* simply include within his spiritual world *direct experiences* (hallucinations, visions, dreams) of "spirits"—e.g., dreaming of a dead relative with whom we communicate, perceiving fairies and ghosts, and other extraordinary experiences such as absorption states (below). All of these direct experiences are amenable to the phenomenological reduction at the level of image consciousness.

HUSSERLIAN PHENOMENOLOGY AND TRANSPERSONAL EXPERIENCES

Husserl's method of phenomenological reduction has gained significant attention by transpersonal psychologists and anthropologists (see Hanna 1993a, Laughlin 1994b, Laughlin and Rock 2021, Malkemus 2012, Robbins *et al.* 2018, Wilber 1996: 70). Indeed, it is hard not to see how Husserlian meditations cannot be relevant to transpersonal studies (see Hanna 1993a). We have already touched on many issues of interest to transpersonal study. First and foremost is Husserl's realization that disciplined application of phenomenological methods (i.e., meditation, contemplation) over the course of months and years inevitably changes the phenomenologist at very fundamental levels (Husserl 1970[1936]: 137; see also Laughlin and Rock 2021). The phenomenological attitude, as we have said, is an altered state which Husserl considered to be more advanced than the natural attitude:

> In one sense, phenomenological reflection becomes radically "abnormal" when it ruptures the concordance of everyday life; it not only reflects on it, but in distinction from everyday "normal" reflection, it no longer yields to the flow of positing meaning, and instead abstains from the presuppositions that it carries out pre-reflectively and reflexively. [...] In another sense, however, phenomenological reflection is "normal"—"hyper-normal," as Edmund Husserl would say—in the sense that it is optimal; for it institutes a new order of experience that is, contextually speaking, "the best possible" even though it is not "concordant" with the natural attitude; it does this by describing the very ways in which the natural attitude unfolds and how objects and the world are there as in-themselves-for-us. Phenomenology is a peculiar kind of reflective attentiveness that distances itself from everyday life in order to get to the root of that very life. (Steinbock 2007: 3)

Four of the personal transformations which we have already introduced are: (1) the realization of the impermanence of the ego, (2) the realization of the distinction between perception and apperception and how they play-out in the organization of intentional acts, (3) realization of essential structures of experience that have evolved over the course of our species' phylogenesis, and (4) the realization that it is the structure of a priori, primordial sensory givenness that grounds our knowledge in reality and keeps us from wafting off into a potentially maladaptive La-La Land.

Husserl, however, was far more involved in transpersonal matters than these realizations, and where he did not do so, his meditative methods can be applied directly to transpersonal phenomena. As a matter of background, it should be noted that Husserl was a religious person, not an agnostic or atheist. Having been raised Jewish, he converted to the Lutheran brand of Protestantism in 1886 (Moran 2005: 16). Despite his Jewish heritage and his Christian faith, he nearly always kept his religiosity apart from his phenomenologizing, except to occasionally play with the very Cartesian idea of a God who is characterized as manifesting absolute reason, absolute knowledge, and absolute omniscience (see various mentions in Husserl 1970[1936]). Husserl was above all a mature contemplative and that course of discovery leads ineluctably to self-realization, regardless of the spiritual tradition being followed. Apropos to his spirituality, this quote from Husserl, translated by Anthony Steinbock, is revealing:

> I also want what the churches want: to lead humanity into the *Aeternitas.*[62] My task is to try to do this through philosophy. Everything that I have written up to now is only preparatory; it is only a development [...] of methods. In the course of one's life, one unfortunately does not arrive at the core, at what is essential. It is so important for philosophy to be led out of liberalism and rationalism, and to be led once more to what is essential, to *truth*. The question concerning ultimate reality, truth, must be the object of every true philosophy. This is my life's work. (Husserl quote from Steinbock 2007: 28)

---

[62] *Aeternitas* in ancient Roman religion was one of many anthropomorphic deities and was considered the personification of eternity.

Being a real phenomenologist, which Husserl equated with "first" philosophizing, is nothing less than a radical shift in goal, a genuine life's *absolute calling*:

> But this absolute radicalism entails, for him who wants to become a philosopher in this most genuine sense, a corresponding absolute and radical life-decision in which his life becomes a *life rooted in an absolute calling*. It is a decision by which the subject commits himself, and indeed simply *as* himself—from the innermost center of his personality—to that in the universal value-realm of cognition that is best in itself, and to a life that is constantly devoted to the idea of what is best in this sense. Or, as we can also say, it is a decision in which the subject in a certain sense "absolutely identifies" himself with what is best in this sense. A correlative expression for this same central and universal self-determination is to say that the subject who defines himself as a philosopher chooses the highest form of cognition, or philosophy, as an absolute final aim of his striving life, as his true "vocation," in terms of which he has defined himself and to which he has committed himself once and for all—to which he, as a practical *Ego*, has given himself over absolutely. (Husserl 2019[1923/24]: 215)

The actual *doing* of phenomenology, like really following any contemplative path towards truth, implies giving oneself up to the internal changes in one's psyche towards which the pursuit of truth inevitably leads.

As we have seen, Husserl used language in unique ways (in German, of course) and it can be difficult on a superficial reading to parse what he was saying vis-à-vis more modern terminology used within interdisciplinary transpersonal studies. For instance, while he often used the term "soul" (Ger.: *die Seele*) to label the psyche in distinction to the body, he also uses it to refer to the spiritual aspects of human mental life. He also uses the term "spirit" (Ger.: *Geist*) and the phrase "spiritual world" (Ger.: *die geistige Welt*) to refer to what we might call spiritual culture or worldview (Husserl 1970[1936]: 6). The soul and the body comprise a monad, a psychophysical unity that includes experiences divorced from or indirectly associated with direct external perception (Husserl 1970[1936]: 214-215, 1993[1931]: §50-54). As Husserl conceived it, the body is the material domain of the monad in which causality reigns while the soul is the domain of motivation (Husserl 1989[1952]: 128-150, 344-349). As an embodied person, I am subject to both causation and motivation, knowing the former by perceiving my body and the latter by observing my intentionality. The two concepts are mangled in my daily natural attitude stream of consciousness, but by means of the epoché I am able to discriminate between the two while practicing genetic phenomenologizing.

One consideration more than any other indicates the penetrating relevance of Husserl to understanding polyphasic cultures. He admits extraordinary experiences into the domain of *ontic meaning* (1970[1936]: 145). The lifeworld is pregiven, as we saw in Chapter 4. The lifeworld is the result of sensory sampled energies that make up the "already thereness" of the *ontic universe*:

> ...the lifeworld, *for us who wakingly live in it*, is always already there, existing in advance for us, the "ground" of all praxis whether theoretical or extratheoretical. The world is pre-given *to us, the waking*, always somehow practically interested subjects, not occasionally but always and necessarily as the universal field of all actual and possible praxis as horizon. To live is always to live-in-certainty-of-the-world. *Waking life is being awake to the world*, being constantly and directly "conscious" of the world and of oneself as living in the world, actually experiencing ... and actually effecting the ontic certainty of the world. (Husserl 1970[1936]: 142-143; emphasis added)

Notice that I have added emphasis where Husserl links perception of the lifeworld with being "awake." One could easily conclude that Husserl was merely reflecting the monophasic ethnocentrism of European society in his day. He seems to be saying that the only periods during which we can be aware of the real world is when we are "awake." However, this would be an egregious error, for soon after this quote he shifts the theme of the meditation from the "what" of the pregiven object—the "what" of the ontic sense—to the "how" of the object and the ontic universe. This is *not* a different topic, but rather a different orientation of the mediation.

> Let us now shape this [meditation] into a new universal direction of interest; let us establish a consistent universal direction in the "how" of the manners of givenness and in the onta themselves, not straightforwardly but rather as objects in respect to their "how"—that is, with our interest exclusively and constantly directed toward how, throughout the alteration of relative validities, subjective appearances, and opinions, the coherent, universal validity world—the world—comes into being for us; how, that is, there arises in us the constant consciousness of the universal existence, of the universal horizon, of real, actually existing objects, *each of which we are conscious of only through the alterations of our relative conceptions [...] of it, of its manners of appearing, its modes of validity, even when we are conscious of it in particularity as something simply being there.* (Husserl 1970[1936]: 144-145; emphasis added)

How is it that I am now perceiving the stack of books on my shelf instead of the view of my keyboard a moment ago? Simple, I turned my head—i.e., I *modified* the structure of my stream of consciousness. If I had not turned my head, I might still imagine the stack of books, but not perceive the actual pregiven sensory object. Yes, a very simplistic example, but now consider this: I have drunk a glass of *ayahuasca* (or a tab of LSD) and in a half hour my perception has been altered such that all the colors around me are deeper and more vibrant in hue and when I move my head rapidly across the lights of the city or a Christmas light display, the lights seem to stream as though they were a liquid flung out behind my shifting gaze. I am "awake"—indeed, I seem to be hyper-awake—but I am no longer able to perceive the ontic universe in the same way that I do when I haven't imbibed a powerful psychedelic drug. Husserl's reduction method still applies, but what "awake" means has expanded into the realm of ASC. The a priori pregivenness of sensory perception remains primordially pregiven, a product of the obduracy of the real world. Yet, I cannot stop the streaking of colored lights no matter how intensely I will it. I cannot willfully order the lights to disappear or the hues to change, their intensity to increase or diminish. In addition, if I fix my gaze at a point in front of me and someone walks across the room perpendicular to my line of sight, I will not perceive one person moving across my field of vision, but multiple images of the person trailing out behind the real person as she moves. This phenomenon, known as "visual trailing," reminds one of Marcel Duchamp's famous painting, *Nude Descending a Staircase* (see Figure 6).

When under the influence of a hallucinatory drug, my sensory systems are still sampling energies in the real world, but how they present in the sensorium is different. Why? We all know why. I modified the biochemistry and organization of the essential structures mediating my sensorium. The drug somehow changes the refresh rate of visual epochs that is so necessary in moving from one "now" to the next "now." In neurophysiological terms, psychologists have offered a variety of partial explanations for visual trailing (Dubois and VanRullen 2011, Frecska *et al.* 2012, Shanon 2002), but the precise mechanism for these phenomena is still unknown—an excellent example of how phenomenology can lead eventually to a neurophenomenological account by discovering the relevant NCC.

Figure 6. *Nude Descending a Staircase.* Painting by Marcel Duchamp from 1912.

Absorption

You may recall that back in Chapter 2 I introduced the advantages of *samatha* ("mind-calming") methods in preparing to carry-out phenomenological reductions. We know that calming the "formations"(chatter, anxiety, scattered focus, etc.) if practiced diligently will enhance the ability of the meditator to focus upon the object of meditation. As time goes on, focus of awareness becomes extraordinarily powerful. Accompanying increased concentration is a gradual gain in lucidity of perception and a stability of orientation as more of the body's energies are channeled into concentration and sensorial production. Eventually, with increased concentration upon the object there may occur a tipping-point when the distinction between subject and object collapses leaving just the object. The unity of subject and object may be accompanied by psychic energy flows up to and including ecstatic bliss, and a release of energy to facilitate continued concentration. In psychology we call this phenomenon *absorption*. In Buddhist phenomenology absorption states are called *jhana* in Pali, *samadhi* in Japanese, and *zuòwàng* in Chinese.

Absorption states range from mundane to extraordinary mystical experiences. If you are like me, you go to the cinema and within seconds after the movie begins the subject-object polarity collapses and there is just the unfolding movie. The same thing happens while reading an "absorbing" book or while "being absorbed in" making love. These are mundane examples because they are absorptions into sensory experiences that may be reduced by you to their primordial givenness. If you do perform a reduction while you are absorbed in an experience being stimulated from the external environing world, you will discover that the obduracy of reality still prevails in the experience. According to Buddhist phenomenology, absorption (or *jhana*) at this level is self-limiting (Anālayo 2017: 109-176, 2020, Arbel 2017, Gunaratana 1988). That is, you are constrained by the obduracy of the environing world such that the "higher" states of absorption cannot occur so long as the object of intentionality is actual. Certain intentional ("yogic") shifts in consciousness must occur in order for concentration to deepen beyond what is possible while orientation is fixed upon a real-world object. For example, if you meditate upon a stationary object (candle flame, bowl of water, photograph, living tree or leaf), the obduracy of the real object limits how absorbed you can become. But if you were to practice scanning the object and then shutting your eyes and focusing upon the after image, it is possible for concentration to be so intense that the after image is retained and may even become more lucid than the actual object. If you continued to concentrate upon the internal image, "higher" absorptions may take place leading eventually to the "highest" absorptions such as those into bounded and unbounded space, nothingness, psychic energy (*kundalini*), and if your karma is right, into Nirvana (see Child 2016, Laughlin 2020a: 139 on so-called "arising yoga" practices).

I mention the pivotal notion of absorption in Buddhist phenomenology only to emphasize that Husserl was on the same track, despite the lack of an explicit calming discipline associated with his methods, not to mention the lack of reliance upon calming to attain extraordinary levels of concentration. Take note here: Buddhist meditators are trained to seek *jhana* states to energize and refresh the mind-body so as to carry on with contemplative explorations. So far as I know, Husserl never included this use of absorption as a tool in developing the phenomenological attitude. The two key points of comparison between Husserl's and Buddhist descriptions of absorption states are: (1) how one interprets the "displacement" of the ego in intentional acts leading to absorption, and (2) the crucial realization *that absorption states are commonly associated with intuitive insights*. Let me explore each of these points in turn.

Point one: Ego displacement and dissociation

For Husserl, everyday consciousness is an "absorption" (or "immersion;" Ger.: *Versunkenheit*) into a world of facts, of natural attitude-ridden experiences (Husserl 1982[1913]). With respect to point one, where does the Watcher (the pure ego) go in absorption states? For Husserl, all ASC (fantasies, imaginings, visions, dreams, hallucinations, etc.) are considered to be modifications of perceptual experiences—that is, they involve modifying the essential structures of experience the principal function of which is adaptive engagement with the real world (see Geniusas 2010, Jansen 2010). As long as we are concentrating upon an object within its perceived horizon and which are sampled from the external environing world, our experiences are limited by the obduracy of reality. But if we "displace" the ego into an intentionality focused memory or make believe, this realistic obduracy is lifted to a great extent (but see the obduracy of the unconscious in the last chapter). This "displacement" of the ego from its principal concern with reality to a "re-presentation" of reality in fantasy or imagination is structurally very similar, especially at the level of hyle and form (Husserl 2005[1898-1925]: Chap. 1). Any perception can be fantasied. If I see the red color of your shirt, I can bring that red shirt back before my mind's eye, either immediately or at some later time. Thus, fantasy is for Husserl an "ability" of consciousness. "Speaking in the sense of ideal possibility, we can characterize it as evident that to every possible perceptual presentation there belongs a possible fantasy presentation that refers to the same object and in a certain sense, even refers to it in precisely the same way" (Husserl 2005[1898-1925]: 17).

But fantasy is not perception, for in the case of perception, experience locates us in the flow of time while fantasy is essentially timeless. That is, the present is replaced by semblances of reality that are not present, either by pure imagination or by image-consciousness. "Husserl develops some meticulous and careful analyses of the relations between these two distinct forms of conscious life, both expressions of *presentification*: imagination, meaning the direct, immediate reference of consciousness to a mental state that is not present; and image-consciousness, indicating the experience of an object (the image), which mediates the relationship to the not-present" (Zippel 2016: 182). This distinction is between what is *present to* consciousness and what is *presentified in* consciousness *as if the presentification were in the perceptual "now"* (see Chapter 6).

It is significant for ethnology that we humans can fantasy things that we have never perceived in the real world (e.g., events on another planet, alien creatures, supernatural beings, etc.). This is why the terms "fantasy" and "imagination" are parallel notions for Husserl. If I fantasize about your red shirt, I can let the mental movie run its own course. The movie is a "simulation" of the perception (Jansen 2010). If I am reading a book that is describing a Hobbit home, my imagination is stimulated by and limited from the real world of the author's text. I imagine the Hobbit home as the writer describes it. If I then stop reading and play with my imagined Hobbit home, I enter the domain of fantasy and image consciousness. And if then I undertake to paint a scene from my fantasied Hobbit home, I have entered the domain of creativity and even art (see next chapter). In every case, my ego has been "displaced" into an intentional act other than perception. But this does not mean, as suggested by Geniusas (2020), that the Watcher is somehow split into two egos, that, "When it comes to any form of intuitive re-presentation, we are confronted with at least a double self-awareness: self-awareness-in-the-now and self-awareness-in-the-then" (2020: 4). Geniusas is making an analytical distinction that is neither necessary for understanding Husserl, nor phenomenologically accurate (see Husserl 1973[1939]: 175-192). I-the-Watcher (pure ego "me") am perfectly able to be aware of perceptual and fantasy content at the same time (Husserl 2005[1898-1925]: 269). We all do it quite naturally. Say that I am talking with an attractive woman, and while doing so I fantasize kissing her in the future. The Watcher is not split off into two Charlies. This is why the displaced ego viewpoint in the fantasy comes embodied—in other words, when I am imagining, I do not leave my body behind. I am speaking with the woman in the real world and kissing her in the fantasy—same "me," same body. To offer another example, being somewhat acrophobic, if I imagine myself standing on the edge of a building or on the lip of a precipice, my body reacts in the same way as if I were perceiving myself in those situations—I feel anxious, I cringe, and my groin shrivels. If I imagine I cut my finger with a butcher knife, my body cringes as if the imagination were actual perception (minus the physical pain). As the old saw goes, wherever I go, there I am—body and soul.

This is not to say that I can be *fully absorbed* in a fantasy, vision, dream or hallucination and maintain awareness of perception at the same time. This is because this higher level of absorption—absorption achieving the *samadhi* level—is made possible by a radical restructuring of intentionality such that the distinction between subject and object collapses and there is only the awareness of the fantasy unfolding. The fantasy takes up, for the duration of the absorption, the entirety of my stream of consciousness. One might say, "I got lost in my day-dream." On top of this, although I have rarely experienced such combinations, it is possible to perceive and hallucinate at the same time—i.e., within the same intentional act (see Schatzman 1982 for the remarkable case of

Ruth). Again, the intensity of concentration (Husserl 1989[1952]: 114-115) is the key variable in determining whether a dream, a phantasm (apparition, illusion, imaginary world), or an image becomes as lucid as a perception. Husserl describes this process clearly and at length, and is worth quoting in its entirety:

> Here I call attention to transitions from a fantasy into a *vision*. The fantasy formations no longer hover before the inner eye as images. Empirical perception, the reality in which the visionary as a bodily organism lives, is suspended; and simultaneously with the suspension the opposition between this reality and the fantasy imagery, the imaging function of the fantasy images, escapes. The visionary is then in a trance state; the world of fantasy is then his real world. He himself takes it to be real; that is to say, his intuitions are perceptions, even endowed with the characteristic of *belief*.

> We will assume the same thing in the case of *dreams*, and not only in the dreaming that occurs in sleep but also in daydreaming. Sometimes we give ourselves up to the attractions of fantasy to such an extent that we begin to react to the fantasy appearances in actions *just as if* perceptions were at stake; our fist clenches, we hold audible dialogues with the imagined persons, and so on. Of course, precisely at that point the dream is in the habit of ending; actual perception chases off imagining. The more frequent case, however, is probably that in which the real world before our eyes is *almost* swallowed up while we pursue the fantasies, although that world makes us aware, in however minimal a way, of its factual existence, so that a faint consciousness that they are semblances constantly colors our fantasy formations. (Husserl 2005[1898-1925]: 45)

When speaking of trance states, Husserl is referring to a range of dissociation states of the kind of interest to transpersonal studies. *Dissociation* is a psychiatric term meaning that some part of the psyche is separated or closed off from other parts of the psyche. In this case, Husserl is referring to dissociation of consciousness from the processes that produce perception. Dissociation in this sense is normal, as is the case with dreaming, and is commonplace among contemplatives. Although he does not say so, it is clear that sufficient absorption into fantasy can produce both dissociation from perception and a lucid dream-like inner reality. This process is of relevance to anthropologists who study such phenomena as spirit possession (Boddy 1994, Bourguignon 1976, Crapanzano and Garrison 1977, Winkelman 1986) and shamanic "journeying" (Flor-Henry, Shapiro and Sombrun 2017, Krippner 2000, Rock and Krippner 2008, 2011, Winkelman 1996, 2010). A note of caution may be relevant here, for it is common for psychologists and anthropologists to confound consciousness with the contents of consciousness. Adam Rock and Stanley Krippner (2007) have emphasized this mangling of the structures of experience with the contents of experience with respect to the practice of shamans. To speak of a "shamanic state of consciousness" reveals this mangling in a way that Husserl too has done. The extraordinariness of shamanic journeys rests with the content of awareness and not the structure of consciousness itself, except for the possibility of absorption states. That the same essential structures of consciousness are operating in transpersonal experiences as in everyday experiences means, for Husserl, that the practice of phenomenology can be exercised in both kinds of experiences.

Dissociation from the perceptual world and intense involvement with fantasy can reach maladaptive extremes. In Husserl's view, a return to perception diminishes or banishes fantasy/dreaming from consciousness. Hence intentional acts directed at the environing world operate *in competition* for dominance. This finding makes sense when we consider intentional acts as trophically costly for the body's metabolic resources (Purves 1990, 2010). Early childhood trauma can lead to dissociation and emphasis upon a fantasy life so great that it results in psychopathology. In a metaphorical sense, one may become "trapped" in fantasy worlds which are preferable to the ego than reality (see Soffer-Dudek, Nirit and Eli Somer 2018, Somer, Somer and Jopp 2016). This tendency reaps its most terrible consequences in violent psychopaths who seek to enact their gruesome fantasies in the real world to the detriment of others (Meloy and Shiva 2008).

Point two: Absorption and intuition

With respect to point two, Husserl discovered that absorption involves not only enhanced concentration, but that absorption states are accompanied by not only sensory objects, their hyletic contents and their relationships, but also intuitive insights. This finding has profound implications for why, as mentioned above, humans seem to seek ASC in initiation ceremonies, spiritual rituals, vision quests, meditation, drug trips and lucidity in dreaming. We may hypothesize that people seek, not only highs and entertaining sensory experiences (body rushes, flashy lights, geometric images, etc.), but also intuitive knowledge often accompanied by numinosity and realization of overarching wisdom, the kind of extraordinary experiences that are at the root of what we in Western culture call "religion" (Robbins 2016). How such experiences are interpreted can vary with personal history and cultural background—the process by which intuition is brought into the natural attitude and shared socially via communication. But at the primordial level, intuitive knowledge has no association with language or concepts, although concepts and words are used to share and "culturize" the knowledge.

To give a common example: Meditation experiences can lead to absorption states in which one realizes with absolute certainty that everything in the world, including oneself, is systemically and causally entangled. This intuition, as we will see below, is a universal element in mystical experiences (Bharati 1976: 25) but is processually no different than the more mundane intuitions we encounter doing a reduction of a coffee cup and its horizon. In the same way that I grasp that there is more to the cup than I can see at the moment (Chapter 3), I suddenly grasp that I am a part of a great, perhaps infinite, whole—the Mother of All Monads. The brainmind has evolved to intuitively know these things in a very human way, which is why: (1) consciousness operates structurally in the same way for everyone regardless of culture, and (2) anyone, regardless of cultural background, can attain the same intuitive realizations, including mystical experiences.

> In this manner we can make into a subject of investigation the invariant general style which this intuitive world, in the flow of total experience, persistently maintains. Precisely in this way we see that, universally, things and their occurrences do not arbitrarily appear and run their course but are *bound* a priori by this style, by the invariant form of the intuitable world. In other words, through a *universal causal regulation, all that is*

together in the world has a universal immediate or mediate way of *belonging together*; through this the world is not merely a totality [...] but an all-encompassing unity [...], a *whole* (even though it is infinite). This is self-evident a priori, no matter how little is actually experienced of the particular causal dependencies, no matter how little of this is known from past experience or is prefigured about future experience. (Husserl 1970[1936]: 31)

It is no great leap to understand that the a priori ground, the lifeworld, upon which spiritual knowledge is based leads to traditional (pre-scientific) cultural worldviews that read almost universally as cosmologies (see Saniotis 2010b). Indeed, as both Husserl and Jung emphasized, the brainmind of humans is "wired" to intuitively know the environing world as a system—a totality confirmed by both contemplation and modern physics. We are born with this intuitive ground of the adult lifeworld (see Brooke 1991: Chap. 3, 1999). However, considerable psychological development may lie between intuitive grasp of entanglement and social wisdom and praxis.

DREAMING

For Husserl, "dreaming" is fantasying while asleep (Husserl 2005 [1898-1925]: 179). As we have seen, fantasy ("daydreaming") and dream are mere "semblances" (Ger.: *Schein*) vis-à-vis the concrete presentation of perception—non-representational experiences with reference to the lifeworld. It is crucial to return to the distinction between *presentment* and *presentification* (Husserl 1964a:63-64). Imagination can resemble perception in that it can produce sensory objects that while being experienced as "present" are derived from memory or anticipation (expectation). Normal dreaming while asleep removes or dissociates the experiential timeline from the flow of pure perception entirely (Zippel 2016). As we have seen above, memories of dreams can be thrust into actuality by blending imagined dream imagery into consideration of the sensory given in perception—a blending of *actual* and *inactual* elements within the stream of consciousness. Not only can I fantasy kissing the attractive woman with whom I am chatting, I can recall having kissed her in my dream last night. I am emphasizing these possible and quite natural intercalations of real and unreal objects within experience to underscore how the actual and inactual can be blended so easily in our everyday natural attitude experiences, feeding into accounting for the range of experiences considered to be real and unreal across cultures.

As transpersonal and dreaming researchers know, as do people who are intensely "into their dream life," dreaming may entail concentration ranging from minimal to intense and recall of experiences from none to vivid (Krippner 1994). The more intense the concentration while dreaming, the more "lucid" the dreams become and the more likely they will be remembered and memorable when awake. A dreamer can become so lucid in their dream state that they can: (1) know they are dreaming while dreaming, (2) learn to control what happens in the dream, and (3) learn to communicate with researchers with eye movements and other actions (see Baird, LaBerge and Tononi 2021, Laughlin 2011a). Most dreaming for most people raised in technocratic societies occurs with a minimum of self-awareness. The dream arises with the Watcher more or less at the center of things, unaware that the experience is not perception but a representation until coming awake (Tougas 2013: 86-89).

Memories can become scrambled. We can easily *confabulate* memories—that is, we can remember events and objects that never actually happened (see Schnider 2018). We can imagine some event, recount it in a story, and some of our audience may recall the story as being real. Nearly a century ago, it was sociologist W. I. Thomas who showed that if an event is thought to be real, its consequences *will be real* (Thomas and Thomas 1928). We can also mangle memories of dreams and memories of actual events. Again, the more lucid the mind state in which the event (real or imagined) occurs, the more likely it will be memorable. Indeed, some of my most memorable experiences occurred in dream and meditative states, and came to me, the Watcher, entirely from within my psyche (Laughlin 2017b), and the consequences of those memories have continued to reverberate in my life to the present day. This is not at all uncommon. Most human cultures recognize the difference, for example, between normal everyday dreams and what anthropologist J. S. Lincoln (1935: 22) called *culture pattern dreams*— dreams that are "big" dreams, memorable dreams, dreams of personal, social, or spiritual significance. In Jungian dream work the distinction is between archetypal dreams and mundane dreams (Kluger 1975). In polyphasic societies, culture pattern dreams tend to be reported and thus become part of common knowledge, perhaps being added to or changing stories recounting worldview level social knowledge.

MYSTICAL EXPERIENCES AND ABSOLUTE UNITARY BEING

Mystical experiences present universal features of human existence that transcend cultural boundaries and historical eras. Husserl's transcendental phenomenology of the genetic sort seems to inevitably entail an eventual consideration of this crucial domain of experiences, one that is of interest to historians of religion and interdisciplinary transpersonal studies.

> Mystical experience has been reported across a wide range of cultures for thousands of years and is among the most powerful and transformative types of experience known. It occurs spontaneously or deliberately, both within and completely outside of established traditions [...]. The intuitive insights of mystical experience have been documented extensively by scholars of anthropology, religion, psychology, and philosophy. To ignore such experience as inconsequential or to dismiss it as delusory is unfortunate indeed. (Hanna 1993a)

Although cultures may impose various interpretive frames upon reported mystical experiences, the core experience is characterized by the following features (see Laughlin 2020a: Chap. 9, Laughlin and Takahashi 2020):

> 1. **Absorption into the void.** The dissolution of the ego or Watcher into Totality (Ott 2007). The primary quality of a mystical experience would seem to be an absorption state which may be an example of what my friend and colleague Eugene d'Aquili liked to call *absolute unitary being* (d'Aquili and Newberg 1998, 1999)—the dissolution of "all boundaries of discrete being" (d'Aquili and Newberg 1999: 95). This is an experience of ego

loss, or the dissolution of apparent boundaries between the ego and the universe (Void, Godhead, the All, etc., depending upon cultural or ideological interpretation).

2. **Time and space distortion.** A profound absorption state will usually collapse time consciousness into a profound present state characterized by loss of "retention" (memory of what has gone on before) and "protention" (anticipation of what is about to occur), two aspects of the normal apprehension of the naïve "now" (Husserl 1964a, Laughlin and Throop 2008; see also Chapter 6). Awareness of past and present, cause and effect, and cyclic interpretation of time cease altogether (Ott 2013). The experience seems timeless but may in fact last seconds to minutes in duration, and its accompanying intuitive insights may last a lifetime.

3. **May occur spontaneously or intentionally.** All mystical experiences are caused, whether or not the subject is aware of the causal factors or not. But some mystical experiences occur spontaneously while others may arise from intentionally "driving" somatic systems by "spiritual technologies" like ritual chanting and dancing, physical ordeals, sexual encounters, dietary proscriptions, psychoactive drug "trips," etc.

4. **Flow, ecstasy, bliss, and numinosity.** Mystical experiences are commonly accompanied by notable psychic energy activity in the brainmind and body. One usually experiences bliss states that can range from pleasurable body rushes to full-blown ecstasy. These feelings of bliss in the body can give one the sense of the body being composed of flowing energy rather than solid tissue or matter (Csikszentmihalyi 2008).

Recall that Husserl's method of reduction requires the disciplined skill of bracketing all thoughts, beliefs, interpretations, and whatnot so as to pave the way to directly "seeing" the primordial sensory given and its inherent intuitive field of knowing. This is the same dictum imposed by all meditative disciplines where discursive thought about what one is experiencing is considered a hindrance, so much verbal chatter to be ignored (Blofeld 1959, Filmer-Lorch 2012, Laughlin 2020a). The reason for this dictum is that the natural attitude layering of meaning atop the primordial given operates as a series of filters that block the direct "seeing" of the way things actually present in consciousness in favor of culturally conditioned ways of understanding via presumptive bias, belief, reason, ideology, praxis, etc. (Husserl 2010[1907]).

Here we need to sound a caution, for although Husserl was perfectly aware of mysticism as a cultural strain going back thousands of years, he specifically denied that mystics, clergies, and ideologies of any sort have a "lock" on the truth (see Kohák 1978: 70). Indeed, anyone with normal intelligence can access the truth of things by paying attention to their stream of consciousness as "absolute data," as evidence (Ger.: *Evidenz*; see Husserl 1982[1913]: §§ 42-46). In a word, for Husserl, *experience is reality*. All any of us have to do is learn to "see" properly to ascertain the truth inherent in the primordial given.

> It is a mark of the type of Being peculiar to experience that perceptual insight can direct its immediate, unobstructed gaze upon every real experience, and to enter into the life of a primordial presence. This insight operates as a "reflexion," and it has this remarkable peculiarity that that which is thus apprehended through perception is, in principle, characterized as something which not only is and endures within the gaze of perception, but *already was before* this gaze was directed to it. "All experiences are conscious experiences:" this tells us specifically with respect to intentional experiences that they are not only the consciousness of something, and as such present not merely when they are objects of a reflective consciousness, but that when unreflected on they are already there in a "background," and therefore in principle, and at first in an analogical sense, *"available for perception,"* like unnoticed things in our external field of vision. (Husserl 1982[1913]: 141-142)

There is an old saying in Buddhist psychology to the effect: "Nirvana is closer to you than your nose." The only difference between individuals who do not know Nirvana and those that do is the maturity of their "seeing." To modify consciousness towards a new object brings with it an alteration of intuitive insight. Mystical knowing is perceiving what actually is and nothing more—at its core is the perception of Absolute Being (Husserl's term). Viewed in this way, Husserl reached the conclusion that what is essentially a mystical way of knowing is foundational to the ultimate success of the natural and social sciences.

> The only true way to explain is to make transcendentally understandable. Everything objective demands to be understood. Natural-scientific knowing about nature thus gives us no truly explanatory, no ultimate knowledge of nature because it does not investigate nature at all *in the absolute framework through which its actual and genuine being reveals its ontic meaning*; thus, natural science never reaches this being thematically. This does not detract in the least from the greatness of its creative geniuses or their accomplishments, just as the being of the objective world in the natural attitude, and this attitude itself, *have lost nothing through the fact that they are, so to speak, "understood back into" [...] the absolute sphere of being in which they ultimately and truly are.* To be sure, the knowledge attained through the constitutive "internal" method, through which all objective-scientific method acquires its meaning and possibility, cannot be without significance for the scientist of nature or any other objective scientist. *It is, after all, a matter of the most radical and most profound self-reflection of accomplishing subjectivity*; how could it not be of service in protecting the naïve, ordinary accomplishment from misunderstandings such as are to be observed in abundance, for example, in the influence of naturalistic epistemology and in the idolization of a logic that does not understand itself? (Husserl 1970[1936]: 189; emphasis added)

For Husserl, the only path to truth about reality is by way of accessing the lifeworld through systematic application of the epoché. Truth is grounded in the intuitive grasp of the Absolute, rather than the relative variations of appearances (Husserl 1982[1913]: 139). What does it mean to say something is "absolute?" It simply means that it exists as it is, not merely as it appears to be. This is why the level of experience and knowing Husserl labeled the "lifeworld" must be foundational in accounting for nature at a higher cortical level.

The absoluteness of my existence (Ger.: *Dasein*) is for me indubitable (Husserl 1999: 38). How I experience myself (how my being appears to me) over time changes—an itch on the leg at time t1 is gone at time t2, replaced by a sneeze which is replaced at time t3 with awareness of the pressure of my rear on the chair, and so forth… to time tn when I feel hungry. All of these appearances of me derive from the concrete, real, imminent me, the absolute embodied me whose existence is independent of consciousness and which I cannot doubt (Husserl 1993[1931]: 28-29). Mystical experience is absorption into transcendental being—universal being, not just my being. Mystical knowledge is grounded *in the direct intuitive grasp of immanent being*, not merely transcendental being which requires adumbrated appearances. Husserl raises the central questions about grasping absolute being in this way:

> But is absolute self-evidence, self-givenness in the act of seeing, present only in the singular experience and its singular moments and parts; can it be only a matter of positing a *"this-here"* in the act of seeing? Could not there also be positing of other forms of givenness as the absolute givenness of, for instance, universals, where a universal would come to self-evident givenness in an act of seeing and any doubt concerning it would be absurd? (Husserl 1999: 38)

The answer to his second question, as anyone who has experienced a mystical state can attest, is a decided "yes." In coming to know my being I come to know all being, and that knowing is not empirical, but experiential and intuitive, and is apodictic, it is beyond doubt. This is why most traditional societies are polyphasic in their cultural understanding of knowing, and why they almost always construct worldviews that are essentially cosmologies.

Here we should give a nod to one of Husserl's students, the phenomenologist and mystic Gerda Walther (1897–1977) who applied her teacher's methods to make sense of her own spiritual experiences (especially in Walther 1923; see also Burns 2020, Calcagno 2018). She accepts Husserl's contention that Western culture is in a crisis, and a major factor of that story—she calls the story the *Sündenfall* or "fall of mankind" (Walther 1923: 31)—is one of loss of contact with direct experience, its inherent essential and intuitive ways of knowing, and a compensatory imbalance toward the hyperrationalism typical of technocratic societies. "This philosophical 'Fall' is typified by an overly rationalistic philosophical approach, in which concepts are over-differentiated, and an original unity of understanding is lost" (Burns 2020: 251). Or as Husserl himself suggested:

> Hence: *as little understanding as possible, as much pure intuition as possible*[63] (*intuitio sine comprehension*). Indeed, we are here reminded of the speech of the mystics when they describe the intellectual act of seeing *that contains no discursive knowledge*. The whole trick here is to let the seeing eye have its way and to exclude all transcendent reference that is interwoven with seeing, those things that are ostensibly given or thought along with what is seen, and, finally, those things that in subsequent reflection get imputed to what is given. The constant question is: *is the intended object also given in the genuine sense, seen and apprehended in the strictest sense, or does the intention go beyond it?* (Husserl 1999: 46-47; emphasis added)

Mystical experiences afford direct access to the truth of things spiritual, but because the truth is attained intuitively by the mystic, the experiences are notoriously ineffable, which accounts for Walther's reliance upon literary and poetical modes of communication. Walther's phenomenology, utilizing Husserl's methods of isolating essential structures in experience, was directed at uncovering universal mystical essences and their unfoldment over the course of the evolution and history of cultures. She was particularly interested in how these experiences, inherently ineffable as they are, come to be shared and communicated within communities. "Guided by the experiences of several mystics, she recognized in her *Zur Phänomenologie der Mystik* (1923) 'a mode of givenness' that is peculiar to the 'primordial phenomenon' of mystical experience as the primordial source of religious experience" (Steinbock 2007: 29).

How reports and memoirs of mystical experiences are used by society is, of course, rife with culturally-loaded interpretations. Polyphasic societies commonly define roles for those adept at interpreting dreams

---

[63] *"[M]öglichst wenig Verstand, aber möglichst reine Intuition."*

and visions had by fellow group members (see Laughlin 2011a: 242-252 for an extended discussion). But also keep in mind that just because an experience is meaningful does not mean that it can be expressed easily in words (see Rodemeyer 2008 and Weiskrantz 1988 on meanings for which there are no words). It is also useful to keep in mind that *there are always multiple interpretations* at the higher cortical level—at the level of the natural attitude and its enculturative influences)—for any given experience, be it mundane or extraordinary.[64] Any experiences that are used as evidence for a belief can be reduced to the level of the a priori pregivenness in experience.

A WORD ABOUT THE PHENOMENOLOGY OF RELIGION

Incidentally, there is a subdiscipline of philosophy and religious studies that touches upon some of the experiences discussed above. The subdiscipline is called the *phenomenology of religion* which has developed a considerable literature (Barua 2009, Cox 2010). As is the case with phenomenology as a whole, the phenomenology of religion provides a variety of "phenomenological" approaches to religion as a way of living and as a sociocultural institution (see Fujiwara, Thurfjell and Engler 2021). Despite offering homage to Husserl as the founder of modern phenomenology, most of these approaches seem to be devoid of any in-depth, mature contemplation of the Husserlian sort. At best they operate upon the presumption (cross-culturally accurate by the way) that religions are founded upon experience. But most writers do not ground their ruminations upon modern ethnology, and when they do speak of "anthropology," it is frequently the quite separate subdiscipline of philosophy known as *philosophical anthropology* (see Giri and Clammer 2013), not the discipline of sociocultural anthropology within which I was trained, nor toward which I am directing this book. Some phenomenology of religion studies are compatible, however, with transpersonal studies and are thus of interest to the ethnology of ASC particularly (see e.g., Allen 2005). And those studies that

---

[64] I call this the *Rule of Multiple Interpretations* (see Laughlin 2011a: 489). This touches on an issue of great importance when doing ethnography and relating direct experiences in various states of consciousness to cultural knowledge systems.

explore more hermeneutical avenues—studies that often give a nod to Martin Heidegger's hermeneutical phenomenology of being and the religious life (see Heidegger 2010[1995]—may have considerable interest for the anthropology of experience. But anthropologists must always be mindful of the fact that most traditional peoples do not have "religions" per se. For instance, the closest you can come to "religion" in traditional Navajo is "moving ceremonially," in other words ritual, myth and spiritual/healing practices. In other words, "religion" defined as Westerners normally do is not a cultural universal, but transpersonal experiences are universal.

Summary and segue

We have now seen that there are at least four aspects of Husserl's theory of knowledge that can guide us in carrying out transpersonal and ethnographic studies of spiritual life: (1) *Möglichst wenig Verstand, aber möglichst reine Intuition*, "as little as possible reason, but as pure as possible intuition," (2) phenomenological reduction may be performed in any state of consciousness where there is sufficient lucidity and concentration present within the intentional act (Eleftheriou and Thomas 2021), (3) absorption experiences accompanied by intuitive insights are commonly considered extraordinary and may result in founding religious institutions, and (4) intuitive realizations may include absolute being which can account for the cosmological structure of world views across cultures. The fact that Husserl usually applied the epoché toward experiences of the external world is an indication of his ethnocentric bias towards materialism. His project was to provide a grounding for natural science and philosophy. He was cognizant that the phenomenological attitude can be applied to ASC of profound importance to spiritual development. Indeed, he considered the disciplined practice of contemplative phenomenology to result in radical alterations of the practitioner's brainmind. Not only that, but as we will soon see, he used the epoché to probe the elements of aesthetic experiences and moral values.

CHAPTER ELEVEN

Husserl and Natural Axiology

Thus, in acts like those of appreciation we have an intentional object of double sense: we must distinguish between the "subject matter" pure and simple and the full intentional object, and corresponding to this, a double intendio, a twofold directedness. If we are directed towards some matter in an act of appreciation, the direction towards the matter in question is a noting and apprehending of it; but we are "directed"—only not in an apprehending way—also to value. Not merely the representing of the matter in question, but also the appreciating which includes the representing, has the modus of actuality.

– Husserl (1982[1913]: 122)

It is fair to say that anthropology has been interested in morality and ethics, as well as aesthetics as topics of ethnographic research since the 19th century. Indeed, it is impossible to do extended ethnographic fieldwork without stumbling across ethical systems, often incorporated with the society's religion and legal system. In addition, the artistic sense is virtually universal to human societies, despite the fact that there may be no word in the local language that precisely glosses "art" in the European sense of an object valued solely for its aesthetic value. For instance, when I was doing fieldwork among the So (Tepes, Tepeth) people of Northeastern Uganda, I spent some time observing tort cases discussed by the council of male elders, and during which customary values pertaining to "good" and "bad," appropriate and inappropriate, rights and obligations, proper gender and social roles, and so forth were revealed and given public expression, usually by males (Laughlin and Allgeier 1979).

ANTHROPOLOGY OF ETHICS

Ethnographic research in the 19th and 20th centuries typically merged ethics with other issues like enculturation of the young, social role, religion, coordination, reciprocity, and the like (see Kapferer and Gold 2018a, Laidlaw 2014 on the history of the "ethical/moral turn" in 21st century anthropology). It took WWII to shake anthropologists out of their ideologically-driven belief in the relativity of ethical/moral cultures and begin to acknowledge that there is such a thing as an immoral culture, or an unethical cultural practice (Kluckhohn 1955). Nobody in their right mind would have advocated that one must evaluate Nazi culture solely from within the value system of National Socialism.

Unlike some anthropologists, I do not make a categorical distinction between "ethics" and "morality" (see Heintz 2021: Chap. 2, Laidlaw 2014, Lambek 2010, Mattingly and Throop 2018, on this issue). For me, as well as for Husserl, the two terms overlap to such a degree that they are considered synonymous. Thus, I will follow Husserl's usage and stick with the term "ethics." Also, despite the profound sense of urgency Husserl felt about the crisis in social, political, and scientific life in pre-WWII Europe, I will not be discussing ethical issues pertaining to *doing* anthropology or in *evaluating* the cultures of technocratic societies. Indeed, following Roy d'Andrade (1995a), I distance a scientific anthropology from the kind of Christian-influenced neoliberalism that has pervaded anthropological rhetoric in the so-called postmodern era (see Carrier 2016, Kapferer and Gold 2018b, Kalb 2018 on this issue). Indeed, for Husserl, the various ideological currents wafting around Europe in the post WWI era were a major root of the crisis he was so concerned about, especially among humanist scientists (Husserl 1970[1936]: 273). As history teaches us, Husserl's and others' calls for cultural renewal proved too little, too late.

One of the hindrances to appreciating a phenomenological perspective on ethics is the natural attitude/social scientific distinction between the individual person and society (see Heintz 2021: 19, Laidlaw 2014, Lambek 2010: 214-217). We so naturally think about how the individual can be pitted against "society" when in fact *there is no such thing as "society" in the real world.*

> Society is an abstract term that connotes the complex of inter-relations that exist between and among the members of the group. Society exists wherever there are good or bad, proper or improper relationships between human beings. These social relationships are not evident, they do not have any concrete form, and *hence society is abstract.* Society is not a group of people; it means in essence a state or condition, a relationship, and is therefore necessarily an abstraction. Society is an organization of relationships. It is the total complex of human relationships. (Hossain and Ali 2014: 131; emphasis added)

For Husserl, "society" is individual group members exercising their intersubjective attitude (see Hart 1992). My "society" are the people with whom I interact in intersubjectively patterned ways. At the root of these interactions is the lifeworld. We interact within the more or less agreed upon reality, grounded and confirmed by the truing effects of our ongoing interrelationship with the environing world. Let us be crystal clear about this matter: Society feels nothing, experiences nothing, doesn't think, create, design, force anyone to do anything against their will. Only people can do this for themselves and for and to each other. This perspective is, of course, the raison d'être for social psychology. This also underscores the importance of a Husserlian phenomenology of intersubjectivity (see Chapter 4).

To speak of a real distinction between individual and social ethics is an exercise in what Alfred North Whitehead (1964) called the *fallacy of misplaced concreteness,* the reification of abstract notions. Social scientific models of causation frequently and unwittingly fall into this fallacy; that is, they reify rational conceptions of social causation upon a process that is essentially subjective, intersubjective, and transcendental (see Laidlaw 2014). Contrary to the classical view of David Hume (1960), causation is demonstrably an attribute of the organization of perception (Whitehead 1947, 1964, Michotte 1963, Mandelbaum 1977, Jaspars, Hewstone and Fincham 1983), and is such from the earliest stages of childhood development (Piaget 1974). In other words, causation is "already there" to perception prior to any rational reflection upon it. Causation is, as Whitehead (1947, 1978: 175-177) rightly taught, an "aboriginal," or primitive aspect of the organization of perceptual awareness—a position mirrored in Husserl's meditations upon the essential structures of perception.

Another problem in understanding the nature and evolution of human axiological systems is the failure of ethnographers to access the experiential dimensions of value (i.e., the "first person" perspective that dominates everyday ethics and problem solving; see Mattingly 2012). Those whose fieldwork methodologies are conditioned by the "culture all the way down" assumption often begin and end their analysis at the sociocultural level of knowledge and ignore the relevance of inherent value-feelings to these more institutional analyses. As a result of these blinders, few sources have anything to offer along a more phenomenological vein (see Throop 2010, 2012 for a notable exception). To get a thumbnail view of the extent to which ethical/moral anthropology avoids the phenomenological grounding of axiology, there are 35 articles in Didier Fassin's 644-page anthology, *A Companion to Moral Anthropology*, of which only two of those articles mention the phenomenology of morality, and one of those pieces leaves the reader with the impression that phenomenology is a useless endeavor. Michael Lambek's edited volume *Ordinary Ethics: Anthropology, Language, and Action* (2010) includes 21 articles, none of which mention phenomenology. Other sources as well ignore phenomenology, even more Husserl's work, touching on the subject in passing (see Heintz 2021), or profoundly misconstruing Husserlian methods (see e.g., Zigon 2009 for discussion of this issue). To state that anthropology has been slow to incorporate phenomenological approaches to ethics/morality is an understatement.

And of course, a seemingly insurmountable problem with contemporary "moral anthropology" stems from the blending of ethnographic research and political activism that has arisen in the wake of the postmodernist turn toward power, class struggle, racism, feminism, anti-colonialism, and so forth which, although they are hugely productive of neoliberal polemics, produce very little in the way of scientifically valid research (see e.g., Carrier 2016, Linstead 1993). This deficit in a phenomenological grounding in axiological anthropology alone argues for the intent of the present book.[65] For this reason, I will not expend space tracking the history of either the anthropology of art or the anthropology of ethics. That has been done by others (see Banks

---

[65] If you wish to find more sources that use phenomenological methods in the anthropological study of *ethics*, see Cassaniti and Hickman 2014, Csordas 2014, Mattingly 2012, Mattingly and Throop 2018, Throop 2010, 2012, Zigon 2010.

and Ruby 2011). Rather, I will introduce you to Husserl's discoveries pertaining to ethics and aesthetics and show how they can apply to a scientific anthropological approach to axiology.

HUSSERLIAN PHENOMENOLOGY OF VALUE AND ETHICS

Husserl's meditations on ethics ("ethical reduction," "ethical epoché") are peppered throughout his English language translations, as well as a number of thus far untranslated German sources[66] and unpublished manuscripts in the *Nachlass*.[67] Early on in his ethical ruminations he was under the influence of his teacher, Franz Brentano, as well as Kant's efforts to build a universal "categorical imperative," but in his later career he came under the considerable influence of Johann Gottlieb Fichte (1762–1814), another German philosopher who was just as concerned with European political developments in his day as was Husserl in the post-WWI era (see Husserl 1995[1917]; see also Hart 1995).

It is typical of discussions of Husserl's account of ethics to split the development of his thought into "early" (pre-WWI) and "later" (post-WWI) phases (see Melle 1991, De Warren 2017, Donohoe 2016: 120-135, Loidolt 2009). Husserl's personal experiences during the First World War were horrendous and tragic, as he lost one son, while another son was critically wounded during the conflict. He then, being born Jewish, had to face the rise of National Socialism in Germany. However, although his concerns about the future development of European societies deepened as a consequence of historical developments and personal travail, many of the root ideas and phenomenological reflections described during the early years remained in play throughout his career (Melle 1991: 116-117).

Husserl found that the root essences underlying ethical systems are to be found in intuitive evaluations in sensory givenness.

---

[66] E.g., Husserl, Edmund, 1988. *Vorlesungen über Ethik und Wertlehre 1908 - 1914*. Husserliana XXVIII. Dordrecht: Kluwer.

[67] If you wish to read more about Husserl's work on *values* and *ethics*, see Husserl 1982[1913], 1988[1908-1914], 2008[1906-1907], 2019[1923/24]: 442ff; see also Costello 2012: 157-172, Donohoe 2018, Ferrarello 2016, Hart 1992, Hart and Embree 1997, Hobbs 2021, Melle 1991. For a bibliography of phenomenological axiology, see Steeves 1997. For a list of all of Husserl's German writings that discuss ethics, see Melle 1991.

In this way, when consciously awake, I find myself at all times, and without my ever being able to change this, set in a relation to a world which, through its constant changes, remains one and ever the same. It is continuously "present" for me, and I myself am a member of it. Therefore, this world is not there for me as a mere *world of facts and affairs*, but, with the same immediacy, as a *world of values*, a *world of goods*, a *practical world*. Without further effort on my part, I find the things before me furnished not only with the qualities that befit their positive nature, *but with value-characters such as beautiful or ugly, agreeable or disagreeable, pleasant or unpleasant, and so forth.* Things in their immediacy stand there as objects to be used, the "table" with its "books," the "glass to drink from," the "vase," the "piano," and so forth. *These values and practicalities, they too belong to the constitution of the "actual present" objects as such, irrespective of my turning or not turning to consider them or indeed any other objects.* The same considerations apply of course just as well to the men and beasts in my surroundings as to "mere things." They are my "friends" or my "foes." My "servants" or "superiors," "strangers" or "relatives," and so forth. (Husserl 1982[1913]:103; emphasis added]

In short, ethics derives, not from reason as Kant and other philosophers would argue, but from the *feelings accompanying objects and events* ("*states of affairs*")—feelings including love, aversion, shock, desire, pleasure, disgust, distress, etc. (see Hart and Embree 1997 on Husserl's value theory). These feelings, paired with the object, constitute the value-feelings intuitively present in the primordial sensory given, which motivate willing and acting relative to the object or event being perceived—what Husserl called the "ethical attitude" that fulfills "value-judgments" (see Husserl 1970 [1900-01], I: 33-34). I am not only aware of this slice of bread on the table before me, but I also note the green mold forming on the slice and feel aversion or disgust relative to the object, so I pitch the slice rather than butter and eat it. This is the value-feeling of the slice of bread for me at this moment.

[A]s Husserl states in his lecture from 1902, there can hardly be "talk of 'good' and 'evil' if one abstracts from feeling." An object must affect us emotionally; otherwise, there is no inducement whatever, no motive for us to be interested in it, to strive for it, or to avoid it. Objects motivate our desire and needs through their value, and their value is given to us originally in value-feelings. (Melle 1991: 118)

In his pre-WWI thinking, Husserl used this finding to argue for a Brentanoesque categorical imperative: "Do the best which is attainable"—as well as a more formal axiology analogous to his work on formal logic.

Husserl formulates it as follows in the lecture from 1911: "Formal praxis leads to a highest formal principle, which in the first-place rests on the principle 'The Best is the enemy of the Good.' This principle says, 'Do the best that is attainable.' That is, of course, a noetic expression. Objectively, the expression would be: the best attainable within the entire practical sphere is not merely the best comparatively speaking—but rather, the sole practical good." (Husserl quote from Melle 1991: 120)

But discussing Husserl's theory of ethics and his take on Brentano's imperative goes beyond our present writ, as does his call for a spiritual "renewal" of European culture. As he states in an article not yet translated into English, "Renewal of man, renewal of both the single person and the community is the chief theme of ethics. Ethical life is essentially and consciously inspired by the idea of renewal; it is a life willfully led and formed by this idea" (translated by Melle 1991: 124). We are not concerned here with how Husserl philosophized about universal ethical principles, however interesting that is at the sociological, cultural, and historical levels. Rather, *we are interested solely in the results of phenomenological meditations on the essential structures of experience underlying value*—groundwork which as we will see below invites a connection with evolutionary processes discussed earlier with respect to communication (see Chapter 7). This is especially so when we get to his later work which, while still supportive of Brentano's ethics, is increasingly influenced by the philosophy and theology of Fichte.

It is my view, and following Husserl, the foundation of ethical systems in all societies derives from the evolutionary selection in favor of *adaptive evaluation, and that we should be able to seek the neurophysiological correlates of valuing within the structure of intentional acts*. Husserl's linking of ethics and emotion runs counter to the prevailing constructivist views of many anthropologists writing about ethics (and morality) who claim that ethics arises in (human) thought (see Reichlin 2012). Perspectives that include biological and neuroscience grounding in ethics are in fact in keeping with Husserl's findings (see e.g., Baumard and Sperber 2012, Damasio 1994, Damasio *et al.* 1994). It is clear from Husserl's writings that the presentation of value-feelings within the essential structures of the intentional act applies as much to animal consciousness as to human. Even solitary species will experience primordial evaluations, although, without a social context, the term "ethics" might seem nonsensical. We hominins were concerned about right and wrong long before we had language, laws, or ethical systems (de Waal 1996, 2006).

It is Husserl's understanding from within the epoché that value is as much a primordially given noetic element as the object. The value of the object precedes any higher cognitive functions. My disgust at the creeping mold on the slice of bread is present virtually instantaneously with the form and hyle of the sensory data. This primordial evaluation is physiologically designed to influence my will and adaptive actions vis-à-vis the object and occurs prior to the exercise of reason or application of culturally formulated and socially shared ethical systems. This foundational evaluative operation is analogous to motor reflexes designed in such a way that an endangered limb is already moving away from the fire as a "reflex" act before higher cortical systems even become aware of the danger (see Libet 2004).

The contemplative who dives deeply into value in the epoché must eventually become changed with respect to personal ethics. The isolation of value-feelings within intentional acts over time should, according to Husserl, result in the building up of positive habits, which over time produce new convictions that perhaps will replace those cultural values learned at the knees of one's parents and social peers.

> For Husserl, personal identity presupposes lasting convictions. Such lasting convictions are habitual sediments of the free, theoretical, axiological and practical position-takings of the

"ego." My person would fragment and disintegrate if my position-takings would not crystallize into habitual convictions. I am "I" only so long as I have harmonious opinions. Only then can I preserve myself as me. "If my life were only a muddle of opinions, then I would not be truly an 'I'—the absolutely identical subject of my acts." *The ethical striving for ultimately justified and thereby non-falsifiable position-takings and convictions is therefore a striving for absolute self-preservation*, a "life of loyalty to the self," of unconditional consistency. (Melle 1991: 126; emphasis added, Husserl quotes translated by Melle)

Just as with scientific knowledge becoming harmonious with adumbrated intuitive knowing, the development of the ethical-self under the influence of the ethical epoché should result in a changed self-identity whose convictions become more harmonious with intuitive value-feelings.

The ethical epoché aims at the validity of each and all acts which constitute my personal being. This, he notes, is quite different from all the validities constituted in the course of my life, especially those by which I have an abiding world. The ethical epoché has to do with "the acts related to the absolute ought and what in this respect is relevant to the universal practical field [...]." (Hart 1992: 31-32; Husserl quote from *The Crisis of European Sciences and Transcendental Phenomenology*)

Thus, one's meditations produce in the long run a more unified identity, much as engagement with the realities of one's unconscious creates a broader and more inclusive ego. This reorganization of the person is by no means an easy task, for the process pits the rational, ethical processes of the brainmind against our fundamental, often unconscious drives, impulses, urges to act-out unconscious complexes, and the like. It takes a force of will for us to dissociate the "lower" level motivations from our actions.

As [Husserl's] ethical lectures from 1920 point out, the ethical will brings about a self-dividing of the ego into the dominant ego of reason and the lowly and sinful ego of drives and impulses.

The ethical life is, in its striving after complete self-preservation and absolute validation, a life of self-discipline, methodical self-cultivation, radical self-critique and self-control. The ideal structure of ethical life is, as Husserl describes it, a "pan-methodicalness" (*Panmethodismus*)—that is, in place of naïveté, of naïve "living-along"—"a life of method." (Melle 1991: 126-127, Husserl quotes translated by Melle)

Perhaps we might take note of a curious fact about the English language. English speakers differentiate the words "consciousness" and "conscience." This is not the case for all Indo-European languages. For example, the Spanish word *conciencia* denotes both "conscience" and "awareness." In German, conscience is expressed with the noun *Gewissen* and consciousness with the noun *Bewusstsein*—as in English, both terms are from the same root. In our collective European heritage, *conscience* is the awareness of value-feelings in intentional acts.

In any event, the phenomenologist who plumbs the depth and variety of value-feelings increasingly develops towards an internal unity of spirit, and in the process may well throw over some of their cultural baggage pertaining to value associated with sensed objects and events, as well as with other people. They may find that their natural attitude, culturally inherited values consist in a blind belief in enculturated evaluations rather than ethics grounded in self-realization. Only after considerable practice of reduction focused upon value-feelings at the primordial level may they come to see that their ethical beliefs may contradict their value-feelings. This congruity testing amounts to a renewal of the individual brought about by the truing effects of revealing the foundational roots of value integral to intentional acts (Donohoe 2016: 128-129).

Beginning perhaps in the early 1920s, Husserl began to deemphasize the formal aspects of ethics and emphasize the importance of love, empathy, and compassion in the process of the phenomenologist's own ethical renewal (Husserl 2014; see also De Warren 2017: 570, Ferrarello 2016: 178-196, Steinbock 2014, 2021):

Husserl's ethics of renewal centers on the generating axis of love. As Husserl reflects: "If we prefer according to our best knowledge and conscience of the best of what is attainable, we have acted ethically, then and only then our will is absolutely right." The new thought here is to conceive of "the best" through an individual's affective conscience and (self)-knowledge of her vocation in view of "absolute values" grounded in love. Of this differentiation between an ethics of reason and an ethics of love (the latter exclusively developed in Husserl's private and unpublished research manuscripts), one example recurs in Husserl's meditations. [...] As Husserl reflects:

> "Should the mother first deliberate and make considerations of the highest possible good? This whole ethics of the highest practical good such as it was derived from Brentano and taken over by me in its essential traits cannot be the last word. Essential determinations are needed! Vocation and inner calling cannot be done justice in this way. There exists an unconditional "you ought and must" that addresses itself to the person and that is not subject to a rational justification and does not depend for its legitimate obligation [...] on such a justification for the one who experiences this absolute affection. This affection [...] precedes all rational explanation even where such an explanation is possible." (de Watten 2017: 570-571; quote from Husserl 2014)

Instead of my ego being uncritically grounded in enculturated values, I come to realize through ethical reduction that value-feelings are primordial—part and parcel of the *absolute givenness* of lived experience. Within the range of affect that arises intuitively within my intentional acts, I recognize the preeminence of love within the range of motivations of practical willing ("position-taking" and judging). I come to realize that love imposes upon me an absolute imperative and is the basis for my ego's status as an ethical person.

> With this turn to a phenomenology of love and absolute values, Husserl offers a transcendental account of moral obligation and its underpinning affective "material" values in conjunction with the

constitution of the self as an ethical project. As Husserl argues in his criticism of Kant's notion of respect for the moral law, the pure (or ethical) will must be motivated by the affection of an absolute value, yet pure affection is itself insufficient to generate the ethical force of moral obligation. *The affectivity of love must be formed through an activity of self-determination, or autonomy, as the project of an individual's deliberate self-constitution.* The affective ground of moral obligation is therefore twofold: the ethical person becomes freely bound to herself in being bound to an absolute value, for which she assumes absolute responsibility in assuming her own ethical vocation, or "person." As Husserl further argues, *a mother's love originates as a "drive" that becomes re-configured into "social" and "ethical" love.* In itself, the drive (love) towards the child, as the subject of care and affection, is neither "ethical" nor "social." It is only through an I–Thou relationship [...] that a person becomes fully constituted such that the mother and child form a primordial "community" [...]: the mother, in her love for her child, establishes an "inner" relationship with her child (and likewise the child with her mother). (De Warren 2017: 571-572; emphasis added)

The point I wish to emphasize is that, for Husserl, the value-feelings from which our ethical sense derives are mediated by an essential structure of intentional acts—part of the absolute givenness of sensory experience—and not the result of cognition at some higher level. A continuity of value experiences produces habits which then may become "convictions" and obviously have some influence upon higher level ethical beliefs and behaviors. Yet it is also quite common for the dictates of cultural, institutional, and occupational ethical judgments to be experienced as contradictory to primordial value-feelings. If I am employed as a police officer, I may be duty-bound to act in ways contrary to my personal "gut" feelings of empathy. A normal human being will experience empathy for another person's suffering, due to the wiring of the brain in those areas with populations of mirror neuron systems (see Chapter 4). Empathy is fundamental to the human lifeworld, as is love. Indeed, as my colleague Melanie Takahashi and I (Laughlin and Takahashi 2020) have shown, it is the capacity for boundless love that leads spiritual practitioners to mystical experiences (see also Steinbock 2014, 2021).

At this juncture, we have to follow Husserl's reasoning carefully, for at the point that value-feelings become ethics, we are entering the phenomenology of intersubjectivity and community (see Chapter 4), as well as culture. When it comes to ethics per se, we are never alone. Indeed, all animals with brains experience value-feelings, but claiming that solitary animals make ethical judgments vis-à-vis conspecifics makes little sense, while social animals certainly do so. It is by blending the essential structurers of intersubjectivity and the ubiquity of value-feelings that Husserl posits love[68] as the glue that cements interpersonal bonds and community. "Text 9 of the second volume *On the Phenomenology of Intersubjectivity* [not yet translated into English] opens with Husserl's description of love as that feeling that ontologically links individuals together as a 'spiritualized corporeity' (172, 175)" (Ferrarello 2016: 198). In other words, primordial love/empathy/compassion and intersubjective experience binds beings into a "community of love" (see Melle 2002). The fact that other highly social animals exhibit this same process demonstrates that we humans inherited our communities of love from earlier hominins, just as they inherited this aspect from pre-hominins (Brooker, Webb and Clay, in press, Decastro, Gaspar and Vicente 2010). This primordial binding force of course has evolved and in Husserl's terms motivates actions under an "absolute ought" at the level of personal ethics and an "absolute command" at the level of community (Melle 2002, Ferrarello 2016: 178-180, Hart 1997).

HUSSERLIAN PHENOMENOLOGY OF VALUE AND AESTHETICS

Husserlian axiology being grounded in the "study of values" also includes *aesthetics*,[69] as it does for many traditional human societies for whom little or no distinction is made between "good" and "beauty" (see below). The ground of aesthetic consciousness (the "aesthetic attitude") is the same as that for ethical consciousness (the "ethical

---

[68] Husserl's value-feeling "love" is the type that Buddhist psychology calls "loving-kindness" (*metta*; see Colzato *et al.* 2012).

[69] If you wish to read more about Husserl's phenomenology of *aesthetics*, see Husserl 1989[1952], 2005[1898-1925]; see also Dufrenne 1973, Hart and Embree 1997, Hobbs 2021, Summa 2014)

attitude"). The aesthetic object (a noetically presented sensory object accompanied by value-feelings of beauty, attractiveness, pleasure, or ugliness, displeasure) is evaluated noematically within the intentional act (Dufrenne 1973). For Husserl, the aesthetic experience is noetically pre-given by a transcendental presentation of object-plus-value-feeling.

The transcendental status of the aesthetic object is independent of other considerations which may potentially dilute the experience in its purest sense. If we gaze at a beautiful painting, say, by Monet—one of his gorgeous garden scenes, like *Le Jardin de l'artiste à Giverny*—we stand moved by the breathtakingly beautiful scene appearing within our sensorium. We experience a pure aesthetic moment in which ideas about the existence or non-existence of the painting, the monetary value of the "piece of art," or for that matter the existence and history of the garden or the artist, are farthest from our minds. Likewise, we sit enthralled at the beauty of a piece of music, say, Jules Massenet's tone poem *Meditation from Thaïs*. If we close our eyes and become totally absorbed in the flow of music, there is nothing before us but the melody and the surge of bliss we may be experiencing. There are no thoughts of Massenet, or the history of the music hall around us, or the historical significance of Massenet's music. In fact, if our absorption is intense enough, gone is the subject as well leaving nothing but the sounds of the music and our value-feelings.

> Husserl insists that taking into account the existence of things that stand in front of us is an attitude of mind which is:

> > [...] the exact opposite of the attitude of mind in purely aesthetic intuition and in the corresponding state of feeling. But it is no less the exact opposite of the purely phenomenological attitude of mind, in which alone can philosophical problems be solved. For the phenomenological method also demands a rigorous exclusion of every existential stand. (Lories 2006: 32; quote translated from Husserl 1994b)

Any object may elicit an aesthetic value-feeling. I have mentioned a painting and a piece of music. But fashion, architecture, landscapes, décor, office, store, plants, animals, etc.—literally anything or any event—may stimulate aesthetic experiences.

> One selects the most favorable appearance. This involves (a) the appearance that contains in itself the maximum stock of sensuous moments and the particular combination of such moments that arouse pleasure; (b) the clear awakening of the consciousness of the object, although the interest does not concern the object as an element of the actual world with respect to its objective properties, relations, and so on, but precisely the appearance alone. However, since the objective apprehension is there and, of course, unavoidable, and since the function of the object, its purposes, and so on, are co-excited, they must be there in clear fashion. The object itself, adapted to its purpose, must be there, or otherwise there would be conflict between the form of the object and its function. (Husserl 2005[1898-1925]: 168)

Here Husserl lays the phenomenological foundations of the aesthetic phenomena encountered by anthropologists across cultures, as we shall see below. Aesthetics can, and in fact in daily life of peoples usually does, blend with other interests in the object. As we will see, the appreciation of aesthetic objects from the attitude of solely aesthetic is culturally atypical when we look at "art" across cultures.

AXIOLOGICAL NEUROPHENOMENOLOGY

It is remarkable how closely a Husserlian phenomenological reduction to the primordial axiological attitude (ethical, aesthetic, or both) parallels what we are coming to know about how the brain mediates this type of perception. By grounding axiology in the phenomenology of value-feelings, Husserl is consonant with the neurophysiology of the affective value of stimuli. The blending of multimodal affect and object within the sensorium would seem to involve both the orbitofrontal region of the prefrontal lobes, that area of cortex that lies just above your eyes, and the amygdala (O'Doherty, Rolls and Kringelbach 2004, Rolls 2018: 66-94). These are areas of the brain within which all sensory modes are represented, and which neuroimaging studies confirm are active when affect is paired with sensory objects and events. From either an evolutionary or an adaptational perspective, it makes sense for selection to favor pairing of affect within immediate, primordial perception to facilitate behavioral responses to significant events in the environing world. Whether these pairings are considered as aesthetic attitudes or ethical attitudes pertain to the judgments and praxis following on from the initial sensory presentation.

It is clear that inherited, a priori knowledge determines how we perceive and evaluate what we perceive. Moreover, as Wolf Singer (2012: 60) emphasizes, evolution is very conservative of systems that function adaptively—especially those that are conducive to adaptational fitness across niches. A priori structures of perception, discovered from the "inside" via phenomenological reduction and "outside" through neuropsychological and psychophysiological research, determine how we experience objects in ways that have been operating in brains for millions of years. Human brains continue to function in these ways although our evolution has resulted in a noticeable complexification of these structures and how they are integrated hierarchically at higher cognitive levels of meaning.

ANTHROPOLOGICAL AXIOLOGY

It is also remarkable how the descriptions of a phenomenological reduction of axiological perceptions mirrors what we have come to know about ethical and aesthetic attitudes evidenced in cultures, especially non-technocratic cultures, across the globe. Along with the research and theoretical turns towards experience and the senses, the anthropology of ethics/morality has become reasonably robust compared with the days nearly forty years ago when David Parkin edited his classic volume, *The Anthropology of Evil* (1985). In his incisive introduction to the book, he points out many problems faced by students of ethical systems when they broaden their studies beyond Christian-influenced cultures, and these problems are foreshadowed in Husserl's reflections on value-feelings. One of the first things a student of ethical systems must do is question the cross-cultural and theoretical utility of English/Christian notions of "good" and "evil" (Parkin 1985: 2-3). The closest one can come in most languages to the former is perfection, structuration, kindness, wholesomeness, happiness, economic plenty, health, etc. and to the latter is imperfection, destruction, disunity, unwholesomeness, self-centeredness, misery, privation, disease, and so forth (see Danchevskaya 2020). Moreover, in many societies, there is no clear binary categorical distinction between good and evil. All of this fits with the role of value-feelings as the roots of ethical judgments, regardless of cultural background. In addition, the unreflective and erroneous theoretical separation of ethical and aesthetic experiences is divulged within the epoché. This is crucial for both the organization of research and retaining the lifeworld reality base for our understanding of peoples' evaluative judgments.

The literature covering ethical/moral anthropology has considerably expanded since the 1980s (see e.g., Cassaniti and Hickman 2014, Fassin 2012, Heintz 2021, Howell 1997, Mattingly 2012, Mattingly and Throop 2018). Unfortunately, some anthropological approaches to ethics/morality still reflect the Durkheimian theory of ethics which has to do primarily with socially defined (constructed) rules and responsibilities (Durkheim 1992). Some anthropologists to this day reify society as though society is real rather than a conceptual abstraction. This is precisely the kind of science bias that Husserl struggled to overcome phenomenologically. As Parkin (1985: 4-5) noted: "[...] Durkheim so conflated the moral with the social that ethnographers could not isolate for analysis those contemplative moments of moral reflexivity that, rather than strict and unambiguous rules, most typify human activity and predicaments."

Turning to aesthetics, one of the most important findings of cross-cultural studies of aesthetics is that virtually no traditional societies conceptually or linguistically separate the value-feeling element from the element of utility. Ethnographers have long known that traditions of "art" on the planet are expressions of the particular society's cosmology. A society's religious art and iconography often reveal the hidden aspects of spirit as glimpsed through the filter of cultural significance. Moreover, traditional art may describe aspects of experiences encountered in ASC. For example, the Huichol peoples of Central Mexico ingest psychoactive peyote in their religious rituals and their yarn paintings, beadwork, basketry and weaving incorporate imagery depicting themes encountered during psychedelic episodes (MacLean 2012). In any such society, any attempt to understand the inner meaning of traditional art is futile without some grasp of the cosmology and perhaps even the direct mystical experiences expressed by the art's iconic form. Traditions of art are in fact systems of symbols that are part of a much greater cultural and experiential context—a context that must at least partially be entered by the ethnologist if they are going to be able to critique the art from anything like an authoritative stance—or for that matter, a Husserlian stance.

Put simply, there are very few traditional societies whose languages have a word for "art" in the Western sense of the term (Mithlo 2012). Moreover, ethnographers have found that aesthetics is almost always entangled conceptually with utility among traditional peoples (see Abiodun 2014 for the case of the Yoruba people of West Africa). As Alfred Gell (1998) has shown, especially for Pacific Island peoples, the principal concern of the people may be upon the use of the object as a kind of technology. Many Pacific peoples create shields, body art, and prow boards for their boats in order to dazzle the beholder and put them at a disadvantage in trade or warfare (Figure 7). We Westerners will collect these artifacts and put them in museums for aesthetic appreciation, thus divorcing their aesthetics from agency.

THE CASE OF NAVAJO AXIOLOGY

Take for instance the ethno-axiology of the Navajo people of the American Southwest (or *Diné* as they call themselves; see Downs 1972), the largest Native American society with a membership roll over 300,000. They are a Western Apache people, related historically and linguistically to the Chiricahua and Jicarilla Apaches, and speak one of the still thriving Athabaskan languages. Approximately 180,000 Navajos inhabit the largest Indian reservation (25,209 square miles) in North America which covers roughly a fifth of the state of Arizona and parts of southern Utah and western New Mexico. The Navajo homeland (*Dinétah*) is mostly semi-arid high desert plateau country, with some forest and mountain areas, and bounded symbolically by

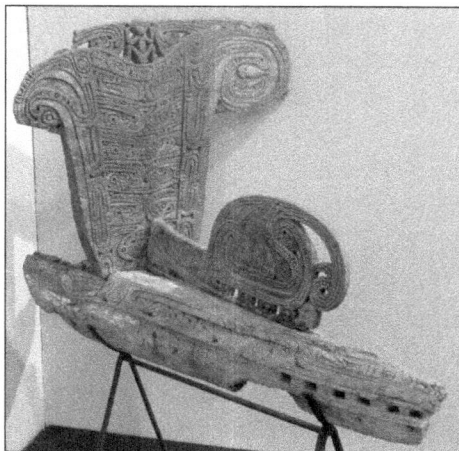

Figure 7. A Pacific Island prow board, removed from its boat and placed in a museum for artistic appreciation.

the four sacred mountains which in English are called Blanca Peak (*Sis Naajíní*), Colorado, to the east, Mount Taylor (*Tsoodził*), New Mexico, to the south, the San Francisco Peaks (*Dookʼoʼoosłííd*), Arizona, to the west and Hesperus Peak (*Dibé Nitsaa*), Colorado, to the north.

The closest one can come in Navajo to our English "good" and "evil" are the terms *hózhó* (a term that is hard to gloss in English, but which is usually translated as "beauty," "healthy," or "good") and *hóchxó* (translated in English variously as "ugly," "destructive," "disharmonious"/"chaotic," "unhealthy," and "bad"). In certain circumstances *hóchxó* is conceived as the polar opposite of *hózhó*, while in other circumstances they may be seen as two opposite poles of a continuum, or as two aspects of the same being or thing. The point here is that *there is little or no distinction among traditional Navajo between aesthetics and ethics, between beauty and "the right thing to do."* If you act ethically then you are *hozho naasha*, "walking in beauty."

Studying the Navajo concept of *hózhó* in depth and in context, which I did among Navajo friends back in the 1990s, takes one into the heart of Navajo philosophy and way beyond the limits of axiology in the way we Euro-american-aussies understand the concept. The term carries with it the connotations of "harmony," "proper order," "health," "goodness" (including the moral and spiritual senses), etc. It is important at the outset to understand that *hózhó* for the Navajo is as much an internal mental state—an existential state of being—as it is a philosophical concept for the metaphysical quality of things "out there" (Witherspoon 1977: 151). *Hózhó* is a spiritual path, a way of life, an ideal and dynamic process of living, and is a quality that one wants to realize in one's being to match its natural counterpart in nature. Nature is inherently in a state of *hózhó*, and when we humans are walking in beauty, we are in synch with the natural state. It is toward celebrating, restoring and maintaining the *hózhó* state of being that virtually all Navajo spiritual practice is directed.

Hózhó refers to the natural state of both perceived external events and the hidden forces behind those events (Farella 1984). The Navajo, like so many other traditional peoples around the globe, have noticed that we cannot actually see the air we breathe. We only know air by its movement and its effects (the rustling of leaves, whirling dust, the sensation of the breeze on our skin, etc.). Not surprising then that in Navajo cosmology the hidden, vital, motivating dimension of things is called *nilch'i*, or Wind (McNeley 1981). Physical reality—indeed, all things in the perceptual world, including people—are motivated by this one, vast, cosmic Holy Wind that flows in and out of all things (*bii'asti*, the "animating energy within"), and that underlies and vitalizes the normally hidden totality of the universe. Wind underlies the vitality, dynamics and movement of nature from the contemplation of which people may attain their intuitions about the purpose of existence. And it is an imbalance or disruption (*hóchxó*) of that portion of the "wind that stands within" (*nilch'i hwii'siziinii*; McNeley 1981) each person that leads to disease and misfortune.

One of the main ways that the sense of *hózhó* can be lost is by forgetting. Thereafter, one may return to the state of beauty by remembering—by literally "*re*-membering," or "*re*-collecting"—by putting it all back together again in the properly healthy and wholesome way. One may again walk in beauty by remembering what the Holy People (*Diyin Diné'e*) taught from the beginning of time, and which is recorded in precise detail in the Sacred Stories handed down from generation to generation. Generally speaking, the Navajo believe that the only route to *hózhó* is to live in accord with the Way of the Holy People. If need be, one may be reminded of the *hózhó* way by instruction from a medicine man or elder, or by singing the appropriate songs, or by doing the proper rituals such as greeting the dawn with an offering of corn pollen and prayer.

Navajo express various views about the relation of the Holy Wind and the Holy People—for instance, the Mountain People, the Star People, the River People, the Rain People, the Corn People, Coyote, Big Fly, etc. For many, the Holy People are the Holy Wind personified, the Wind imagined (and sometimes directly experienced). For others, the Holy People exist in their own right and like everything else in reality are motivated by the Holy Wind. In either case, one of the major mnemonic devices for reminding people of the hidden aspects of the way of beauty is the imagery in iconographic art—that is, art works that resemble and invoke heroic figures (e.g., the Holy People or *yee'ii*), sacred themes and processes (e.g., the open circle) and mythological events (e.g., slaying of monsters by the Hero Twins) that reveal the causally powerful, but hidden spiritual dimensions of the world. Mnemonic imagery is depicted in statues, masks, prayer sticks, textile designs, jewelry, basketry and sandpaintings. A piece of sacred art reminds the viewer of the teachings of the Holy People, and thus the mind is guided, in the presence of the object and its narrative associations, back onto the path of beauty, harmony and health.

Among the Navajo people, as with numerous other peoples whose ethnographies we might consult, there is little or no distinction made between ethics and aesthetics. In each and every one of these societies, one would search in vain for abstract notions that would match our social scientifically and philosophically generated abstract notions of either ethics or aesthetics, for what most people in traditional societies cognize has to do with feeling states relative to objects and events in their direct experience of the world.

THE CRISIS OF EXPANDING CONSCIOUSNESS, REDUX

At this point, let us return to the crisis of expanding consciousness I introduced in Chapter 7. Not only did complexification of communication, especially language, enhance sociality in response to expanding consciousness, it also made possible the sharing and standardization of axiological oughts and convictions among group members. This would have marked the origin of group ethical systems however primitive they may have been in practice. So long as the consciousness of local group members were limited by their perceptual horizon, the intuited value-feelings embedded within the structure of individual intentional acts would have been sufficient to result in concerted social action, for they would have been automatically available within the lifeworld of the group. But when the evolution of the brains of our ancestors reached a level of complexity such that their individual experienced worlds began to diverge and threaten social unity and social action, then selection would have increased for more intersubjective communication and thus greater interpersonal standardization of attitudes and behaviors. This increased selection in favor of standardization of attitude and behaviors would have resulted in a potential divergence between subjective value-feelings and the standardized social ("cultural") oughts and ought-nots.

As we saw above, humans have lived with this tension between potentially diverse subjective values and the adaptive power of sociality ever since. I feel afraid of something and would naturally avoid that something, but the ethics of my job will not let me back away from that something. "Bootcamp," "retraining," and "initiation" type institutions are constructed to recondition individuals into line with standardized oughts, often at the expense of suppressing the inherited a priori value feelings accompanying subjective intentional acts. I emphasize axiological here, instead of merely ethical, for the same process would have increased standardized aesthetic tastes as well as ethical oughts. As the anthropology of art amply shows, what we call "art" among traditional peoples is highly standardized and, as we have seen, intermingled with group worldviews and social actions. Consider the social pressures for just the right kind of iconography involved in producing prow boards such as the one in Figure 7. While virtually all traditional art across the globe is "abstract," there are virtually zero degrees of freedom in style, intent, execution, utility, and appreciation of such aesthetic productions (Dissanayake 1992, Gell 1998, Laughlin 2004). To offer another example, Navajo healers construct elaborate mandalas from ground stone—their famous sandpaintings—within a hut for use in healing ceremonies. At a certain point in the ceremony the patient is asked to sit in the middle of the mandala, after which, and at the end of the ceremony, the painting is destroyed and the ground stone cast to the winds. Traditionally—that is, before there was an Anglo market for such paintings—the healer would never think of conserving the painting because for them the image is a portal to powerful spiritual energies evoked for the purpose of healing the patient and would be a dangerous opening into the spirit world if it was left assembled. The construction of the mandala is done to specific standards, and for it to work at all, it must follow guidelines precisely. "Sandpaintings" constructed for the art market these days *always* incorporate an intentional error, which render them safe and useless in healing (see Samuels 1995, Witherspoon 1977).

THE QUESTION OF NATURAL ETHICS

In my opinion, a scientific anthropology of ethics should incorporate the perspectives in the sibling sciences commonly known as *natural morality* (Baumard and Sperber 2012, Boehm 2012, Churchland 2019, Joyce 2007, Tomasello 2016, Wong 2006), as well as the new subdiscipline of neuroscience termed *neuroethics* (Inglese and Lavazza 2022, Lavazza 2016). Viewed in this natural or biological light, human ethics is not an invention of culture, but rather due to selective pressures on social consciousness and behavior over the course of millions of years and left its structural basis in the neurognostic organization of the human brainmind. The biogenetic view of the origins of morality date back at least to Charles Darwin who discussed the origins of moral norms in the inherent empathy animals feel for each other, as opposed to the individual's proclivity for selfishness (Darwin 2008[1871]). In short, ethics/morality did *not* suddenly appear as a product of human cultural construction. Morality is *not* "culture all the way down," but is the result of millions of years of evolution. I argue that a turn in anthropology towards natural morality is implied by Husserl's phenomenological axiology, although so far as I know he never got into the biology of the issue. It is clear now that other social animals exhibit norms of behavior, empathy for fellow group members, a sense of fairness in interaction, and an attitude of cooperation (de Waal 1996, Hauser 2006). It is also clear that our brains are "wired" for a moral sense in the form of value-feelings, and that the biogenetic structure underlying moral judgments and actions is evident in babies (Bloom 2013). It is my view, as it was for Husserl by implication, that the neural networks mediating value-feelings are inherited and are then modified in interaction with the world and group during development (Hauser 2006: 165). This does not mean that neural structures are inherited but are empty of function. Indeed, again, neural networks are not microchips. There is no such thing as a cellular network, neurophysiological or otherwise, that does not function.

We have to be cautious here, for if empathy and other value-feelings were not connected to motor activity (e.g., altruism)—if they did not produce adaptively relevant behavior—there would be no selection for or against these value-feelings, either at the individual or group levels. Biologically speaking, structures in the body are selected for or against based upon the behaviors that increase or decrease the fitness of the local reproductive population. Selective pressures among social animals are both more complex and depend upon mechanisms leading to cooperation among members of the group—social cooperation including altruistic behaviors (Baumard and Sperber 2012, Boehm 2012: 7-18, Joyce 2007: Chap. 1, Tomasello 2016: Chap. 2).

As I mentioned above, from Husserl's genetic phenomenological viewpoint, value-feelings influence judgments, judgements influence willing and willing produces behavior which in turn results in negative or positive feedback into the structures of consciousness, all of which unfolds in time. In a very real sense, Husserl's meditations upon empathy and behavior within the context of intersubjective intentionality supports a kind of phenomenological *consequentialism*—consequentialism being the school of moral philosophy that holds that, "[...] the moral quality of action and character is determined by the *effects* of the action or character trait [...]" (Driver 2012: 1). On this account, actions and traits are good or bad relative to how those around us conceive of the effects of our proclivities, judgments and actions.

> Somewhat more precisely, we may think of a consequentialist theory of this kind as coming in two parts. First, it gives some principle for ranking overall states of affairs from best to worst

from an impersonal standpoint, and then it says that the right act in any given situation is the one that will produce the highest-ranked state of affairs that the agent is in a position to produce. (Scheffler 1988: 1)

Remember Husserl's reworking of Kant's categorical imperative, now to read: "Do the best which is attainable." What he is saying in his early pre-WWI manuscripts is that an ethical act is one that is the best available which can actually be accomplished by the agent. Shift this reasoning to an evolutionary perspective, and the "impersonal" evaluator becomes *natural selection, rather than the group*. Thanks to group selection among social animals, those traits and actions that support sociality, cooperation, altruistic behaviors, and (keeping the crisis of expanding consciousness in mind) synchronized value-feelings and judgements will have been selected for. A case in point: "Altruism exists. If by altruism we mean traits that evolve by virtue of benefitting whole groups, despite being selectively disadvantageous within groups, then altruism indubitably exists and accounts for the group-level functional organization that we see in nature" (Wilson 2015: 141).

CHAPTER TWELVE

Concluding Reflections: Grounding Scientific Anthropology in the Structures of the Senses

What we must do now is something that has never been done seriously on either side and has never been done radically and consistently: we must go from the scientific fundamental concepts back to the contents of "pure experience," we must radically set aside all presumptions of exact science, all its peculiar conceptual superstructures—in other words, we must consider the world as if these sciences did not yet exist, the world precisely as lifeworld, just as it maintains its coherent existence in life throughout all its relativity, as it is constantly outlined in life in terms of validity.

– Husserl (1970[1936]: 216)

Modern humans possess remarkable cognitive abilities, including abstract reasoning, creativity, and social intelligence. These abilities enabled humans to develop sophisticated technologies, express themselves through language and art, and examine the world through science and philosophy, ultimately culminating into a rapid and ongoing cultural evolution that, for better or worse, sets humans apart from any other species on the planet.

– Ewoud Schmidt and Franck Polleux (2022: 1)

Over the past chapters, I have attempted to give you a feeling for both the wide scope of Husserl's meditations and tips on how you might apply them yourself as a contemplative phenomenologist. I have been concerned with the challenges and advantages of being able to carry out Husserlian reductions within the context of either training to do, or doing anthropological and other social science research, a valuable addition to the qualitative methods toolbox.

With the exception of Schutz, Jung and Eugene Fink, I have purposely ignored other phenomenological approaches, especially those that are not based upon mature contemplation. Once again, I quote Don Ihde's words: "Without doing phenomenology, it may be practically impossible to understand phenomenology" (Ihde 2012: 3).

We have seen that the principal result of performing the epoché is to convince the researcher by analyzing their own direct perception that experience is *not* "culture all the way down," that there is a real structural basis to human perception—and thus apperception—which is present and operating in every moment of consciousness, regardless of state of consciousness or enculturative background. I have argued that experience is structured the way it is because that is how the brain is organized, namely, to present samples of what is going on in the environing world at the moment, structures that have passed the evolutionary tests of time by leading to thousands of generations of adaptive fitness.

I have shown you how to go about contemplating your own intentionality, whether the object of your perception is a coffee cup, your pet, or a fellow human being. We have seen that if you direct this process toward your ego, you can prove to yourself with absolute certainty that no permanent "me" exists apart from an awareness—the Watcher—that is always present as an integral structure within your intentional acts. In addition, we have explored how the brainmind constructs objects from non-random patterns within percepts as portrayed in the sensorium. What makes objects, including other humans, real to experience is the way the brainmind fills in the form of the object with sensuous "stuff" or hyle, and we saw that the hyle arises and passes with each sensory epoch as a field of contiguous pixelated units. Thus, we have seen that sensuous experience is realized as a kind of plenum void within which reality appears as dynamically concrete and as instantiations of our ideas. These concatenations of hyletically filled and formed eidetic units are accompanied by intuitive knowledge that commonly becomes the keystones for higher cognitive processes within the cortex of the brain, and for individual and "cultural" variability.

In addition, we have seen that all that is required to enter the phenomenological attitude is to apply and retain sufficient awareness within the state of consciousness to control the focus of attention and bracket extraneous mental operations so that pure experience can be observed single-mindedly, studied, and described. This exercise is made easier by learning to calm the body and mind by whatever means available to you before performing a reduction, a skill that Husserl never practiced and never seems to have mentioned explicitly, but only implied. The researcher who develops these contemplative skills is richly rewarded, for they may be used to study any state of consciousness within which intense awareness is possible, including hypnagogic/hypnopompic, dream, vision, entheogen trip, and ritually driven ASC (e.g., Sufi dancing, drumming, ordeal, trance-running, meditation experiences, rebirthing).

Over several chapters, we explored the appropriate use of Husserlian methods to a variety of conscious-related issues of interest to anthropology and social science. The essentially symbolic nature of intentionality was underscored as crucial to understanding how we know reality—how the brainmind constructs a meaningful world that allows our species to adapt to a dynamic environing world. Fundamental to that process is the function of primordial sensuous patterns to operate as keys into higher brain structures that generate meaning, retain and contribute information stored in memory, and assign appropriate responses within the environing world. But we humans have a very social brain and are motivated as much by stability and continuity of meaning as we are by the effort after truth. I took the opportunity to suggest a theory—the crisis of expanding consciousness—that may explain why we humans, alone among the other social animals, developed the capacity for complex communication, especially spoken language. We delved into the roots of knowing, using Husserl's guidance, and found the most primitive kind of knowing within the structure of intentionality—primordial intuitions. Intuition is as much a part of the irreducible a priori as is form and hyle, and as such is the foundation of truth-value upon which higher cognitive operations depend. It is not merely the form, hyle and perceptual field relationships upon which higher forms of knowing are grounded, but also essential intuition. The function of intuition, as with the form and filling of the object and its relations, is to ground our knowing in reality.

We discovered that Husserl recognized certain limitations to phenomenological inquiries, so-called limit-problems. When we try to remember our earliest experiences as a child, we come to a kind of precipice of memory beyond which we cannot go. Thus, there exists an absolute boundary to genetic phenomenology we cannot under normal circumstances penetrate.[70] This goes as well for unconscious brainmind operations. Husserl emphasized the "sinking-in" of phenomena as we lose data from retentive memory, and as our attention wanders from object to object in the stream of consciousness. These now unconscious data may or may not be retrievable. There are also unconscious activities that are forever hidden from awareness.

Husserl was cognizant of course of the relevance of the epoché vis-à-vis ASC, including dreaming, absorption, and mystical experiences. Again, one has to keep in mind that for Husserl phenomenology results in changes in the psychology of the practicing contemplative, a fact that has overwhelming support from today's neuropsychology. Hence, Husserlian phenomenology is a transpersonal enterprise that may continue for a lifetime and result in spontaneous transformations in consciousness up to and including mystical experiences.

We explored some of the shifts in "attitude" (Husserl's term for state of consciousness) within which the application of the epoché may be successfully applied. Two of the most important for Husserl and for anthropology are the ethical attitude and the aesthetic attitude; the two may or may not occur simultaneously. If simultaneous awareness of beauty and duty occur, this might be considered an "axiological" attitude, for in many cultures the two attitudes are two sides of the same coin—i.e., the good and the beautiful may be considered the same quality.

Husserl and Anthropology

I wish to close this exploration of the relevance of Husserl's phenomenology to both neuropsychology and neuroanthropology by returning to the central theme of the book: In order for anthropology to become a nomological science, it must ground its methods and theories in reality.

---

[70] Although of course we can retrieve previously unconscious information about our birth, and even our mental-physical life in utero by practicing holotropic breathwork and other esoteric techniques with which Husserl was unfamiliar.

The only source of information we have about reality is experience—direct naturalistic experience through our senses and technologically augmented observations transduced to sensuous experience. For instance, on a really clear Arizona night with no light pollution, I can see the Andromeda Galaxy with my "naked eye." I can obtain a more complex view of our sister galaxy using binoculars, even more complex via a telescope. Astronomers can increase the complexity of view using space-based telescopes, including the new Webb infrared instrument. Each of these methods depends upon producing a sample of light frequencies impinging upon somebody's retinae. No matter how complex the technology, the information (patterns of energy) they allow us to collect must be transduced via our visual system into a direct experience—an image of the object, measurements of variables on a computer screen, the visual effects of a probe colliding with a celestial object.

Does this mean I envision anthropology to be a science just like astrophysics? Hardly (see McIntyre 2018: Chap. 2). What I am saying is that like any other nomological science, anthropology and its sibling disciplines must be grounded in experience of the real world, transduced to what can be perceived with our senses. Those social sciences (anthropology, sociology, psychology, geography, political science and economics) that focus upon our species are including in their scope of inquiry the productions of *the most complex system in the known universe, the human brain*. Compared with the complexity of the brain, astrophysical systems are child's play. In the brain and its evolution, the universe becomes aware of itself, and in becoming aware, it is forced to recognize its experiential and empirical limitations (McIntyre 1993, 2018). None-the-less, as challenging as the project may appear, we have to face this systemic complexity head-on, and not veer away from it the way anthropology has done for generations.

Let me make myself clearer. What do I mean by nomological science? Philosophers of science have various views and definitions of "nomology." The term is rooted in the ancient Greek roots meaning "lawful" and "reason." In other words, the application of our rational faculties to the study of the world should result in uncovering the lawful behavior of the scope (earthworms, galaxy clusters, wetland ecosystems, economic recessions, humans and other social animals performing rituals, and so forth). The lawful nature of the world can be modeled by reasonable people. Narrowing it down a bit, we are primarily concerned with the field of anthropology, and hence are mostly concerned with the *nomology of brainmind*—the study of the laws or structures underlying the operations of the brainmind that produce ideas, perceptions, knowledge, and behaviors (see Brugha 2015, McIntyre 2018). What this means for our present topic is that we are arguing for a nomological anthropology (see d'Andrade 1995a, Dow 1996, Jarvie 1967, Kuznar 2008, Lett 1997, Spaulding 1988, Spiro 1986)—an anthropology that is grounded in experience (à la William James) and *that searches for and models the universal laws of brainmind functioning in interaction with the environing world under natural conditions.*

The advent of the neuro-turn demands nothing less of us than to construct a scientific anthropology, grounded in something like a Husserlian neurophenomenology. The alternative is to split anthropology off from any status as a science and allow other disciplines to fill in the gaps, as for instance the "new" science of neuroethics purports to do (Inglese and Lavazza 2022). To allow that to happen would be a failure in a major part of our mission, which to my mind is: (1) to educate the other sciences, as well as humanity as a whole, about the role of social learning in our species' adaptation to discrete niches and historical contingencies, (2) to constantly complexify scientific understanding of human lived experience in its natural setting through the evidence of participant observation, and (3) expose cultural and theoretical biases produced by ethnocentric projections, presumptions, and beliefs:

> When anthropologists speak of the impossibility of being objective, they have in mind the secondary meaning of the term, which is "to be unbiased." (The primary meaning of the term "objective" is "pertaining to the object"—that is, about something external to oneself, rather than about one's feelings about something.) And it is true that people doing science, like people everywhere, are often biased. But "bias" does not destroy science. On the contrary, because of the constant checking on other's accounts, it is doing science that destroys bias. Science is a public activity in which people check on each other's observations and reasoning, and it is this that gives science a chance at the truth. Science is the best bias destroyer we have. (d'Andrade 1995a: 4)

As we all know, the essence of science is the disciplined testing of ideas about the world by observing the world. A train of explanations within a theory is like a suspension bridge. Theoretical work must touch down into the bedrock of reality frequently enough to maintain the truing effects of the lifeworld. Too broad the spans, the bridge eventually fails, i.e., the anomalous data piles up too fast. As Husserl noted, in the company of others (see Feyerabend 2010), our theories of the world pre-determine the appropriate empirical methods used to test explanations. Among other things, this has the effect of alienating science from everyday experience as well as the direct awareness of the primordial sensuous given upon which all science must be grounded. As Jan Patočka (2016: 3) emphasized, this has left modern technocratic society without a unifying worldview. Also, this is why science can never become or ever replace a worldview in the traditional sense. As philosopher Steven Goldman notes:

> That theories are true because they correspond with reality is a misrepresentation of science, useful perhaps in gaining for science the status it enjoys in society, and public funding for research, *but with harmful social consequences*. As became evident in the political struggle in the United States over a national policy with respect to global warming and again with the COVID-19 pandemic, when scientific theories are revised even as policy options are being discussed, people conclude that the scientists do not yet know, that they are guessing, and that this guessing reflects a hidden social or political agenda. Significant portions of the public interpret theory change as a sign that the changed theory was false, so why accept the new one as true? This is a direct consequence of ignorance of the conjectural, corrigible, and evolving nature of scientific knowledge, subject as it is to available information. And this ignorance is exploited by those with a political agenda that would benefit from thwarting or limiting scientific input into a policy decision. (Goldman 2022: 256; emphasis added)

Once again, most humans and most human social groups are motivated by the effort after meaning and rarely by the effort after truth. This became, in my opinion, an inevitable consequence of the crisis of expanding consciousness. Selective pressure for enhanced communication and coordinated, consensus meaning systems led to normatized (institutionalized) and conservative views relative to change; in other words, more emphasis upon social homeostasis rather than the more individual, perceptual fieldframes, adaptive *homeorhesis* (Waddington 1957). I do not mean to imply that worldviews don't change, for if they were set in concrete, so to speak, they would eventually be confronted by so many anomalies they would become irrelevant at best and maladaptive at worst. As the great psychological anthropologist, Anthony F. C. Wallace, showed, consensus worldviews must undergo periodic *revitalization* to retain their connection with an ever-changing physical and social reality (Wallace 1957, 2003).

Science is perhaps the world's only social institution that privileges the effort after truth over the effort after meaning, and hence is in a constant state of revitalization of views. The scientific method requires the scientist to pay attention primarily to anomalies rather than merely the results that confirm some theory. "A scientific anomaly happens, basically, when a phenomenon is observed, within the scope of a theory, i.e., a fact which the theory was supposed to explain, but that cannot be inferred from its current laws and auxiliary hypotheses" (Silvestre and Pequeno 2003). In fact, theories function to create anomalies, anomalies to further research, the results of which require the theory be changed (Maffie 2005). A traditional society's worldview on the other hand is a story of reality that resists change, for it provides the framework for explaining events in terms of history, be that history in the form of myth or revelation.

As we have seen, the primordial structures of consciousness have evolved over countless millions of years to perform that crucial function—to link our ideas with percepts, to true our ideas, to keep our reasoning rooted in the primordial sensuous given. The further our ideas, apperceptions, understandings, conclusions, and theories stray from access to the lifeworld, the more likely they will accumulate errors and produce anomalous experiences. Philosophies that rely mostly or entirely upon cerebration with no primordial sensuous input from the sensorium will at best be contentious and lead to endless polemics, and at worst may produce destructive ideologies. As Husserl repeatedly emphasized, skillful phenomenology of the contemplative kind is not just interesting, it is essential to maximizing the truth value of our theory-building.

The brainmind is a system—in fact an intelligent complex adaptive system (Chapter 5)—everything in the brainmind affects everything else in the brainmind as a whole. How we go about testing our ideas about the world when we do science is usually conditioned by those very ideas. As Paul Feyerabend (2010) showed us, theories purport not only to explain their scope, but they also determine how the truth value of the ideas and propositions are to be tested or falsified. Theory and method are two sides of the same empirical coin. This is why Husserl argued so strenuously for applying pure phenomenology *before* applying empirical research so that the scientist realizes from their own direct experience the relationship between ideas and sensuous reality. By exercise of the epoché the scientist or philosopher learns to parse what is given from sensuous reality and what is provided by the meaning-layering processes of cognition. By learning this the scientist can better control for the empirical bias inherent in theory construction. Put another way, most people, including most scientists, cannot perceive the distinction between their ideas and what their senses are portraying in their sensorium. As Husserl emphasized repeatedly, this is a learned skill which should in principle precede training on the application of the "scientific method" in any discipline.

Husserl often spoke of "anthropology" and one of his essays is indeed entitled "Phenomenology and Anthropology" (Husserl 1981[1941]). But like many other philosophers, he was usually not referring to what we call "sociocultural" anthropology, or ethnology. Rather, he was referring to the quite separate subdiscipline of philosophy known as *philosophical anthropology* (see Giri and Clammer 2013). Philosophical anthropology tracks its roots back through Max Scheler, a follower of Husserl, from there to various schools of both Western philosophy and Christian theology back to the classical Greek philosophers. They make very few references to those thinkers who have guided ethnology or biological anthropology.

An interesting exception for Husserl was his interest in and dialog with Lucien Lévy-Bruhl (1857-1939), a fellow philosopher who later in his career developed a keen interest in the writings of Émile Durkheim (1858-1917) and ethnologists interested in the human mind (Levy-Bruhl 1966[1923]). In fact, Levy-Bruhl was among the audience when Husserl gave his 1929 Paris Lectures (Husserl 1964b). Husserl (2008) sent Levy-Bruhl a very revealing letter pertaining to the latter's take on "primitive" mentality in which Husserl wrote:

> For me, in the present state of the life's work I have incessantly carried out, this perspective is of the highest interest, because many years ago I put to myself the problem of the correlation… between We and environing world as a "transcendental-phenomenological" problem with regard to the possible manifold "we," and in fact as a problem that ultimately refers back to the problem of the absolute ego. For it is in its horizon of consciousness that all social units and the environing worlds relative to them have constructed sense and validity… and, in changing, continue to build them always anew. I feel certain that on this path of an intentional analysis, which I have already worked out extensively, historical relativism proves to be undoubtedly justified (as an anthropological fact), but also that anthropology, like every positive science and its universality…, though the first, is not the final word of knowledge—scientific knowledge. Positive science is consistently… objective science; it is science within the taken-for-grantedness… of the being of the objective world and of human being as real factual existence… in the world. Transcendental phenomenology is the radical and consistent science of subjectivity, which ultimately constitutes the world in itself. In other words, it is the science that reveals the *universal taken-for-grantedness* "world and we human beings in the world" to be an *obscurity…*, thus an enigma, a problem, and that makes it scientifically intelligible… in the solely possible way of radical self-examination. It is a scientificity that is novel by virtue of this radicality; it proceeds as a systematic analysis, which systematically shows the ABCs and the elementary grammar of the formation… of "objects" as unities of validity…, the formation of object-manifolds and infinities as valid… "worlds" for sense bestowing subjects, and thereby, as a philosophy, it ascends from below into the heights.

Very succinctly put, this was Husserl's challenge to sociocultural anthropology—to analyze the processes and structures by which the brainmind constructs both the experienced environing world for itself, and the transcendental "We" that collectively operate upon the sensuous and fundamental lifeworld.[71]

ANTHROPOLOGY AND THE INTERSUBJECTIVE GIVEN

With respect to sociocultural anthropology and the doing of phenomenologically oriented ethnography, let me be more specific lest my colleagues miss the point here. Henry A. Murray said it best I think (see Kluckhohn and Murray 1948). Paraphrasing Murray: *in some ways all humans are alike, in some ways some humans are alike, and in some ways no humans are alike.* We humans share universal mental properties because we share the same brainmind organization, groups of humans can vary in their lifeways from other groups of humans because of social learning, and each human brainmind becomes unique due to myriad experiences had over the course of their lives (see Prat 2022 on the uniqueness of the individual brain). Anthropology has specialized in the middle perspective, and during the 20th century has made the discovery of intergroup differences its stock-in-trade. This is why, when anthropologists do turn to phenomenology (e.g., Ram and Houston 2015a, Jackson 1996, 2012), they almost always gravitate toward those philosophers who tend to espouse existential/hermeneutical approaches such as Heidegger, Ricoeur, Sartre, Simone de Beauvoir, Merleau-Ponty, and others, most of whom forswore contemplation of the Husserlian sort, claiming each in their own way that "existence precedes essence" and then failing to study the essences or structures of perception or cognition using anything like contemplation. This is unfortunately predictable, for if one remains at the level of interpretation, one can proceed as though phenomenology is another way to study culture (e.g., Jackson 2012: 20-21). As I discussed at the outset of this book, this bias has created an unfortunate distortion of the anthropological view of human nature and led to the fiction that human psychology is "culture all the way down."

---

[71] Alas, Levy-Bruhl's erroneous categorical distinction between primitive and civilized psychology rubbed off on Husserl, although to a very minor extent (see 1970[1936]: 279 for Husserl's notion of "extrascientific culture," meaning, culture that has not been enlightened via philosophy and science).

As anthropologist, Melford Spiro, argued in a number of essays (see Spiro 1992), prior to the unfortunate shift to its nihilistic postmodernist fad, anthropologists at least considered peoples reared in other societies to be more like us than different, as siblings rather than "Others." For anthropologists who got caught-up in postmodernism, other people became incomprehensible, and "culture" ceased to be a dependent variable for the purposes of theory-building and methodology. For them, other people became utterly incomprehensible and "culture" became an independent variable that "explains" that incomprehensibility. These anthropologists painted themselves into a corner from which no structures or universal processes were available from which to build theory, and given their assumptions, they often spent energy telling us that we cannot do ethnology anymore because only our hosts can tell their story. This of course was precisely what Bastian, and in turn, Boas and his students taught us to do all along. But unlike those two great thinkers, cultural constructivist anthropologists seem to have lost track of the simple fact that we are equipped with a brainmind conditioned through hundreds of thousands of years to "see" reality in a veridical way.

As Husserl repeatedly emphasized, anthropology in the company of all the other sciences loses track of the pregiven world for the very lack of proper awareness, a failure that can only be addressed by practicing reductive contemplation (see Husserl 1970[1936]: 48-51). Husserl, of course, studied interpretation as well, and its role in the intentional act. But because he was a mature contemplative he saw too the essential structures of perception, and, as we have discussed, revealed from within the epoché that the amount of interpretive (meaning) operations increased the further removed consciousness gets from pure sensory experience (the noesis; see especially Luft 2011: 14).

Over the course of the last few decades, some anthropologists have shifted focus more and more away from social structure, institutional organization and habitual behavior to a more first-person, subjective level of analysis emphasizing experience. As we saw earlier, this led to the need for appropriate phenomenological methods which led to the occasional conversation about Husserlian methods. But applying Husserlian methods to experience reveals a layer of structural essence—some of the ways that all humans are alike—thus creating an ontological quandary for many anthropologists who persist in taking an absolutist position on cultural relativity. Does this mean we should get rid of the concept of "culture" in order to solve the problem? Hardly, as British social anthropology did not take to the concept until the writings of Edwin Ardener (2017). Even Husserl uses the term in his writing and was cognizant of the source of the natural attitude—the doxic "universal taken-for-grantedness"—of everyday consciousness of people living in groups. A result of his shift to genetic reduction revealed the pivotal importance of social learning in constructing the layers of meaning with which we mindlessly blanket the a priori, primordial sensuous world.

HUSSERL ON "CULTURE"

We have touched upon Husserl's use of the concept of "culture" in previous chapters.[72] Indeed, Husserl was cognizant of the role of social learning in "constituting," "achieving," "accomplishing," or as we anthropologists would say, *constructing* the layers of shared beliefs that are projected upon sensuous and intersubjective experiences.[73] As we saw when explaining the crisis of expanding consciousness in Chapter 7, the crucial function of communication was to become the enhanced sharing of information about individual experiences and knowledge so that the group was able to retain, as Husserl terms it, a "common surrounding world:"

> The *common* surrounding world acquires communal characteristics of a new sense and at a higher level by means of acts of personal mutual determination which arise on the basis of mutual comprehension. This results in possibilities not only for a parallel and mutually understood component to objects as the ones of the community's surrounding world but also for a joint-unitary comportment of persons to such objects, a comportment in which

---

[72] If you wish to read more about Husserl's understanding of *culture*, see Husserl 1989[1952]: 200-219, 250, 365-366, 1977[1925]: 170-179, 1970[1936]: 278-279; also see various articles in Jensen and Moran 2013a, Kohak 1978.

[73] Husserl spoke of *Kulturgebilde* or *Kulturgestalt*, "culture formation," *Kultur-Phänomen*, "cultural phenomenon," and *Kulturwissenschaft*, "science of culture" (Cairns 1973).

they participate communally as members of a whole that binds
them together. Persons apprehend themselves comprehensively not
only in the certainly first and fundamental way, namely that the
one understands, as Body, the Corporeality of the other belonging
to his surrounding world and its spiritual sense, thereby interpreting
the facial expressions, gestures, and spoken worlds as intimations
of personal life, but also in such a way that they "determine one
another" and are active not just as individuals but communally,
i.e., as personally united. (Husserl 1989[1952]: 201-202)

By "acts of personal mutual determination" we might include communal
rituals and ceremonies, interpersonal discussions about future plans,
training exercises to learn shared techniques,[74] group hunting or
horticultural strategies, and other forms of social cooperation—
sociality adding to "the total stock of 'pass it along' type information"
(d'Andrade 1981). Notice that Husserl emphasizes the importance
of shared comprehension to attaining these communal acts. Also,
he means by "determine one another" that we each and all of us as
members of a group have a causal influence upon the interpretations,
decisions and actions of each other. As we saw, over evolutionary time,
humans gradually superseded the primacy of the perceptual field with
communicated, vicarious experiences that became incorporated in the
group's normatized perspective on reality.

    How we act towards, and reach an understanding of, each other
depends first and foremost upon our shared lifeworld perceptions.
Regardless of how varied our cultural backgrounds, we still share the
same lifeworld because we share the same sensory systems, sensorium,
and brainmind:

And when I, in the act of empathy, experience others, I do not take
them only as the experienced of my experiences, as my possession,
but as subjects like myself, hence as subjects for their surrounding
world, valid for them, and at the same time as subjects for the
one same world which in the "appearances" we all have of our
surrounding worlds (in the worlds having subjective validity) is,

---

[74] As an interesting sidenote, see Heidegger 1977 on techniques and technology
re consciousness.

as a result of an all-encompassing validity, valid for each of us as an identical world [read lifeworld], showing itself to one in this way, to others in that way. But this self-same world can still be relative, for even if we may all be in agreement on a certain content (as an identical, actually existing world) over and against what is subjective and changing, yet in the progress of history this content itself can indeed change, *though we do remain convinced that it is the one identical world that it was always, which only "appeared" to us historically or to people of different cultures at one time in one way, at another time differently.* If this manner of consideration is carried out universally and consistently to the end, we then attain the universal and absolute human science—transcendental phenomenology. (Husserl 1989[1952]: 365, emphasis added)

Husserl made an interesting distinction between *natural* objects and *cultural* objects of intentional acts (Husserl 1977[1925]: 111, 1982[1913]: Chap. 4, Kohak 1978: 40, Nenon 2013a, Pulkkinen 2013). These are not exclusive categories, for they overlap like a Venn diagram. Their relationship gives us a further clue to how what we call "culture" is generated subjectively and intersubjectively and maintained across generations. Natural objects encountered as sensuous givens may or may not be modified through "cultural achievement" (i.e., cultural construction) to become cultural objects by way of building intersubjectively shared meaning that crops up in other group members' intentional acts. On the other hand, people can and do construct meaningful objects that have no concrete material instantiations, or only artistic existence, e.g., superheroes, fantasy gardens, world trees, spirits like the tooth fairy, etc. It is this kind of imaginative activity that may lead to a categorical distinction between a people's "culture" and their actual environing world, a false dichotomy if there ever was one (see Croll and Parkin 1992).

What Husserl has shown us is the mechanism by which different social groups seemingly vary in the meaning contents of their natural attitudes—they quite naturally mangle cognitive-affective knowing and perception because, like everybody else on the planet, we are usually concerned with meaning, not with truth. The application of pure phenomenology in a disciplined program of contemplative study inevitably shows us the many ways all humans are alike, much as does the study of Jungian archetypes and of evolutionary psychology. This new way of seeing the ways that all people are alike and the ways that some people are alike (*and the reasons why*) makes anthropology conducive to a *nomology of brainmind*, and by programmatic extension, a scientific anthropology.

THE NECESSITY OF AN ETHNOLOGICAL TURN IN HUSSERLIAN NEUROPHENOMENOLOGY

The actual doing of phenomenology in a Husserlian way—yes, we are back to that issue again!—virtually begs for an ethnological perspective. Why? Because phenomenologists in company with other philosophers and with non-anthropological social scientists tend to be ethnocentric in their views—usually projecting often unconscious assumptions about the experience as had and reported by non-Western peoples, especially the more traditional peoples around the globe (Giorgi 2020). We are all that way, as Husserl described (Chapter 4). This is why I consider ethnology and ethnography valuable to science, even when wearing the cultural constructivist blinkers that have hamstrung theory construction for generations. If ethnology did not exist, so the old saw has it, we would have to invent it, even as Bastian and others had to do generations ago. Aside from exploring the lifeways of peoples around the world, ethnology operates as a necessary corrective for the ethnocentrism and lack of cross-cultural understanding that pervades technocratic societies today.

What I am advocating is a mature science of humanity that controls for the ways that all of us are the same and for the ways some of us are the same, across social groups and nations, with our roots firmly buried in the methods of transcendental phenomenology. I would suggest that being informed by a contemplative phenomenology can help the ethnologist and fieldworker in the following ways:

1. See clearly the distinction between what primordial sensuous data and intuitive *eidos* are, and what is layered on from social learning in acts of experience.

2. Comprehend how essential structures of brainmind operate as building blocks to more complex levels of interpretation in experience.
3. Avoid the perpetual debate between "essentialism" and "constructivism" among ethnological theorists.
4. Avoid the inevitable ethnocentrism of philosophical assumptions and scientific methods.

Few are better equipped than a phenomenological anthropologist to contribute in these ways (see Spiegelberg 1975: 177-187, Chap. 14). And yet anthropologists could potentially do so much more for neurophenomenological research (Kuznar 2008: Chap. 8). Don't get me wrong. I am not a political conservative railing against left-wing attitudes. In fact, I am a democratic socialist. Indeed, applying anthropology to the ills of modern technocratic society is perfectly appropriate. Every science has its applied arm. Biology, ecology, geography, astrophysics, meteorology all have useful perspectives to contribute to understanding the issues of climate change, loss of biodiversity, endangered species, distribution of scarce resources, water conservation, threats of meteor strikes, and so on. The difference is that all of these disciplines have mature science behind them, and *we anthropologists do not*. We could have, but we don't! As a direct consequence of this failure, all sorts of pseudo-ethnographic studies have spread within and beyond anthropology with no scientific core upon which to distinguish them from the real deal (Ingold 2014).

As I have mentioned before, in order for anthropology to become a nomological science it must *in principium* be able to float theories that are grounded in universal structures (dare we say, human nature) and that are falsifiable by standard scientific methods (McIntyre 1996: Chap.4). Let us not get lost in jargon here. By "universal structures" I mean the architecture of reality. For biology it might refer to the fact that many genetically varied animals ranging from bats to turtles, dolphins to humans have five phalanges fore and aft. In astrophysics we see that asteroids often orbit around each other. In ecology we find that many species evolve mutually, like aphids and ants. These are "structures." Anyone who cares to do so may seek out and confirm or falsify these findings. Scientific theories are grounded in and often explain such structures. Where do we find the universal structures grounding anthropology? We cannot find those structures because of all the relativist blinders I have discussed in the pages above. We continue to reproduce what Herbert Simon (2019[1981]) called an "artificial science." The late social anthropologist, Edwin Ardener, said it well when discussing the extreme relativism of anthropological accounts of language:

> Consequently, much of this work has been judged to have painted itself into a corner, appearing to favor: 1) extreme cultural relativism; 2) separate cultural realities; 3) the cultural determination of both knowledge and "experience;" and even, as we have seen, 4) linguistic determination of cultural experience. These extreme positions (if actually held) would obviously make arguments for the existence of cultural universals more difficult, and stand in opposition to ideas of cultural change, as well as to more subtle views of the relation of language to culture and culture to reality. (Ardener 2012: 164)

In fact, the structures upon which to ground anthropology are right before our eyes and some have been studied, described, and hypothesized about by other sciences. They are found in the physiology of the body, in the neurophysiology of the nervous system, in the evolution and architecture of our very social brainmind. They are found in our deep interactions with our environing worlds (Ingold 1902). Since we humans have become a sort of *Homo technicus*, we cannot live anywhere without profoundly changing our environments. Even the previous sites of the Pygmies of the Ituri Rainforest in the Democratic Republic of the Congo for years after their habitation are detectible by the crop of cannabis growing where once their huts stood (Putnam 1954). These effects upon our environing worlds are structures.

I have focused upon one scope of universal structures in this book— the essential structures of sensory perception, discernable to anyone who applies Husserlian methods. That focus requires that we learn how to "see" through the mind of a neurophenomenologist, a perspective within which I use the methods of Husserl's transcendental phenomenology. I have challenged you to learn to see in a Husserlian way—to perfect within your own brainmind the phenomenological attitude—and to link the essential structures of perception with neural correlates of your sensory systems. If you have done this, then you have seen one vast scope of universal structures upon which an anthropology of the senses can be grounded (Pink 2009). If you are an ethnologist and do not follow in Husserl's footsteps, you may fall victim to the "culture all the way down" presumption and conclude that there is nothing structural or universal about perception. Let me offer an example from Mary Douglas' famous book, *Purity and Danger*, in which she wrote:

> As perceivers we select from all the stimuli falling on our senses only those which interest us, and our interests are governed by a pattern-making tendency, sometimes called a schema. *In a chaos of shifting impressions*, each of us constructs a stable world in which objects have recognizable shapes, are located in depth, and have permanence. (Douglas 1966: 36; emphasis added)

Douglas's implication is that perception is chaotic until we imposed our interests upon the stimuli which then coalesce into a perception. Only by projecting the world we want onto the chaos of stimuli that is assumed to be the nature of the world "out there" can we "have permanence." If you have followed Husserlian findings over the past chapters, you know: (1) there is no "booming, buzzing" chaos of raw sensuous perception, (2) any object of interest is perceived within its highly ordered and ever changing horizon, (3) a culturally determined will cannot change the order that comprises the form, the hyle, the relations among objects, the intuitive associations, and the object's horizon (or total perceptual field), (4) my primordial sensuous perception exhibits essential structures that cannot be altered "culturally," and (5) my primordial sensuous perception is structurally the same as yours, and as a lifeworld is the same as all other persons with normal neural systems, regardless of cultural background. Rather, had Douglas said something on the order of *our socially influenced interests cause us to select some objects over others in our intentional acts*, she would have been closer to the truth about how perception actually works, and far less inclined to presume "it's culture all the way down."

Anthropology has gotten closer to a realistic methodology with the advent of the anthropology of experience, and then the anthropology of the senses (see Chapter 1). Anthropologists still have to apply, or at least become conversant with neuroscience to find the NCC of phenomena within the ethnological scope—i.e., ritual states, ASC, empathy, perceptions, reasoning, categorical ideas, and so forth. Of immediate necessity is an ethnography that is productive of cross-cultural Husserlian phenomenology to explore similarities and variations in sensuous experiences among members of different societies, and the neuropsychology that might explain those findings. I give credence to the universality of the lifeworld, not because the theory of the lifeworld has been tested across cultures using Husserlian methods (they haven't), but because Buddhist methods, similar to Husserl's in many respects, have proven to have similar results regardless of the cultural backgrounds of practitioners (see Houshmound *et al.* 2002, Laughlin 2020a, Tran *et al.* 2014, Yaden *et al.* 2018; but cf. Karl *et al.* 2020 on cross-cultural measurement problems). Of course, experiences had during meditation sessions may vary in interpretation with the religious or cultural frame of the practitioner.

OPERATIONALIZING HUSSERLIAN METHODS IN ETHNOGRAPHY

Husserlian methods have the advantage of not being linked to any spiritual or religious ideology. As I have taken pains to show, doing pure phenomenology is a scientific method which can be easily and endlessly replicated and can be mastered by anyone, regardless of sociocultural background, who is both willing and possessed of sufficient discipline and single-minded focus. One of the problems we face, however, is that so far as I know, virtually all of the data collected by contemplative phenomenologists have come from people in Western technocratic societies. This ethnocentric bias is so common among philosophers and researchers in the human sciences (other than anthropologists) that it is commonly overlooked (Henrich, Heine and Norenzayan 2010). In American-style psychology, for instance, the results of studies of Americans are commonly generalized to the entire species:

> Yet a striking feature of research in American psychology is that its conclusions are based not on a broad cross-section of humanity but on a small corner of the human population—mainly, persons

living in the United States. Recently the population of the United States reached 300 million persons (U.S. Bureau of the Census, 2007). The current world population is about 6.5 billion persons (Population Reference Bureau [PRB], 2006). Consequently, by concentrating primarily on Americans, psychological researchers in the United States restrict their focus to less than 5% of the world's total population. The rest of the world's population, the other 95%, is neglected. (Arnett 2008: 601)

Of course, psychology developed its own corrective for ethnocentrism in what is now called *cross-cultural psychology* (see Keith 2019). But applying certain methods developed while doing work with Western populations has proved problematic when they are applied to non-Western subjects. Not only that, but little cross-cultural psychological research is done by researchers living within the host society and learning a holistic context for their data by way of participant observation.

In a sense, the ethnographer who has become a seasoned mature contemplative, either through Husserlian methods or by way of some other meditative discipline, has already operationalized contemplation within the context of their fieldwork (Ram and Houston 2015b: 2-3). They have become a different and more enlightened person.

[A]nyone who seriously considers becoming a philosopher must once in his life withdraw into himself and then, from within attempt to destroy and rebuild all previous learning. Philosophy is the supremely personal affair of the one who philosophizes. It is the question of *his sapiential universalis*, the aspiration of *his* knowledge for the universal. (Husserl 1964b: 3-4)

When I did my lengthy stays in monasteries in Nepal among fellow Buddhist monks of the Tibetan Sakya tradition, I was already a mature contemplative, and this factor conditioned how I observed, the questions I asked, and interpretations I offered (Laughlin 2020a). When I later did fieldwork among the Navajo people of the American southwest, my own experiences conditioned my approach to their teachings, especially about their experience of *hozho*, the central concept of Navajo philosophy, and how that experience influences their healing practices (Farella 1984). I already knew from my own Buddhist contemplative work, especially so-called *arising yoga*, what power the mandalas bring to bear when utilized by Navajo healing shamans in their "sings." Believe me, it becomes much easier for a contemplative phenomenologist to discern what is given in experience and what is interpretation from within the host's cultural frame.

But we do not want to limit ourselves to the phenomenology of pure perception of things. Recall that Husserl developed methods for studying both the ego and the structures involved in intersubjective experiencing, the latter being of great interest to ethnology. Pure phenomenology is inseparable from the phenomenology of the person or subject. As we have seen, the object and subject are two poles of the structure of the intentional act. The ethnographer who has done the work of reducing their ego to the Watcher will enter the field from a different standpoint when studying self or cultural identity issues among his hosts. The ethnographer who has realized that the roots of sociality is in the structure of intersubjective acts will be less likely to treat sociality as an "objective" field of facticity—of status, role, kinship relations, social category, etc.; that is to say, sociality as an epiphenomenon where issues of individual subjectivity are of no consequence.

The anthropologist who wishes to operationalize Husserlian methods will need to explore human relationships from the standpoint of the structure of intersubjectivity and gain a deep realization (from within the epoché) of the structures of their own intersubjective intentional acts. Sociality does not merely involve social behavior. Sociality involves social consciousness and the flow of intersubjective intentional acts that arise in that flow. As we have seen, the social act involves deep structures that are wired-in to the brainmind below the layer of social category attributions, social strategies, conditioned behaviors, and patterns of reciprocity. The phenomenological ethnologist will be interested in social bonding and awareness at the root of social consciousness among their hosts. Of prime interest will be expressions of empathy (see e.g., Hollan and Throop 2011, Throop 2008, 2016), and how the host experiences that essence, perhaps in its pure state or only after layers of cultural interpretation.

Of great interest perhaps will be any data that may be teased out by way of conversations about the lifeworld. This will take us into studies of social attribution: to what extent does the host perceive themselves as "like the other." Questions may involve attribution of causation in social relations, and how are those experienced within the intentional act. To what extent does the host perceive a cross-cultural other as sharing with them the same world of experience? The ideal, of course, is if the ethnographer can find a host who is interested and willing to learn to do reductions and report out their discoveries. This would not only provide a kind of ethno-phenomenology, but also produce the kinds of data that are comparable across cultures. This will be an easier task in today's world with so many of our previously host peoples now producing their own anthropologists and allied social scientists who may be willing to collaborate (see Kim 1990, Ntarangwi 2010).

Anthropologists who seek to apply the insights and methods of hermeneutical phenomenologists like Paul Ricoeur, Martin Heidegger, Maurice Merleau-Ponty, among others, do so because it allows them to immediately focus upon the production of meaning without having to pay attention through the phenomenological attitude and study of the layers of experience below meaning. Their interests tend to center on how meaning is socially constructed and how it is organized and thematized such that meaning becomes culturally normative vis à vis projection and action (see Crowell 2013: Chap. 5, 2016, Luft 2011). Because these philosophers were critical of Husserl's grounding of science and hermeneutics in the essential structures of sensory experience, social scientists can simply ignore those issues and debates. They thus lose track of the world and the embodied Watcher, and focus on symbolic interaction, narrative, communication, belief, etc. They run into trouble of course when they wish to incorporate consciousness into the mix, for these philosophers distance themselves from those issues. Heidegger for example sought to detach consciousness from his *Dasein* (Luft 2011: 129-135). This removed any contemplation (phenomenological epoché) of the sensuous given in experience. Merleau-Ponty (1962[1945]), while in my opinion understanding Husserl's project better than the other hermeneuticists, rejected Husserl's discovery of the intentional structure of conscious experience, Husserl's transcendental subjectivity, Husserl's method of the reduction—he claimed a reduction can never be completed, as though that were an argument against the method. All of these positions were, in my opinion, their authors' rationalizations for not *doing* phenomenology. The results have been predictable, for the hermeneuticists take a stance within the natural attitude and try to reason their way back to the world, instead of entering the rare state in which one may see directly the structures of perception that allow the world to be present in experience. This is a serious flaw, for it perpetuates the "culture all the way down" fiction and becomes fatal when their models are: (1) mapped upon how we know the brainmind works, and (2) considered from the biological question of how the human brainmind evolved to adapt to the world by constituting knowledge.

As we have seen in earlier chapters, Husserl too was interested in interpretation and meaning as they take a role in the intentional act. But unlike the philosophers above, his method and model do not lose sight of the world, they work their way up from the world as it presents itself in the sensorium. His transcendental subjectivity approach retains a balance of world and mind that is better suited for anthropological issues when those issues remain embodied in reality and evolutionary in scope. Let me give you a poignant example. Where in the ethnographic literature do fieldworkers report on their hosts' understanding of intuition? What is the role of intuition in the constitution of cultural knowledge? Where is our anthropology or ethnography of intuition? There is none (see Laughlin 1997b). The reason for this absence in my opinion is that the typical fieldworker and ethnologist mangles intuition and cognition. The failing is greater than that, however. Many anthropologists still equate knowledge with language—implying that other animals don't construct knowledge. Yet as we have seen, following as we have done the course of Husserlian phenomenology, intuition is inherent in the intentional act of humans—and presumably chimps, dolphins, and elephants—and depends neither upon higher cognition nor language. So, shouldn't the anthropology of knowledge make room for an ethnography of intuition?

PIAGET'S "CLINICAL INTERVIEW" USING HUSSERLIAN METHODS

Returning to the operationalization of Husserlian methods while doing ethnographic research, the application is easy, for it does not entail instruments, questionnaires, computer software, or quantitative measures. The problem is straightforward: When our host is invited to "return to the things," and is shown the way to achieve this, what will they discover and how do they share their knowledge? The approach might be something like the *clinical interview* designed by Jean Piaget to obtain data from children and teens about how their cognitive systems work (Duveen 2000). This method is more like a conversation about a problem the investigator poses for the subject (see Ginsburg 1997). When applying the method to adult host volunteers, it presumes that the researcher is a skilled contemplative. The problem set for the host collaborator would be to "reduce" a simple sensory experience; for example, a coconut shell lying atop a table. By reduce I mean to coax the collaborator to do an "intentional peeling" of the layers of meaning until all that is left is the experience of the primordial given. This should occur within the context of a conversation, preferably in the host's own language (Boas-style). The object would be to collect data about how the host describes what they "see" (or touch or smell). Can the collaborator understand the project and to what extent can they "see" the sensuous a priori?

The collaborator's reported experiences could potentially enrich a more "thick description" (the native's perspective) of each individual's study of their own sensuous experiences (Geertz 1985, Duveen and Lloyd 1993), and give depth to the data we use in the anthropology of the senses. A hypothetical example might be tracking through the layers of a sensory intentional act with a host from a "hot and cold" society: "In many parts of the world the concepts of hot and cold play a central role in disease etiologies. In these systems 'hot' and 'cold' do not usually refer to actual temperature states but to abstract qualities. Foods, bodily states and diseases are classified as being hot or cold and diseases are thought to be caused by excess heat or cold in the body" (Pool 1987: 389). The problem would be to discern at what point in an intentional act does the category of hot or cold become attributed to a food or a malady. At what point in perception is the attribution added to influence the host's judgement?

There is nothing really radical about using a Husserlian methodology in the field. We ethnographers do seemingly peculiar things all the time as when we ask informants about things they have never been asked about, and perhaps never thought about. When I was doing fieldwork among the So (Tepeth) people in Karamoja District, Uganda, it was during what became a terrible ten-year drought period in East Africa. I was interested in how families adapted to this stress and so collected a random sample of "household budgets" to find out where they obtained money and other resources and how they distributed and used them (see Laughlin and Allgeier 1979). I am sure that the So people had never been asked to remember and report this kind of information before or since.

In a brilliant piece of cross-cultural research, ethnologist James Hamill used a kind of clinical interview to study how people in different societies reason ("ethno-logic"). He set up situations in which his hosts were presented syllogisms and discussed how they processed them. His findings are fascinating reading (Hamill 1990). We ethnographers routinely manipulate social situations in order to see how they influence the data. It is one thing to ask a woman in more traditional societies her point of view while in the company of males, and another to ask that same woman her views when only females are present (S. Ardener 1975).

A realistic option for applying Husserlian methods in the field is as part of a team. As we anthropologists know, the heroic image of a "Lone Ranger" loner carrying out lengthy participant observations of "their" tribe is rarely the case (Erickson and Stull 1997: 2). When I did my fieldwork among the So, I was accompanied by my wife at the time and three children, all of whom in one way or another contributed to the collection of data. My wife, the late Elizabeth Allgeier, later to become a renowned sexologist, was then a psychology student and was interested in sexual behavior. All of the data we published on the subject in our two-volume ethnography of the So (Laughlin and Allgeier 1979) were collected by her. In addition, the chapter of the ethnography describing the ecology of the So was guest written by biologist John Wilson who we felt would do a better job than we could do. Thus, "my" fieldwork experience was actually accomplished by a team.

Ken Erickson and Donald Stull's (1998) little book, *Doing Team Ethnography: Warnings and Advice*, offers numerous examples of applied and pure research projects using the team approach. They note of course the early days of ethnology when large teams were sent out by government agencies on the "expeditions" we all learned about in Anthro 101: the British Torres Strait expedition and the US Bureau of Ethnology expeditions to Native American tribes in the 19th century. They also discuss the many family teams like the one of my own described above who carried out research throughout the 20th century. Probably the best designed team research program in psychology that is of interest to anthropology—there is a long history of "life-history" methods used in ethnography (Caughey 2006)—was created by Henry A. Murray to operationalize his holistic *personology* approach to the psychology of personality. Personology was and is the method of studying the psyche of an individual as a whole person and the person as a whole—the unit of study was the individual's entire lifetime (Murray *et al.* 1938). He became the director of the Harvard Psychological Clinic which was staffed with researchers of various backgrounds and specialties, both pure and clinical, some of whom carried out research on each of the subjects selected for study.

What I am suggesting here is that the principal ethnographer need not be the one doing phenomenological assessment during the research period, nor the neuroscience for that matter. There is no reason why one of a team might not be a Husserlian cross-cultural phenomenologist using contemplative methods to ascertain what elements of the host volunteer's experiences are universal and which show cultural variation. The phenomenologist would not have to spend the entire research period in the field. The bottom line is that although certain types of "phenomenology" are being increasingly applied in the field among non-Western peoples, few if any are applying Husserlian methods (Katz and Csordas 2003). When Husserlian cross-cultural methods are added to the ethnographer's training and field kit, new vistas of scope will open up and potentially ground a scientific approach to the study of humanity as a whole.

HUSSERLIAN METHODS AND THE ANTHROPOLOGY OF THE SENSES

If you have followed my take on Husserl's project, then you will understand when I say, sensory ethnology should be at the very center of the ethnological enterprise, not at its periphery, or perish the thought, not a mere fad—how easily anthropologists gravitate to new fads, a sign of the lack of anything like a scientific paradigm within the discipline. It is via the senses that we know anything about the world, that we can true our beliefs, that we can build knowledge that allows us to adapt to the environing world. By turning out attention to the senses we become able (at least potentially able) to study and discover the structures of the brainmind that ground us in the world as present to us in each moment of consciousness. I am hoping that as the anthropology of the senses gains momentum (see Classen 1997, Geurts 2002, Good *et al.* 1992, Goody 2002, Howes 1991a, Pink 2009, 2010, Stoller 1989, 2010):

1. It will not fall victim to the "culture all the way down" fiction.
2. It will incorporate phenomenological methods capable *in principium* of describing the primordial sensuous level of experience.
3. It will seek-out in each society the level of sensory experience that conforms to the biogenetic structure of pure perception.
4. It will include the entire sensorium of sensory experience in each society, not just the major exteroceptive senses—particularly vision— the sense(s) that are the most iconic in that society (see Stoller 2010: 3, 55). The methods used should be as applicable to the kinesthetic as to the visual sense, auditory as well as pain (Howes 1991b, Potter 2008).
5. And it will develop its models of sensory culture in conjunction with neuroscience.

Thus far, however, anthropologists seeking methods appropriate to their tasks have been confused by the highly superficial, but common claim that "there are as many phenomenologies as there are phenomenologists"—a catchy phrase originating from an article published 54 years ago by Willard Oztoby (1968). That would be the same as saying there are as many anthropologies as there are anthropologists. Remember the challenge, "if you want to know this, do this... ." There are very few phenomenologies that will provide the "do this" if what we wish to know is how the brainmind structures sensuous experience—how the brainmind constitutes its stream of consciousness. By now I would hope that my answer to this challenge is obvious. Only a scientific, contemplative phenomenology will answer that injunction (see Giorgi 2020), and to my knowledge there is no phenomenology more likely to pass muster than Husserl's. Indeed, I believe that a Husserlian transcendental phenomenology combined with neuroscience is exactly the "sophisticated phenomenology" envisioned by Robert Desjarlais and Jason Throop in their excellent assessment of phenomenology in anthropology:

> What is most called for are careful, sophisticated phenomenological approaches in anthropology, realized through ethnographic field research methods, that attend at once to the tangible realities of people's lives and to the often interrelated social, biological, corporeal, sensorial, discursive, cultural, political, economic, psychological, and environmental dimensions of those realities. This phenomenology would rebut conventional ideas of self, society, consciousness, memory, and the human more generally. This anthropology would be attuned to both particular situations and the common threads of existence that weave through all our lives. (Desjarlais and Throop 2011: 97)

If you want to realize the roots of your sense of reality, then bracket your natural attitude, enter the phenomenological attitude, and perform the reduction as many times it takes for you *to get it*. If you want to know why it is so easy for people to understand each other across sociocultural, linguistic, and geographical boundaries, then reduce your own intersubjectivity as many times as it takes for you *to get it*. If you want to know how your brainmind links ideas with reality, then reduce your experiences of the sensuous world to its recurrent intentional acts as often as it takes for you *to get it*. If you wish to find out what your ego is really like, then reduce your empirical ego until all that's left is the Watcher and do this as many times as it takes for you *to get it*. After you accomplish all of this, then apply the insights gained to your research efforts in the field. Need I say more?

GLOSSARY

act

> When Husserl speaks of acts, he is referring to operations (or mediations) producing certain types of experiences within the stream of consciousness. Thus, one may refer to an act of reason, an act of feeling, an act of meaning, and so forth. By implication, all "acts" in Husserl's sense are embodied and therefore are trophic; that is, they require effort.

attitude (Ger.: *Einstellung*)

> Husserl speaks of an "attitude" as a state of mind, standpoint, view, or stance with respect to intentional acts. Used in a phrase, like "aesthetic attitude," "ethical attitude," "phenomenological attitude," etc., the term signals that Husserl is speaking of the principal orientation of the stream of consciousness at the moment—in other words, a state of consciousness.

brainmind

> I use Earl W. Count's (1973, 1976c) term *brainmind* when I wish to refer to the structure and function of the brain mediating "mind" or "psyche." It is a non-dualistic way of talking about the mind and body simultaneously.

cognit

> Cognit is short for "cognitive neural network." A cognit is a very complex neural structure whose connections often range over a large area of the cortex of the brain (see Fuster 2003, 2013).

doxa, doxic

> Knowledge that is taken for granted, like a presumption, belief, or opinion. The natural attitude is rife with doxic material.

environing world

> By *environing world*, or *surrounding world* (Ger.: *Umwelt*; Frings 2012, von Uexküll 1909, 2018[1926], Sebeok 1991, Sebeok, Umiker-Sebeok

and Young 1992) I am referring to the real world within which an animal adapts. I explicitly refer to that part of the real world within which an animal finds its niche, and with which it has an adaptively relevant interaction. It is the world the animal senses and acts within (von Uexküll 2018[1926]: 126-127).

horizon

Horizon is a metaphor for the limits of experience or intentionality, in the moment or potentially. Just as the visual horizon limits how far we can see, a phenomenological horizon refers to the limits of phenomenological meditation within any given perceptual field, or any possible perceptual field.

hyle (hyletic matter, hyletic data)

Hyle is Husserl's term for the sensuous content of sensory objects. Hyle (aka: "stuff," "matter," "primary content," or in modern parlance, "qualia") is what "fulfill" forms and ideas, both physical and social, within the sensorium—the colors, textures, odors, sounds, etc.

immanence

Immanence is another way Husserl refers to *absolute being*, which is contrary to *transcendence*, the latter being a product of consciousness and intersubjectivity, as in the lifeworld. It is the task of pure phenomenology to uncover the layer of pure immanence, which is the ground of all knowledge about the world.

intentionality

The very essence of phenomenology is the discovery that every state of consciousness is about something. Intentionality consists of the object or event being experienced and the subject or "ego" doing the intending.

lifeway

I use the term *lifeway* as a rather loose label for the way people go about their daily lives. It is not to be confused with Husserl's notion of *lifeworld*.

lifeworld

> The lifeworld (Ger: *Lebenswelt*) is constituted by all of the universal, essential structures that we as humans share, within a group and across groups.

mature contemplation

> A *mature contemplative* is a meditator who has developed sufficient skill that they become what Charles Tart has called a "state-specific" scientist (Tart 1972; see also d'Aquili, Laughlin and McManus 1993; Laughlin, McManus and d'Aquili 1990: Chap. 11). As Husserl noted, the phenomenological attitude is an alternative state of consciousness in which the contemplative is capable of routinely discriminating between the primordial given and the natural attitude elements of experience. More precisely, a mature contemplative has reached the level of contemplation at which they realize the impermanence of the empirical ego.

neural correlate of consciousness (NCC)

> A neural correlate of consciousness (NCC) is the neural network, or network of neural cells, that mediate or produce some aspect of consciousness.

noesis, noema

> Noesis and noema are the two poles of any intentional act. Noesis (noetic) refers to the sensuous given constituting perception and noema (noematic) covers the idea(s) and meanings associated in apperception, focused on the noetic.

ontic sense or meaning

> The term Husserl uses to emphasize that the object is part of the real world. Objects in the real world are "constantly actuality for us" (Husserl 1970[1936]: 145).

primordial sensory given

> By "primordial" Husserl means that it is already there in my experience as a type of perceptual intuition—the primordial sensory given is

irreducible, presenting to the Watcher as a priori, and mediated by the essential structures of the nervous system's sensory systems.

sensorium

> The sensorium is that part of the brain where unimodal and multimodal perceptions come together presenting the sensory world in the moment. The sensorium is likely located in the prefrontal cortex of the brain.

solipsism

> Solipsism is a view in philosophy that all that exists is the self. Because of his use of pure phenomenological methods which focus upon experiences had by the individual of their environing world with ontological questions and knowledge bracketed, critics have mistakenly accused Husserl of being a solipsist.

transcendent (transcendence, transcendental)

> I use Husserl's concept to mean that the objects in the environing world that we perceive exist in the real world. So too with all essential structures of experience, for we never perceive them directly, but only via induction. The whole world and all the things in it are transcendental relative to our experiences of them. When Husserl uses the term "transcendence" or "transcendental," he is referring, after Kant, to the a priori, essential nature of the object of consciousness, or to the pure ego. The transcendental nature of consciousness is our ticket to knowing the objective world. Transcendence is contrasted with immanence (see above) which does not require consciousness.

Watcher

> The Watcher is *my term* (not Husserl's) for the searchlight awareness that is the subject of every act of perception. We realize the Watcher when we learn that the Watcher's gaze can be directed toward every attribute of the empirical ego thought to be permanent and discover that none of them is in fact permanent (see Carr 1987). All that remains is the Watcher. In Husserl's terms, the Watcher is the "absolute transcendental ego" (1993[1931]: 89).

BIBLIOGRAPHY

Abiodun, Rowland, 2014. *Yoruba Art and Language: Seeking the African in African Art.* Cambridge: Cambridge University Press.

Ackman, James B., Timothy J. Burbridge and Michael C. Crair, 2012. "Retinal Waves Coordinate Patterned Activity Throughout the Developing Visual System." *Nature* 490(7419): 219-225.

Adam, B., 1990. *Time and Social Theory.* Philadelphia: Temple University Press.

Adams, William Y., 1998. *The Philosophical Roots of Anthropology.* Stanford, CA: CSLI Publications.

Addison A (2009) "Jung, Vitalism and 'the Psychoid:' An Historical Reconstruction." *Journal of Analytical Psychology* 54(1): 123-142.

Aggleton, John P., 2008. "Understanding Anterograde Amnesia: Disconnections and Hidden Lesions." *The Quarterly Journal of Experimental Psychology* 61(10): 1441-1471.

Agor, Weston H., 1985. "Intuition as a Brain Skill in Management." *Public Personnel Management* 14(1): 15-24.

Ajina, Sara, Miriam Pollard and Holly Bridge, 2020. "The Superior Colliculus and Amygdala Support Evaluation of Face Trait in Blindsight." *Frontiers in Neurology* 11: 769.

Albertazzi, Liliana, 2018. "Naturalizing Phenomenology: A Must Have?" *Frontiers in Psychology* 9: 1933.

Aldea, A. S., 2013. "Husserl's Struggle with Mental Images: Imaging and Imagining Reconsidered." *Continental Philosophy Review* 46: 371–394.

Allen, Colin and Michael Trestman, 2017. "Animal Consciousness." In *The Blackwell Companion to Consciousness,* ed. by Susan Schneider and Max Velmans. Oxford: Blackwell, pp. 63-76.

Allen, Douglas, 2005. "Phenomenology of Religion." In *The Routledge Companion to the Study of Religion*, ed. by John R. Hennells. London: Routledge, pp. 194-219.

Allman, W. F., 1989. *Apprentices of Wonder: Inside the Neural Network Revolution.* New York: Bantam.

Allport, D. A., 1968. "Phenomenological Simultaneity and the Perceptual Moment Hypothesis." *British Journal of Psychology* 59: 395–406.

Allport, D. A., 1985. "Distributed Memory, Modular Systems and Dysphasia." In *Current Perspectives in Dysphasia,* ed. by S. K. Newman and R. Epstein. Edinburgh: Churchill Livingstone, pp. 32-60.

Almeder, Robert, 1990. "On Naturalizing Epistemology." *American Philosophical Quarterly* 27(4): 263-279.

Altobello, Robert, 2007. "Concentration and Contemplation: A Lesson in Learning to Learn." *Journal of Transformative Education* 5(4): 354-371.

Arnhart, Larry, 2001. "The Truth, Goodness, and Beauty of Darwinism." *Zygon* 36(1): 77-92.

Anālayo, Bhikkhu, 2017. *Early Buddhist Meditation Studies.* Barre, MA: Barre Center for Buddhist Studies.

Anālayo, Bhikkhu, 2020. "A Brief History of Buddhist Absorption." *Mindfulness* 11(3): 571-586.

Andresen, J., 2001. "Conclusion: Religion in the Flesh: Forging New Methodologies for the Study of Religion." In *Religion in Mind: Cognitive Perspectives on Religious Belief, Ritual, and Experience*, ed. by J. Andresen. Cambridge: Cambridge University Press, pp. 257–287.

Andrews, Kristin, 2018. "Apes Track False Beliefs but Might Not Understand Them." *Learning and Behavior* 46(1): 3-4.

Antweiler, Christoph, 2019. "On the Human Addiction to Norms: Social Norms and Cultural Universals of Normativity." In *The Normative Animal?: On the Anthropological Significance of Social, Moral, and Linguistic Norms*, ed. by Neilo Roughley and Kurt Bayertz. London: Oxford University Press, pp. 83-100.

Anzulewicz, Anna, Dariusz Asanowicz, Bert Windey, Borysław Paulewicz, Michał Wierzchoń and Axel Cleeremans, 2015. "Does Level of Processing Affect the Transition from Unconscious to Conscious Perception?" *Consciousness and Cognition* 36: 1-11.

Arbel, K., 2017. *Early Buddhist Meditation: The Four Jhānas as the Actualization of Insight*. London: Routledge.

Arbib, Michael A., 1972. *The Metaphorical Brain: An Introduction to Cybernetics As Artificial Intelligence and Brain Theory*. New York: Wiley-Interscience.

Arbib, Michael A., 1985. "Schemas for the Temporal Organization of Behaviour." *Human Neurobiology* 4(2): 63-72.

Arbib, Michael A., 1987. *Brains, Machines, and Mathematics* (second edition). Berlin: Springer-Verlag.

Arbib, Michael A., 2012. *How the Brain Got Language: The Mirror System Hypothesis*. Oxford: Oxford University Press.

Arbib, Michael A., Péter Érdi and János Szentagothai, 1998. *Neural Organization: Structure, Function, and Dynamics*. Cambridge, MA: MIT press.

Arbib, Michael A. and Mary B. Hesse, 1986. *The Construction of Reality*. Cambridge University Press.

Ardener, Edwin, 2017. *The Voice of Prophecy and Other Essays* (2nd ed). Oxford: Berghahn.

Ardener, Shirley, 1975. *Perceiving Women*. London: Malaby Press.

Armstrong, Este, 1991. "The Limbic System and Culture." *Human Nature* 2(2): 117-136.

Armstrong, Este and Dean Falk (eds.), 1982. *Primate Brain Evolution*. New York: Plenum Press.

Armstrong, Este and Mary Anne Shea, 1997. "Brains of New-World and Old-World Monkeys." In *New World Primates: Ecology, Evolution, and Behavior*, ed. by Warren G. Kinzey. New York: Routledge, pp. 25-44.

Arnett, Jeffrey J., 2008. "The Neglected 95%: Why American Psychology Needs to Become Less American." *American Psychologist*, 63(7): 602–614.

Arterberry, Martha E. and Phillip J. Kellman, 2016. *Development of Perception in Infancy: The Cradle of Knowledge Revisited*. Oxford: Oxford University Press.

Arvidson, P. Sven, 1996. "Toward a Phenomenology of Attention." *Human Studies* 19(1): 71-84.

Atkinson, Will, 2018. "Bourdieu and Schutz: Bringing Together Two Sons of Husserl." *The Oxford Handbook of Pierre Bourdieu*, ed. by T. Medvetz and J. J. Sallaz. Oxford: Oxford University Press.

Atleo, Marlene Renate, 2006. "The Ancient Nuu-Chah-Nulth Strategy of Hahuulthi: Education for Indigenous Cultural Survivance." *International Journal of Environmental, Cultural, Economic and Social Sustainability* 2(1): 153-162.

Atran, Scott, 1998. "Folk Biology and the Anthropology of Science: Cognitive Universals and Cultural Particulars." *Behavioral and Brain Sciences* 21(4): 547-569.

Atran, Scott and Douglas Medin, 2008. *The Native Mind and the Cultural Construction of Nature.* Cambridge, MA: MIT Press.

Aurora, Simone, 2018. "Structural Phenomenology: A Reading of the Early Husserl." *Cognitive Semiotics* 11(2):1-12.

Aurora, Simone and Patrick Flack, 2016. "Phenomenology and Linguistics." *Metodo: International Studies in Phenomenology and Philosophy* 4(2): 7-12.

Austin, James H., 1998. *Zen and the Brain: Toward an Understanding of Meditation and Consciousness.* Cambridge, MA: MIT Press.

Austin, John Langshaw, 1975. *How to Do Things with Words.* Oxford: Oxford University Press.

Austin, John Langshaw, 1979. *Philosophical Papers* (3rd edition). Oxford: Oxford University Press.

Azevedo, Frederico A. C. , Ludmila R. B. Carvalho, Lea T. Gribergb, José Marcelo Farfel, Renata E. L. Ferretti, Renata E. P. Leite, Wilson Jacob Filho, Roberto Lent and Suzana Herculano-Houzel, 2009. "Equal Numbers of Neuronal and Nonneuronal Cells Make the Human Brain an Isometrically Scaled-Up Primate Brain." *The Journal of Comparative Neurology* 513: 532-541.

Azzouni, Jody, 2015. *Semantic Perception: How the Illusion of a Common Language Arises and Persists.* Oxford: Oxford University Press.

Bachelard, Suzanne, 1968. *A Study of Husserl's Formal and Transcendental Logic.* Evanston, IL: Northwestern University Press.

Baird, Benjamin, Stephen LaBerge and Giulio Tononi, 2021. "Two-Way Communication in Lucid REM Sleep Dreaming." *Trends in Cognitive Sciences* 25(6): 427-428.

Banks, Marcus and Jay Ruby (eds). 2011. *Made to be Seen: Perspectives on the History of Visual Anthropology.* Chicago: University of Chicago Press.

Bar, Moshe, 2004. "Visual Objects in Context." *Nature Reviews Neuroscience* 5(8): 617-629.

Barber, Michael D., 2009. "Genetic Phenomenology and Potentiality: A New Insight to the Theory of Empathy in Husserl." *Análisis: Revista Colombiana de Humanidades* 75: 61-89.

Barkow, Jerome, 1989. *Darwin, Sex and Status: Biological Approaches to Mind and Culture.* Toronto: University of Toronto Press.

Barkow, Jerome, 1992. "Beneath New Culture Is Old Psychology." In *The Adapted Mind. Evolutionary Psychology and the Generation of Culture*, ed. by J. H. Barkow, L. Cosmides, and J. Tooby. pp. 627-637. New York: Oxford University Press.

Barkow, J., L. Cosmides and J. Tooby (eds), 1992. *The Adapted Mind: Evolutionary Psychology and the Generation of Culture.* Oxford: Oxford University Press.

Baron-Cohen, Simon, 1997. *Mindblindness: An Essay on Autism and Theory of Mind.* Cambridge, MA: MIT Press.

Barrett, Deirdre, 1991. "Flying Dreams and Lucidity: An Empirical Study of Their Relationship." *Dreaming: Journal of the Association for the Study of Dreams* 1(2): 129-134.

Barrow, J. and F. Tipler, 1986. *The Anthropic Cosmological Principle.* Oxford: Oxford University Press. New York.

Barth, Fredrik, 2002. "An Anthropology of Knowledge." *Current Anthropology* 43(1): 1-18.

Barth, Friedrich G., Patrizia Giampieri-Deutsch and Hans-Dieter Klein (eds), 2012. *Sensory Perception: Mind and Matter.* Vienna: Springer.

Bartlett, F. C., 1932. *Remembering: A Study in Experimental and Social Psychology.* Cambridge, UK: Cambridge University Press.

Bartra, Roger, 2014. *Anthropology of the Brain: Consciousness, Culture, and Free Will.* Cambridge: Cambridge University Press.

Barua, Archana, 2009. *Phenomenology of Religion.* London: Lexington.

Basar, E., C. Basar-Eroglu, S. Karakas and M. Schurmann, 2000. "Brain Oscillations in Perception and Memory." *International Journal of Psychophysiology* 35(2–3): 95–124.

Basso, Anna, 2003. *Aphasia and Its Therapy.* Oxford: Oxford University Press.

Bateson, Gregory, 1972. *Steps to an Ecology of Mind.* San Francisco, CA: Chandler.

Bateson, Gregory, 1979. *Mind and Nature.* New York: E.P. Dutton.

Batson, C. D., 2011. "These Things Called Empathy." In *The Social Neuroscience of Empathy*, ed. by J. Decety and W. Ickes. Cambridge, MA: The MIT Press, pp. 3-16.

Baumard, Nicolas and Dan Sperber, 2012. "Evolutionary and Cognitive Anthropology." In *A Companion to Moral Anthropology*, ed. by Didier Fassin. London: Wiley, pp. 611-627.

Baumgardt, E., 1972. "Threshold Quantal Problems." *Handbook of Sensory Physiology* 7(4): 29-55.

Bayne, Tim, Jakob Hohwy and Adrian M. Owen, 2016. "Are There Levels of Consciousness?" *Trends in Cognitive Sciences* 20(6): 405-413.

Beck, A. T. and G. Emery, 1985. *Anxiety Disorders and Phobias: A Cognitive Perspective.* New York: Basic Books.

Becker, Ernest, 1973. *The Denial of Death.* New York: Free Press.

Beckers, R., O. E. Holland and J. L. Deneubourg, 1994. "From Local Actions to Global Tasks: Stigmergy and Collective Robotics." In *Artificial Life IV*, ed. by R. Brooks and P. Maes. *Proceedings of the Fourth International Workshop on the Synthesis and Simulation of Living Systems.* Cambridge, MA: MIT Press.

Bekoff, Marc, 2002. *Minding Animals: Awareness, Emotions and Heart.* Oxford: Oxford University Press.

Bekoff, Marc, 2007. *The Emotional Lives of Animals.* Navato, CA: New World Library.

Bekoff, Marc and C. Allen, 1997. "Intentional Communication and Social Play: How and Why Animals Negotiate and Agree to Play." In *Animal Play: Evolutionary, Comparative, and Ecological Perspectives*, ed. by Marc Bekoff and John A. Byers. Cambridge: Cambridge University Press, pp. 97-114.

Bell, David, 1990. *Husserl.* London: Routledge.

Bello, Angela Ales, 2004. "The Function of Intentionality and the Function of Creativity; A.-T. Tymieniecka and E. Husserl: A Confrontation." In *Imaginatio Creatrix*, ed. by Anna-Teresa Tymieniecka. Dordrecht: Springer, pp. 543-552.

Bender, J. and D. E. Wellbery (eds), 1991. *Chronotypes: The Construction of Time.* Stanford, CA: Stanford University Press.

Benedek, Mathias, Till Schües, Roger E. Beaty, Emanuel Jauk, Karl Koschutnig, Andreas Fink and Aljoscha C. Neubauer, 2018. "To Create or to Recall Original Ideas: Brain Processes Associated with the Imagination of Novel Object Uses." *Cortex* 99: 93-102.

Benovsky, Jiri, 2013. "The Present vs. the Specious Present." *Review of Philosophy and Psychology* 4(2): 193-203.

Berger, H. M., 1997. "The Practice of Perception: Multi-functionality and Time in the Musical Experiences of a Heavy Metal Drummer." *Ethnomusicology* 41(3): 464–88.

Berger, H. M., 1999. *Metal, Rock, and Jazz: Perception and the Phenomenology of Musical Experience.* Middletown, CT: Wesleyan University Press.

Bergson, H., 1910 [1889]. *Time and Free Will: An Essay on the Immediate Data of Consciousness* (trans. by F.L. Pogson). Oxford: Oxford University Press.

Berlin, Brent and Paul Kay, 1969. *Basic Color Terms: Their Universality and Evolution*. Berkeley: University of California Press.

Berndtsson, Inger, Silwa Claesson, Febe Friberg and Joakim Öhlén, 2007. "Issues About Thinking Phenomenologically While Doing Phenomenology." *Journal of Phenomenological Psychology* 38(2): 256-277.

Bernet, Rudolf, 2002. "Unconscious Consciousness in Husserl and Freud." *Phenomenology and the Cognitive Sciences* 1(3): 327-351.

Bernhardt, B.C. and T. Singer, 2012. "The Neural Basis of Empathy." *Annual Review of Neuroscience* 35: 1-23.

Beveridge W. I. B., 1950. *The Art of Scientific Investigation*, New York: Heinemann.

Bharati, Agehananda, 1976. *The Light at the Center: Context and Pretext of Modern Mysticism*. Sant Barbara, CA: Ross Erikson.

Bickerton, Derek, 1990. *Language and Species*. Chicago: University of Chicago Press.

Birch, Jonathan, Alexandra K. Schnell and Nicola S. Clayton, 2020. "Dimensions of Animal Consciousness." *Trends in Cognitive Sciences* 24(10): 789-801.

Bishop, Michael A. and J. D. Trout, 2005. *Epistemology and the Psychology of Human Judgment*. Oxford: Oxford University Press.

Bizley, Jennifer K. and Yale E. Cohen, 2013. "The What, Where and How of Auditory-Object Perception." *Nature Reviews Neuroscience* 14(10): 693-707.

Blakemore, Sarah-Jayne and Uta Frith, 2004. "How Does the Brain Deal with the Social World?" *Neuroreport* 15(1): 119-128.

Blanke, O., T. Landis, L. Spinelli and M. Seeck, 2004. "Out-of-Body Experience and Autoscopy of Neurological Origin." *Brain* 127(2): 243-258.

Block, Maurice, 1977. "The Past and the Present in the Present." *Man* 12(2): 278–92.

Blofeld, John Eaton Calthorpe, 1959. *The Zen Teaching of Huang Po: On the Transmission of the Mind*. New York: Grove Press.

Blonder, Lee Xenakis, 1991. "Human Neuropsychology and the Concept of Culture." *Human Nature* 2(2): 83-116.

Bloom, Paul, 2013. *Just Babies: The Origins of Good and Evil*. New York: Broadway Books.

Boddy, J., 1994. "Spirit Possession Revisited: Beyond Instrumentality." *Annual Review of Anthropology* 23: 407-434.

Boehm, Christopher, 2012. *Moral Origins: The Evolution of Virtue, Altruism, and Shame*. New York: Basic Books.

Bond, Peter, 2017. "The Biology of Technology: An Exploratory Essay 1." In *Theory of Technology*, ed. by David Clarke. New York: Routledge, pp. 99-118.

Book, Angela, Tabitha Methot, Nathalie Gauthier, Ashley Hosker-Field, Adelle Forth, Vernon Quinsey and Danielle Molnar, 2015. "The Mask of Sanity Revisited: Psychopathic Traits and Affective Mimicry." *Evolutionary Psychological Science* 1(2): 91-102.

Bostar, Leo, 1993. "Reading Ingarden Read Husserl: Metaphysics, Ontology, and Phenomenological Method." *Husserl Studies* 10(3): 211-236.

Bouchard, Denis, 2013. *The Nature and Origin of Language*. Oxford: Oxford University Press.

Bourdieu, Pierre, 1977. *Outline of a Theory of Practice*. Cambridge: Cambridge University Press.

Bourguignon, Erica, 1976. *Possession*. San Francisco: Chandler and Sharp.

Bourguignon, E. and T. I. Evascu, 1977. "Altered States of Consciousness Within a General Evolutionary Perspective: A Holocultural Analysis." *Behavior Science Research* 12: 197-216.

Bower, Matt, 2014. "Husserl's Motivation and Method for Phenomenological Reconstruction." *Continental Philosophy Review* 47(2): 135-152.

Bowerman, Melissa and Stephen C. Levinson (eds), 2001. *Language Acquisition and Conceptual Development.* Cambridge: Cambridge University Press.

Boyd, R. and J. B. Silk, 2000. *How Humans Evolved.* New York: Norton.

Boyer, Pascal, 1999. "Cognitive Tracks of Cultural Inheritance: How Evolved Intuitive Ontology Governs Cultural Transmission." *American Anthropologist* 100(4): 876–889.

Boyer, Pascal, 2003. "Religious Thought and Behaviour as By-Products of Brain Function." *Trends in Cognitive Sciences* 7(3): 119-124.

Boyer, Pascal, 2019. "Informal Religious Activity Outside Hegemonic Religions: Wild Traditions and their Relevance to Evolutionary Models." *Religion, Brain and Behavior* 10(4): 459-472.

Bradbury, Jack W. and Sandra L. Vehrencamp, 2011. *Principles of Animal Communication* (2nd edition). Sunderland, MA: Sinauer Associates.

Brandmeyer, Tracy, Arnaud Delorme and Helané Wahbeh, 2019. "The Neuroscience of Meditation: Classification, Phenomenology, Correlates, and Mechanisms." *Progress in Brain Research* 244: 1-29.

Brannon, Elizabeth M., L. W. Roussel, W. H. Meck and W. Woldorff, 2004. "Timing in the Baby Brain." *Cognitive Brain Research* 21: 227–33.

Brannon, Elizabeth M., and Herbert S. Terrace, 2000. "Representation of the Numerosities 1–9 by Rhesus Macaques (*Macaca mulatta*)." *Journal of Experimental Psychology: Animal Behavior Processes* 26(1): 31.

Brefczynski-Lewis, J. A., A. Lutz, H. S. Schaefer, D. B. Levinson and R. J. Davidson, 2007. "Neural Correlates of Attentional Expertise in Long-Term Meditation Practitioners." *Proceedings of the National Academy of Sciences USA* 104: 11483–11488.

Brereton, Derek P., 2009. "Why Sociocultural Anthropology Needs John Dewey's Evolutionary Model of Experience." *Anthropological Theory* 9(1): 5-32.

Brewer, Judson A. *et al.*, 2011. "Meditation Experience Is Associated with Differences in Default Mode Network Activity and Connectivity." *Proceedings of the National Academy of Sciences USA* 108(50): 20254-20259.

Breyer, Thiemo, 2020. "Empathy, Sympathy and Compassion." In *The Routledge Handbook of Phenomenology of Emotion*, ed. by Thomas Szanto and Hilge Landweer. New York: Routledge, pp. 429-440.

Broadfield, Douglas, Michael Yuan, Kathy Schick and Nicholas Toth (eds), 2010. *The Human Brain Evolving: Paleoneurological Studies in Honor or Ralph L. Holloway.* Gosport, IN: Stone Age Institute Press.

Brooke, Roger, 1991. *Jung and Phenomenology.* New York: Routlidge.

Brooke, Roger, 1999. "Jung's Recollection of the Life-World." In *Pathways into the Jungian World: Phenomenology and Analytic Psychology*, ed. by Roger Brooke. New York: Routledge, pp. 13-24.

Brooker, J. S., C. E. Webb and Z. Clay, in press. "Primate Empathy: A Flexible and Multi-Componential Phenomenon." In *Primate Cognitive Studies*, ed. by B. L. Schwartz and M. J. Beran. London: Cambridge University Press.

Brown, Cecil H., 1983. "Where Do Cardinal Direction Terms Come From?" *Anthropological Linguistics* 25(2): 121-161.

Brown, D. E.,1991. *Human Universals.* New York: McGraw Hill.

Brown, R., H. Lau and J. E. LeDoux, 2019. "Understanding the Higher-Order Approach to Consciousness." *Trends in Cognitive Science* 23: 754–768.

Brugha, Cathal MacSwiney, 2015. "Foundation of Nomology." *European Journal of Operational Research* 240(3): 734-747.

Bruner, Jerome, 1986. *Actual Minds, Possible Worlds*. Cambridge, MA: Harvard University Press.

Bruner, Jerome, 1990. *Acts of Meaning*. Cambridge, MA: Harvard University Press.

Bryer, Margaret AH, Sarah E. Koopman, Jessica F. Cantlon, Steven T. Piantadosi, Evan L. MacLean, Joseph M. Baker, Michael J. Beran *et al.* 2022. "The Evolution of Quantitative Sensitivity." *Philosophical Transactions of the Royal Society* B 377(1844): 20200529.

Bruzina, Ronald, 1989. "Solitude and Community in the Work of Philosophy: Husserl and Fink, 1928–1938." *Man and World* 22(3): 287-314.

Bruzina, Ronald, 1990. "The Last Cartesian Meditation." *Research in Phenomenology* 20(1): 167-184.

Bruzina, Ronald, 1995. "Translator's Introduction." In *Sixth Cartesian Meditation: the Idea of a Transcendental Theory of Method*, Eugen Fink. Bloomington, IN: Indiana University Press, pp. vii-xcii.

Bruzina, Ronald, 1997. "The Transcendental Theory of Method in Phenomenology: The Meontic and Deconstruction." *Husserl Studies* 14(2): 75-94.

Bruzina, Ronald, 2004. *Edmund Husserl and Eugen Fink: Beginnings and Ends in Phenomenology*, 1928-1938. New Haven, CT: Yale University Press.

Bucke, Richard Maurice, 2009[1961]. *Cosmic Consciousness: A Study in the Evolution of the Human Mind*. New York: Courier Corporation.

Buddhaghosa, B., 1976. *The Path of Purification (Visuddhimagga)*, Volumes I and II. Berkeley: Shambhala.

Buhusi, C. V. and W. H. Meek, 2005. "What Makes Us Tick? Functional and Neural Mechanisms of Interval Timing." *Neuroscience* 6: 755–65.

Bulkeley, K., 1995. *Spiritual Dreaming: A Cross-Cultural and Historical Journey*. New York: Paulist Press.

Bundgaard, Peer F., 2004. "The Ideal Scaffolding of Language: Husserl's Fourth Logical Investigation in the Light of Cognitive Linguistics." *Phenomenology and the Cognitive Sciences* 3: 49–80.

Bundgaard, Peer F., 2010. "Husserl and Language." In *Handbook of Phenomenology and Cognitive Science*, ed. by Shaun Gallagher. Dordrecht: Springer, pp. 368-399.

Bunzl, Matti, 1996. "Franz Boas and the Humboldtian Tradition: From *Volksgeist* and *Nationalcharakter* to an Anthropological Concept of Culture." In *Volksgeist as Method and Ethic: Essays on Boasian Ethnography and the German Anthropological Tradition*, ed. by George Stocking. Madison, WI: University of Wisconsin Press, pp. 17-78.

Burge, Tyler, 2010a. "Origins of Perception." *Disputatio* 4(29): 1-38.

Burge, Tyler, 2010b. "Steps Toward Origins of Propositional Thought." *Disputatio* 4(29): 39-67.

Burnet, John (trans.), 1930. "Fragments of Heraclitus." In *From Early Greek Philosophy*, 3rd ed. London: A. & C. Black.

Burns, Niamh, 2020. "A Modernist Mystic: Philosophical Essence and Poetic Method in Gerda Walther (1897–1977)." *German Life and Letters* 73(2): 246-269.

Burr, D. and C. Morrone, 2006. "Time Perception: Space-time in the Brain." *Current Biology* 16(5): R171–R173.

Burtt, E. A., 1954. *The Metaphysical Foundations of Modern Science* (Revised Edition). Garden City, NY: Doubleday Anchor Book.

Buss, David M., 2004. *Evolutionary Psychology: The New Science of the Mind*. Boston: Pearson.

Buttelmann, David, Frances Buttelmann, Malinda Carpenter, Josep Call and Michael

Tomasello, 2017. "Great Apes Distinguish True from False Beliefs in an Interactive Helping Task." *PLoS One* 12(4): e0173793.

Byrne, Thomas, 2017. "Surrogates and Empty Intentions: Husserl's 'On the Logic of Signs' as the Blueprint for his First Logical Investigation." *Husserl Studies* 33(3): 211-227.

Cacioppo, J. T., G. G. Berntson, R. Adolphs, C. S. Carter *et al.* (eds), 2002. *Foundations in Social Neuroscience.* Cambridge, MA: MIT Press.

Cairns, Dorion, 1939. "Some Results of Husserl's Investigations." *The Journal of Philosophy* 36(9): 236-238.

Cairns, Dorion, 1940. "An Approach to Phenomenology," In *Essays in Memory of Edmund Husserl,* ed. by Marvin Farber. Cambridge, MA: Harvard University Press, p. 17.

Cairns, Dorion, 1941. "The Ideality of Verbal Expressions." *Philosophy and Phenomenological Research* 1(4): 453-462.

Cairns, Dorion, 1976. *Conversations with Husserl and Fink.* The Hague: Martinus Nijhoff.

Cairns, Dorion, 1973. *Guide for Translating Husserl.* The Hague: Martinus Nijhoff.

Calitoiu, D., B. J. Oommen and D. Nussbaum, 2012. "Large-Scale Neuro-Modeling for Understanding and Explaining Some Brain-Related Chaotic Behavior." *Simulation* 88: 1316–1337.

Calcagno, Antonio (ed), 2018. *Gerda Walther's Phenomenology of Sociality, Psychology, and Religion.* Dordrecht: Springer.

Call, Josep and Michael Tomasello, 2008. "Does the Chimpanzee Have a Theory of Mind?: 30 Years Later." *Trends in Cognitive Sciences* 12(5): 187-192.

Callebaut, W. R. and Pinxten (eds), 2012. *Evolutionary Epistemology: A Multiparadigm Program.* New York: Springer Science & Business Media.

Callen, Kenneth E., 1983. "Auto-Hypnosis in Long Distance Runners." *American Journal of Clinical Hypnosis* 26(1): 30-36.

Calvert, G., C. Spence and B. E. Stein (eds), 2004. *The Handbook of Multisensory Processes.* Cambridge, MA: MIT Press.

Čapek, Jakub, 2017. "Oneself through Another: Ricœur and Patočka on Husserl's Fifth Cartesian Meditation." *Meta: Research in Hermeneutics, Phenomenology, and Practical Philosophy* 9(2): 387-415.

Carafides, John L., 1974. "H. Spiegelberg on the Phenomenology of C. G. Jung." *Journal of Phenomenological Psychology* 5(1): 75.

Card, Nicholas S. and Omar A. Gharbawie, 2022. "Cortical Connectivity Is Embedded nn Resting State at Columnar Resolution." *Progress in Neurobiology* 213: 102263.

Cardeña, Etzel, S. J. Lynn and S. Krippner (eds.), 2000. *Varieties of Anomalous Experience: Examining the Scientific Evidence.* Washington, DC: American Psychological Association.

Čargonja, Hrvoje, 2013. "Bodies and Worlds: An Outline of Phenomenology in Anthropology." *Studia Ethnologica Croatica* 25: 19-60.

Carr, David, 1974. *Phenomenology and the Problem of History: A Study of Husserl's Transcendental Philosophy.* Evanston, IL: Northwestern University Press.

Carr, David, 1987. "The Problem of the Non-Empirical Ego: Husserl and Kant." In *Interpreting Husserl,* ed. by David Carr. Dordrecht: Springer, pp. 137-156.

Carrier, James G. (ed), 2016. *After the Crisis: Anthropological Thought, Neoliberalism and the Aftermath.* London: Routledge.

Carter, Brandon, 1983. "The Anthropic Principle and Its Implications for Biological Evolution." *Philosophical Transactions of the Royal Society of London.* Series A, *Mathematical and Physical Sciences* 310(1512): 347-363.

Carter, Brandon, 2006[1974]. *Anthropic Principle in Cosmology*. Cambridge: Cambridge University Press.

Carvalho, Gil B. and Antonio Damasio, 2021. "Interoception and the Origin of Feelings: A New Synthesis." *BioEssays* 24 March issue: 2000261.

Casey, Edward S., 1971. "Expression and Communication in Art." *The Journal of Aesthetics and Art Criticism* 30(2): 197-207.

Casey, Edward S., 1976. "The Image/Sign Relation in Husserl and Freud." *The Review of Metaphysics* 30(2): 207-225.

Casper, Stephen T., 2014. History and Neuroscience: An Integrative Legacy." *Isis* 105(1): 123-132.

Cassaniti, Julia L. and Jacob R. Hickman, 2014. "New Directions in the Anthropology of Morality." *Anthropological Theory* 14(3): 251-262.

Cassirer, Ernst, 1957. *The Philosophy of Symbolic Forms*, Volume 3: *The Phenomenology of Knowledge*. New Haven: Yale University Press.

Castaldi, Elisa, Antonella Pomè, Guido Marco Cicchini, David Burr and Paola Binda, 2021. "The Pupil Responds Spontaneously to Perceived Numerosity." *Nature Communications* 12(1): 1-8.

Caughey, John L., 2006. *Negotiating Cultures and Identities: Life History Issues, Methods, and Readings*. Lincoln: University of Nebraska Press.

Černis, Emma, Esther Beierl, Andrew Molodynski, Anke Ehlers, and Daniel Freeman. "A new perspective and assessment measure for common dissociative experiences:'Felt Sense of Anomaly'." *PloS One* 16, no. 2 (2021): e0247037.

Chang, Garma C. C. (ed), 2004. *Teachings and Practice of Tibetan Tantra*. North Chelmsford, MA: Courier Corporation.

Chapple, Elliot D., 1970. *Culture and Biological Man*. New York: Holt, Rinehart and Winston.

Chapple, Eliot D. and Carleton S. Coon, 1942. *Principles of Anthropology*. New York: Holt, Rinehart and Winston.

Chase, Philip G., 1999. "Symbolism as Reference and Symbolism as Culture." In *The Evolution of Culture*, ed. by Dunbar, Robin I. M., Chris Knight and Camilla Power. New Brunswick, NJ: Rutgers University Press, pp. 34-49.

Chelstrom, Eric S., 2012. *Social Phenomenology: Husserl, Intersubjectivity, and Collective Intentionality*. Washington, DC: Lexington Books.

Chen, Si, Zheng Tan, Wenran Xia, Carlos Alexandre Gomes, Xilei Zhang, Wenjing Zhou, Shuli Liang, Nikolai Axmacher and Liang Wang, 2021. "Theta Oscillations Synchronize Human Medial Prefrontal Cortex and Amygdala during Fear Learning." *Science Advances* 7(34): eabf4198.

Chiao, J. Y., S. C. Li, R. Seligman and R. Turner (eds), 2016. *The Oxford Handbook of Cultural Neuroscience*. Oxford: Oxford University Press.

Child, Louise, 2016. *Tantric Buddhism and Altered States of Consciousness: Durkheim, Emotional Energy and Visions of the Consort*. New York: Routledge.

Childers, D. G. and N. W. Perry, 1971. "Alpha-Like Activity in Vision." *Brain Research* 25: 1–20.

Choe, Yoonsuck, Jaerock Kwon and J. I. Ryang Chung, 2012. "Time, Consciousness, and Mind Uploading." *International Journal of Machine Consciousness* 4(1): 257-274.

Chomsky, Noam, 1965. *Aspects of the Theory of Syntax*. Cambridge, MA: MIT Press.

Christiansen, Morten H. and Simon Kirby (eds), 2003. *Language Evolution*. Oxford: Oxford University Press.

Church, R. M., 1999. "Evaluation of Quantitative Theories of Timing." *Journal of the Experimental Analysis of Behavior* 71: 253–91.

Churchland, Patricia, 1985. "Reduction, Qualia, and the Direct Introspection of Brain States." *The Journal of Philosophy* 82(1): 8-28.

Churchland, Patricia, 2013. *Touching a Nerve: Our Brains, Our Selves.* New York: Norton.

Churchland, Patricia, 2019. *Conscience: The Origins of Moral Intuition.* New York: Norton.

Churchland, Patricia and Terrence J. Sejnowski, 1992. *The Computational Brain.* Cambridge, MA: MIT Press/Bradford Books.

Claffert, Pieter F., 2019. "The Supernatural: A Range of Neurocultural Phenomena." In *The Supernatural after the Neuro-Turn.*, ed. by P. F. Claffert, J. R. Baker and M. J. Winkelman. New York: Routledge, pp. 12-28.

Claffert, Piere F., John R. Baker and Michael J. Winkelman (eds), 2019. *The Supernatural after the Neuro-Turn.* New York: Routledge.

Clark, Andy, 2013. "Whatever Next? Predictive Brains, Situated Agents, and the Future of Cognitive Science." *Behavioral and Brain Sciences* 36(3): 181-204.

Classen, Constance, 1997. "Foundation for an Anthropology of the Senses." *International Social Science Journal* 153: 401-412.

Cohen, Emma, 2010. "Anthropology of Knowledge." *Journal of the Royal Anthropological Institute* 16: S193-S202.

Cole, Jonathan, 1998. *About Face.* Cambridge, MA: MIT Press.

Colzato, Lorenza S., Hilmar Zech, Bernhard Hommel, Rinus Verdonschot, Wery P. M. Van den Wildenberg and Shulan Hsieh, 2012. "Loving-Kindness Brings Loving-Kindness: The Impact of Buddhism on Cognitive Self–Other Integration." *Psychonomic Bulletin and Review* 19(3): 541-545.

Connolly, Patrick J., 2014. "Newton and God's Sensorium." *Intellectual History Review* 24(2): 185-201.

Conroy, S. A., 2003. "A Pathway for Interpretive Phenomenology." *International Journal of Qualitative Methods* 2(3): 36-62.

Conway Morris, Simon, 2003a. "The Navigation of Biological Hyperspace." *International Journal of Astrobiology* 2(2): 149.

Conway Morris, Simon, 2003b. *Life's Solution: Inevitable Humans in a Lonely Universe.* Cambridge, UK: Cambridge University Press.

Conway Morris, Simon, 2009. "The Predictability of Evolution: Glimpses into a Post-Darwinian World." *Naturwissenschaften* 96(11): 1313-1337.

Conway Morris, Simon, 2010. "Evolution: Like Any Other Science It Is Predictable." *Philosophical Transactions of the Royal Society B: Biological Sciences* 365(1537): 133-145.

Conway Morris, Simon, 2015. *The Runes of Evolution: How the Universe Became Self-Aware.* West Conshohocken, PA:Templeton Press.

Costello, Peter R., 2012. *Layers in Husserl's Phenomenology: On Meaning and Intersubjectivity.* Toronto, ON: University of Toronto Press.

Costelloe, Timothy M., 2003. "Husserl's Attitude Problem: Intersubjectivity in Ideas II and the Fifth Cartesian Meditation." *Journal of the British Society for Phenomenology* 34(1): 74-86.

Count, Earl W., 1958. "The Biological Basis of Human Sociality." *American Anthropologist* 60: 1049-1085.

Count, Earl W., 1973. *Being and Becoming Human.* New York: Van Nostrand Reinhold.

Count, Earl W., 1976a. "Man in Search of His Image," *Reviews in Anthropology* 3(3): 269-276.

Count, Earl W., 1976b. "Languages of Organism." In *Origins and Evolution of Language and Speech*, ed. by S. R. Harnad *et al. Annals of the New York Academy of Sciences* 280: 456-466.

Count, Earl W., 1976c. "Man in Search of His Image." *Reviews in Anthropology* 3(3): 269-276.

Cox, James L., 2010. *An Introduction to the Phenomenology of Religion*. London: Continuum.

Cozolino, Louis, 2014. *The Neuroscience of Human Relationships: Attachment and the Developing Social Brain*. New York: Norton.

Crapanzano, V. and V. Garrison (eds), 1977. *Case Studies in Spirit Possession*. New York: Wiley.

Crick, Malcolm R., 1982. "Anthropology of Knowledge." *Annual Review of Anthropology* 11(1): 287-313.

Croll, Elizabeth and David Parkin, 1992. "Cultural Understanding of the Environment." In *Bush Base, Forest Farm: Cultural Environment and Development,* ed. By E. Croll and D. Parkin. London: Routledge, pp. 11-36.

Crowell, Steven, 2013. *Normativity and Phenomenology in Husserl and Heidegger*. Cambridge: Cambridge University Press.

Crowell, Steven, 2016. "Phenomenology, Meaning, and Measure: Response to Maxime Doyon and Thomas Sheehan," *Philosophy Today*, 60 (1): 237–252.

Csibra, Gergely and György Gergely, 2006. "Social Learning and Social Cognition: The Case for Pedagogy." *Processes of Change in Brain and Cognitive Development: Attention and Performance XXI*, ed by Y. Munakata and M. H. Johnson. London: Oxford University Press, pp. 249-274.

Csibra, Gergely and György Gergely, 2011. "Natural Pedagogy as Evolutionary Adaptation." *Philosophical Transactions of the Royal Society B: Biological Sciences* 366(1567): 1149-1157.

Csikszentmihalyi, M., 2008. *Flow: The Psychology of Optimal Experience*. New York: Harper.

Csordas, Thomas J., 1990. "Embodiment as a Paradigm for Anthropology" *Ethos* 18:5-47.

Csordas, Thomas J., 1993. "Somatic Modes of Attention." *Cultural Anthropology* 8:135-56

Csordas, Thomas J. (ed), 1994a. *Embodiment and Experience: The Existential Ground of Culture and Self.* Cambridge: Cambridge University Press.

Csordas, Thomas J., 1994b. "Introduction: The Body as Representation and Being-in-the-World." In *Embodiment and Experience: The Existential Ground of Culture and Self,* Thomas Csordas (ed.). Cambridge: Cambridge University Press, pp. 1-24.

Csordas, Thomas J., 1994c. *The Sacred Self: A Cultural Phenomenology of Charismatic Healing.* Berkeley, CA: University of California Press.

Csordas, Thomas J., 2011. "Cultural Phenomenology. Embodiment: Agency, Sexual Difference, and Illness." In *A Companion to the Anthropology of the Body and Embodiment*, ed. by F. E. Mascia-Lees. Oxford: Willey-Blackwell, pp. 137–157.

Csordas, Thomas J., 2014. "Afterword: Moral Experience in Anthropology." *Ethos* 42(1): 139-152.

Cunningham, Paul F., 2022. *Introduction to Transpersonal Psychology: Bridging Spirit and Science.* New York: Routledge.

Czeisler, C. A. *et al.*, 1999. "Stability, Precision, and Near-24–Hour Period of the Human Circadian Pacemaker." *Science* 284: 2177–2181.

D'Agostino, Fred, 2009. *Naturalizing Epistemology: Thomas Kuhn and the 'Essential Tension'.* Berlin: Springer.

Dainton, B., 2006. *Stream of Consciousness: Unity and Continuity in Conscious Experience.* London: Routledge.

Daley, Christine E. and Anthony J. Onwuegbuzie, 2011. "Race and Intelligence." In *The Cambridge Handbook of Intelligence*, ed. by Robert J. Sternberg and Scott B. Kaufman. Cambridge: Cambridge University Press, pp. 293-308.

D'Alfonso, A. A. L., J. Van Honk, D. J. L. G. Schutter, A. R. Caffe, A. Postma and E. H. F. de Haan, 2002. "Spatial and Temporal Characteristics of Visual Motion Perception Involving V5 Visual Cortex." *Neurological Research* 24(3): 266-270.

Daly, Martin, and Margo Wilson, 1983. *Sex, Evolution, and Behavior* (2nd ed.). Boston: Willard Grant.

Damasio , Antonio, 1994. *Descartes' Error: Emotion, Reason, and the Human Brain*. New York: Putnam.

Damasio, Antonio, 1999a. "Time-locked Multiregional Retroactivation: A Systems-level Proposal for the Neural Substrates of Recall and Recognition." *Cognition* 33(1–2): 25–62.

Damasio, Antonio, 1999b. *The Feeling of What Happens: Body and Emotion in the Making of Consciousness*. New York: Harcourt.

Damasio, Hanna, Thomas Grabowski, Randall Frank, Albert M. Galaburda and Antonio R. Damasio, 1994. "The Return of Phineas Gage: Clues about the Brain from the Skull of a Famous Patient." *Science* 264(5162): 1102-1105.

Danchevskaya, Oksana Y., 2020. "Good and Evil in Native American Mythology." In *Native Legacies in the Twenty-First Century. Proceedings of the Thirteenth Native American Symposium*, ed. by Matthew J. Sparacio. Durant, OK: Southeastern Oklahoma State University, pp. 23-28.

D'Andrade, Roy G., 1981. "The Cultural Part of Cognition." *Cognitive Science* 5(3): 179-195.

D'Andrade, Roy G., 1995a. "What do you think you're doing?" *Anthropology Newsletter* 36(7): 1.

D'Andrade, Roy G., 1995b. "Moral Models in Anthropology." *Current Anthropology* 36(3): 399-408.

Daneman, Richard and Alexandre Prat, 2012. "The Blood–Brain Barrier." *Cold Spring Harbor Perspectives in Biology* 7(1): a020412.

D'Aquili, Eugene G., 1982. "Senses of Reality in Science and Religion: A Neuroepistemological Perspective." *Zygon* 17(4): 361-384.

D'Aquili, Eugene G., 1985. "Human Ceremonial Ritual and the Modulation of Aggression." *Zygon* 20(1): 21-30.

D'Aquili, Eugene G., 1986. "Myth, Ritual, and the Archetypal Hypothesis." *Zygon* 21(2): 141-160.

D'Aquili, Eugene G., Charles D. Laughlin and John McManus, 1993. "Mature Contemplation." *Zygon* 28(2): 133-176.

D'Aquili, Eugene G. and Andrew B. Newberg, 1993. "Religious and Mystical States: A Neuropsychological Model." *Zygon* 28: 177-200.

D'Aquili, Eugene G. and Andrew B. Newberg, 1998. "The Neuropsychological Basis of Religions, or Why God Won't Go Away." *Zygon* 33: 187-201.

D'Aquili, Eugene G. and Andrew B. Newberg, 1999. *The Mystical Mind: Probing the Biology of Religious Experience*. Minneapolis: Fortress Press.

D'Aquili, Eugene G. and Andrew B. Newberg, 2000. "The Neuropsychology of Aesthetic, Spiritual, and Mystical States." *Zygon* 35: 39-51.

Darwin, Charles, 2008[1871]. *The Descent of Man, And Selection in Relation to Sex*. Princeton, NJ: Princeton University Press.

David-Neel, Alexandra, 1971. *Magic and Mystery in Tibet* (originally in French, Paris, 1929). New York: Dover Publications.

Davidson, J. M., 1976. "The Physiology of Meditation and Mystical States of Consciousness." *Perspectives in Biology and Medicine* 19: 345-379.

Davidson, Richard J., 2003. "Alterations in Brain and Immune Function Produced by Mindfulness Meditation." *Psychosomatic Medicine* 65: 564–570.

Davis, Hank, 2009. *Caveman Logic: The Persistence of Primitive Thinking in a Modern World.* New York: Prometheus.

Davis-Floyd, Robbie E. and Charles D. Laughlin, 2016. *Power of Ritual.* Brisbane, Australia: Daily Grail.

Dawkins, Richard and John R. Krebs, 1978. "Animal Signals: Information or Manipulation." *Behavioural Ecology: An Evolutionary Approach*, ed. by J. R. Krebs and N. B. Davies. Oxford: Blackwell, pp. 282-309.

Deacon, Terrence W., 1997. *The Symbolic Species: The Co-Evolution of Language and the Brain.* New York: Norton.

DeCasper, Anthony J., Jean-Pierre Lecanuet, Marie-Claire Busnel, Carolyn Granier-Deferre and Roselyne Maugeais, 1994. "Fetal Reactions to Recurrent Maternal Speech." *Infant Behavior and Development* 17(2): 159-164.

Decastro, Rita, Augusta Gaspar and Luís Vicente, 2010. "The Evolving Empathy: Hardwired Bases of Human and Non-Human Primate Empathy." *Psicologia* 24(2): 131-152.

Decety, Jean, Chenyi Chen, Carla Harenski and Kent A. Kiehl, 2013. "An fMRI Study of Affective Perspective Taking in Individuals with Psychopathy: Imagining Another in Pain Does Not Evoke Empathy." *Frontiers in Human Neuroscience* 7: 489.

Decety, Jean and William Ickes (eds.), 2009. *The Social Neuroscience of Empathy.* Cambridge, MA: MIT Press.

Deeley, Peter Q., 2004. "The Religious Brain: Turning Ideas into Convictions." *Anthropology & Medicine* 11(3): 245-267.

Degenaar, J. and E. Myin, 2014. "The Structure of Color Experience and the Existence of Surface Colors." *Philosophical Psychology* 27(3): 384-400.

Dehaene, S., 2014. *Consciousness and the Brain: Deciphering How the Brain Codes Our Thoughts.* New York: Viking.

Dehaene, S. and J.-P. Changeux, 2011. "Experimental and Theoretical Approaches to Conscious Processing." *Neuron* 70: 200–227.

Dehay, Colette and Henry Kennedy, 2020. "Evolution of the Human Brain." *Science* 369(6503): 506-507.

Deikman, Arthur J., 1966. "De-Automatization and the Mystical Experience." *Psychiatry* 29: 324-338.

Dempsey, William P. *et al.*, 2022. "Regional Synapse Gain and Loss Accompany Memory Formation in Larval Zebrafish." *Proceedings of the National Academy of Sciences* 119(3): e2107661119.

Denzin, Norman K. and Yvonna S. Lincoln (eds), 2005. *The Sage Handbook of Qualitative Research* (3rd edition). London: Sage Publications.

Derrida, Jacques, 1973. *Speech and Phenomena, and Other Essays on Husserl's Theory of Signs.* Evanston, IL: Northwestern University Press.

Derrida, Jacques, 2003[1990]. *The Problem of Genesis in Husserl's Philosophy.* Chicago: University of Chicago Press.

De Santis, Daniele, 2020. "'Self-Variation': A Problem of Method in Husserl's Phenomenology." *Husserl Studies* 36(3): 255-269.

DeSantis, Larisa RG, Rachel A. Beavins Tracy, Cassandra S. Koontz, John C. Roseberry and Matthew C. Velasco, 2012. "Mammalian Niche Conservation Through Deep Time."

PLoS One 7(4): e35624.

De Saussure, Ferdinand, 2011[1916]. *Course in General Linguistics.* New York: Columbia University Press.

Descartes, René, 2008. *Meditations on First Philosophy: With Selections from the Objections and Replies,* trans. Michael Moriarty. Oxford: Oxford University Press.

Desjarlais, Robert and C. Jason Throop, 2011. "Phenomenological Approaches in Anthropology." *Annual Review of Anthropology* 40: 87-102.

Devereux, Paul, 1992. *Symbolic Landscapes.* Sumerset, England: Gothic Image Publications.

Devereux, Paul, 2008. *The Long Trip: A Prehistory of Psychedelia.* Brisbane, Australia: Daily Grail.

Devereux, Paul, 2013. "Dreamscapes: Topography, Mind, and the Power of Simulacra in Ancient and Traditional Societies." *International Journal of Transpersonal Studies* 32(1): 51-63.

De Waal, Frans, 1996. *Good Natured: The Origins of Right and Wrong in Humans and Other Animals.* Cambridge, MA: Harvard University Press.

De Waal, Frans, 2006. "The Animal Roots of Human Morality." *New Scientist* 192(2573): 60-61.

De Warren, Nicolas, 2017. "Husserl and Phenomenological Ethics." In *The Cambridge History of Moral Philosophy,* ed. by Sacha Golob and Jens Timmermann. New York: Cambridge University Press, pp. 562-576.

Dico, Giuseppe Lo, 2018. "Self-Perception Theory, Radical Behaviourism, and the Publicity/ Privacy Issue." *Review of Philosophy and Psychology* 9(2): 429-445.

Di Gregorio, Francesco, Jelena Trajkovic, Cristina Roperti, Eleonora Marcantoni, Paolo Di Luzio, Alessio Avenanti, Gregor Thut and Vincenzo Romei, 2022. "Tuning Alpha Rhythms to Shape Conscious Visual Perception." *Current Biology* 32(5): 988-998.

Dissanayake, Ellen, 1992. *Homo Aestheticus: Where Art Comes From and Why.* Seattle: University of Washington Press.

Dobkin de Rios, Marlene, 1984. *Hallucinogens: Cross Cultural Perspectives.* Albuquerque, N.M.: University of New Mexico Press.

Dobkin de Rios, Marlene and Michael Winkelman (eds.), 1989. *Shamanism and Altered States of Consciousness.* Special issue of the *Journal of Psychoactive Drugs* 21(1).

Domínguez Duque, Juan F., Robert Turner, E. Douglas Lewis, and Gary Egan, 2010. "Neuroanthropology: A Humanistic Science for the Study of the Culture–Brain Nexus." *Social Cognitive and Affective Neuroscience* 5(2-3): 138-147.

Donald, Merlin, 1991. *Origins of the Modern Mind.* Cambridge, MA: Harvard University Press.

Donald, Merlin, 2003. *A Mind So Rare: The Evolution of Human Consciousness.* New York: Norton.

Donohoe, Janet, 2018. *Husserl on Ethics and Intersubjectivity.* Toronto, ON: University of Toronto Press.

Dornan, Jennifer, 2004. "Beyond Belief: Religious Experience, Ritual, and Cultural Neurophenomenology in the Interpretation of Past Religious Systems." *Cambridge Archaeological Journal* 14(1): 25-36.

Dorsey, George Amos, 1905. *The Ponca Sun Dance.* Vol. 7, no. 2. Field Columbian Museum.

Doty, R. W., 1975. "Consciousness from Neurons." *Acta Neurobiologiae Experimentalis* 35: 791-804.

Doty, William G., 1986. *Mythography: The Study of Myths and Rituals.* Tuscaloosa: University of Alabama Press.

Douglas, Mary, 1966. *Purity and Danger*. New York: Praeger.

Dow, James W., 1996. "The Cultural Context of Scientific Anthropology." *Anthropology Newsletter* 37(2): 48.

Downs, James F., 1972. *The Navajo*. New York: Holt, Rinehart and Winston.

Dreher, Jochen, 2003. "The Symbol and the Theory of the Life-World: 'The Transcendences of the Life-World and Their Overcoming by Signs and Symbols'." *Human Studies* 26(2): 141-163.

Driver , Julia, 2012. *Consequentialism*. London: Routledge.

Droit-Volet, S., 2002. "Scalar Timing in Temporal Generalization in Children with Short and Long Stimulus Durations." *Quarterly Journal of Experimental Psychology* A 55A: 1193–1209.

Duarte, André, 2004. "Heidegger and the Possibility of an Existential Anthropology." *Natureza Humana* 6(1): 29-51.

Dubois, Julien and Rufin VanRullen, 2011. "Visual Trails: Do the Doors of Perception Open Periodically?" *PLoS Biology* 9(5): e1001056.

Dufour, Darna L., 2006. "Biocultural Approaches in Human Biology." *American Journal of Human Biology* 18 (1): 1–9.

Dufrenne, Mikel, 1973. *The Phenomenology of Aesthetic Experience*, trans. by Edward S. Casey *et al*. Evanston, IL: Northwestern University Press.

Dunbar, Robin I. M., 2003. "The Social Brain: Mind, Language, and Society in Evolutionary Perspective." *Annual Review of Anthropology* 32(1): 163-181.

Dunbar, Robin I. M., 2016. *Human Evolution: Our Brains and Behavior*. Oxford: Oxford University Press.

Dunbar, Robin I. M., C. Gamble and J. A. Gowlett, 2010. *Social Brain, Distributed Mind*. Oxford: Oxford University Press.

Dunbar, Robin I. M., Chris Knight and Camilla Power (eds), 1999. *The Evolution of Culture*. New Brunswick, NJ: Rutgers University Press.

Dunbar, Robin I. M. and Susanne Shultz, 2007. "Evolution in the Social Brain." *Science* 317(5843): 1344-1347.

Duranti, Alessandro, 2009. "The Relevance of Husserl's Theory to Language Socialization." *Journal of Linguistic Anthropology* 19(2): 205-226.

Duranti, Alessandro, 2010. "Husserl, Intersubjectivity and Anthropology." *Anthropological Theory* 10(1-2): 16-35.

Durham, William H., 1982. "Toward a Co-evolutionary Theory of Human Biology and Culture." In *Biology and the Social Sciences*, ed. by T. C. Wiegele. Boulder, Colorado: Westview Press, pp. 39-59.

Durham, William H., 1991. *Coevolution: Genes, Culture, and Human Diversity*. Stanford, CA: Stanford University Press.

Durkheim, Émile, 1992. *Professional Ethics and Civil Morals*. London: Routledge.

Duveen, Gerard, 2000. "Piaget Ethnographer." *Social Science Information* 39(1): 79–97.

Duveen, Gerard and Barbara Lloyd, 1993. "An Ethnographic Approach to Social Representations." In *Empirical approaches to social representations,* ed. by Glynis Marie Breakwell and David V. Canter. Oxford: Oxford University Press, pp. 90–109.

Easterlin, Nancy, 1999. "Making Knowledge: Bioepistemology and the Foundations of Literary Theory." *Mosaic: A Journal for the Interdisciplinary Study of Literature* 32(1): 131-147.

Edelman, David B. and Anil K. Seth, 2009. "Animal Consciousness: A Synthetic Approach." *Trends in Neurosciences* 32(9): 476-484.

Edelman, Gerald M., 1987. *Neural Darwinism: The Theory of Neuronal Group Selection*. New York: Basic Books.

Edelman, Gerald M., 1992. *Bright Air, Brilliant Fire: On the Matter of Mind*. New York: Basic Books.

Edelman, Gerald M., 2006. *Second Nature: Brain Science and Human Knowledge*. Hew Haven, CT: Yale University Press.

Edelman, Gerald M and Vernon B. Mountcastle, 1978. *The Mindful Brain*. Cambridge, MA: MIT Press.

Edelman, Gerald M. and G. Tononi, 2000. *A Universe of Consciousness: How Matter Becomes Imagination*. New York: Basic Books.

Edie, James M., 1963. "Expression and Metaphor." *Philosophy and Phenomenological Research* 23(4): 538-561.

Edie, James M., 1976. *Speaking and Meaning: The Phenomenology of Language*. Bloomington, IN: Indiana University Press.

Edie, James M., 1987. *Edmund Husserl's Phenomenology: A Critical Commentary*. Bloomington, IN: Indiana University Press.

Edie, James M., Francis H. Parker and Calvin O. Schrag, 1970. *Patterns of the Life-World: Essays in Honor of John Wild*. Evanston: IL: Northwestern University Press.

Edinger, E. F., 1972. *Ego and Archetype: Individuation and the Religious Function of the Psyche*. New York: G.P. Putnam's.

Edwards, P., 1967. *The Encyclopedia of Philosophy*. London: Collier MacMillan.

Efron, R., 1970. "The Minimum Duration of a Perception." *Neuropsychologia* 8:57–63.

Ekman, Paul, 1993. "Facial Expression and Emotion." *American Psychologist* 48(4): 384.

Elden, Stuart, 2008. "Eugen Fink and the Question of the World." *Parrhesia: A Journal of Critical Philosophy* 5: 48-59.

Eleftheriou, Maria Eleni and Emily Thomas, 2021, "Examining the Potential Synergistic Effects Between Mindfulness Training and Psychedelic-Assisted Therapy." *Frontiers in Psychiatry* : 12: 707057.

Eliade, Mircea, 1964[1951]. *Shamanism: Archaic Techniques of Ecstasy*. New York: Pantheon Books. (Original work published as *Le Chamanisme et les techniques archaïques de l'extase,* 1951)

Elkholy, Ramsey, 2016. *Being and Becoming: Embodiment and Experience Among the Orang Rimba of Sumatra*. New York: Berghahn Books.

Ellul, Jacques, 2018[1977]. *The Technological System*. Eugene, OR: Wipf and Stock.

Embree, Lester E., 1972. *Life-World and Consciousness: Essays for Aron Gurwitsch*. Evanston: IL: Northwestern University Press.

Engel, A. K., P. Fries, P. Konig, M. Brecht and W. Singer, 1999. "Temporal Binding, Binocular Rivalry, and Consciousness." *Consciousness and Cognition* 8(2): 128–51. (Entire issue pertains to temporal binding.)

Engel, A. K. and W. Singer, 2001. "Temporal Binding and the Neural Correlates of Sensory Awareness." *Trends in Cognitive Sciences* 5(1): 16–25.

Engelien, Almut *et al.*, 2000. "The Neural Correlates of 'Deaf-Hearing' in Man: Conscious Sensory Awareness Enabled by Attentional Modulation." *Brain* 123(3): 532-545.

Engelhardt, H. Tristram, 1977. "Husserl and the Mind-Brain Relation." In *Interdisciplinary Phenomenology*, ed. by Don Ihde and Richard M. Zaner. Dordrecht: Springer, pp. 51-70.

Erickson, Ken C. and Donald D. Stull, 1997. *Doing Team Ethnography: Warnings and Advice*. London: Sage Publications.

Escamilla, Michael, 2020. "Neuroscience and Jung." In *The Professional Practice of Jungian Coaching*, ed. by Nada O'Brian and John O'Brian. New York: Routledge, pp. 44-56.

Evans-Pritchard, E. E., 1937. *Witchcraft, Oracles and Magic Among the Azande.* Oxford: Clarendon Press.

Evans-Pritchard, E. E., 1939. "Nuer Time Reckoning." *Africa* 12(2): 189–216.

Falk, Dean, 1992. *Braindance: What New Findings Reveal About Human Origins and Brain Evolution.* New York: Henry Holt.

Färber, Marvin, 1943. *The Foundation of Phenomenology. Edmund Husserl and the Quest for a Rigorous Science of Philosophy.* Albany, NY: State University of New York Press.

Färber, Marvin, 1967. "Husserl and Philosophic Radicalism." In *Phenomenology*, ed. by Joseph J. Kockelmans. Garden City, NY: Doubleday, pp. 37-57.

Farella, J. R., 1984. *The Main Stalk: A Synthesis of Navajo Philosophy.* Tucson, AZ: University of Arizona Press.

Fassin, Didier (ed), 2012. *A Companion to Moral Anthropology.* John Wiley & Sons, 2012.

Fazakas, I. and T. Gozé, 2020. "The Promise of the World: Towards a Transcendental History of Trust." *Husserlian Studies* 36: 169–189.

Feinberg, Todd E. and Jon M. Mallatt, 2016. *The Ancient Origins of Consciousness: How the Brain Created Experience.* Cambridge, MA: MIT Press.

Ferguson, H., 2006. *Phenomenological Sociology: Experience and Insight in Modern Society.* London: Sage.

Fernandez, J. W. (ed), 1991. *Beyond Metaphor: The Theory of Tropes in Anthropology.* Stanford, CA: Stanford University Press

Ferrarello, Susi, 2016. *Husserl's Ethics and Practical Intentionality.* Oxford: Bloomsbury.

Ferrari, P. F. and G. Rizzolatti, 2014. "Mirror Neuron Research: The Past and the Future." *Philosophical Transactions of the Royal Society London B: Biological Sciences* 369: 20130169.

Feyerabend, Paul, 2010. *Against Method: Outline of an Anarchistic Theory of Knowledge* (4th edition). New York: Verso.

Fields, R. Douglas, Alfonso Araque, Heidi Johansen-Berg, Soo-Siang Lim, Gary Lynch, Klaus-Armin Nave, Maiken Nedergaard, Ray Perez, Terrence Sejnowski and Hiroaki Wake, 2014. "Glial Biology in Learning and Cognition." *The Neuroscientist* 20(5): 426-431.

Filmer-Lorch, A., 2012. *Inside Meditation: In Search of the Unchanging Nature Within.* Leicester, UK: Troubador Publishing.

Fingelkurts, A. A., A. A. Fingelkurts and C. F. Neves, 2010. "Natural World Physical, Brain Operational, and Mind Phenomenal Space–Time." *Physical Life Review* 7: 195–249.

Fink, Andreas and Mathias Benedek, 2013. "The Creative Brain: Brain Correlates Underlying the Generation of Original Ideas." *Neuroscience of Creativity*, ed. by Oshin Vartanian, Adam S. Bristol, James C. Kaufman. Cambridge, MA: MIT Press, pp. 207-232.

Fink, Eugen, 1960. "The Ontology of Play." *Philosophy Today* 4(2): 95-109.

Fink, Eugen, 1968. "The Oasis of Happiness: Toward an Ontology of Play." *Yale French Studies* 41: 19-30.

Fink, Eugen, 1970. "The Phenomenological Philosophy of Edmund Husserl and Contemporary Criticism." In *The Phenomenology of Husserl: Selected Critical Readings*, ed. by R. O. Elveton. Chicago: Quandrangle Books,

Fink, Eugen, 1972. "What Does the Phenomenology of Edmund Husserl Want to Accomplish? The Phenomenological Idea of Laying-a-Ground." *Research in Phenomenology* 2: 5-27.

Fink, Eugen, 1981a. "The Problem of the Phenomenology of Edmund Husserl." In *Apriori and World*, ed. by W. McKenna, R. M. Harlan and L. E. Winters. The Hague: Martinus Nijhoff, pp. 21-55.

Fink, Eugen, 1981b. "Operative Concepts in Husserl's phenomenology." In *Apriori and World*, ed. by W. Mckenna, R. M. Harlan and L.E. Winters. Dordrecht: Springer, pp. 56-70.

Fink, Eugen, 1995. *Sixth Cartesian Meditation: The Idea of a Transcendental Theory of Method*. Bloomington: Indiana University Press.

Fink, Eugen, 2016[1960]. *Play as Symbol of the World and Other Writings* (I. A. Moore and C. Turner, Trans.). Bloomington, IN: Indiana University Press.

Finnegan, Ruth and Robin Horton, 1973. *Modes of Thought in Western and Non-Western Societies*. Eugene, OR: Wipf and Stock.

Fischer, Roland, 1971. "A Cartography of the Ecstatic and Meditative States." *Science* 174(4012): 897-904.

Flinn, Mark V., 1997. "Culture and the Evolution of Social Learning." *Evolution and Human Behavior* 18(1): 23-67.

Flinn, Mark V., 2006. "Cross-Cultural Universals and Variations: The Evolutionary Paradox of Informational Novelty." *Psychological Inquiry* 17(2): 118-123.

Flinn, Mark V., 2011. "Evolutionary Anthropology of the Human Family." In *The Oxford Handbook of Evolutionary Family Psychology*, ed. by Catherine Salmon and Todd K. Shackelford. Oxford: Oxford University Press, pp. 12-32.

Flor-Henry, Pierre, Yakov Shapiro and Corine Sombrun, 2017. "Brain Changes during a Shamanic Trance: Altered Modes of Consciousness, Hemispheric Laterality, and Systemic Psychobiology." *Cogent Psychology* 4(1): 1313522.

Foa, M., 2015. *Georges Seurat: The Art of Vision*. New Haven: Yale University Press.

Føllesdal, Dagfinn, 1969. "Husserl's Notion of Noema." *Journal of Philosophy* 66: 680–687.

Føllesdal, Dagfinn, 1978. "Brentano and Husserl on Intentional Objects and Perception." *Grazer Philosophische Studien* 5: 83-94.

Føllesdal, Dagfinn, 1990. "Noema and Meaning in Husserl." *Philosophy and Phenomenological Research* 1 (Supplement, fall): 263–71.

Føllesdal, Dagfinn, 2006. "Husserl's Reductions and the Role They Play in His Phenomenology." *A Companion to Phenomenology and Existentialism*, ed. by Hubert L. Dreyfus and Mark A. Wrathall. New York: Wiley, pp. 240-252.

Forster, Kenneth I., 1970. "Visual Perception of Rapidly Presented Word Sequences of Varying Complexity." *Perception and Psychophysics* 8(4): 215-221.

Fox, Kieran C. R. *et al.*, 2014. "Is Meditation Associated with Altered Brain Structure? A Systematic Review and Meta-Analysis of Morphometric Neuroimaging in Meditation Practitioners." *Neuroscience and Biobehavioral Reviews* 43: 48-73.

Fox, N. A., S. D. Calkins and M. A. Bell, 1994. "Neural Plasticity and Development in the First Two Years of Life: Evidence from Cognitive and Socioemotional Domains of Research." *Development and Psychopathology* 6: 677–696.

Frecska, Ede, Csaba E. Móré, András Vargha and Luis E. Luna, 2012. "Enhancement of Creative Expression and Entoptic Phenomena as After-Effects of Repeated Ayahuasca Ceremonies." *Journal of Psychoactive Drugs* 44(3): 191-199.

Freeman, Walter J., 2000. "Mesoscopic Neurodynamics: From Neuron to Brain." *Journal of Physiology-Paris* 94(5-6): 303-322.

Fricke, C., 2018. "Constructivism in Epistemology—On the Constitution of Standards of Normality." In *Husserl's Phenomenology of Intersubjectivity*, ed. by F. Kjosavik, C. Beyer and C. Fricke. New York: Routledge, pp. 283-301.

Frings, Manfred S., 1978. "Husserl and Scheler: Two Views on Intersubjectivity." *Journal of the British Society for Phenomenology* 9(3): 143-149.

Frings, S. 2012. 'Sensory cells and sensory organs.' In Barth, F. G., Giampieri-Deutsch, P.

and Klein, H.-D. (eds), *Sensory Perception*. (pp. 5-21). Vienna: Springer.

Frith, Christopher D. and Uta Frith, 2005. "Theory of Mind." *Current Biology* 15(17): R644-R645.

Fujiwara, Satoko, David Thurfjell and Steven Engler (eds), 2021. *Global Phenomenologies of Religion: An Oral History in Interviews*. Bristol, CT: Equinox.

Funke, Gerhard, 1984. "The Primacy of Practical Reason in Kant and Husserl." In *Kant and Phenomenology*, ed. by Thomas M. Seebohm and Joseph J. Kockelmans. New York: University Press of America, pp. 1-29.

Funke, Gerhard, 1987. *Phenomenology: Metaphysics or Method?* Athens, OH: Ohio University Press.

Fusar-Poli, P. and G. Stanghellini, 2009. "Maurice Merleau-Ponty and the 'Embodied Subjectivity' (1908-61)." *Medical Anthropology Quarterly* 23(2): 91-93.

Fuster, Joaquín M., 1993. "Frontal Lobes." *Current Opinion in Neurobiology* 3(2): 160-165.

Fuster, Juaquin M., 2002. "Physiology of Executive Functions: The Perception-Action Cycle." In *Principles of Frontal Lobe Function,* ed. by Donald T. Stuss and Robert T. Knight. Oxford: Oxford University Press, pp. 96-108.

Fuster, Joaquín M., 2003. *Cortex and Mind: Unifying Cognition*. Oxford: Oxford University Press.

Fuster, Joaquín M., 2013. *The Neuroscience of Freedom and Creativity: Our Predictive Brain*. Cambridge University Press, 2013.

Fuster, Joaquin M., 2014. "The Prefrontal Cortex Makes the Brain a Preadaptive System." *Proceedings of the IEEE* 102(4): 417-426.

Fuster, Joaquín M., 2015. *The Prefrontal Cortex* (5th edition). New York: Elsevier.

Fuster, Joaquín M., 2017. "Prefrontal Executive Functions Predict and Preadapt." In *Executive Functions in Health and Disease*, ed. by Elkhonon Goldberg. New York: Academic Press, pp. 3-19.

Fuster, Joaquín M. and Steven L. Bressler, 2012. "Cognit Activation: A Mechanism Enabling Temporal Integration in Working Memory." *Trends in Cognitive Sciences* 16(4): 207-218.

Fuster, Joaquín M. and Steven L. Bressler, 2015. "Past Makes Future: Role of PFC in Prediction." *Journal of Cognitive Neuroscience* 27(4): 639-654.

Gable, Eric, 2010. *Anthropology and Egalitarianism: Ethnographic Encounters from Monticello to Guinea-Bissau*. Bloomington, IN: Indiana University Press.

Galanter, E., 1962. *Contemporary Psychophysics*. New York: Holt, Rinehart, Winston.

Gallagher, Shaun, 1986. "Hyletic Experience and the Lived Body." *Husserl Studies* 3(2): 131-166.

Gallagher, Shaun, 2008. "Direct Perception in the Intersubjective Context." *Consciousness and Cognition* 17(2): 535-543.

Gallagher, H. L. and C. D. Frith, 2003. "Functional Imaging of 'Theory of Mind'." *Trends in Cognitive Science* 7(2): 77– 83.

Gallese, V., M. Morris, M. N. Eagle and P. Migone, 2007. "Intentional Attunement: Mirror Neurons and the Neural Underpinnings of Interpersonal Relations." *Journal of the American Psychoanalytic Association* 55: 131-176.

Gangestad, Steven W., Martie G. Haselton and David M. Buss, 2006. "Evolutionary Foundations of Cultural Variation: Evoked Culture and Mate Preferences." *Psychological Inquiry* 17(2): 75-95.

Gardner, Howard, 2004[1983]. *Frames of Mind: The Theory of Multiple Intelligences*. London: Paladin.

Garro, L. C., 1992. "Chronic Illness and the Construction of Narratives." In *Pain as Human Experience: An Anthropological Perspective*, ed. by Mary-Jo DelVecchio Good, Paul Brodwin, Byron Good and Arthur Kleinman. Los Angeles: University of California Press, pp. 100-137.

Garro, L. C., 1994. "Narrative Representations of Chronic Illness Experience: Cultural Models of Illness, Mind, and Body in Stories Concerning the Temporomandibular Joint (TMJ)." *Social Science and Medicine* 38(6): 775–88.

Garro, L.C. and Mattingly, C., 2000. "Narrative as Construct and Construction." In *Narrative and the Cultural Construction of Illness and Healing*, ed. by C. Mattingly and L.C. Garro. Berkeley: University of California Press, pp. 1–49.

Gazzaniga, Michael S., 1985. *The Social Brain: Discovering the Networks of the Mind*. New York: Basic Books.

Gazzaniga Michael S., 1995. "Principles of Human Brain Organization Derived from Split-Brain Studies." *Neuron* 14: 217-28.

Gazzaniga Michael S., J. D. Holtzman, M. D. F. Deck and B. C. P. Lee, 1985. "MRI Assessment of Human Callosal Surgery with Neuropsychological Correlates." *Neurology* 35: 1763-1766.

Ge, Xinxin, Kathy Zhang, Alexandra Gribizis, Ali S. Hamodi, Aude Martinez Sabino and Michael C. Crair, 2021. "Retinal Waves Prime Visual Motion Detection by Simulating Future Optic Flow." *Science* 373(6553): eabd0830.

Gebuis, Titia, Roi Cohen Kadosh and Wim Gevers, 2016. "Sensory-Integration System Rather Than Approximate Number System Underlies Numerosity Processing: A Critical Review." *Acta Psychologica* 171: 17-35.

Geertz, Clifford, 1985. *Local Knowledge* (3rd edition). New York: Basic Books.

Geertz, Clifford, 2017. *The Interpretation of Cultures* (3rd edition). New York: Basic Books.

Gegenfurtner, Karl, 2001. "Color in the Cortex Revisited." *Nature Neuroscience* 4(4): 339-340.

Gell, Alfred, 1992. *The Anthropology of Time*. Oxford: Berg.

Gell, Alfred, 1998. *Art and Agency: An Anthropological Theory*. Oxford: Clarendon.

Gellhorn, Ernst, 1967. *Principles of Autonomic-Somatic Integration*. Minneapolis: University of Minnesota Press.

Gellhorn, Ernst, 1970. "The Emotions and the Ergotropic and Trophotropic Systems: II. The Tuning of the Central Nervous System and its Psychological Implication." *Psychologische Forschung* 34: 67-94.

Gellhorn, Ernst. and W. F. Kiely, 1972. "Mystical States of Consciousness: Neurophysiological and Clinical Aspects." *Journal of Nervous and Mental Diseases* 154: 399-405.

Gellhorn, Ernst, and G. N. Loofbourrow, 1963. *Emotions and Emotional Disorders*. New York: Harper and Row.

Gelman, Rochel and Sara Cordes, 2001. "Counting in Animals and Humans." In *Language, Brain, and Cognitive Development: Essays in Honor of Jacques Mehler*, ed. by E. Dupoux. Cambridge, MA: MIT Press, pp. 279–301.

Geniusas, Saulius, 2011. "William James and Edmund Husserl on the Horizontality of Experience." In *Transcendentalism Overturned: From Absolute Power of Consciousness Until the Forces of Cosmic Architectonics*, ed. by Anna-Teresa Tymieniecka. Dordrecht: Springer, pp. 481-494.

Geniusas, Saulius, 2012. *The Origins of the Horizon in Husserl's Phenomenology*. Dordrecht: Springer.

Geniusas, Saulius, 2020. "Towards a Phenomenology of the Unconscious: Husserl and Fink on *Versunkenheit."* *Journal of the British Society for Phenomenology* DOI:10.1080/00071 773.2020.1834334.

Gepshtein, Sergei, Ambarish Pawar, Sunwoo Kwon, Sergey Savelev and Thomas D. Albright, 2021. "Spatially Distributed Computation in Cortical Circuits." *bioRxiv* preprint version, https://doi.org/10.1101/2021.12.13.472322.

Gescheider, G. A., 2013. *Psychophysics: The Fundamentals.* Washington, DC: Psychology Press.

Geurts, Kathryn Linn, 2002. "On Rocks, Walks, and Talks in West Africa: Cultural Categories and an Anthropology of the Senses." *Ethos* 30(3): 178-198.

Ghigi, Nicoletta, 2004. "Creativity in Husserl's Impulsive Intentionality." In *Imaginatio Creatrix,* ed. by Anna-Teresa Tymieniecka. Dordrecht: Springer, pp. 553-564.

Gho, M. and F. J. Varela, 1988/89. "A Quantitative Assessment of the Dependency of the Visual Temporal Frame upon the Cortical Rhythm." *Journal of Physiology* (Paris) 83(2): 95–101.

Gibbon, J., R. M. Church and W. H. Meck, 1984. "Scalar Timing in Memory." *Annals of the New York Academy of Sciences* 423: 52–77.

Gibbon, J., C. Malapani, C. L. Dale and C. R. Gallistel, 1997. "Toward a Neurobiology of Temporal Cognition: Advances and Challenges." *Current Opinion in Neurobiology* 7(2): 170–84.

Gibbs, Raymond W., 2006. "Introspection and Cognitive Linguistics: Should We Trust Our Own Intuitions?" *Annual Review of Cognitive Linguistics* 4(1): 135-151.

Gibson, J. J., 1977. "The Theory of Affordances." In *Perceiving, Acting, and Knowing: Toward an Ecological Psychology,* ed. by R. S. John and B. John. Hillsdale, NJ: Lawrence Erlbaum, pp. 67–82.

Gibson, J. J., 1979. *The Ecological Approach to Visual Perception.* Boston: Houghton Mifflin.

Gibson, J. J., 1982. "Notes on Affordances." In *Reasons for Realism,* ed. by E. Reed and R. Jones. Hillsdale, NJ: Lawrence Erlbaum, pp. 401–30.

Gieser, Thorsten, 2018. "The Experience of 'Being a Hunter:' Towards a Phenomenological Anthropology of Hunting Practices." *Hunter Gatherer Research* 3(2): 227-251.

Gillespie-Lynch, Kristen, Patricia M. Greenfield, Heidi Lyn and Sue Savage-Rumbaugh, 2014. "Gestural and Symbolic Development Among Apes and Humans: Support for a Multimodal Theory of Language Evolution." *Frontiers in Psychology* 5: 1228.

Ginot, Efrat, 2015. *The Neuropsychology of the Unconscious: Integrating Brain and Mind in Psychotherapy.* Noe York: Norton.

Ginsburg, Herbert, 1997. *Entering the Child's Mind: The Clinical Interview in Psychological Research and Practice.* Cambridge: Cambridge University Press.

Giorgi, Amedeo, 2007. "Concerning the Phenomenological Methods of Husserl and Heidegger and Their Application in Psychology." *Collection du Cirp* 1(1): 63-78.

Giorgi, Amedeo, 2009. *The Descriptive Phenomenological Method in Psychology: A Modified Husserlian Approach.* Pittsburgh, PA: Duquesne University Press.

Giorgi, Amedeo, 2020. "In Defense of Scientific Phenomenologies." *Journal of Phenomenological Psychology* 51(2): 135-161.

Giorgi, Amedeo and B. Giorgi, 2008. "Phenomenological Psychology." In *The SAGE Handbook of Qualitative Research in Psychology,* ed. by K. Chamberlain, M. Murray, C. Willig and W. S. Rogers. London: Sage, pp.165-178.

Giri, Ananta Kumar and John Clammer (eds), 2013. *Philosophy and Anthropology: Border Crossing and Transformations.* New York: Anthem Press.

Givón, T. and Bertram F. Malle (eds), 2002. *The Evolution of Language Out of Pre-Language.* New York: Benjamins

Glasser, Solange, 2016. "Synesthesia and Prodigiousness: The Case of Olivier Messiaen." *Musical Prodigies: Interpretations from Psychology, Education, Musicology, and Ethnomusicology*, ed. by Gary E. McPherson. Oxford: Oxford University Press, p. 453.

Glenberg, Arthur M., 2010. "Embodiment as a Unifying Perspective for Psychology." *Wiley Interdisciplinary Reviews: Cognitive Science* 1(4): 586-596.

Godsoe, William, Jill Jankowski, Robert D. Holt and Dominique Gravel, 2017. "Integrating Biogeography with Contemporary Niche Theory." *Trends in Ecology and Evolution* 32(7): 488-499.

Goldman, Steven L., 2022. *Science Wars: The Battle over Knowledge and Reality*. Oxford: Oxford University Press.

Goleman, Daniel, 1977. *Varieties of the Meditative Experience*. New York: Dutton.

Goleman, Daniel and Richard J. Davidson, 2017. *Altered Traits: Science Reveals How Meditation Changes Your Mind, Brain, and Body*. New York: Penguin.

Gómez-Robles, Aida, William D. Hopkins, Steven J. Schapiro and Chet C. Sherwood, 2015. "Relaxed Genetic Control of Cortical Organization in Human Brains Compared with Chimpanzees." *Proceedings of the National Academy of Sciences* 112(48): 14799-14804.

Good, B. J., 1994. *Medicine, Rationality and Experience: An Anthropological Perspective*. Cambridge: Cambridge University Press.

Good, M-J. D. *et al.* (eds), 1992. *Pain as Human Experience: An Anthropological Perspective*. Berkeley: University of California Press.

Goodenough, Ward H., 1971. *Culture, Language, and Society*. Reading, MA: Addison-Wesley.

Goodwyn, Erik D., 2012. *The Neurobiology of the Gods: How Brain Physiology Shapes the Recurrent Imagery of Myth and Dreams*. New York: Routledge.

Goodwyn, Erik D., 2016. *Healing Symbols in Psychotherapy: A Ritual Approach*. New York: Routledge.

Goody, Jack, 1968. "Time: Social Organization." *International Encyclopedia of the Social Sciences* 16: 30–42.

Goody, Jack, 2002. "The Anthropology of the Senses and Sensations." *La ricerca folklorica* 45: 17-28.

Goswami, Usha, 2013. *Analogical Reasoning in Children*. Washington, DC: Psychology Press.

Green, Adam E., David J. M. Kraemer, Jonathan A. Fugelsang, Jeremy R. Gray and Kevin N. Dunbar, 2012. "Neural Correlates of Creativity in Analogical Reasoning." *Journal of Experimental Psychology: Learning, Memory, and Cognition* 38(2): 264-272.

Gribizis, Alexandra, Xinxin Ge, Tanya L. Daigle, James B. Ackman, Hongkui Zeng, Daeyeol Lee and Michael C. Crair, 2019. "Visual Cortex Gains Independence from Peripheral Drive Before Eye Opening." *Neuron* 104(4): 711-723.

Grossberg, S. and A. Grunewald, 1997. "Cortical Synchronization and Perceptual Framing." *Journal of Cognitive Neuroscience* 9: 117–32.

Goulet, Jean-Guy, 1987. "Ways of Knowing: Towards a Narrative Ethnography of Experiences among the Dene Tha." *Journal of Anthropological Research* 50(2): 113-139.

Goulet, Jean-Guy, 1998. *Ways of Knowing: Experience, Knowledge, and Power Among the Dene Tha*. Lincoln, NE: University of Nebraska Press.

Govinda, A., 1974. *The Psychological Attitude of Early Buddhist Philosophy*. New York: Samuel Weiser.

Grant, Colin B., 2007. *Uncertainty and Communication: New Theoretical Investigations*. Berlin: Springer.

Gray, C .M. W. and Singer, 1989. "Stimulus-Specific Neuronal Oscillations in Orientation

Columns of Cat Visual Cortex." *Proceedings of the National Academy of Sciences USA* 86(5): 1698–1702.

Graziano, Michael S. A., 2013. *Consciousness and the Social Brain.* Oxford: Oxford University Press.

Green, Celia, 1968. *Lucid Dreams.* Oxford: Institute of Psychophysical Research.

Green, Elmer and Alyce Green, 1977. *Beyond Biofeedback.* Toronto, ON: Delacorte.

Griffin, Donald R., 2013. *Animal Minds: Beyond Cognition to Consciousness.* Chicago: University of Chicago Press.

Grimes, Ronald L., 2003. "Ritual Theory and the Environment." *The Sociological Review* 51(S2): 31-45.

Gros, Alexis Emanuel, 2017. "Alfred Schutz on Phenomenological Psychology and Transcendental Phenomenology." *Journal of Phenomenological Psychology* 48(2): 214-239.

Grossberg, S. and Grunewald, A., 1997. "Cortical Synchronization and Perceptual Framing." *Journal of Cognitive Neuroscience* 9: 117–32.

Gunaratana, Benepola Henepola, 1988. *The Jhanas in Theravada Buddhist Meditation.* Kandy, Sri Lanka: Buddhist Publication Society.

Gur, Moshe and D. Max Snodderly, 1997. "A Dissociation Between Brain Activity and Perception: Chromatically Opponent Cortical Neurons Signal Chromatic Flicker That Is Not Perceived." *Vision Research* 37(4): 377-382.

Gurwitsch, Aron, 1964. *The Field of Consciousness.* Pittsburgh. PA: Duquesne University Press.

Gurwitsch, Aron, 1966. *Studies in Phenomenology and Psychology.* Evanston, IL: Northwestern University Press.

Gurwitsch, Aron, 1967. "On the Intentionality of Consciousness." In *Phenomenology*, ed. by Joseph J. Kockelmans. Garden City, NY: Doubleday, pp. 118-137.

Gurwitsch Aaron, 1970. "Problems of the Life-World." In *Phenomenology and Social Reality*, ed. by M. Natanson. Dordrecht: Springer, pp. 35-61.

Gurwitsch, Aron, 1979. *Phenomenology and Theory of Science.* Evanston, IL: Northwestern University Press.

Habermas, Jürgen, 1992. *Postmetaphysical Thinking: Philosophical Essays.* Cambridge, MA: MIT Press.

Hageman, Joan H., Stanley Krippner and Ian Wickramasekera, 2008. "Sympathetic Reactivity During Meditation." *Subtle Energies and Energy Medicine Journal Archives* 19(2): 23-48.

Haier, Richard J., 2017. *The Neuroscience of Intelligence.* Cambridge: Cambridge University Press.

Hallowell, A. I., 2002[1960]. "Ojibwa Ontology, Behavior, and World View." *Readings in Indigenous Religions* 22: 17-49.

Hamill, James F., 1990. *Ethno-Logic: The Anthropology of Human Reasoning.* Urbana, IL: University of Illinois Press.

Hamilton, G., 2008. "Mythos and Mental Illness: Psychopathy, Fantasy, and Contemporary Moral Life." *Journal of Medical Humanities* 29: 231–242.

Hammer, Rubi, Erick J. Paul, Charles H. Hillman, Arthur F. Kramer, Neal J. Cohen and Aron K. Barbey, 2019. "Individual Differences in Analogical Reasoning Revealed by Multivariate Task-Based Functional Brain Imaging." *Neuroimage* 184: 993-1004.

Han, S., 2017. *The Sociocultural Brain: A Cultural Neuroscience Approach to Human Nature.* Oxford: Oxford University Press.

Haney, Kathleen, 2002. "The Role of Intersubjectivity and Empathy in Husserl's Foundational Project." In *Phenomenology World-Wide*, ed. by Anna-Teresa Tymieniecka. Dordrecht: Springer, pp. 146-158.

Hanna, Fred J., 1993a. "The Transpersonal Consequences of Husserl's Phenomenological Method." *The Humanistic Psychologist* 21(1): 41-57.

Hanna, Fred J., 1993b. "Rigorous Intuition: Consciousness, Being, and the Phenomenological Method." *Journal of Transpersonal Psychology* 25(2): 181-197

Hanna, Fred J., 1995. "Husserl on the Teachings of the Buddha." *The Humanistic Psychologist* 23(3): 365-372.

Hanna, Fred J., Brett D. Wilkinson and Joel Givens, 2017. "Recovering the Original Phenomenological Research Method: An Exploration of Husserl, Yoga, Buddhism, and New Frontiers in Humanistic Counseling." *The Journal of Humanistic Counseling* 56(2): 144-162.

Hanna, Robert, 2013. "Transcendental Idealism, Phenomenology, and the Metaphysics of Intentionality." *The Impact of Idealism: The Legacy of Post-Kantian German Thought* 1: 191-224.

Hannah, Barbara, 2015[1981]. *Encounters with the Soul: Active Imagination as Developed by C. G. Jung*. Ashville, NC: Chiron.

Harding, Brian, 2005. "Epoché, the Transcendental Ego, and Intersubjectivity in Husserl's Phenomenology." *Journal of Philosophical Research* 30: 141-156.

Harding, Douglas E., 1961. *On Having No Head*. New York: Arkana.

Hardy, Lee, 1999. "Translator's Introduction." In *The Idea of Phenomenology*, by Edmund Husserl. Dordrecht: Kluwer, pp. 1-13.

Harrington, D. L. *et al.*, 1998. "Cortical Networks Underlying Mechanisms of Time Perception." *Journal of Neuroscience* 18(3): 1085–95.

Harrington, D. L. *et al.*, 1999. "Specialized Neural Systems Underlying Representations of Sequential Movements." *Journal of Cognitive Neuroscience* 12: 56–77.

Harrington, D. L. *et al.*, 2004. "Does the Representation of Time Depend on the Cerebellum? Effect of Cerebellar Stroke." *Brain* 127: 561–74.

Harris, Martin (ed.), 2007. *Ways of Knowing: New Approaches in the Anthropology of Experience and Learning*. New York: Berghahn Books.

Hart, James G., 1992. *The Person and the Common Life: Studies in Husserlian Social Ethics*. Dordtecht: Kluwer.

Hart, James G., 1995. "Husserl and Fichte: With Special Regard to Husserl's Lectures on 'Fichte's Ideal of Humanity'." *Husserl Studies* 12(2): 135-163.

Hart, James G., 1997. "The *Summum Bonum* and Value-Wholes: Aspects of a Husserlian Axiology and Theology." In *Phenomenology of Values and Valuing*, ed. by James G. Hart and Lester Embree. Dordrecht: Kluwer, pp. 193-230.

Hart, James G. and Lester Embree (eds), 1997. *Phenomenology of Values and Valuing*. Dordrecht: Kluwer.

Hartelius, Glenn, Mariana Caplan and Mary Anne Rardin, 2007. "Transpersonal Psychology: Defining the Past, Divining the Future." *The Humanistic Psychologist* 35(2): 135-160.

Hartelius, Glenn, Holly Adler, Marie Isabelle Thouin-Savard, Gretchen Stamp, Maureen Harrahy and Seth Pardo, 2021. "Is Transpersonal Psychology in its Second Wave? Evidence from Bibliometric and Content Analyses of Two Transpersonal Journals." *The Journal of Transpersonal Psychology* 53(1): 9-30.

Harter, M., 1967. "Excitability Cycles and Cortical Scanning: A Review of two Hypotheses of Central Intermittency in Perception." *Psychological Bulletin* 68: 47–58.

Hartimo, Mirja, 2017. "Husserl and Hilbert." In *Essays on Husserl's Logic and Philosophy of Mathematics*, ed. by Stefania Centrone. Dordrecht: Springer, pp. 245-263.

Harvey, Oscar Jewel, David E. Hunt and Harold M. Schroder, 1961. *Conceptual Systems and Personality Organization*. New York: Wiley.

Hatfield, Elaine, Richard L. Rapson and Yen-Chi L. Le, 2011. "Emotional Contagion and Empathy." *The Social Neuroscience of Empathy*, ed. by Jean Decety and William John Ickes. Cambridge, MA: MIT Press, pp. 19-30.

Hauser, Marc, 2006. *Moral Minds: How Nature Designed Our Universal Sense of Right and Wrong*. Ecco/HarperCollins Publishers, 2006.

Havlík, Marek, 2017. "From Anomalies to Essential Scientific Revolution? Intrinsic Brain Activity in the Light of Kuhn's Philosophy of Science." *Frontiers in Systems Neuroscience* 11: 7.

Hawes, Leonard C., 1992. "The Politics of Articulation and Critical Communication Theory." *Annals of the International Communication Association* 15(1): 582-594.

Hayek, Friedrich A., 2014[1952]. *The Sensory Order and Other Writings on the Foundations of Theoretical Psychology*. Chicago: University of Chicago Press.

Hayman, Genevieve, 2016. "Mirror Neurons, Husserl, and Enactivism: An Analysis of Phenomenological Compatibility." *Perspectives: International Postgraduate Journal of Philosophy* 6 (1): 13-23.

Hecht, Erin E., Richard Patterson and Aron K. Barbey, 2012. "What Can Other Animals Tell Us About Human Social Cognition? An Evolutionary Perspective on Reflective and Reflexive Processing." *Frontiers in Human Neuroscience* 6: 224.

Heidegger, Martin, 1977. "The Question Concerning Technology." In *Basic Writings* (trans. by D. Krell). New York: Harper and Row.

Heidegger, Martin, 1996[1927]. *Being and Time*, Joan Stambaugh (trans.). Albany: State University of New York Press.

Heidegger, Martin, 2010[1995]. *The Phenomenology of Religious Life*. Bloomington, IN: Indiana University Press.

Heintz, Monica, 2021. *The Anthropology of Morality: A Dynamic and Interactionist Approach*. New York: Routledge.

Held, Klaus, 2003a. "Husserl's Phenomenology of the Life-World." In *The New Husserl: A Critical Reader*, ed. by Donn Weldon. Bloomington, IN: Indiana University Press, pp. 32-62.

Held, Klaus, 2003b. "Husserl's Phenomenological Method." In *The New Husserl: A Critical Reader*, ed. by Donn Weldon. Bloomington, IN: Indiana University Press, pp. 3-31.

Heller, Laurence and Aline LaPierre, 2012. *Healing Developmental Trauma: How Early Trauma Affects Self-Regulation, Self-Image, and the Capacity for Relationship*. North Atlantic Books.

Henrich, Joseph, Steven J. Heine and Ara Norenzayan, 2010. "The Weirdest People in the World?" *Behavioral and Brain Sciences* 33(2-3): 61-83.

Herculano-Houzel, Suzana, 2009. "The Human Brain in Numbers: A Linearly Scaled-Up Primate Brain." *Frontiers in Human Neuroscience* 3: 31. https://doi.org/10.3389/neuro.09.031.2009

Hertrich, Ingo, Susanne Dietrich, Corinna Blum and Hermann Ackermann, 2021. "The Role of the Dorsolateral Prefrontal Cortex for Speech and Language Processing." *Frontiers in Human Neuroscience* 15: 645209.

Hess, W. R., 1925. *On the Relations between Psychic and Vegetative Functions*. Zurich: Schabe.

Hewlett, Barry S., Hillary N. Fouts, Adam H. Boyette and Bonnie L. Hewlett, 2011. "Social Learning among Congo Basin Hunter–Gatherers." *Philosophical Transactions of the Royal Society B: Biological Sciences* 366(1567): 1168-1178.

Hickey, A. and C. Smith, 2020. "Working the Aporia: Ethnography, Embodiment and the Ethnographic Self." *Qualitative Research* 20(6): 819-36.

Hill, Kim, 2009. *The Question of Animal Culture.* Cambridge, MA: Harvard University Press.

Hill, S. J., 2019. *Confrontation with the Unconscious: Jungian Depth Psychology and Psychedelic Experience.* London: Aeon Books.

Hillman, James, 2021. *Archetypal Psychology: A Brief Account.* Dallas, TX: Spring Publications.

Hilton, Courtney B., Cody J. Moser, Mila Bertolo, Harry Lee-Rubin, Dorsa Amir, Constance M. Bainbridge, Jan Simson et al., 2022. "Acoustic Regularities in Infant-Directed Speech and Song Across Cultures." *Nature Human Behaviour* 18 July 2022: 1-12. https://doi.org/10.1038/s41562-022-01410-x

Hinton, S. C. and W. H. Meck, 1997. "The 'Internal Clocks' of Circadian and Interval Timing." *Endeavour* 21: 82.

Hobbs, Dave J., 2021. *Towards a Phenomenology of Values: Investigations of Worth.* New York: Routledge.

Hobeika, L., C. Diard-Detoeuf, B. Garcin, R. Levy and E. Volle, 2016. "General and Specialized Brain Correlates for Analogical Reasoning: A Meta-Analysis of Functional Imaging Studies." *Human Brain Mapping* 37(5): 1953-69.

Hobson, R. F., 2018. "The Archetypes of the Collective Unconscious." In *Analytical Psychology: A Modern Science,* ed. by M. Fordham. New York: Routledge, pp. 66-75.

Hodges, Matt, 2008. "Rethinking Time's Arrow: Bergson, Deleuze and the Anthropology of Time." *Anthropological Theory* 8(4): 399-429.

Hoffman, Donald D., 1998. *Visual Intelligence: How We Create What We See.* New York: Norton.

Hoffmeyer, Jesper, 2008. *Biosemiotics: An Examination into the Signs of Life and the Life of Signs.* Scranton, PA: University of Scranton Press.

Hofman, Michel A., 2014. "Evolution of the Human Brain: When Bigger is Better." *Frontiers in Neuroanatomy* 8: 15.

Holland, John H., 1992. "Complex Adaptive Systems." *Daedalus* 121(1): 17-30.

Hollan, Douglas W. and C. Jason Throop (eds), 2011. *The Anthropology of Empathy: Experiencing the Lives of Others in Pacific Societies.* Oxford: Berghahn Books.

Holloway, Ralph L., 1981. "Culture, Symbols, and Human Brain Evolution: A Synthesis." *Dialectical Anthropology* 5: 287 303.

Holloway, Ralph L., 1983a. "Human Brain Evolution." *Canadian Journal of Anthropology* 2: 215 230.

Holloway, Ralph L., 1983b. "Human Paleontological Evidence Relevant to Language Behavior." *Human Neurobiology* 2(3): 105-114.

Holloway, Ralph L., 1995. "Toward a Synthetic Theory of Human Brain Evolution." In *Origins of the Human Brain,* ed. by Jean-Pierre Changeux and Jean Chavaillon. Oxford: Clarenden, pp. 42-60.

Holloway, Ralph L., 2008. "The Human Brain Evolving: A Personal Retrospective." *Annual Review of Anthropology* 37: 1-19.

Holloway, Ralph L. and Marie Christine De La Costelareymondie, 1982. "Brain Endocast Asymmetry in Pongids and Hominids: Some Preliminary Findings on the Paleontology of Cerebral Dominance." *American Journal of Physical Anthropology* 58(1): 101-110.

Homer, W. J., 1964. *Seurat and the Science of Painting.* Cambridge, MA: MIT Press.

Hopp, Walter, 2008. "Husserl on Sensation, Perception, and Interpretation." *Canadian Journal of Philosophy* 38(2): 219-245.

Horst, Steven, 2010. "The Role of Phenomenology in Psychophysics." In *Handbook of Phenomenology and Cognitive Science*, ed by ed. by D. Schmicking and S. Gallagher. Dordrecht: Springer, pp. 446-469.

Horton, Robin, 1967. "African Traditional Thought and Western Science." *Africa: Journal of the International African Institute* Part 1, 37(1): 50–71; Part 2, 37(2): 155–187.

Hossain, F. M. Anayet and Korban Ali, 2014. "Relation Between Individual and Society." *Open Journal of Social Sciences* 2(8): 130-137.

Houshmound, Zara, Anne Harrington, Clifford Saron and Richard J. Davidson, 2002. "Training the Mind: First Steps in a Cross-Cultural Collaboration in Neuroscientific Research." In *Visions of Compassion: Western Scientists and Tibetan Buddhists Examine Human Nature*, ed. by the Dalai Lama XIV and Tenzin Gyatsho. Oxford: Oxford University Press, pp. 3-17.

Howard, Marc W. *et al.*, 2003. "Gamma Oscillations Correlate with Working Memory Load in Humans." *Cerebral Cortex* 13: 1369–1374.

Howell, Signe (ed), 1997. *The Ethnography of Moralities*. London: Routledge.

Howes, D., 1991a. *The Varieties of Sensory Experience: A Sourcebook in the Anthropology of the Senses*. Toronto, ON: University of Toronto Press.

Howes, D., 1991b. "Introduction: 'To Summon All the Senses'." In *The Varieties of Sensory Experience: A Sourcebook in the Anthropology of the Senses*, ed. By David Howes. Toronto, ON: University of Toronto Press, pp. 3-21.

Huberman, Andrew D., Marla B. Feller and Barbara Chapman, 2008. "Mechanisms Underlying Development of Visual Maps and Receptive Fields." *Annual Review of Neuroscience* 31: 479-509.

Hughes, D. O. and T. R. Trautmann (eds), 1995. *Time: Histories and Ethnologies*. Ann Arbor: University of Michigan Press.

Hunt, Harry T., 1995. *On the Nature of Consciousness: Cognitive, Phenomenological, and Transpersonal Perspectives*. New Haven, CT: Yale University Press.

Hunt, Harry T., 2012. "A Collective Unconscious Reconsidered: Jung's Archetypal Imagination in the Light of Contemporary Psychology and Social Science." *Journal of Analytical Psychology* 57(1): 76-98.

Hurford, James R., 1999. "The Evolution of Language and Languages." In *The Evolution of Culture*, ed. by Dunbar, Robin I. M., Chris Knight and Camilla Power. New Brunswick, NJ: Rutgers University Press, pp. 173-193.

Hurley, S. L., 1998. *Consciousness in Action*. Cambridge, MA: Harvard University Press.

Hussein, Basel Al-Sheikh, 2012. "The Sapir-Whorf Hypothesis Today." *Theory and Practice in Language Studies* 2(3): 642-646.

Husserl, Edmund, 1964a. *The Phenomenology of Internal Time-Consciousness*. Bloomington: Indiana University Press.

Husserl, Edmund, 1964b. "The Paris Lectures." In *The Paris Lectures*. Dordrecht: Springer, pp. 1-39.

Husserl, Edmund, 1969[1929]. *Formal and Transcendental Logic*, Trans. by Dorion Cairns. The Hague: Nijhoff.

Husserl, Edmund, 1970 [1900-01]. *Logical Investigations* (2 volumes), translated by J.N. Findley. New York: Humanities Press.

Husserl, Edmund, 1970[1936]. *The Crisis in European Sciences and Transcendental Phenomenology*. Evanston: Northwestern University Press.

Husserl, Edmund, 1973[1939]. *Experience and Judgment: Investigations in a Genealogy of Logic*. Evanston, IL: Northwestern University Press.

Husserl, Edmund, 1977[1925]. *Phenomenological Psychology: Lectures, Summer Semester, 1925*. Berlin: Springer.

Husserl, Edmund, 1980[1952]. *Ideas Pertaining to a Pure Phenomenology and to a Phenomenological Philosophy*. Third Book: *Phenomenology and the Foundation of the Sciences*. Translated by Ted Klein and William Pohl. The Hague: Nijhoff.

Husserl. Edmund, 1981[1917]. "Husserl's Inaugural Lecture at Freiburg im Breisgau (1917)." In *Husserl: Shorter Works*, ed. by Peter McCormick and Frederick Elliston. Notre Dame, IN: University of Notre Dame Press, pp. 10-17.

Husserl. Edmund, 1981[1941]. "Phenomenology and Anthropology." In *Husserl: Shorter Works*, ed. by Peter McCormick and Frederick Elliston. Notre Dame, IN: University of Notre Dame Press, pp. 315-323.

Husserl, Edmund, 1982[1913]. *Ideas Pertaining to a Pure Phenomenology and to a Phenomenological Philosophy*. First Book: *General Introduction to a Pure Phenomenology*, trans. by F. Kersten. The Hague: Nijhoff.

Husserl, Edmund, 1988[1908-1914]. *Vorlesungen über Ethik und Wertlehre 1908 - 1914*, trans. by Ullrich Melle, *Husserliana* XXVIII. Dordrecht: Kluwer.

Husserl, Edmund, 1989[1952]. *Ideas Pertaining to a Pure Phenomenology and to a Phenomenological Philosophy*. Second Book: *Studies in the Phenomenology of Constitution*. New York: Springer.

Husserl, Edmund, 1993[1931]. *Cartesian Meditations: An Introduction to Phenomenology*. The Hague: Martinus Nijhoff.

Husserl, Edmund, 1994a. *Early Writings in the Philosophy of Logic and Mathematics* [1890-1901]. Dordrecht: Kluwer.

Husserl, Edmund, 1994b. *Briefwechsel*. Band VII: *Wissenschaftlerkorrespondenz*, ed. by Karl Schuhmann. *Husserliana Dokumente* III, 7. Dordrecht: Kluwer, pp. 133–6.

Husserl, Edmund, 1995[1917]. "Fichte's Ideal of Humanity [Three Lectures]." *Husserl Studies* 12(2): 111-133.

Husserl, Edmund, 1997. *Psychological and Transcendental Phenomenology and the Confrontation with Heidegger (1927-1931)*. Dordrecht: Kluwer.

Husserl, Edmund, 1997[1907]. *Thing and Space: Lectures of 1907*. Dordrecht: Kluwer.

Husserl, Edmund, 1999. *The Idea of Phenomenology*. Dordrecht: Kluwer.

Husserl, Edmund, 2001[1920/24]. *Analyses Concerning Passive and Active Synthesis: Lectures on Transcendental Logic* (trans. by A. J. Steinbock). Dordrecht: Kluwer. [the "passive synthesis" lectures]

Husserl, Edmund, 2002[1910]. "Philosophy as Rigorous Science." In *New Yearbook for Phenomenology and Phenomenological Philosophy* 2, ed. by Burt Hopkins and Steven Crowell. New York: Routledge, pp. 249-295.

Husserl, Edmund, 2003[1887-1901]. *Philosophy of Arithmetic: Psychological and Logical Investigations with Supplementary Texts from 1887-1901* (trans. by D. Willard). Dordrecht: Kluwer.

Husserl, Edmund, 2005[1898-1925]. *Phantasy, Image Consciousness, and Memory* (trans. by J. B. Brough). Dordrecht: Springer.

Husserl, Edmund, 2006[1910-1911]. *The Basic Problems of Phenomenology*. Dordrecht: Springer.

Husserl, Edmund, 2008[1906-1907]. *Introduction to Logic and Theory of Knowledge, Lectures 1906/07*. Dordrecht: Springer.

Husserl, Edmund, 2008. "Edmund Husserl's Letter to Lucien Lévy-Bruhl" (trans. by D. Moran and L Steinacher). *New Yearbook for Phenomenology and Phenomenological Philosophy* 8: 349-354.

Husserl, Edmund, 2010[1907]. *The Idea of Phenomenology*. Dordrecht: Kluwer.

Husserl, Edmund, 2014. *Grenzprobleme der Phänomenologie*, ed. Rocus Sowa and Thomas Vongehr. Dordrecht: Springer.

Husserl, Edmund, 2019[1917/18]. *Logic and General Theory of Science*. Cham, Switzerland: Springer Nature.

Husserl, Edmund, 2019[1923/24]. *First Philosophy: Lectures 1923/24 and Related Texts from the Manuscripts (1920-1925)*. Dordrecht: Springer.

Hutcheson, Peter, 1980. "Husserl's Problem of Intersubjectivity." *Journal of the British Society for Phenomenology* 11(2): 144-162.

Hutchinson, G. E., 1965. "The Niche: An Abstractly Inhabited Hypervolume." In *The Ecological Theatre and the Evolutionary Play*, ed. by G. E. Hutchinson. New Haven: Yale University Press, pp. 26-78.

Hayek, Friedrich A., 2014[1952]. *The Sensory Order: An Inquiry into the Foundations of Theoretical Psychology*. Mansfield Center, MD: Martino.

Ihde, Don, 1991. *Instrumental Realism*. Bloomington: Indiana University Press.

Ihde, Don, 2012. *Experimental Phenomenology: Multistabilities*. Albany, NY: State University of New York Press.

Ihde, Don, 2016. *Husserl's Missing Technologies*. New York: Fordham University Press.

Immordino-Yang, Mary Helen, 2013. "Studying the Effects of Culture by Integrating Neuroscientific with Ethnographic Approaches." *Psychological Inquiry* 24(1): 42-46.

Inaba, D. S., and W. E. Cohen, 2004. *Uppers, Downers, and All Arounders: Physical and Mental Effects of Psychoactive Drugs*. Ashland, Oregon: CNS Productions.

Inglese, Silvia and Andrea Lavazza, 2022. "Neuroethics as a New Kind of Scientific Anthropology." *AJOB Neuroscience* 13(1): 40-43.

Ingold, Tim, 1992. "Culture and the Perception of the Environment." In *Bush Base, Forest Farm*, ed. by Elizabeth Croll and David Parkin. New York: Routledge, pp. 51-68.

Ingold, Tim, 2014. "That's Enough About Ethnography!" *Hau: Journal of Ethnographic Theory* 4(1): 383-395.

Inkpin, Andrew, 2016. *Disclosing the World: On the Phenomenology of Language*. Cambridge, MA: MIT Press.

Isenman, Lois D., 1997. "Toward an Understanding of Intuition and Its Importance in Scientific Endeavor." *Perspectives in Biology and Medicine* 40(3): 395-403.

Ito, Masao, 2004. "Historical Overview: The Search for inhibitory neurons and their function." In *Excitatory-Inhibitory Balance*, ed. by Takao K. Hensch and Michela Fagiolini. Boston, MA: Springer, pp. 1-10.

Ivry, R. B. and S. W. Keele, 1989. "Timing Functions of the Cerebellum." *Journal of Cognitive Neuroscience* 1: 136–52.

Jackson, Michael, ed., 1996. *Things as They Are: New Directions in Phenomenological Anthropology*. Washington, D. C.: Georgetown University Press.

Jackson, Michael, 2012. *Lifeworlds: Essays in Existential Anthropology*. Chicago: University of Chicago Press.

James, Wendy and David Mills (eds), 2020. *The Qualities of Time: Anthropological Approaches*. New York: Routledge.

James, William, 1890. *The Principles of Psychology* (1981 edition). Cambridge, MA.: Harvard University Press.

James, William, 1976 [1912]. *Essays in Radical Empiricism*. Cambridge, MA: Harvard University Press.

Jansen, Julia, 2005. "On the Development of Husserl's Transcendental Phenomenology of Imagination and Its Use for Interdisciplinary Research." *Phenomenology and the Cognitive Sciences* 4(2): 121-132.

Jansen, Julia, 2010. "Phenomenology, Imagination and Interdisciplinary Research." In *Handbook of Phenomenology and Cognitive Science*, ed. by S. Gallagher and D. Schmicking. Dordrecht: Springer, pp. 141–158.

Jantzen, K. J., F. L. Steinberg and J. A. S. Kelso, 2005. "Functional MRI Reveals the Existence of Modality and Coordination-Dependent Timing Networks." *NeuroImage* 25: 1031–42.

Jardine, James, 2014. "Husserl and Stein on the Phenomenology of Empathy: Perception and Explication." *Synthesis Philosophica* 29(2): 273–288.

Jarvie, Ian Charles. 1967. *The Revolution in Anthropology.* London: Routledge.

Jaspars, J., M. Hewstone and F.D. Fincham, 1983. "Attribution Theory and Research: The State of the Art." In *Attribution Theory and Research: Conceptual, Developmental and Social Dimensions,* ed. by J. Jaspars, F. D. Fincham and M. Hewstone. New York: Academic Press.

Jensen, R. T. and D. Moran (eds), 2013a. *The Phenomenology of Embodied Subjectivity.* New York: Springer.

Jensen, R. T. and D. Moran, 2013b. "Introduction: Some Themes in the Phenomenology of Embodiment." In *The Phenomenology of Embodied Subjectivity*, ed. by R. T. Jensen and D. Moran. New York: Springer, pp. vii-xxxiii.

Jerison, Harry J., 1973. *Evolution of the Brain and Intelligence.* New York: Academic Press.

Jerison, Harry J., 1985. "On the Evolution of Mind." In *Brain and Mind*, ed. by D.A. Oakley. New York: Methuen, pp. 1-31.

Jerison, Harry J., 2007. "Evolution of the Frontal Lobes." In *The Human Frontal Lobes: Functions and Disorders*, ed. by B. L. Miller and J. L. Cummings. New York: Guilford, pp. 107-120.

John, E. R., P. Easton and R. Isenhart, 1997. "Consciousness and Cognition May Be Mediated by Multiple Independent Coherent Ensembles." *Consciousness and Cognition* 6(1): 3-39.

Johnson, Galen A., 1980. "Husserl and History." *Journal of the British Society for Phenomenology* 11(1): 77-91.

Joliot, M., U. Ribary and R. Llinas, 1994. "Human Oscillatory Brain Activity near 40 Hz Coexists with Cognitive Temporal Binding." *Proceedings of the National Academy of Sciences USA* 91: 11748–11751.

Jones, D. N., 2014. "Predatory Personalities as Behavioural Mimics and Parasites: Mimicry Deception Theory." *Perspectives on Psychological Science* 9: 445-451.

Jones, Edward E., 1986. "Interpreting Interpersonal Behavior: The Effects of Expectancies." *Science* 234(4772): 41-46.

Jordan, Gabriele and John Mollon, 2019. "Tetrachromacy: The Mysterious Case of Extra-Ordinary Color Vision." *Current Opinion in Behavioral Sciences* 30: 130-134.

Jorgensen, Dan, 1980. "What's in a Name: The Meaning of Nothingness in *Telefolmin*." *Ethos* 8(4): 349-366.

Joseph, Rhawn, 2013. *The Right Brain and the Unconscious: Discovering the Stranger Within.* New York: Springer.

Joyce, Richard, 2007. *The evolution of morality.* Cambridge, MA: MIT Press.

Jung, Carl G., 1953 [1943/45]. *Two Essays on Analytical Psychology.* London: Routledge & Kegan Paul.

Jung, Carl G., 1954. *The Development of Personality.* London: Routledge and Kegan Paul. (Collected Works No. 17).

Jung, Carl G., 1956 [1912]. *Symbols of Transformation: An Analysis of the Prelude to a Case of Schizophrenia*. London: Routledge and Kegan Paul (Collected Works No. 5).

Jung, Carl G., 1965. *Memories, Dreams, Reflections*. New York: Vintage Books.

Jung, Carl G., 1968a. *The Archetypes and the Collective Unconscious* (Collected Works No. 9). Princeton, NJ: Princeton University Press.

Jung, Carl G., 1968b [1934, revised 1954]. "Archetypes of the Collective Unconscious." In *The Archetypes and the Collective Unconscious*. Princeton, NJ: Princeton University Press, pp. 3-41 (Collected Works No. 9).

Jung, Carl G., 1968c [1936/37]. "The Concept of the Collective Unconscious." In *The Archetypes and the Collective Unconscious*. Princeton, NJ: Princeton University Press, pp. 42-53 (Collected Works No. 9).

Jung, Carl G., 1969a. *The Structure and Dynamics of the Psyche*. Princeton, NJ: Princeton University Press (Collected Works No. 8).

Jung, Carl G., 1969b[1946]. "On the nature of the psyche." In *The Structure and Dynamics of the Psyche*. Princeton, NJ: Princeton University Press, pp. 159-234 (Collected Works No. 8).

Jung, Carl G., 1969c[1919]. "Instinct and the Unconscious." in *The Structure and Dynamics of the Psyche*. Princeton, NJ: Princeton University Press, pp. 129-138 (Collected Works No. 8).

Jung, Carl G., 1970 [1955/56]). *Mysterium Coniunctionis: An Inquiry into the Separation and Synthesis of Psychic Opposites in Alchemy*. Princeton, NJ: Princeton University Press (Collected Works No. 14).

Jung, Carl G., 1971. *Psychological Types*. Princeton, N.J.: Princeton University Press (Collected Works No. 6).

Kagan, Jerome, 2013. *The Human Spark: The Science of Human Development*. New York: Basic Books.

Kahane, Sylvain, 2001. "What Is a Natural Language and How To Describe It? Meaning-Text Approaches in Contrast with Generative Approaches." In *International Conference on Intelligent Text Processing and Computational Linguistics*, ed. by Alexander Gelbukh. Berlin: Springer, pp. 1-17.

Kalb, Don, 2018. "Why I Will Not Make It as a 'Moral Anthropologist'." In *Moral Anthropology: A Critique*. Oxford: Berghahn Books, pp. 65-76.

Kanizsa, Gaetano, 1955. "Margini quasi-percettivi in campi con stimolazione omogenea." *Rivista di Psicologia* 49(1): 7–30.

Kapferer, Bruce and Marina Gold (eds), 2018a. *Moral Anthropology: A Critique*. Oxford: Berghahn Books.

Kapferer, Bruce and Marina Gold (eds), 2018b. "Introduction: Reconceptualizing the Discipline." In *Moral Anthropology: A Critique*. Oxford: Berghahn Books, pp. 1-24.

Kapoor, Vishal, Abhilash Dwarakanath, Shervin Safavi, Joachim Werner, Michel Besserve, Theofanis I. Panagiotaropoulos and Nikos K. Logothetis, 2022. "Decoding Internally Generated Transitions of Conscious Contents in the Prefrontal Cortex without Subjective Reports." *Nature Communications* 13(1): 1-16.

Karecki, Madge, 1997. "Discovering the Roots of Ritual." *Missionalia* 25(2): 169-177.

Karl, Johannes A. *et al.*, 2020. "The Cross-Cultural Validity of the Five-Facet Mindfulness Questionnaire Across 16 Countries." *Mindfulness* 11(5): 1226-1237.

Katz, J. and T. J. Csordas, 2003. "Phenomenological Ethnography in Sociology and Anthropology." *Ethnography* 4(3): 275–288.

Kay, Paul and Luisa Maffi, 1999. "Color Appearance and the Emergence and Evolution of Basic Color Lexicons." *American Anthropologist* 101(4): 743-760.

Kays, Jill L., Robin A. Hurley and Katherine H. Taber, 2012. "The Dynamic Brain: Neuroplasticity and Mental Health." *The Journal of Neuropsychiatry and Clinical Neurosciences* 24(2): 118-124.

Kearney, Michael, 1975. "World View Theory and Study." *Annual Review of Anthropology* 4(1): 247-270.

Keith, Kenneth D. (ed), 2019. *Cross-Cultural Psychology: Contemporary Themes and Perspectives.* New York: Wiley.

Keijzer, Fred A., 2017. "Evolutionary Convergence and Biologically Embodied Cognition." *Interface Focus* 7(3): 20160123, http://dx.doi.org/10.1098/rsfs.2016.0123.

Kendler, Kenneth S., L. M. Karkowski and C. A. Prescott, 1999. "Fears and Phobias: Reliability and Heritability." *Psychological Medicine* 29(3): 539-553.

Kern, Iso, 2019. "Husserl's Phenomenology of Intersubjectivity." In *Husserl's Phenomenology of Intersubjectivity,* ed. by Frode Kjosevik, Christian Beyer and Christel Fricke. New York: Routledge, pp. 11-89.

Kersten, Frederick, 1973. "Husserl's Doctrine of Noesis-Noema." In *Phenomenology: Continuation and Criticism,* ed. by F. Kersten and Richard M. Zaner. Dordrecht: Springer, pp. 114-144.

Kevan, Peter G., Lars Chittka and Adrian G. Dyer, 2001. "Limits to the Salience of Ultraviolet: Lessons from Colour Vision in Bees and Birds." *Journal of Experimental Biology* 204(14): 2571-2580.

Keysers, Christian and Luciano Fadiga (eds.), 2017. *The Mirror Neuron System: A Special Issue of Social Neuroscience.* Washington, D. C.: Psychology Press.

Kilner, James M. and R. N. Lemon, 2013. "What We Know Currently about Mirror Neurons." *Current Biology* 23(23): R1057-R1062.

Kilpatrick, Lisa A. *et al.*, 2011. "Impact of Mindfulness-Based Stress Reduction Training on Intrinsic Brain Connectivity." *Neuroimage* 56(1): 290-298.

Kim, Choong Soon, 1990. "The Role of the Non-Western Anthropologist Reconsidered: Illusion Versus Reality." *Current Anthropology* 31(2): 196-201.

King, Charles, 2020. *Gods of the Upper Air: How a Circle of Renegade Anthropologists Reinvented Race, Sex, and Gender in the Twentieth Century.* New York: Anchor.

Kjosevik, Frode, Christian Beyer and Christel Fricke (eds), 2019. *Husserl's Phenomenology of Intersubjectivity.* New York: Routledge.

Klopf, A. H., 1982. *The Hedonistic Neuron: A Theory of Memory, Learning and Intelligence.* New York: Hemisphere.

Klopf, A. H., James S. Morgan and Scott E. Weaver, 1993. "Modeling Nervous System Function with a Hierarchical Network of Control Systems that Learn." In *From Animals to Animats 2: Proceedings of the Second International Conference on Simulation of Adaptive Behavior* (Vol. 2), ed. by Jean-Arcady Meyer, Herbert L. Roitblat, Stewart W. Wilson and Stewart W. Wilson. Cambridge, MA: MIT Press, pp. 254-261.

Kluckhohn, Clyde, 1955. "Ethical Relativity: *sic et non.*" *The Journal of Philosophy* 52(23): 663-677.

Kluckhohn, Clyde E. and Henry A. Murray, 1948. *Personality in Nature, Society, and Culture.* New York: Knopf.

Kluger, H. Y., 1975. "Archetypal Dreams and 'Everyday' Dreams: A Statistical Investigation into Jung's Theory of the Collective Unconscious." *The Israel Annals of Psychiatry and Related Disciplines* 13(1): 6-47.

Knibbe, Kim and Els van Houtert, 2018. "Religious Experience and Phenomenology." *The International Encyclopedia of Anthropology,* ed. by H. Callen. New York: Wiley, pp. 1-10.

Knibbe, Kim and Peter Versteeg, 2008. "Assessing Phenomenology in Anthropology: Lessons from the Study of Religion and Experience." *Critique of Anthropology* 28(1): 47-62.

Knight, Daniel M., 2021. *Vertiginous Life: An Anthropology of Time and the Unforeseen.* New York: Berghahn Books.

Knorr-Cetina, Karin D. 2013. *The Manufacture of Knowledge: An Essay on the Constructivist and Contextual Nature of Science.* Amsterdam: Elsevier.

Koch, Christof, 2004. *The Quest for Consciousness: A Neurobiological Approach.* Englewood, CO: Roberts.

Koch, Christof, 2005. "The Movie in Your Head." *Scientific American Mind*, October.

Koch, Christof, 2019. *The Feeling of Life Itself: Why Consciousness Is Widespread but Can't Be Computed.* Cambridge, MA: MIT Press.

Koch, Christof, Marcello Massimini, Melanie Boly and Giulio Tononi, 2016. "Neural Correlates of Consciousness: Progress and Problems." *Nature Reviews Neuroscience* 17(5): 307-321.

Kockelmans, J. J., 1967. *Phenomenology: The Philosophy of Edmund Husserl.* Garden City, New York: Doubleday.

Koepping, Klaus-Peter, 1983. *Adolf Bastian and the Psychic Unity of Mankind: The Foundations of Anthropology in Nineteenth Century Germany.* St. Lucia: University of Queensland Press.

Koepping, Klaus-Peter, 1995. "Enlightenment and Romanticism in the Work of Adolf Bastian: The Historical Roots of Anthropology in the Nineteenth Century." In *Fieldwork and Footnotes: Studies in the History of European Anthropology,* ed. by Arturo Alvarez Roldan and Han Vermeulen. New York: Routledge, pp. 89-106.

Kohak, Erazim V., 1978. *Idea and Experience: Edmund Husserl's Project of Phenomenology in Ideas I.* Chicago: University of Chicago Press.

Kolb, Bryan, Allonna Harker and Robbin Gibb, 2017. "Principles of Plasticity in the Developing Brain." *Developmental Medicine and Child Neurology* 59(12): 1218-1223.

Kolk, Sharon M. and Pasko Rakic, 2022. "Development of Prefrontal Cortex." *Neuropsychopharmacology* 47(1): 41-57.

König, Viola, 2007. "Adolf Bastian and the Sequel: Five Companions and Successors as Collectors for Berlin's Royal Museum of Ethnology." *Adolf Bastian and His Universal Archive of Humanity: The Origins of German Anthropology,* ed. by Manuela Fischer, Peter Bolz and Susan Kamel. Zürich: Georg Olms Verlag, pp. 127-139.

Kortooms, Toine, 2002. *Phenomenology of Time: Edmund Husserl's Analysis of Time-Consciousness.* Dortrecht: Kluwer.

Koukal, D. R., 2008. "The Necessity of Communicating Phenomenological Insights and Its Difficulties." In *Meaning and Language: Phenomenological Perspectives,* ed. by Filip Mattens. Dordrecht: Springer, pp. 256-279.

Krieger, Nancy M., 2014. *Bridges to Consciousness: Complexes and Complexity.* New York: Routledge.

Krippner, Stanley, 1994. "Waking Life, Dream Life, and the Construction of Reality." *Anthropology of Consciousness* 5(3): 17-23.

Krippner, Stanley, 1997. "The Varieties of Dissociative Experience." In *Broken Images, Broken Selves: Dissociative Narratives in Clinical Practice,* ed. by S. Krippner and S. M. Powers. Washington, DC: Brunner/Mazel, pp. 336-362.

Krippner, Stanley, 2000. "The Epistemology and Technologies of Shamanic States of Consciousness." *Journal for Consciousness Studies* 7(11–12): 93–118.

Krippner, Stanley and Allan Combs, 2002. "The Neurophenomenology of Shamanism: An essay review." *Journal of Consciousness Studies* 9(3): 77-82.

Kronenfeld, David B., Giovanni Bennardo, Victor C. De Munck and Michael D. Fischer (eds), 2015. *A Companion to Cognitive Anthropology.* New York: Wiley.

Krug, Kristine, 2012. "Principles of Function in the Visual System." In *Sensory Perception: Mind and Matter,* ed. by Friedrich G. Barth, Patrizia Giampieri-Deutsch and Hans-Dieter Klein. Vienna: Springer, pp 41-56.

Kuhn, Thomas, 1977. *The Essential Tension.* Chicago: University of Chicago Press.

Kulenović, Nina, 2021. "The Explanatory Power of the Concept of Embodiment in Anthropology." *Issues in Ethnology and Anthropology* 16(2): 325-351.

Kuo, Wen-Jui, Tomas Sjöström, Yu-Ping Chen, Yen-Hsiang Wang and Chen-Ying Huang, 2009. "Intuition and Deliberation: Two Systems for Strategizing in the Brain." *Science* 324(5926): 519-522.

Kuznar, Lawrence A., 2008. *Reclaiming a Scientific Anthropology.* Walnut Creek, CA: Rowman Altamira.

Kwant, Remy C., 1965. *Phenomenology of Language.* Pittsburgh, PA: Duquesne University Press.

LaBerge, Stephen, L. Levitan and W. C. Dement, 1986. "Lucid Dreaming: Physiological Correlates of Consciousness during REM Sleep." *Journal of Mind and Behavior* 7: 251-258.

Labov, W., 1972. "The Transformation of Experience in Narrative Syntax," In *Language in the Inner City,* ed. by W. Labov. Philadelphia: University of Pennsylvania Press, pp. 354–96.

Lahood, Gregg, 2007. "One Hundred Years of Sacred Science: Participation and Hybridity in Transpersonal Anthropology." *ReVision* 29(3): 37-49.

Laidlaw, James, 2014. *The Subject of Virtue: An Anthropology of Ethics and Freedom.* Cambridge: Cambridge University Press.

Laland, Kevin N. and Bennett G. Galef (eds), 2009. *The Question of Animal Culture.* Cambridge, MA: Harvard University Press.

Lambek, Michael, 2010. *Ordinary Ethics: Anthropology, Language, and Action.* New York: Fordham University Press.

Landgrebe, Ludwig, 1949. "Phenomenology and Metaphysics." *Philosophy and Phenomenological Research* 10(2): 197-205.

Landgrebe, Ludwig, 1981. *The Phenomenology of Edmund Husserl: Six Essays.* Ithaca, NY: Cornell University Press.

Latour, P. L., 1967. "Evidence of Internal Clocks in the Human Operator." *Acta Psycholgica* 27: 341–348.

Laughlin, Charles D., 1988a. "The Prefrontosensorial Polarity Principle: Toward a Neurophenomenology of Intentionality." *Biology Forum* 81(2): 243-260.

Laughlin, Charles D. 1988b. "Transpersonal Anthropology: Some Methodological Issues." *Western Canadian Anthropologist* 5: 29-60.

Laughlin, Charles D., 1989a. "Brain, Culture and Evolution: Some Basic Issues in Neuroanthropology." In *A Different Drummer,* ed. by B. Cox, V. Blundell and J. Chevalier. Ottawa, Ontario: Carleton University Press, pp. 145-156.

Laughlin, Charles D., 1989b. "Ritual and the Symbolic Function: A Summary of Biogenetic Structural Theory." *Journal of Ritual Studies* 4(1): 15-39.

Laughlin, Charles D., 1990a. "At Play in the Fields of the Lord: The Role of Metanoia in the Development of Consciousness." *Play and Culture* 3(3): 173-192.

Laughlin, Charles D., 1990b. "Ritual and the Symbolic Function: A Summary of Biogenetic Structuralism." *Journal of Ritual Studies* 4(1): 15-39.

Laughlin, Charles D., 1991. "Pre- and Perinatal Brain Development and Enculturation: A Biogenetic Structural Approach." *Human Nature* 2(3): 171-213.

Laughlin, Charles D., 1992a. "Time, Intentionality, and a Neurophenomenology of the Dot." *Anthropology of Consciousness* 3(3 & 4): 14-27.

Laughlin, Charles D., 1992b. *Scientific Explanation and the Life-World: A Biogenetic Structural Theory of Meaning and Causation*, Report No. CP-2. Sausalito, CA: Institute of Noetic Sciences.

Laughlin, Charles D., 1992c. "Consciousness in Biogenetic Structural Theory." *Anthropology of Consciousness* 3(1-2): 17-22.

Laughlin, Charles D., 1993. "Fuzziness and Phenomenology in Ethnological Research: Insights from Fuzzy Set Theory." *Journal of Anthropological Research* 49(1): 17-37.

Laughlin, Charles D., 1994a. "Psychic Energy and Transpersonal Experience: A Biogenetic Structural Account of the Tibetan *Dumo* Practice." In *Being Changed by Cross-Cultural Encounters*, ed. by D. E. Young and J.-G. Goulet. Peterborough, Ontario: Broadview Press, pp. 99-134.

Laughlin, Charles D. 1994b. "Apodicticity: The Problem of Absolute Certainty in Transpersonal Anthropology." *Anthropology and Humanism* 19(2): 1-15.

Laughlin, Charles D., 1994c. "Transpersonal Anthropology, Then and Now." *Transpersonal Review* 1(1): 7-10.

Laughlin, Charles D., 1996. "Archetypes, Neurognosis and the Quantum Sea." *Journal of Scientific Exploration* 10(3): 375-400.

Laughlin, Charles D., 1997a. "Body, Brain, and Behavior: The Neuroanthropology of the Body Image." *Anthropology of Consciousness* 8(2-3): 49-68.

Laughlin, Charles D., 1997b. "The Nature of Intuition: A Neuropsychological Approach." in *Intuition: The Inside Story*, ed. by Robbie E. Davis-Floyd and P. Sven Arvidson. New York: Routledge, pp. 19-37.

Laughlin, Charles D., 1997c. "The Cycle of Meaning: Some Methodological Implications of Biogenetic Structural Theory." In *Anthropology of Religion: Handbook of Theory and Method*, ed. by S. Glazier. Westport, CT: Greenwood Press, pp. 471-488.

Laughlin, Charles D., 2004. "Art and Spirit: Brain, the Navajo Concept of *Hozho*, and Kandinsky's 'Inner Necessity'." *International Journal of Transpersonal Studies* 23: 1-20.

Laughlin, Charles D., 2011a. *Communing with the Gods: Consciousness, Culture and the Dreaming Brain*. Brisbane, Australia: Daily Grail.

Laughlin, Charles D., 2011b. "Communing with the Gods: The Dreaming Brain in Cross-Cultural Perspective." *Time and Mind* 4(2): 155-188.

Laughlin, Charles D., 2012. "Transpersonal Anthropology: What Is It, and What Are the Problems We Face Doing It?" In *Paranthropology: Anthropological Approaches to the Paranormal*, ed. by Jack Hunter. Bristol, UK: Paranthropology, pp. 67-95.

Laughlin, Charles D., 2013a. "The Ethno-Epistemology of Transpersonal Experience: The View from Transpersonal Anthropology." *International Journal of Transpersonal Studies* 32(1): 43-50.

Laughlin, Charles D., 2013b. "The Self: A Transpersonal Neuroanthropological Account." *International Journal of Transpersonal Studies* 32(1): 100-116.

Laughlin, Charles D., 2017a. "Conceptual Systems Theory: A Neglected Perspective for the Anthropology of Consciousness." *Anthropology of Consciousness* 28(1): 31-68.

Laughlin, Charles D., 2017b. "Sensory Dots, No-Self and Stream-Entry: The Significance of Buddhist Contemplative Development for Transpersonal Studies." *International Journal of Transpersonal Studies* 36(1), 4-38.

Laughlin, Charles D., 2020a. *The Contemplative Brain: Meditation, Phenomenology and Self-Discovery from a Neuroanthropological Point of View*. Brisbane, Australia: Daily Grail.

Laughlin, Charles D., 2020b. "Supernatural and the Invisible: A Biogenetic Structural Account." In *The Supernatural After the Neuro-Turn*, ed. by Pieter F Craffert, John R. Baker and Michael James Winkelman. New York: Routledge, pp. 29-47.

Laughlin, Charles D., n.d. "Consciousness as an Intelligent Complex Adaptive System." Forthcoming.

Laughlin, Charles D. and Elizabeth R. Allgeier, 1979. *An Ethnography of the So of Northeastern Uganda* (2 vols.). New Haven, CT: HRAF Press.

Laughlin, Charles D. and Ivan A. Brady, eds., 1978. *Extinction and Survival in Human Populations*. New York: Columbia University Press.

Laughlin, Charles D. and Eugene, G. d'Aquili, 1974. *Biogenetic Structuralism*. New York: Columbia University Press.

Laughlin, Charles D. and J. H. N. Loubser, 2010. "Neurognosis: The Development of Neural Models, and the Study of the Ancient Mind." *Time and Mind* 3(2): 135-158.

Laughlin, Charles D. and John McManus, 1995. "The Relevance of the Radical Empiricism of William James to the Anthropology of Consciousness." *Anthropology of Consciousness* 6(3): 34–46.

Laughlin, Charles D., John McManus and Eugene G. d'Aquili, 1990. *Brain, Symbol and Experience: Toward a Neurophenomenology of Consciousness*. New York: Columbia University Press.

Laughlin, Charles D., John McManus and Eugene G. d'Aquili, 1993. "Mature Contemplation." *Zygon* 28(2): 133-176.

Laughlin, Charles D., John McManus and Jon Shearer, 1983. "Dreams, Trance and Visions: What a Transpersonal Anthropology Might Look Like." *Phoenix: The Journal of Transpersonal Anthropology* 7(1/2): 141-159.

Laughlin, Charles D., John McManus and Jon Shearer, 1993a. "The Function of Dreaming in the Cycles of Cognition." In *The Function of Dreaming*, ed. by A. Moffitt *et al*. Albany: SUNY Press.

Laughlin, Charles D., John McManus and Jon Shearer, 1993b. "Transpersonal Anthropology." In *Paths Beyond Ego: The Transpersonal Vision*, ed. by R. Walsh and F. Vaughan. Los Angeles, CA: Tarcher, pp. 190-195.

Laughlin, Charles D., John McManus and Christopher D. Stephens, 1981. "A Model of Brain and Symbol." *Semiotica* 33(3/4): 211 236.

Laughlin, Charles D., John McManus and Mark Webber, 1984. "Neurognosis, Individuation, and Tibetan Arising Yoga Practice." *Phoenix: The Journal of Transpersonal Anthropology* 8: 91-106.

Laughlin, Charles D. and Adam J. Rock, 2013. "Neurophenomenology: Enhancing the Experimental and Cross-Cultural Study of Brain and Experience." In *The Wiley-Blackwell Handbook of Transpersonal Psychology*, ed. by H. Friedman and G. Hartelius. New York: Wiley, pp. 261-280.

Laughlin, Charles D. and Adam Rock, 2014. "What Can We Learn from Shamans' Dreaming? A Cross-Cultural Exploration." *Dreaming* 24(4): 233-252.

Laughlin, Charles D. and Adam Rock, 2021. "Transpersonal Phenomenology: The Cosmological and Spiritual Dimensions of the Husserlian Epoché." *Transpersonal Psychology Review* 23(2): 41-62.

Laughlin, Charles D. and Christopher D. Stephens, 1980. "Symbolism, Canalization and P-Structure." In *Symbol as Sense*, ed. by M. L. Foster and S. Brandis. New York: Academic Press, pp. 323-363.

Laughlin, Charles D. and Melanie Takahashi, 2020. "Mystical Love: The Universal Solvent." *Anthropology of Consciousness* 31(1): 5-62.

Laughlin, Charles D. and C. Jason Throop, 2001. "Imagination and Reality: on the Relations between Myth, Consciousness, and the Quantum Sea." *Zygon* 36(4): 709–36.

Laughlin, Charles D. and C. Jason Throop, 2003. "Experience, Culture, and Reality: The Significance of Fisher Information for Understanding the Relationship between Alternative States of Consciousness and the Structures of Reality." *International Journal of Transpersonal Studies* 22: 7–26.

Laughlin, Charles D. and C. Jason Throop, 2006. "Cultural Neurophenomenology: Integrating Experience, Culture and Reality through Fisher Information." *Journal Culture & Psychology* 12(3): 305-337.

Laughlin, Charles D. and C. Jason Throop, 2008. "Continuity, Causation and Cyclicity: A Cultural Neurophenomenology of Time-Consciousness." *Time and Mind* 1: 159-186.

Laughlin, Charles D. and C. Jason Throop, 2009. "Husserlian Meditations and Anthropological Reflections: Toward a Cultural Neurophenomenology of Experience and Reality." *Anthropology of Consciousness* 20(2): 130-170.

Laughlin, Charles D. and Vincenza A. Tiberia, 2012. "Archetypes: Toward a Jungian Anthropology of Consciousness." *Anthropology of Consciousness* 23(2): 127-157.

Laughlin, Charles D. and Vincenza A. Tiberia, 2016. "Dream Incubation: The Roles of Instinct and Archetype in Ritual." *Journal of Social Sciences* (Kuwait) 28: 458-486.

Lavazza, Andrea (ed), 2016. *Frontiers in Neuroethics: Conceptual and Empirical Advancements.* Cambridge: Cambridge Scholars Publishing.

Laycock, Steven W., 1994. *Mind as Mirror and the Mirroring of Mind: Buddhist Reflections on Western Phenomenology.* Albany, NY: State University of New York Press.

Leach, Edmund R., 1966. "G. Ritualization in Man: Ritualization in Man in Relation To Conceptual and Social Development." *Philosophical Transactions of the Royal Society of London.* Series B, *Biological Sciences* 251(772): 403-408.

Leder, Drew, 1990. *The Absent Body.* Chicago: University of Chicago Press.

LeDoux, J. E., 2020a. "How Does the Non-Conscious Become Conscious?" *Current Biology* 30: R196–R199.

LeDoux, J. E., 2020b. "Thoughtful Feelings." *Current Biology* 30: R619–R623.

LeDoux, J. E, and R. Brown, 2017. "A Higher-Order Theory of Emotional Consciousness." *Proceedings of the National Academy of Sciences USA* 114: E2016–E2025.

LeDoux, J. E. and W. Hirst (eds), 1986. *Mind and Brain: Dialogues in Cognitive Neuroscience.* Cambridge: Cambridge University Press.

Lee, Nam-In, 2010. "Phenomenology of Language Beyond the Deconstructive Philosophy of Language." *Continental Philosophy Review* 42(4): 465-481.

Lee, Nam-In, 2019. "The Pluralistic Concept of the Life-World and the Various Fields of the Phenomenology of the Life-World in Husserl." *Husserl Studies* 36: 47–68.

Legerstee, Maria, David W. Haley and Marc H. Bornstein (eds.), 2013. *The Infant Mind: Origins of the Social Brain.* New York: Guilford Press.

Lehar, S., 2003. *Gestalt Isomorphism and the Primacy of Subjective Conscious Experience: A Gestalt Bubble Model.* Mahwah, NJ: Erlbaum.

Lehar, S., 2004. "Gestalt Isomorphism and the Primacy of Subjective Conscious Experience: A Gestalt Bubble Model." *Behavioral and Brain Sciences* 26(4): 375–444.

Lejeune, H. and J. H. Wearden, 2006. "Scalar Properties in Animal Timing: Conformity and Violations." *Quarterly Journal of Experimental Psychology* 59(11): 1875–1908.

Lende, Daniel H. and Greg Downey, 2012. *The Encultured Brain: An Introduction to Neuroanthropology.* Cambridge, MA: MIT Press.

Lengermann, Patricia M. and Jill Niebrugge, 1995. "Intersubjectivity and Domination: A Feminist Investigation of the Sociology of Alfred Schutz." *Sociological Theory* 13(1): 25-36.

Lenneberg, E. H., 1967. *Biological Foundations of Language.* New York: Wiley.

Lett, James, 1997. *Science, Reason, and Anthropology: The Principle of Rational Inquiry.* New York: Rowman & Littlefield.

Leuven, Husserl-Archives, 2007. "The Rescue of Husserl's Nachlass and the Founding of the Husserl-Archives." *History of the Husserl-Archives Leuven.* Dordrecht: Springer, pp. 39-69.

LeVasseur, Jeanne J., 2003. "The Problem of Bracketing in Phenomenology." *Qualitative Health Research* 13(3): 408-420.

Levering, Bas and Max Van Manen, 2002. "Phenomenological Anthropology in the Netherlands and Flanders." In *Phenomenology World-Wide,* ed. by Anna-Teresa Tymieniecka. Dordrecht: Springer, pp. 274-286.

Levinas, Emmanuel, 1967. "Intuition of Essences." In *Phenomenology,* ed. by Joseph J. Kockelmans. Garden City, NY: Doubleday, pp. 83-105.

Levinas, Emmanuel, 1995. *The Theory of Intuition in Husserl's Phenomenology* (second edition), trans. A. Orianne. Evanston, IL: Northwestern University Press.

Lévi-Strauss, Claude, 2021[1962]. *Wild Thought: A New Translation of "La Pensée sauvage".* Chicago: University of Chicago Press.

Levitan, Carmel A., Yih-Hsin A. Ban, Noelle RB Stiles and Shinsuke Shimojo, 2015. "Rate Perception Adapts Across the Senses: Evidence for a Unified Timing Mechanism." *Scientific Reports* 5(1): 1-6.

Levy-Bruhl, Lucein, 1966[1923]. *Primitive Mentality.* Boston: Beacon Press.

Lewis, P. A. and R. C. Miall, 2006. "Remembering the Time: A Continuous Clock." *Trends in Cognitive Science* 10(9): 401–6.

Lewis, P. A. and V. Walsh, 2005. "Time Perception: Components of the Brain's Clock." *Current Biology* 24: R384–R391.

Lex, Barbara W., 1979. "The Neurobiology of Ritual Trance." In *The Spectrum of Ritual,* ed. by Eugene G. d'Aquili, Charles D. Laughlin and John McManus. New York: Columbia University Press, pp. 117-151.

Li, Charles N., 2002. "Missing Links, Issues and Hypotheses in the Evolutionary Origin of Language." In *The Evolution of Language Out of Pre-Language,* ed. by T. Givón and Bertram F. Malle. New York: Benjamins, pp. 83-106.

Li, Jingjing, 2016. "Buddhist Phenomenology and the Problem of Essence." *Comparative Philosophy* 7(1): 59-89.

Libet, B., 2004. *Mind Time: The Temporal Factor in Consciousness.* Cambridge, MA: Harvard University Press.

Lilienfeld, Scott O., 2007. "Psychological Treatments That Cause Harm." *Perspectives on Psychological Science* 2(1): 53-70.

Lillard, Angeline, 1998. "Ethnopsychologies: Cultural Variations in Theories of Mind." *Psychological Bulletin* 123(1): 3-32.

Lin, L. C. and E. H. Telzer, 2018. "An Introduction to Cultural Neuroscience." In *The Handbook of Culture and Biology,* ed. by J. M. Causadias, E. H. Telzer and N. A. Gonzales. New York: Wiley-Blackwell, pp. 399–420.

Lincoln, J. S., 1935. *The Dream in Primitive Culture.* London: Cresset.

Linstead, Stephen, 1993. "From Postmodern Anthropology to Deconstructive Ethnography." *Human Relations* 46(1): 97-120.

Liston, Delores D., 1998. "Quantum Metaphors and the Study of the Mind-Brain." In *The Paideia Archive: Twentieth World Congress of Philosophy* 29: 228-234.

Littlefield, Melissa M., and Jenell Johnson (eds.), 2012. *The Neuroscientific Turn: Transdisciplinarity in the Age of the Brain.* Ann Arbor, MI: University of Michigan Press.

Liu, Huaping, Yupei Wu, Fuchun Sun and Di Guo, 2017. "Recent Progress on Tactile Object Recognition." *International Journal of Advanced Robotic Systems* 14(4). https://doi.org/10.1177/1729881417717056.

Livesey, A. C., M. B. Wall and A. T. Smith, 2007. "Time Perception: Manipulation of Task Difficulty Dissociates Clock Functions from other Cognitive Demands." *Neuropsychologia* 45: 321–31.

Livingston, Paul, 2002. "Husserl and Schlick on the Logical Form of Experience." *Synthese* 132(3): 239-272.

Llinas, R. R. and D. Pare, 1991. "Of Dreaming and Wakefulness." *Neuroscience* 44(3): 521–35.

Llinas, R. R. and U. Ribary, 1993. "Coherent 40 Hz Oscillation Characterizes Dream State in Humans." *Proceedings of the National Academy of Sciences USA* 90(5): 2078–81.

Lockwood, M., 1989. *Mind, Brain and the Quantum: The Compound "I."* Oxford: Blackwell.

Lohmann, Roger Ivar, 2019. "Culture and Dreams." *Cross-Cultural Psychology: Contemporary Themes and Perspectives*, ed. by Kenneth D. Keith. New York: Wiley, pp. 327-341.

Lohmann, Roger Ivar and Jane C. Goodale, 2003. *Dream Travelers: Sleep Experiences and Culture in the Western Pacific.* New York: Palgrave Macmillan.

Lohmar, Dieter, 2006. "Mirror Neurons and the Phenomenology of Intersubjectivity." *Phenomenology and the Cognitive Sciences* 5(1): 5-16.

Loidolt, Sophie, 2009. "Husserl and the Fact of Practical Reason–Phenomenological Claims Toward a Philosophical Ethics." *Santalka: Filologija, Edukologija* 17(3): 50-61.

Lombo, José Angel and Francesco Russo, 2014. *Philosophical Anthropology: An Introduction.* Downers Grove, IL: Midwest Theological Forum.

Lonergan, B. J. F., 1958. *Insight: A Study of Human Understanding.* New York: Harper and Row.

Lories, Danielle, 2006. "Remarks on Aesthetic Intentionality: Husserl or Kant." *International Journal of Philosophical Studies* 14(1): 31-49

Losin, Elizabeth A. Reynolds, Mirella Dapretto and Marco Iacoboni, 2009. "Culture in the Mind's Mirror: How Anthropology and Neuroscience Can Inform a Model of the Neural Substrate for Cultural Imitative Learning." *Cultural Neuroscience: Cultural Influences on Brain Function*, ed. by J. Y. Chiao. New York: Elsevier, pp. 175-190.

Luft, Sebastian, 2004. "Husserl's Theory of the Phenomenological Reduction: Between Life-World and Cartesianism." *Research in Phenomenology* 34(1): 198-234.

Luft, Sebastian, 2011. *Subjectivity and Lifeworld in Transcendental Phenomenology.* Evanston: Northwestern University Press.

Luft, Sebastian, 2015. "Laying Bare the Phenomenal Field: The Reductions as Ways to Pure Consciousness." In *Commentary on Husserl's Ideas I*, ed. by A. Staiti. Berlin-Boston: De Gruyter, 133–157.

Luft, Sebastian, 2016. "Reconstruction and Reduction: Natorp and Husserl on Method and the Question of Subjectivity." *Meta: Research in Hermeneutics, Phenomenology, and Practical Philosophy* 8: 326-370.

Lukács, Georg, 1967. *History and Class Consciousness.* London: Merlin Press.

Lumpkin, Tara W., 2001. "Perceptual Diversity: Is Polyphasic Consciousness Necessary for Global Survival?" *Anthropology of Consciousness* 12(1): 37–70.

Lusthaus, Dan, 2014. *Buddhist Phenomenology: A Philosophical Investigation of Yogacara Buddhism and the Ch'eng Wei-shih Lun.* New York: Routledge.

Lyman, R. Lee and Michael J. O'Brien, 2004. "Nomothetic Science and Idiographic History in Twentieth-Century Americanist Anthropology." *Journal of the History of the Behavioral Sciences* 40(1): 77-96.

MacDonald, Douglas A. and Manuel Almendro (eds), 2021. *Transpersonal Psychology and Science: An Evaluation of Its Present Status and Future Direction.* Newcastle upon Tyne, UK: Cambridge Scholars.

MacDonald, J. L., 1981. "Theoretical Continuities in Transpersonal Anthropology." *Phoenix: The Journal of Transpersonal Anthropology* 5(1): 31-47.

Mach, Ernst, 1959[1897]. *The Analysis of Sensations* (trans. by C.M. Williams and S. Waterlow. New York: Dover Books.

Machado, Sergio, Marlo Cunha, Bruna Velasques, Daniel Minc, Silmar Teixeira, Clayton A. Domingues, Julio G. Silva *et al.*, 2010. "Sensorimotor Integration: Basic Concepts, Abnormalities Related to Movement Disorders and Sensorimotor Training-Induced Cortical Reorganization." *Revue Neurologique* 51(7): 427-436.

MacLean, Hope, 2012. *The Shaman's Mirror: Visionary Art of the Huichol.* Austin, TX: University of Texas Press.

MacWhinney, Brian, 2002. "The Gradual Emergence of Language." In *The Evolution of Language Out of Pre-Language,* ed. by T. Givón and Bertram F. Malle. New York: Benjamins, pp. 233-263.

Maffie, James, 1995. "Towards an Anthropology of Epistemology." *The Philosophical Forum* 26: 218-241. Maffie, James. "Recent work on naturalized epistemology." American Philosophical Quarterly 27, no. 4 (1990): 281-293.

Maffie, James, 2005. "Ethnoepistemology." *Internet Encyclopedia of Philosophy.* http://www.iep.utm.edu/ethno-ep/

Maffie, James, 2014. *Aztec Philosophy: Understanding a World in Motion.* Boulder, CO: University Press of Colorado.

Mahasi Sayadaw, 1978. *The Progress of Insight: A Treatise on Buddhist Satipatthana Meditation.* Kandy, Sri Lanka: Buddhist Publication Society.

Maisson, David J-N., Tyler V. Cash-Padgett, Maya Z. Wang, Benjamin Y. Hayden, Sarah R. Heilbronner and Jan Zimmermann, 2021. "Choice-Relevant Information Transformation along a Ventrodorsal Axis in the Medial Prefrontal Cortex." *Nature Communications* 12(1): 1-14.

Malkemus, Samuel Arthur, 2012. "Toward a General Theory of Enaction: Biological, Transpersonal, and Phenomenological Dimensions." *Journal of Transpersonal Psychology* 44(2): 201-223.

Malmierca, Manuel S., Lucy A. Anderson and Flora M. Antunes, 2015. "The Cortical Modulation of Stimulus-Specific Adaptation in the Auditory Midbrain and Thalamus: A Potential Neuronal Correlate for Predictive Coding." *Frontiers in Systems Neuroscience* 9: 19.

Mamo, Laura, 1999. "Death and Dying: Confluences of Emotion and Awareness." *Sociology of Health and Illness* 21(1): 13-36.

Mandelbaum, M., 1977. *The Anatomy of Historical Knowledge.* Baltimore: Johns Hopkins University Press.

Marbach, Eduard, 2019. "On Husserl's Genetic Method of Constitutive Deconstruction and Its Application in Acts of Modified Empath into Children's Minds." In *Husserl's*

Phenomenology of Intersubjectivity, ed. by Frode Kjosavik, Christian Beyer and Christel Fricke. New York: Routledge, pp. 142-162.

Markram, H., Maria Toledo-Rodriguez, Yun Wang, Anirudh Gupta, Gilad Silberberg and Caizhi Wu, 2004. "Interneurons of the Neocortical Inhibitory System." *Nature Reviews Neuroscience* 5(10): 793-807.

Marlowe, Frank W., 2005. "Hunter-Gatherers and Human Evolution." *Evolutionary Anthropology: Issues, News, and Reviews* 14(2): 54-67.

Marosan, B. P., 2020. "Edmund Husserl's Constructive Phenomenology in the C-Manuscripts and Other Late Research Manuscripts." *Phainomena* 29(112/113): 5-23.

Marti, Sébastien, Jérôme Sackur, Mariano Sigman and Stanislas Dehaene, 2010. "Mapping Introspection's Blind Spot: Reconstruction of Dual-Task Phenomenology Using Quantified Introspection." *Cognition* 115(2): 303-313.

Martindale, Colin, 1978. "Sit with Statisticians and Commit a Social Science: Interdisciplinary Aspects of Poetics." *Poetics* 7(3): 273-282.

Masataka, Nobuo, 2009. "The Origins of Language and the Evolution of Music: A Comparative Perspective." *Physics of Life Reviews* 6(1): 11-22.

Mascia-Lees, Frances E. (ed.), 2011. *A Companion to the Anthropology of the Body and Embodiment.* New York: John Wiley & Sons.

Mashour, G. A., P. Roelfsema, J.-P. Changeux and S. Dehaene, 2020. "Conscious Processing and the Global Neuronal Workspace Hypothesis." *Neuron* 105: 776–798.

Mateos-Aparicio, Pedro and Antonio Rodríguez-Moreno, 2019. "The Impact of Studying Brain Plasticity." *Frontiers in Cellular Neuroscience* 13: 66.

Matt, Daniel Chanan, 1995. *The Essential Kabbalah: The Heart of Jewish Mysticism.* San Francisco: San Francisco: Harper One."

Mattens, Filip (ed), 2008a. *Meaning and Language: Phenomenological Perspectives.* Dordrecht: Springer.

Mattens, Filip, 2008b. "Introductory Remarks." In *Meaning and Language: Phenomenological Perspectives*, ed. by Filip Mattens. Dordrecht: Springer, pp. ix-xix.

Mattingley, Jason B. and Anina N. Rich, 2004. "Behavioral and Brain Correlates of Multisensory Experience in Synesthesia." In *The Handbook of Multisensory Processes*, ed. by Gemma A, Calvert, Charles Spence and Barry E. Stein. Cambridge, MA: MIT Press, pp. 851-865.

Mattingly, Cheryl, 1994. "The Concept of Therapeutic 'Emplotment.'" *Social Science and Medicine* 38(6): 811–22.

Mattingly, Cheryl, 1998. *Healing Dramas and Clinical Plots: The Narrative Structure of Experience.* Cambridge: Cambridge University Press.

Mattingly, Cheryl, 2012. "Two Virtue Ethics and the Anthropology of Morality." *Anthropological Theory* 12(2): 161-184.

Mattingly, Cheryl and L. Garro, 2000. *Narrative and the Cultural Construction of Illness and Healing.* Berkeley: University of California Press.

Mattingly, Cheryl, and C. Jason Throop, 2018. "The Anthropology of Ethics and Morality." *Annual Review of Anthropology* 47: 475-492.

Maturana, H. and F. Varela, 1980. *Autopoiesis and Cognition.* Boston: Reidel.

Maunsell, John H. R., 1995. "The Brain's Visual World: Representation of Visual Targets in Cerebral Cortex." *Science* 270(5237): 764-769.

Mays, Wolfe, 1977. "Genetic Analysis and Experience: Husserl and Piaget." *Journal of the British Society for Phenomenology* 8(1): 51-55.

Mazzoni, Giuliana, Jean-Roch Laurence and Michael Heap, 2014. "Hypnosis and Memory: Two Hundred Years of Adventures and Still Going!" *Psychology of Consciousness: Theory, Research, and Practice* 1(2): 153-167.

McCulloch, W. S., 1965. *Embodiments of Mind*. Cambridge, MA: MIT Press.

McGrew, W. C., 2010. "New Theaters of Conflict in the Animal Culture Wars: Recent Findings from Chimpanzees." In *The Mind of the Chimpanzee: Ecological and Experimental Perspectives*, ed. by Elizabeth V. Lonsdorf, Stephen R. Ross and Tetsuro Matsuzawa. Chicago, IL: University of Chicago Press, pp. 168-177.

McIntyre, Lee C., 1993. "Complexity and Social Scientific Laws." *Synthese* 97: 209-227.

McIntyre, Lee C., 2018. *Laws and Explanation in the Social Sciences: Defending a Science of Human Behavior*. New York: Routledge.

McKilliam, Andy Kenneth, 2020. "What Is a Global State of Consciousness?" *Philosophy and the Mind Sciences* 1(2), https://doi.org/10.33735/phimisci.2020.II.58.

McNeill, David. 2012. *How Language Began: Gesture and Speech in Human Evolution*. Cambridge: Cambridge University Press.

McNeley, James K., 1981. *Holy Wind in Navajo Philosophy*. Tucson: University of Arizona Press.

Mead, Margaret, 1952. "The Training of the Cultural Anthropologist." *American Anthropologist* 54(3): 343-346.

Mead, Margaret, 1963. "Socialization and Enculturation." *Current Anthropology* 4(2): 184-188.

Melle, Ulrich, 1991. "The Development of Husserl's Ethics." *Études phénoménologiques* 7(13/14): 115-135.

Melle, Ullrich, 1997. "Husserl's Phenomenology of Willing." In *Phenomenology of Values and Valuing*, ed. by James G. Hart and Lester Embree. Dordrecht: Springer, pp. 169-192.

Melle, Ullrich, 2002. "Edmund Husserl: From Reason to Love." In *Phenomenological Approaches to Moral Philosophy*, ed. by J.J. Drummond and Lester Embree. Dordrecht: Springer, pp. 229-248.

Mellmann, Katja, 2012. "Is Storytelling a Biological Adaptation." In *Telling Stories: Literature and Evolution*, ed. by Carsten Gansel and Dirk Vanderbeke. Berlin: de Gruyter, pp. 30-49.

Meloy, J. Reid and Andrew Shiva, 2008. "A Psychoanalytic View of the Psychopath." In *International Handbook of Psychopathic Disorders and the Law*, ed. by Alan Felthous and Henning Sass. New York: Wiley, pp. 335-346.

Meltzoff, Andrew N. and Patricia K. Kuhl, 2016. "Exploring the Infant Social Brain: What's Going on in There." *Zero to Three* 36(3): 2-9.

Menzel, Emil W., 1967. "Naturalistic and Experimental Research on Primates." *Human Development* 10: 170-186.

Merchant, C., 1980. *The Death of Nature*. New York: Harper and Row.

Merchant, Hugo, Deborah L. Harrington and Warren H. Meck, 2013. "Neural Basis of the Perception and Estimation of Time." *Annual Review of Neuroscience* 36: 313-336.

Merleau-Ponty, Maurice, 1962[1945]. *Phenomenology of Perception*. London: Routledge and Kegan Paul.

Merleau-Ponty, Maurice, 1968. *The Visible and the Invisible*. Evanston, IL: Northwestern University Press.

Meschiari, Matteo, 2009. "Roots of the Savage Mind. Apophenia and Imagination as Cognitive Process." *Quaderni di semantica* 30: 183-222.

Metzinger, Thomas (ed), 2000. *Neural Correlates of Consciousness: Empirical and Conceptual Questions*. Cambridge, MA: MIT Press.

Meyer, R. A., M. Ringkamp, J. N. Campbell and S. N. Raja, 2006. "Peripheral Mechanisms of Cutaneous Nociception." In *Wall and Melzak's Textbook of Pain*, ed. by S. B. Mahon and M. Koltzenburg. Amsterdam: Elsavier, pp 3-34.

Michotte, A., 1963. *The Perception of Causality*. New York: Basic Books.

Miller, George A., 1956. "The Magical Number of Seven, Plus or Minus Two: Some Limit on Our Capacity for Processing Information." *Psychological Review* 63: 81–97.

Miller, George. A., E. H. Galanter and K. H. Pribram, 1960. *Plans and the Structure of Behavior.* New York: Holt, Rinehart and Winston.

Miller, Earl K. and Jonathan D. Cohen, 2001. "An Integrative Theory of Prefrontal Cortex Function." *Annual Review of Neuroscience* 24(1): 167-202

Miller, Izshak, 1984. *Husserl, Perception, and Temporal Awareness*. Cambridge, MA: MIT Press.

Mimica, Jadran, 2010. "Un/knowing and the Practice of Ethnography: A Reflection on Some Western Cosmo-Ontological Notions and their Anthropological Application." *Anthropological Theory* 10(3): 203-228.

Miracle, Andrew W. and Dan Southard, 1993. "The Athlete and Ritual Timing: An Experimental Study." *Journal of Ritual Studies* 7(1): 125-138.

Mishara, Aaron L., 1990. "Husserl and Freud: Time, Memory and the Unconscious." *Husserl Studies* 7(1): 29-58.

Mizumoto, Masaharu, Jonardon Ganeri and Cliff Goddard (eds), 2020. *Ethno-Epistemology: New Directions for Global Epistemology*. London: Routledge.

Moeran, Brian, 2009. "From Participant Observation to Observant Participation." In *Organizational ethnography: Studying the complexity of everyday life*, ed. by S. Ybema, D. Yanow, H. Wels and F. H. Kamsteeg. New York: Sage, pp. 139-155.

Mohanty, Jitendranath Nath, 1959. "Individual Fact and Essence in Edmund Husserl's Philosophy." *Philosophy and Phenomenological Research* 20, no. 2 (1959): 222-230.

Mohanty, Jitendranath Nath, 1972. "Phenomenology and Existentialism: Encounter with Indian Philosophy." *International Philosophical Quarterly* 12(4): 485-511.

Mohanty, Jitendra Nath, 1978. "Husserl's Transcendental Phenomenology and Essentialism." *The Review of Metaphysics* 31(2): 299-321.

Mohanty, Jitendra Nath, 1991. "Method of Imaginative Variation in Phenomenology." In *Thought Experiments in Science and Philosophy*, ed. by Tamara Horowitz and Gerald J. Massey. Washington, DC: Rowman and Littlefield, pp. 261-272.

Møller, Aage R., 2014. *Sensory Systems: Anatomy and Physiology* (second edition). Richardson, TX: Aager Møller Publications.

Molnár, Z. and K. S. Rockland, 2020. "Cortical Columns." In *Neural Circuit and Cognitive Development*, ed. by J. Rubenstein and P. Rakic. New York: Academic Press, pp. 103-126.

Moore, Lila, 2015. "Fields of Networked Mind: Ritual Consciousness and the Factor of Communitas in Networked Rites of Compassion." *Technoetic Arts* 13(3): 331-339.

Moran, Dermot, 2000. *Introduction to Phenomenology*. New York: Routledge.

Moran, Dermot, 2005. *Edmund Husserl: Founder of Phenomenology*. Cambridge: Polity Press.

Moran, Dermot, 2013a. "From the Natural Attitude to the Life-World." In *Husserl's Ideen, Contributions to Phenomenology* 66, ed. by L. Embree and T. Nenon. Dordrecht: Springer, pp. 105-124.

Moran, Dermot, 2013b. "The Phenomenology of Embodiment: Intertwining and Reflexivity." In *The Phenomenology of Embodied Subjectivity*, ed. by Rasmus Thybo Jensen and Dermot Moran. Berlin: Springer, pp. 285-303.

Moran, Dermot and Joseph Cohen, 2012. *The Husserl Dictionary*. Oxford: Bloomsbury.

Morrison, Steven J. and Steven M. Demorest, 2009. "Cultural Constraints on Music Perception and Cognition." *Progress in Brain Research* 178: 67-77.

Mountcastle, Vernon B., 1988. "Representations and the Construction of Reality." *Transactions of the American Clinical and Climatological Association* 99: 70-90.

Mountcastle, Vernon B. and M. A. Steinmetz, 1990. "The Parietal Visual System and Some Aspects of Visuospatial Perception." In *From Neuron to Action*, ed. by V. B. Mountcastle, M. A. Steinmetz, L. Deecke and J. C. Eccles. Berlin: Springer, pp. 193-209.

Munn, N. D., 1992. "The Cultural Anthropology of Time: A Critical Essay." *Annual Review of Anthropology* 21: 93–123.

Murphy, William P., 1980. "Secret Knowledge as Property and Power in Kpelle Society: Elders Versus Youth." *Africa* 50(2): 193-207.

Murray, Henry A. *et al.*, 1938. *Explorations in Personality: A Clinical and Experimental Study of Fifty Men of College Age*. Oxford: Oxford University Press.

Naidu, Maheshvari, 2013. "Anthropology of Experience: Touring the Past at Robben Island." *Journal of Human Ecology* 43(1): 51-60.

Nase, G., W. Singer, H. Monyer and A. K. Engle, 2003. "Features of Neuronal Synchrony in Mouse Visual Cortex." *Journal of Neurophysiology* 90: 1115–23.

Natanson, Maurice, 1970. *Phenomenology and Social Reality: Essays in Memory of Alfred Schutz*. The Hague: Martinus Nijhoff.

Natanson, Maurice, 1973. *Edmund Husserl: Philosopher of Infinite Tasks*. Evanston, IL: Northwestern University Press.

Natanson, Maurice, 1981. "The World Already There: An Approach to Phenomenology." *Philosophical Topics* 12(Supplement): 101-116.

Neckar, M. and P. Bob, 2014. "Neuroscience of Synesthesia and Cross-Modal Associations." *Reviews in the Neurosciences* 25(6): 833-840.

Neisser, U., 1976. *Cognition and Reality: Principles and Implications of Cognitive Psychology*. San Francisco: Freeman.

Nelson, Charles A. and Laurel J. Gabard-Durnam, 2020. "Early Adversity and Critical Periods: Neurodevelopmental Consequences of Violating he Expectable Environment." *Trends in Neurosciences* 43(3): 133-143.

Nenon, Thomas, 2013a. "Intersubjectivity, Interculturality, and Realities in Husserl's Research Manuscripts on the Life-World (Hua XXXIX)." In *The Phenomenology of Embodied Subjectivity*, ed. by Rasmus Thybo Jensen and Dermot Moran. Berlin: Springer, pp. 143-163.

Nenon, Thomas, 2013b. "Edmund Husserl: Nature and Spirit: Lectures Summer Semester 1919, Husserliana Materials vol IV, ed Michael Weiler." *Husserl Studies* 29(3): 231-237.

Neumann, Erich, 1969. *The Origins and History of Consciousness*. Princeton, NJ: Princeton University Press.

Newberg, Andrew B., 2010. *Principles of Neurotheology*. London: Ashgate Publishing.

Newberg, Andrew B., and Eugene G. d'Aquili. 2000. "The Neuropsychology of Religious and Spiritual Experience." *Journal of Consciousness Studies* 7(11-12): 251-266.

Newberg, Andrew B. and Eugene G. d'Aquili, 2008. *Why God Won't Go Away: Brain Science and the Biology of Belief*. New York: Ballantine Books.

Noé, Keiichi, 1992. "The 'Hermeneutic turn' in Husserl's Phenomenology of Language." *Human Studies* 15(1): 117-128.

Norenzayan, Ara and Steven J. Heine, 2005. "Psychological Universals: What Are They and How Can We Know?" *Psychological Bulletin* 131(5): 763.

Nozaradan, Sylvie, Isabelle Peretz and André Mouraux, 2012. "Steady-State Evoked Potentials as an Index of Multisensory Temporal Binding." *Neuroimage* 60(1): 21-28.

Ntarangwi, Mwenda, 2010. *Reversed Gaze: An African Ethnography of American Anthropology.* University of Illinois Press.

Nunez, Paul L., 2010. *Brain, Mind, and the Structure of Reality.* Oxford: Oxford University Press.

Nyamnjoh, Francis B., 2015. "Beyond an Evangelizing Public Anthropology: Science, Theory and Commitment." *Journal of Contemporary African Studies* 33(1): 48-63.

Nyanaponika Thera, 2005. *The Power of Mindfulness.* Sri Lanka: Buddhist Publication Society.

Obermayer, Klaus, Terrence Sejnowski and Gary G. Blasdel, 1995. "Neural Pattern Formation Via a Competitive Hebbian Mechanism." *Behavioural Brain Research* 66(1-2): 161-167.

Ochs, E. and L. Capps, 2001. *Living Narrative: Creating Everyday Storytelling.* Cambridge, MA: Harvard University Press.

O'Doherty, J., E. T. Rolls and M. Kringelbach, 2004. "Neuroimaging Studies of Cross-Modal Integration for Emotion." *The Handbook of Multisensory Processes*, ed. by G. Calvert, C. Spence and B. E. Stein. London: Bradford, 563-579.

Ogden, C.K. and I.A. Richards, 1923. *The Meaning of Meaning* (8th edition). New York: Harcourt Brace Jovanovich.

Okawa, H. and A. P. Sampath, 2007. "Optimization of Single-Photon Response Transmission at the Rod-To-Rod Bipolar Synapse." *Physiology* 22(4): 279-86.

Ormont, Louis R., 1986. "Adopting Roles to Resolve Resistances in Group Analysis." *Group Analysis* 19(4): 311-325.

Ott, Ulrich, 2007. "States of Absorption: In Search of Neurobiological Foundations." In *Hypnosis and Consciousness States: The Cognitive-Neuroscience Perspective*, ed. by G. A. Jamieson. New York: Oxford University Press, pp. 257–270.

Ott, Ulrich, 2013. "Time Experience during Mystical States." *The Evolution of Time in Science, Anthropology, Theology*, ed. by A. Nicolaidis and W. Achtner. London: Bentham Science Publishers, pp. 104-116.

Over, David E. (ed), 2003. *Evolution and the Psychology of Thinking: The Debate.* New York: Psychology Press.

Overgaard, Søren, 2002. "Epoché and Solipsistic Reduction." *Husserl Studies* 18(3): 209-222.

Oxtoby, Willard, 1968. "*Religionswissenschaft* Revisited." In *Religion in Antiquity*, ed. by J. Neusner. Leiden: Brill, pp. 591-608.

Ozturk, Ozge, Shakila Shayan, Ulf Liszkowski and Asifa Majid, 2013. "Language Is Not Necessary for Color Categories." *Developmental Science* 16(1): 111-115.

Paci, Enzo, 1970. "The Lebenswelt as Ground and as *Leib* in Husserl: Somatology, Psychology, Sociology." In *Patterns of the Life-World: Essays in Honor of John Wild*, ed. by James M. Edie, Frances H. Parker and Calvin O. Schrag. Evanston, IL: Northwestern University Press, pp. 123-138.

Paci, Enzo, 1972. *The Function of the Sciences and the Meaning of Man.* Evanston, IL: Northwestern University Press.

Page, Scott E., 2007. *The Difference: How the Power of Diversity Creates Better Groups, Firms, Schools, and Societies.* Princeton, NJ: Princeton University Press.

Pareti, G. and A. Palma, 2004. "Does the Brain Oscillate? The Dispute on Neuronal Synchronization." *Neurological Sciences* 25(2): 41–7.

Parker, Francis H. and Calvin O. Schrag (eds), 1970. *Patterns of the Life-World: Essays in Honor of John Wild.* Evanston, IL: Northwestern University Press.

Paravahera Vajiranana Mahathera, 1987. *Buddhist Meditation in Theory and Practice: A*

General Exposition According to the Pali Canon of the Theravada School. Kuala Lumpur, Malaysia: Buddhist Missionary Society.

Parkin, David J. (ed), 1985. *The Anthropology of Evil*. Oxford: Blackwell.

Pastor, M. *et al.*, 2004. "The Functional Neuroanatomy of Temporal Discrimination." *Journal of Neuroscience* 24(10): 2585–91.

Patel, Aniruddh D., 2008. *Music, Language, and the Brain*. Oxford: Oxford University Press.

Patočka, Jan, 1996. *An Introduction to Husserl's Phenomenology*. Chicago: Open Court.

Patočka, Jan, 1998. *Body, Community, Language, World*. Chicago: Open Court.

Patočka, Jan, 2016. *The Natural World as a Philosophical Problem*. Evanston, IL: Northwestern University Press.

Peregrine, Peter, Yolanda T. Moses, Alan Goodman, Louise Lamphere and James Lowe Peacock, 2012. "What Is Science in Anthropology?" *American Anthropologist* 114(4): 593-597.

Persinger, Michael A. and C. Lavallee C., 2012. "The Σn=n Concept: And the Quantitative Support for the Cerebral-Holographic and Electromagnetic Configuration of Consciousness". *Journal of Consciousness Studies* 19: 128–253.

Petitot, Jean, 1999. *Naturalizing Phenomenology: Issues in Contemporary Phenomenology and Cognitive Science*. Stanford, CA: Stanford University Press.

Petrus, Theodore S., 2006. "Engaging the World of the Supernatural: Anthropology, Phenomenology and the Limitations of Scientific Rationalism in the Study of the Supernatural." *Indo-Pacific Journal of Phenomenology* 6(1): 1-12.

Pfänder, Alexander and Herbert Spiegelberg, 1967. *Alexander Pfander: Phenomenology of Willing and Motivation*. Evanston, IL: Northwestern University Press.

Phelps, Elizabeth A. and Michael S. Gazzaniga, 1992. "Hemispheric Differences in Mnemonic Processing: The Effects of Left Hemisphere Interpretation." *Neuropsychologia* 30(3): 293-297.

Piaget, Jean, 1969. *The Child's Conception of Time*. New York: Basic Books.

Piaget, Jean, 1971. *Biology and Knowledge*. Chicago: University of Chicago Press.

Piaget, Jean, 1980. *Adaptation and Intelligence*. Chicago: University of Chicago Press.

Piaget, Jean and Bärbel Inhelder, 2013. *The Growth of Logical Thinking from Childhood to Adolescence: An Essay on the Construction of Formal Operational Structures*. New York: Routledge.

Picton, Terence W., Claude Alain and Anthony R. McIntosh, 2002. "The Theater of the Mind: Physiological Studies of the Human Frontal Lobes." In *Principles of Frontal Lobe Function*, ed. by Donald T. Stuss and Robert T. Knight. Oxford: Oxford University Press, pp. 109-126.

Pink, Sarah, 2009. *An Anthropology of the Senses: Doing Sensory Ethnography*. London: Sage.

Pink, Sarah, 2010. "The Future of Sensory Anthropology/The Anthropology of the Senses." *Social Anthropology* 18(3): 331-333.

Pinker, Steven, 1994. *The Language Instinct: How the Mind Creates Languages*. New York: William Morrow.

Pinker, Steven, 1995. "Facts About Human Language Relevant to Its Evolution." In Jean-Pierre Changeux and Jean Chavaillon (eds), *Origins of the Human Brain*. Oxford: Clarenden, pp. 262-285.

Pinker, Steven, 2003. *The Blank Slate: The Modern Denial of Human Nature*. New York: Penguin.

Pinker, Steven and Paul Bloom, 1990. "Natural Language and Natural Selection." *Behavioral and Brain Sciences* 13: 707-784.

Pinker, Steven and Ray Jackendoff, 2005. "The Faculty of Language: What's Special About It?" *Cognition* 95(2): 201-236.

Pockett, Susan, 2003. "How Long Is "Now"? Phenomenology and the Specious Present." *Phenomenology and the Cognitive Sciences* 2(1): 55-68.

Poincaré, Henri, 1914[1904]. *Science and Method*. London: Thomas Nelson.

Polanyi, M., 1965. "The Structure of Consciousness." *Brain* 88: 799-810.

Pool, Robert, 1987. "Hot and Cold as an Explanatory Model: The Example of Bharuch District in Gujarat, India." *Social Science and Medicine* 25(4): 389-399.

Pöppel, E., 1988. *Mindworks: Time and Conscious Experience*. Boston: Harcourt Brace Jovanovich.

Postill, J., 2002. "Clock and Calendar Time: A Missing Anthropological Problem." *Time and Society* 11(2/3): 251–70.

Potter, Caroline, 2008. "Sense of Motion, Senses of Self: Becoming a Dancer." *Ethnos* 73(4): 444-465.

Powers, W. T., 2005. *Behavior: The Control of Perception* (second edition). Escondido, CA: Benchmark Publications.

Prat, Chantel, 2022. *The Neuroscience of You: How Every Brain Is Different and How to Understand Yours*. New York: Dutton.

Premack, D. and G. Woodruff, 1978. "Does the Chimpanzee Have a Theory of Mind?" *The Behavioral and Brain Sciences* 4: 515–526.

Pribram, Karl H., 1971. *Languages of the Brain: Experimental Paradoxes and Principles in Neuropsychology*. Englewood Cliffs, NJ: Prentice-Hall.

Pribram, Karl H., 1980. "Unpacking Some Dualities Inherent in a Mind/Brain Dualism." *Philosophy of the Social Sciences* 109(3): 295.-308

Pribram, Karl H., 1991. *Brain and Perception: Holonomy and Structure in Figural Processing*. Hillscale, NJ: Lawrence Erlbaum.

Pronin, Emily and Matthew B. Kugler, 2007. "Valuing Thoughts, Ignoring Behavior: The Introspection Illusion as a Source of the Bias Blind Spot." *Journal of Experimental Social Psychology* 43(4): 565-578.

Proust, Marcel, 2003[1913]. *In Search of Lost Time: The Way by Swann's*. London: Penguin UK.

Psathas, George, 2004. "Alfred Schutz's Influence on American Sociologists and Sociology." *Human Studies* 27(1): 1-35.

Pulkkinen, Simo, 2013. "Lifeworld, as an Embodiment of Spiritual Meaning: The Constitutive Dynamics of Activity and Passivity in Husserl." In *The Phenomenology of Embodied Subjectivity*, ed. by Rasmus Thybo Jensen and Dermot Moran. Berlin: Springer, pp. 121-141.

Purves, Dale, 1990. *Body and Brain: A Trophic Theory of Neural Connections*. Cambridge, MA: Harvard University Press.

Purves, Dale, 2010. *Brains: How They Seem to Work*. Upper Saddle River, NJ: Pearson Education.

Putnam, Anne Eisner, 1954. *Madami: My Eight Years of Adventure with the Congo Pygmies*. New York: Prentice Hall.

Rabanaque, Luis Román, 2003. "Hyle, Genesis and Noema." *Husserl Studies* 19(3): 205-215.

Raghavachari, S. *et al.*, 2001. "Gating of Human Theta Oscillations by a Working Memory Task." *Journal of Neuroscience* 21(9): 3175–83.

Ram, Kalpana and Christopher Houston (eds.), 2015a. *Phenomenology in Anthropology: A sense of Perspective*. Bloomington, IN: Indiana University Press.

Ram, Kalpana and Christopher Houston, 2015b. "Introduction: Phenomenology's Methodological Invitation." In *Phenomenology in Anthropology: A sense of Perspective*, ed. by Kalpana Ram and Christopher Houston. Bloomington, IN: Indiana University Press, pp 1-25.

Rao, S. M., A. R. Mayer and D. L. Harrington, 2001. "The Evolution of Brain Activation during Temporal Processing." *Nature Neuroscience* 4: 317–323.

Rappaport, Roy A., 1984. *Pigs for the Ancestors* (second edition). New Haven, CT: Yale University Press.

Rasmussen, David M., 2012. *Mythic-Symbolic Language and Philosophical Anthropology: A Constructive Interpretation of the Thought of Paul Ricœur*. New York: Springer.

Rathbun, Brian C. and Caleb Pomeroy, 2021. "See No Evil, Speak No Evil? Morality, Evolutionary Psychology, and the Nature of International Relations." *International Organization* 19 October issue: 1-34. doi:10.1017/S0020818321000436.

Reichlin, Massimo, 2012. "Neuroethics." In *A Companion to Moral Anthropology*, ed. by Didier Fassin. London: Wiley, pp. 595-610.

Reinach, Adolf, 1969. "Concerning Phenomenology." *The Personalist* 50(2): 194-221.

Reinach, Adolf and John Crosby (eds), 2013. *The Apriori Foundations of the Civil Law: Along with the Lecture 'Concerning Phenomenology'*. Aletheia 8. Berlin: de Gruyter.

Rensch, Bernhard, 1959. *Evolution Above the Species Level*. New York: Columbia University Press.

Rentzeperis, Ilias, Andrey R. Nikolaev, Daniel C. Kiper and Cees van Leeuwen, 2014. "Distributed Processing of Color and Form in the Visual Cortex." *Frontiers in Psychology* 5: 932.

Reynaert, Peter, 2001. "Intersubjectivity and Naturalism: Husserl's Fifth Cartesian Meditation Revisited." *Husserl Studies* 17(3): 207-216.

Richards, J. and E. von Glasersfeld, 1979. "The Control of Perception and the Construction of Reality." *Dialectica* 33(1): 37–58.

Richelle, Marc, Helga Lejeune, Daniel Defays, P. Greenwood, F. Macar and H. Mantanus, 2013. *Time in Animal Behaviour*. New York: Elsevier.

Ricoeur, Paul, 1970. *Freud and Philosophy: An Essay on Interpretation*. (D. Savage, Trans.). New Haven, CT: Yale University Press.

Ricoeur, Paul, 1980. "Narrative time." *Critical Inquiry* 7(1): 169-190.

Ricoeur, Paul, 1984. *Time and Narrative*. Chicago: University of Chicago Press.

Rigby, Peter, 1995. "Time and Historical Consciousness: The Case of the *Ilparakuyo* Maasai." In *Time: Histories and Ethnographies*, ed. by D.O. Hughes and T.R. Trautmann. Ann Arbor: University of Michigan Press.

Rilling, James K. and Thomas R. Insel, 1999. "Differential Expansion of Neural Projection Systems in Primate Brain Evolution." *Neuroreport* 10(7): 1453-1459.

Rizal, Yan *et al.*, 2020 "Last Appearance of *Homo erectus* at Ngandong, Java, 117,000–108,000 Years Ago." *Nature* 577(7790): 381-385.

Robbins, Brent Dean, Harris L. Friedman, Chad V. Johnson and Zeno Franco, 2018. "Subjectivity Is No Object: Can Subject-Object Dualism Be Reconciled Through Phenomenology?" *International Journal of Transpersonal Studies* 37(2): 144-167.

Robbins, Joel, 2016. "What Is the Matter with Transcendence? On the Place of Religion in the New Anthropology of Ethics." *Journal of the Royal Anthropological Institute* 22(4): 767-781.

Roberts, Bernadette, 1993. *The Experience of No-Self: A Contemplative Journey*. Albany, NY: State University of New York Press.

Robinson, Maria, 2007. *Child Development from Birth to Eight: A Journey Through the Early Years*. London: McGraw-Hill Education.

Rochat, Philippe, 2001. *The Infant's World*. Cambridge, MA: Harvard University Press.

Rock, Adam J. and Stanley Krippner, 2007. "Shamanism and the Confusion of Consciousness with Phenomenological Content." *North American Journal of Psychology* 9(3): 485-500.

Rock, Adam J. and Stanley Krippner, 2008. "Some Rudimentary Problems Pertaining to the Construction of an Ontology and Epistemology of Shamanic Journeying Imagery." *International Journal of Transpersonal Studies* 27: 12-19.

Rock, Adam J. and Stanley Krippner, 2011. *Demystifying Shamans and Their World: A Multidisciplinary Study*. Luton, UK: Andrews UK Limited.

Rodd, Robin, 2002. "*Märipa teui*: A radical empiricist approach to Piaroa shamanic training and initiation." *Antropológica* 96: 53-82.

Rodd, Robin, 2004. *The Biocultural Ecology of Piaroa Shamanic Practice*. Perth: University of Western Australia.

Rodd, Robin, 2006. "*Piaroa* Sorcery and the Navigation of Negative Affect: To Be Aware, To Turn Away." *Anthropology of Consciousness* 17(1): 35-64.

Rodemeyer, Lanei M., 2008. "'I Don't Have the Words:' Considering Language (and the Lack Thereof) Through the Phenomenological Paradigms nof Temporality and Corporeality. In *Meaning and Language: Phenomenological Perspectives*, ed. by Filip Mattens. Dordrecht: Springer, pp. 195-212.

Rogers, Richard A., 1994. "Rhythm and the Performance of Organization." *Text and Performance Quarterly* 14(3): 222-237.

Rogers, Timothy T. and James L. McClelland, 2014. "Parallel Distributed Processing At 25: Further Explorations in the Microstructure of Cognition." *Cognitive Science* 38(6): 1024-1077.

Rolfs, Martin, Michael Dambacher and Patrick Cavanagh, 2013. "Visual Adaptation of the Perception of Causality." *Current Biology* 23(3): 250-254.

Rolls, Edmund T., 2018. *The Brain, Emotion, and Depression*. Oxford: Oxford University Press.

Rosch, E., 1977. "Human Categorization." *Studies in Cross-Cultural Psychology* 1: 1-49.

Rosch, E., 1978. "Principles of Categorization." In *Cognition and Categorization*, ed. by E. Rosch and B. B. Lloyd. Hillsdale, NJ: Erlbaum, pp. 27-48.

Rosch, E. *et al.*, 1976. "Basic Objects in Natural Categories." *Cognitive Psychology* 8: 382-439.

Rosen, R., 1985. *Anticipatory Systems: Philosophical, Mathematical & Methodological Foundations*. Oxford: Pergamon Press.

Rubinstein, Robert A., 1981. "Toward the Anthropological Study of Cognitive Performance." *Human Relations* 34(8): 677-703.

Rubinstein, Robert A. and Charles D. Laughlin, 1977. "Bridging Levels of Systemic Organization." *Current Anthropology* 18(3): 459-481.

Rubinstein, Robert A., Charles D. Laughlin and John McManus, 1984. *Science as Cognitive Process: Toward an Empirical Philosophy of Science*. Philadelphia: University of Pennsylvania Press.

Ruck, C. A. P., J. Bigwood, D. Staples, J. Ott and R. G. Wasson, 1979. "Entheogens." *Journal of Psychoactive Drugs* 11(1-2): 145-146.

Rudrauf, David, Antoine Lutz, Diego Cosmelli, Jean-Philippe Lachaux and Michel Le Van Quyen, 2003. "From Autopoiesis to Neurophenomenology: Francisco Varela's Exploration of the Biophysics of Being." *Biological Research* 36(1): 27-65.

Ruthrof, Horst, 2021. *Husserl's Phenomenology of Natural Language: Intersubjectivity and Communality in the* Nachlass. New York: Bloomsbury Publishing.

Samson, Will, 2015. "On the Neuro-Turn in the Humanities." *Chiasma: A Site for Thought* 2(1): 29-45.

Samuels, Jeffrey, 1995. "Healing Sand: A Comparative Investigation of Navajo Sandpaintings and Tibetan Sand Mandalas." *Journal of Ritual Studies* 9(1): 101-126.

Sanford, J. A., 1971. "A Periodic Basis for Perception and Action." In *Biological Rhythms and Human Performance,* ed. by W. Colquhuon. New York: Academic Press, pp. 179-209.

Sangster, Rodney B., 2013. *Reinventing Structuralism: What Sign Relations Reveal about Consciousness.* Berlin: Walter de Gruyter.

Saniotis, Arthur, 2009. "Evolving Brain: Neuroanthropology, Emergence, and Cognitive Frontiers." *NeuroQuantology* 7(3): 482-490.

Saniotis, Arthur, 2010a. "Evolutionary and Anthropological Approaches Towards Understanding Human Need for Psychotropic and Mood-Altering Substances." *Journal of Psychoactive Drugs* 42(4): 477-484.

Saniotis, Arthur, 2010b. "Making Connectivities: Neuroanthropology and Ecological Ethics." *NeuroQuantology* 8(2): 200-205.

Sasaki, George H., 1956. "The Concept of *Kamma* in Buddhist Philosophy." *Oriens Extremus* 3(2): 185-204.

Sauce, Bruno and Louis D. Matzel, 2017. "Inductive Reasoning." *Encyclopedia of Animal Cognition and Behavior* 6: 1-8.

Scanlon, John D., 1972[1941]. "The *Epoche* and Phenomenological Anthropology." *Research in Phenomenology* 2(1): 95-109.

Scarantino, Andrea, 2013. "Animal Communication as Information-Mediated Influence." In *Animal Communication Theory: Information and Influence,* ed. by Ulrich E. Stegmann. Cambridge: Cambridge University Press, pp. 1-39.

Scharlau, Ingrid, 2002. "Leading, But Not Trailing, Primes Influence Temporal Order Perception: Further Evidence for an Attentional Account of Perceptual Latency Priming." *Perception and Psychophysics* 64(8): 1346-1360.

Schatzman, Morton, 1982. *The Story of Ruth.* New York: Penguin Books.

Scheffler, Samuel (ed), 1988. *Consequentialism and its Critics.* Oxford: Oxford University Press.

Scheler, Max, 1994[1961]. *Ressentiment.* Milwaukee, WI: Marquette University Press.

Scheper-Hughes, Nancy, 1995. "The Primacy of the Ethical: Propositions for a Militant Anthropology." *Current Anthropology* 36: 409–440.

Scherer, Klaus R. and Harald G. Wallbott, 1994. "Evidence for Universality and Cultural Variation of Differential Emotion Response Patterning." *Journal of Personality and Social Psychology* 66(2): 310-328.

Schmicking, D., 2010. "A Toolbox of Phenomenological Methods." In *Handbook of Phenomenology and Cognitive Science,* ed. by D. Schmicking and S. Gallagher. Dordrecht: Springer, pp. 35-55.

Schmidt, Ewoud R. E. and Franck Polleux, 2022. "Genetic Mechanisms Underlying the Evolution of Connectivity in the Human Cortex." *Frontiers in Neural Circuits* 15: 1-16.

Schmidt, Marcia and Michael Tweed (eds.), 2012. *Perfect Clarity: A Tibetan Buddhist Anthology of Mahamudra and Dzogchen.* New York: North Atlantic Books.

Schmidt, Richard, 1967. "Husserl's Transcendental-Phenomenological Reduction." In *Phenomenology,* ed. by Joseph J. Kockelmans. Garden City, NY: Doubleday, pp. 58-67.

Schnell, Alexander, 2010. "Intersubjectivity in Husserl's Work." *META: Research in Hermeneutics, Phenomenology, and Practical Philosophy* 2(1): 9-31.

Schnider, Armin, 2018. *The Confabulating Mind: How the Brain Creates Reality.* Oxford: Oxford University Press.

Schoenemann, P. Thomas, 1999. "Syntax as an Emergent Characteristic of the Evolution of Semantic Complexity." *Minds and Machines* 9(3): 309-346.

Schore, Allan N., 2004. "The Human Unconscious: The Development of the Right Brain and Its Role in Early Emotional Life." In *Emotional Development in Psychoanalysis, Attachment Theory and Neuroscience,* ed. by Viviane Green. New York: Routledge, pp. 33-62.

Schrödinger, Erwin, 1946. *What Is Life?* Cambridge: Cambridge University Press.

Schroll, Mark A. and Stephan A. Schwartz, 2005. "Whither Psi and Anthropology? An Incomplete History of SAC's Origins, Its Relationship with Transpersonal Psychology and the Untold Stories of Castaneda's Controversy." *Anthropology of Consciousness* 16(1): 6-24.

Schutz, Alfred, 1962. "Some Leading Concepts of Phenomenology." In *Collected Papers* I, Dordrecht: Springer, pp. 99-117.

Schutz, Alfred, 1967[1932]. *The Phenomenology of the Social World.* Evanston: Northwestern University Press.

Schutz, Alfred, 1970. "Some Structures of the Life-World." In *Collected Papers* III Dordrecht: Springer, pp. 116-132.

Schutz, Alfred, 1966. *The Problem of Transcendental Intersubjectivity in Husserl.* The Hague: Martinus.

Schutz, Alfred and T. Luckman, 1973. *The Structures of the Life-World*: Vol. I. Evanston, IL: Northwestern University Press.

Schutz, A. and T. Luckmann, 1989. *The Structures of the Life-World*: Vol. II. Evanston, IL: Northwestern University Press.

Schwab, Ivan R., 2011. *Evolution's Witness: How Eyes Evolved.* Oxford: Oxford University Press.

Schweder, Richard A. 1991. *Thinking Through Cultures.* Cambridge, MA: Harvard University Press.

Scriven, Michael,1977. *Reasoning.* New York: McGraw Hill.

Searcy, William A. and Stephen Nowicki, 2010. *The Evolution of Animal Communication.* Princeton, NJ: Princeton University Press.

Sebeok, Thomas A., 1976. "Foreword." In *Contributions to the Doctrine of Signs,* ed. by Thomas A. Sebeok. Lisse, Netherlands: Peter de Ridder Press.

Sebeok, Thomas A., 1991. *A Sign Is Just a Sign.* Bloomington, IN: Indiana University Press.

Seligman, Martin, 1971. "Phobias and Preparedness." *Behavior Therapy* 2: 307-320.

Seligman, Martin, 1975. *Helplessness: On Development, Depression and Death.* San Francisco: Freeman.

Seligman, Martin and J. Hager, 1972. *Biological Boundaries of Learning.* New York: Appleton-Century-Crofts.

Seligman, Rebecca, 2014. *Possessing Spirits and Healing Selves: Embodiment and Transformation in an Afro-Brazilian Religion.* New York: Palgrave Macmillan.

Seligman, Rebecca and Ryan A. Brown, 2010. "Theory and Method at the Intersection of Anthropology and Cultural Neuroscience." *Social Cognitive and Affective Neuroscience* 5(2-3): 130-137.

Senkowski, Daniel, Till R. Schneider, John J. Foxe and Andreas K. Engel, 2008. "Crossmodal Binding Through Neural Coherence: Implications for Multisensory Processing." *Trends in Neurosciences* 31(8): 401-409.

Serafin, Andrzej, 2016. "Heidegger's Phenomenology of the Invisible." *Argument: Biannual Philosophical Journal* 6(2): 313-322.

Seth, Anil, 2021. *Being You: A New Science of Consciousness*. New York: Dutton.

Seung, H. Sebastian, 2003. "Learning in Spiking Neural Networks by Reinforcement of Stochastic Synaptic Transmission." *Neuron* 40(6): 1063-1073.

Seyfarth, Robert M. and Dorothy L. Cheney, 1990. "The Assessment by Vervet Monkeys of Their Own and Another Species' Alarm Calls." *Animal Behaviour* 40(4): 754-764.

Seyfarth, Robert M. and Dorothy L. Cheney, 2003. "Signalers and Receivers in Animal Communication." *Annual Review of Psychology* 549(1): 145-173.

Shannon, C. E. and W. Weaver, 1963. *The Mathematical Theory of Communication*. Urbana, IL: University of Illinois Press.

Shanon, Benny, 2002. *The Antipodes of the Mind Charting the Phenomenology of the Ayahuasca Experience*. Oxford: Oxford University Press.

Shapley, Robert and Michael Hawken, 2002. "Neural Mechanisms for Color Perception in the Primary Visual Cortex." *Current Opinion in Neurobiology* 12(4): 426-432.

Sheets-Johnstone, Maxine, 2009. "Consciousness: A Natural History." In *The Corporeal Turn: An Interdisciplinary Reader*, ed. by M. Sheets-Johnstone. Charlottesville, VA: Imprint Academic, pp. 149-194.

Sheneman, Leigh, Jory Schossau and Arend Hintze, 2019. "The Evolution of Neuroplasticity and the Effect on Integrated Information." *Entropy* 21(5): 524.

Shepard, R. N., 1992. "The Perceptual Organization of Colors: An Adaptation to Regularities of the Terrestrial World?" In *The Adapted Mind: Evolutionary Psychology and the Generation of Culture*, ed. by J. H. Barkow, L. Cosmides and J. Tooby. Oxford: Oxford University Press, pp. 495–532.

Sheppard, E., 2007. "Anthropology and the Development of the Transpersonal Movement: Finding the Transpersonal in Transpersonal Anthropology." *Transpersonal Psychology Review* 11(1): 59-69.

Shore, Bradd, 1998. *Culture in Mind: Cognition, Culture, and the Problem of Meaning*. Oxford: Oxford University Press.

Sidhu, Premeet and Marcus Carter, 2021. "Pivotal Play: Rethinking Meaningful Play in Games Through Death in Dungeons & Dragons." *Games and Culture* (2021): 15554120211005231, doi:10.1177/15554120211005231.

Sieroka, Norman, 2015. *Leibniz, Husserl and the Brain*. Dordrecht: Springer.

Silvestre, Ricardo Sousa and Tarcisio H. C. Pequeno, 2003. "A Logical Treatment of Scientific Anomalies or Artificial Intelligence Meets Philosophy of Science." In *IC-AI*, pp. 669-675.

Silvia, Paul J. and Guido HE Gendolla, 2001. "On Introspection and Self-Perception: Does Self-Focused Attention Enable Accurate Self-Knowledge?" *Review of General Psychology* 5(3): 241-269.

Simon, Herbert A., 2019[1981]. *The Sciences of the Artificial*, reissue of the third edition with a new introduction by John Laird. Cambridge, MA: MIT Press.

Singer, T., B. Seymour, J. O'Doherty, H. Kaube, R. J. Dolanand C. D. Frith, 2004. "Empathy for Pain Involves the Affective But Not the Sensory Components of Pain." *Science* 303(2004):1157-1161.

Singer, Wolf, 1999. "Neuronal Synchrony: A Versatile Code for the Definition of Relations?" *Neuron* 24: 49–65.

Singer, Wolf, 2001. "Consciousness and the Binding Problem." *Annals of the New York Academy of Sciences* 929: 123–46.

Singer, Wolf, 2007. "Understanding the Brain: How Can Our Intuition Fail So Fundamentally When It Comes to Studying the Organ to Which It Owes Its Existence?" *EMBO Reports* 8(S1): S16-S19.

Singer, Wolf, 2012. "What Binds It All Together? Synchronized Oscillatory Activity in Normal and Pathological Cognition." In *Sensory Perception*, ed. by F. G. Barth, P. Giampieri-Deutsch and H.-D. Klein. Vienna: Springer, pp. 57-70.

Singh, Manvir and Luke Glowacki, 2022. "Human Social Organization During the Late Pleistocene: Beyond the Nomadic-Egalitarian Model." *Evolution and Human Behavior* 43 (in press).

Slater, Alan, 2002. "Visual Perception in the Newborn Infant: Issues and Debates." *Intellectica* 34(1): 57-76.

Smith, A. R., 2021. *A Biography of the Pixel*. Cambridge, MA: MIT Press.

Smith, Barry, 1987a. "Adolf Reinach: An Annotated Bibliography," In *Speech Act and Sachverhalt. Reinach and the Foundations of Realist Phenomenology*, ed. by K. Mulligan. Dordrecht: Nijhoff, pp. 299–332.

Smith, Barry, 1987b. "On the Cognition of States of Affairs," In *Speech Act and Sachverhalt. Reinach and the Foundations of Realist Phenomenology*, ed. by K. Mulligan. Dordrecht: Nijhoff, pp. 189–225.

Smith, Barry, 1990. "Towards a History of Speech Act Theory," In *Speech Acts, Meaning and Intentions*, ed. by A. Burkhardt. Berlin: de Gruyter, pp. 29–61.

Smith, Barry, 1997. "Realistic Phenomenology." In *Encyclopedia of Phenomenology*, ed. by L. Embree. Dordrecht: Kluwer, pp. 586–590.

Smith, Barry. 2001. "Husserlian Ecology." *Human Ontology* (Kyoto) 7: 9-24.

Smith, David Woodruff, 2013. *Husserl* (second edition). New York: Routledge.

Smith, M. L., F. Gosselin and P. G. Schyns, 2006. "Perceptual Moments of Conscious Visual Experience Inferred from Oscillatory Brain Activity." *Proceedings of the National Academy of Sciences* (USA) 103(4): 5626–31.

Smith, W. John, 1981. "Referents of Animal Communication." *Animal Behaviour* 29(4): 1273-1275.

Smuts, Barbara, 2001. "Encounters with Animal Minds." *Journal of Consciousness Studies* 8(5-6): 293-309.

Soffer-Dudek, Nirit and Eli Somer, 2018. "Trapped in a Daydream: Daily Elevations in Maladaptive Daydreaming Are Associated with Daily Psychopathological Symptoms." *Frontiers in Psychiatry* 9, article 194.

Sokolowski, Robert, 1964. *The Formation of Husserl's Concept of Constitution*. The Hague: Nijhoff.

Soltani, Alireza and Etienne Koechlin, 2022. "Computational Models of Adaptive Behavior and Prefrontal Cortex." *Neuropsychopharmacology* 47(1): 58-71.

Somer, Eli, Liora Somer and Daniela S. Jopp, 2016. "Parallel Lives: A Phenomenological Study of the Lived Experience of Maladaptive Daydreaming." *Journal of Trauma and Dissociation* 17(5): 561-576.

Soon, Chun Siong, Marcel Brass, Hans-Jochen Heinze and John-Dylan Haynes, 2008. "Unconscious Determinants of Free Decisions in the Human Brain." *Nature Neuroscience* 11(5): 543-545.

Southgate, Victoria, Gergely Csibra, Jordy Kaufman and Mark H. Johnson, 2008. "Distinct Processing of Objects and Faces in the Infant Brain." *Journal of Cognitive Neuroscience* 20(4): 741-749.

Spaulding, Albert C., 1988. "Distinguished Lecture: Archeology and Anthropology." *American Anthropologist* 90(2): 263-271.

Sperber, Dan, 1985. *On Anthropological Knowledge*. Cambridge: Cambridge University Press.

Spezio, Michael L., 2001. "Understanding Biology in Religious Experience: The Biogenetic Structuralist Approach of Eugene d'Aquili and Andrew Newberg." *Zygon* 36(3): 477-484.

Spiegelberg, Herbert, 1965. "A Phenomenological Approach to the Ego." *The Monist* 49(1): 1-17.

Spiegelberg, Herbert, 1975. *Doing Phenomenology: Essays On and In Phenomenology*. The Hague: Nijhoff.

Spiegelberg, Herbert, 1981. "What William James Knew About Edmund Husserl: On the Credibility of Pitkin's Testimony." In *The Context of the Phenomenological Movement*, ed. by H. Spiegelberg. Dordrecht: Springer, pp. 105-118.

Spiegelberg, Herbert, 1983. *The Phenomenological Movement: A Historical Introduction* (3rd edition). The Hague: Nijhoff.

Spiro, Melford E., 1986. Cultural Relativism and the Future of Anthropology. Cultural Anthropology 1: 259-286.

Spiro, Melford E., 1992. *Anthropological Other or Burmese Brother: Studies in Cultural Analysis*. New Brunswick: Transaction Publishers.

Staiti, Andrea (ed), 2017. *Commentary on Husserl's* Ideas I. Berlin: De Gruyter.

Stawarska, B., 2020. *Saussure's Linguistics, Structuralism, and Phenomenology*. London: Palgrave.

Steeves, H. Peter, 1997. "A Bibliography of Axiology and Phenomenology." In *Phenomenology of Values and Valuing,* ed. by James G. Hart and Lester Embree. Dordrecht: Kluwer, pp. 231-244.

Stegmann, Ulrich E., 2013. "Introduction: A Primer on Information and Influence in Animal Communication." In *Animal Communication Theory: Information and Influence*, ed. by Ulrich E. Stegmann. Cambridge: Cambridge University Press, pp. 1-39.

Stein, Barry F., Wan Jlang and Terrence R. Stanford, 2004. "Multisensory Integration in Single Neurons of the Midbrain." In *The Handbook of Multisensory Processes*, ed. by Gemma A, Calvert, Charles Spence and Barry E. Stein. Cambridge, MA: MIT Press, pp. 243 264.

Stein, Edith, 1989 [1917]. *On the Problem of Empathy* (3rd edition). Washington, D.C.: ICS Publications.

Steinbock, Anthony J., 1995. *Home and Beyond: Generative Phenomenology After Husserl*. Evanston, IL: Northwestern University Press.

Steinbock, Anthony J., 2014. *Moral Emotions: Reclaiming the Evidence of the Heart*. Evanston, IL: Northwestern University Press.

Steinbock, Anthony J., 2017. *Limit-Phenomena and Phenomenology in Husserl*. New York: Rowman & Littlefield.

Steinbock, Anthony J., 2021. *Knowing By Heart: Loving as Participation and Critique*. Evanston, IL: Northwestern University Press.

Steriade, M. and M. Deschenes, 1985. "The Thalamus as a Neuronal Oscillator." *Brain Research Reviews* 8: 1–63.

Stevens. Anthony, 1982. *Archetypes: A Natural History of the Self.* New York: William Morrow.

Stocking, George W., 1968. *Race, Culture, and Evolution: Essays in the History of Anthropology*. New York: Free Press.

Stoller, Paul, 1989. *The Taste of Ethnographic Things: The Senses in Anthropology*. Philadelphia: University of Pennsylvania Press.

Stoller, Paul, 2010. *Sensuous Scholarship*. Philadelphia: University of Pennsylvania Press.

Straddon, J. E. R. and J. J. Higa, 1999. "Time and Memory: Towards a Pacemaker-Free Theory of Internal Timing." *Journal of the Experimental Analysis of Behavior* 71: 215–51.

Strauss, Claudia and Naomi Quinn, 1997. *A Cognitive Theory of Cultural Meaning*. Cambridge: Cambridge University Press.

Stroud, J. M., 1967. "The Fine Structure of Psychological Time." *Annals of the New York Academy of Sciences* 138: 623–31.

Sturdy, Christopher B. and Richard Mooney, 2000. "Bird Communication: Two Voices Are Better Than One." *Current Biology* 10(17): R634-R636.

Stuss, Donald T. and D. F. Benson, 1986. *The Frontal Lobes.* New York: Raven.

Stuss, Donald T. and Robert T. Knight (eds), 2002. *Principles of Frontal Lobe Function.* Oxford: Oxford University Press.

Summa, Michela, 2014. *Spatio-Temporal Intertwining: Husserl's Transcendental Aesthetic.* New York: Springer.

Summa, Michela, 2021. "Husserl's Phenomenology of Acts of Imagination." In *The Husserlian Mind*, ed. by H. Jacobs. London: Routledge, pp. 208-219.

Suzuki, Shunryū, 1970. *Zen Mind, Beginner's Mind.* New York: Weatherhill.

Taipale, Joona, 2012. "Twofold Normality: Husserl and the Normative Relevance of Primordial Constitution." *Husserl Studies* 28(1): 49-60.

Talsma, Durk, Daniel Senkowski, Salvador Soto-Faraco and Marty G. Woldorff, 2010. "The Multifaceted Interplay Between Attention and Multisensory Integration." *Trends in Cognitive Sciences* 14(9): 400-410.

Tang, Wenbo, Justin D. Shin and Shantanu P. Jadhav, 2021. "Multiple Time-Scales of Decision-Making in the Hippocampus and Prefrontal Cortex." *Elife* 10: e66227.

Tart, Charles T., 1972. "States of Consciousness and State-Specific Sciences." *Science* 176(4040): 1203-1210.

Taylor, Eugene, 1994. "Radical Empiricism and the Conduct of Research." In *New Metaphysical Foundations of Modern Science*, ed. by E. A. Burtt. Sausalito, CA: Institute of Noetic Sciences.

Tedlock, Barbara, 1991. "From Participant Observation to the Observation of Participation: The Emergence of Narrative Ethnography." *Journal of Anthropological Research* 47(1): 69-94.

TenHouten, Warren D., 1991. "Into the Wild Blue Yonder: On the Emergence of the Ethnoneurologies—The Social Science-Based Neurologies and the Philosophy-Based Neurologies." *Journal of Social and Biological Structures* 14(4): 381-408.

TenHouten, Warren D., 2005. *Time and Society.* Albany, NY: State University of New York Press.

Thanem, T. and D. Knights, 2019. *Embodied Research Methods.* London: Sage.

Thanissaro, B., 1997. "One Tool Among Many: The Place of Vipassana in Buddhist Practice." From *The Access to Insight* Website. Retrieved on 21 March 2014 from: http://www.accesstoinsight.org/lib/authors/thanissaro/onetool.html.

Thanissaro, B. (trans), 2003. *Dhammapada: A Translation* (third edition). Kandy, Sri Lanka: Dhamma Dana Publications.

Theeuwes, Jan, 1991. "Exogenous and Endogenous Control of Attention: The Effect of Visual Onsets and Offsets." *Perception and Psychophysics* 49(1): 83-90.

Theise, Neil D. and Menas Kafatos, 2013. "Sentience Everywhere: Complexity Theory, Panpsychism and the Role of Sentience in Self-Organization of the Universe." *Journal of Consciousness Exploration and Research* 4(4): 378-390.

Thoen, Hanne H., Martin J. How, Tsyr-Huei Chiou and Justin Marshall, 2014. "A Different Form of Color Vision in Mantis Shrimp." *Science* 343(6169): 411-413.

Thomas, William Isaac and Dorothy Swaine Thomas, 1928. "The Methodology of Behavior Study." In *The Child in America: Behavior Problems and Programs*, ed. by William I. Thomas and Dorothy S. Thomas. New York: Knopf, pp. 553-576.

Thomasson, Amie L., 2017. "Husserl on Essences: A Reconstruction and Rehabilitation." *Grazer Philosophische Studien* 94(3): 436-459.

Throop, C. Jason, 2000. "Shifting from a Constructivist to an Experiential Approach to the Anthropology of Self and Emotion." *Journal of Consciousness Studies* 7(3): 27-52.

Throop, C. Jason, 2002. "Experience, Coherence, and Culture: The Significance of Dilthey's Descriptive Psychology for the Anthropology of Consciousness." *Anthropology of Consciousness* 13: 2-26.

Throop, C. Jason, 2003a. "Minding Experience: An Exploration of The Concept of "Experience" in the Early French Anthropology of Durkheim, Lévy-Bruhl, and Lévi-Strauss." *Journal of the History of the Behavioral Sciences* 39(4): 365-382.

Throop, C. Jason, 2003b. "Articulating Experience." *Anthropological Theory* 3(2): 219-241.

Throop, C. Jason, 2008. "On the Problem of Empathy: The Case of Yap, Federated States of Micronesia." *Ethos* 36(4): 402-426.

Throop, C. Jason, 2009. "Gradations of Experience: Toward a Diltheyan View of Cultural Subjectivity and Social Action." In *Narrative, Self, and Social Practice*, ed. by Uffe Jensen and Cheryl Mattingly. New York: Philosophia Press.

Throop, C. Jason, 2010. *Suffering and Sentiment: Exploring the Vicissitudes of Experience and Pain in Yap*. Berkeley, CA: University of California Press.

Throop, C. Jason, 2012. "Moral Sentiments." In *A Companion to Moral Anthropology*, ed. by Didier Fassin. London: Wiley Blackwell, pp. 150-168.

Throop, C. Jason, 2016. "Pain and Otherness, the Otherness of Pain." In *Anthropology and Alterity*, ed. by Bernhard Leistle. New York: Routledge, pp. 195-216.

Throop, C. Jason and Charles D. Laughlin, 2002. "Ritual, Collective Effervescence and the Categories: Toward a Neo Durkheimian Model of the Nature of Human Consciousness, Feeling and Understanding." *Journal of Ritual Studies* 16(1): 40 63.

Throop, C. Jason and Charles D. Laughlin, 2007. "Anthropology of Consciousness." In *Cambridge Handbook of Consciousness*, ed. by P. D. Zelazo, M. Moscovitch and E. Thompson. New York: Cambridge University Press, pp. 631-669.

Throop, C. Jason and K. M. Murphy, 2002. "Bourdieu and Phenomenology: A Critical Assessment." *Anthropological Theory* 2(2): 185–207.

Tiberia, Vincenza A. and Charles D. Laughlin, 2016. "Dream Incubation: The Roles of Instinct and Archetype in Ritual." *Journal of Human Sciences* (Kuwait) 28: 458-486.

Tobias, Phillip V., 1971. *Evolutionary Anthropology: The Brain in Hominid Evolution*. New York: Columbia University Press.

Togni, Alice, 2018. "Husserl on the Unconscious and Reduction." *AVANT. Pismo Awangardy Filozoficzno-Naukowej* 2: 75-86.

Tomasello, Michael, 2008. *Origins of Human Communication*. Cambridge, MA: MIT Press.

Tomasello, Michael, 2014. *A Natural History of Human Thinking*. Cambridge, MA: Harvard University Press.

Tomasello, Michael, 2016. *A Natural History of Human Morality*. Cambridge, MA: Harvard University Press.

Tononi, Giulio and Christof Koch, 2008. "The Neural Correlates of Consciousness: An Update." *Annals of the New York Academy of Sciences* 1124(1): 239-261.

Tooby, J. and L. Cosmides, 1989. "Evolutionary Psychology and the Generation of Culture. Part I: Theoretical Considerations." *Ethology and Sociobiology* 10: 29 49.

Tougas, Cedile T., 2013. *The Phenomena of Awareness: Husserl, Canto, Jung*. New York: Routledge.

Tran, U. S. *et al*, 2014. "The Serenity of the Meditating Mind: A Cross-Cultural Psychometric Study on a Two-Factor Higher Order Structure of Mindfulness, Its Effects, and Mechanisms Related to Mental Health among Experienced Meditators." *PloS One*, 9(10): e110192.

Trencher, Susan R., 2002. "The American Anthropological Association and the Values of Science, 1935-70." *American Anthropologist* 104(2): 450-462.

Turnbull, Oliver, 2018. "Emotion, False Beliefs, and the Neurobiology of Intuition." In *Revolutionary Connections: Psychotherapy and Neuroscience*, edited by Jenny Corrigall and Heward Wilkinson. New York: Routledge, pp. 135-162.

Turner, Trudy R. (ed), 2005. *Biological Anthropology and Ethics: From Repatriation to Genetic Identity*. Albany, NY: State University of New York Press.

Turner, Victor, 1974. *Dramas, Fields, and Metaphors: Symbolic Action in Human Society*. Ithaca: Cornell University Press.

Turner, Victor, 1977. "Process, System, and Symbol: A New Anthropological Synthesis." *Daedalus* 106(3): 61-80.

Turner, Victor, 1982. "Images of Anti-Temporality: An Essay in the Anthropology of Experience." *Harvard Theological Review* 75(2): 243-265.

Turner, Victor, 1983. "Body, Brain, and Culture." *Zygon* 18(3): 221-245.

Turner, Victor, 1985. *On the Edge of the Bush: Anthropology as Experience*. Tucson, AZ: University of Arizona Press.

Turner, Victor, 1992. *Blazing the Trail: Way Marks in the Exploration of Symbols*. Tucson, AZ: University of Arizona Press.

Turner, Victor and E. M. Bruner, 1986. *The Anthropology of Experience*. Urbana, Ill: University of Illinois Press.

Uemura, Genki and Alessandro Salice, 2018. "Motives in Experience: Pfänder, Geiger, and Stein." In *Phenomenology and Experience*, ed. by A. Cimino and C. Leijenhorst. Leiden, Netherlands: Brill, pp. 129-149.

Vagle, Mark D., 2018. *Crafting Phenomenological Research* (second edition). New York: Routledge.

Van den Bos, Ruud, 2000. "General Organizational Principles of the Brain As Key to the Study of Animal Consciousness." *Psyche* 6(5): February issue.

Van De Pitte, M. M., 1977. "Husserl's Solipsism." *Journal of the British Society for Phenomenology* 8(2): 123-125.

Vandervert, Larry R., 1988. "Systems Thinking and a Proposal for a Neurological Positivism." *Systems Research* 5(4): 313-321.

Vandervert, Larry R., 1995. "Chaos Theory and the Evolution of Consciousness and Mind: A Thermodynamic-Holographic Resolution to the Mind-Body Problem." *New Ideas in Psychology* 13(2): 107-127.

Van Leeuwen, N. and M. Van Elk, 2019. "Seeking the Supernatural: The Interactive Religious Experience Model." *Religion, Brain and Behavior* 9(3): 221-51.

Van Manen, Michael, 2018. *Phenomenology of the Newborn: Life from Womb to World*. London: Routledge.

Van Peursen, Cornelis, 1959. "Some Remarks on the Ego in the Phenomenology of Husserl." In *For Roman Ingarden*, ed. by Anna-Teresa Tymieniecka. Dordrecht: Springer, pp. 29-41.

Varela, Francisco J., 1979. *Principles of Biological Autonomy*. New York: North Holland.

Varela, Francisco J., 1997. "The Naturalization of Phenomenology as the Transcendence of Nature: Searching for Generative Mutual Constraints." *Alter: revue de phénoménologie* 5: 355-385.

Varela, Francisco J., 1999. "The Specious Present: The Neurophenomenology of Time Consciousness." In *Naturalizing Phenomenology*, ed. by J. Petitot, F. J. Varela, B. Pachoud and J. M. Roy. Stanford, CA: Stanford University Press, pp. 266–314.

Varela, Francisco J., L. P. Lachaux, E. Rodriguez and J. Martinerie, 2001. "The Brainweb: Phase Synchronization and Large-scale Integration." *Nature Reviews Neuroscience* 2: 229–239.

Varela, Francisco J., Evan Thompson and Eleanor Rosch, 1991. *The Embodied Mind: Cognitive Science and Human Experience*. Cambridge, MA: MIT Press.

Varela, Francisco J., Alfredo Toro, E. Roy John, and Eric L. Schwartz, 1981. "Perceptual Framing and Cortical Alpha Rhythm." *Neuropsychologia* 19(5): 675-686.

Yaden, David Bryce, Mostafa Meleis, Andrew B. Newberg, Dave R. Vago and Justin McDaniel, 2018. "Cross-Cultural Contributions to Psychology and Neuroscience: Self, Mind, and Mindfulness in Buddhism." *Pacific World* 3(19): 53-68.

Vedantam, Shankar, 2010. *The Hidden Brain: How Our Unconscious Minds Elect Presidents, Control Markets, Wage Wars, and Save Our Lives*. New York: Random House Digital.

Vermersch, Pierre, 2011. "Husserl the Great Unrecognized Psychologist! A Reply to Zahavi." *Journal of Consciousness Studies* 18, no. 2 (2011): 20-23.

Vogeley, K. and C. Kupke, 2007. "Disturbances of Time Consciousness from a Phenomenological and a Neuroscientific Perspective." *Schizophrenia Bulletin* 33(1): 157–65.

Voget, Fred W., 1984. *The Shoshoni-Crow Sun Dance*. Norman, OK: University of Oklahoma Press.

Voland, Eckart 2007. "We Recognize Ourselves as Being Similar to Others: Implications of the "Social Brain Hypothesis" for the Biological Evolution of the Intuition of Freedom." *Evolutionary Psychology* 5(3): 147470490700500301.

Von Uexküll, Jakob, 1909. *Umwelt und Innewelt der Tierre*. Berlin: Julius Springer.

Von Uexküll, Jakob, 2018[1926]. *Theoretical Biology*. New York: Forgotten Books.

Waddington, C. H., 1957. *The Strategy of the Genes*. London: George Allen and Unwin.

Wade, Nicholas, 2010. "Anthropology a Science? Statement Deepens a Rift." *New York Times* December 9, 2010, issue.

Wagner, Helmut R., 1983. "Toward an Anthropology of the Life-World: Alfred Schutz's Quest for the Ontological Justification of the Phenomenological Undertaking." *Human Studies* 6(1): 239-246.

Wajman, José Roberto, 2018. "Evolutionary Traits of Human Cognition: An Introductory Essay on the Interface between Cultural Neuroscience and Neuroanthropology." *International Journal of Brain and Cognitive Sciences* 7(1): 17-29.

Walker, G., 2012. "Sociological Theory and Jungian Psychology." *History of the Human Sciences* 25(1): 52-74.

Wall, Patrick David, Horace Basil Barlow and Raymond Michael Gaze, 1977. "The Presence of Ineffective Synapses and the Circumstances Which Unmask Them." *Philosophical Transactions of the Royal Society of London. B, Biological Sciences* 278(961): 361-372.

Wallace, Anthony F. C., 1957. "Study of Processes of Organization and Revitalization of Psychological and Socio-Cultural Systems." *American Philosophical Society Yearbook*. Philadelphia: American Philosophical Society, pp. 310-311.

Wallace, Anthony F. C., 2003. *Revitalizations and Mazeways*. Lincoln: University of Nebraska Press.

Walsh, Roger, 2011. "The Varieties of Wisdom: Contemplative, Cross-Cultural, and Integral Contributions." *Research in Human Development* 8(2): 109-127.

Walsh, Roger, 2018. "Exploring Consciousness: Fifty Years of Transpersonal Studies." *Journal of Transpersonal Psychology* 50(1): 1-10.

Walsh, Roger and F. Vaughan, 1980. *Beyond Ego: Transpersonal Dimensions in Psychology*. Los Angeles, CA: J.P. Tarcher.

Walther, Gerda, 1923. *Zur Phänomenologie der Mystik*. Halle: Niemeyer.

Wearden, J. H., 2003. "Applying the Scalar Timing Model to Human Time Psychology: Progress and Challenges," In *Time and Mind II: Information-Processing Perspectives*, ed. by H. Helfrich. Göttingen: Hogrefe and Huber, pp. 21–39.

Weber, M., 1978. *Economy and Society*. Berkeley: University of California Press.

Weiner, James F., 1992. "Anthropology Contra Heidegger Part I: Anthropology's Nihilism." *Critique of Anthropology* 12(1): 75-90.

Weiskrantz, Lawrence (ed.), 1988. *Thought Without Language*. Oxford: Clarendon Press.

Weiss, Gail, 2016. "De-Naturalizing the Natural Attitude: A Husserlian Legacy to Social Phenomenology." *Journal of Phenomenological Psychology* 47(1): 1-16.

Welton, Donn, 1982. "Husserl's Genetic Phenomenology of Perception." *Research in Phenomenology* 12: 59-83.

Welton, Donn (ed.), 1999. "The Systematicity of Husserl's Transcendental Philosophy." In *The Essential Husserl: Basic Writings in Transcendental Phenomenology*. Bloomington, IN: Indiana University Press, pp. 255-288.

Welton, Donn, 2000. *The Other Husserl: The Horizons of Transcendental Phenomenology*. Bloomington, IN: Indiana University Press.

Welton, Donn, 2003. *The New Husserl: A Critical Reader*. Bloomington, IN: Indiana University Press.

Werner, Gerhard, 2013. "Consciousness Viewed in the Framework of Brain Phase Space Dynamics, Criticality, and the Renormalization Group." *Chaos, Solitons and Fractals* 55: 3-12.

West, Louis Jolyon and Ian P. Howard, 2021. "Movement Perception." *Encyclopedia Britannica* 9 May. 2016, https://www.britannica.com/science/movement-perception. Accessed 30 October 2021.

Wheatcroft, David and Trevor D. Price, 2013. "Learning and Signal Copying Facilitate Communication Among Bird Species." *Proceedings of the Royal Society B: Biological Sciences* 280(1757): 1-7.

Whitehead, Alfred N., 1947. "Uniformity and Contingency." In *Essays in Science and Philosophy*, ed. by A. N. Whitehead. New York: Philosophical Library, pp. 132-148.

Whitehead, Alfred N., 1964. *Concept of Nature*. Cambridge: Cambridge University Press.

Whitehead, Alfred N., 1978. *Process and Reality: An Essay in Cosmology* (corrected edition by D. R. Griffin and D. W Sherburne). New York: Free Press.

Whitehead, Charles, 2004. "Everything I Believe Might Be a Delusion. Whoa! Tucson 2004: Ten years on, and are we any nearer to a Science of Consciousness?" *Journal of Consciousness Studies* 11(12): 68-88.

Whitehead, Patrick, 2015. "Phenomenology Without Correlationism: Husserl's Hyletic Material." *Indo-Pacific Journal of Phenomenology*. 15(2): 1-12.

Whorf, B. L., 1956. *Language, Thought, and Reality*. Cambridge, MA: MIT Press.

Wiens, John J. and Catherine H. Graham, 2005. "Niche Conservatism: Integrating Evolution, Ecology, and Conservation Biology." *Annual Review of Ecology, Evolution, and Systematics* 36: 519-539.

Wilber, Ken, 1996. *The Atman Project: A Transpersonal View of Human Development*. New York: Quest Books.

Wilber, Ken, 2005[1983]. *A Sociable God: Toward a New Understanding of Religion*. Boulder, CO: Shambhala.

Wild, Markus, 2020. "Conceptual Thought Without Language? The Case from Animal Cognition." *Concepts in Thought, Action, and Emotion: New Essays*, ed. by Christoph Demmerling and Dirk Schröder. New York: Routledge, pp. 94.

Wilkinson, S., 2020. "The Agentive Role of Inner Speech in Self-Knowledge." ORE Open Research Exeter. Accessed on May 15, 2021 at http://hdl.handle.net/10871/121914.

Willen, Sarah S. and Don Seeman, 2012. "Introduction: Experience and Inquietude." *Ethos* 40(1): 1–23.

Williams, Heath, 2016. "Husserlian Phenomenological Description and the Problem of Describing Intersubjectivity." *Journal of Consciousness Studies* 23(7-8): 254-277.

Williams, Paul, Anthony Francis and Robert Durham, 1976. "Personality and Meditation." *Perceptual and Motor Skills* 43(3): 787-792.

Wilshire, Bruce, 1978. "The Phenomenology of Language." *Journal of the British Society for Phenomenology* 9(2): 130-133.

Wilson, David Sloan, 2015. *Does Altruism Exist?: Culture, Genes, and the Welfare of Others.* New Haven: Yale University Press.

Wilson, Edward O., 1975. *Sociobiology: The New Synthesis.* Cambridge, MA: Harvard University Press.

Wimmer, Marina C. and Martin J. Doherty, 2011. "The Development of Ambiguous Figure Perception." *Monographs of the Society for Research in Child Development*, pp: i-130.

Winkelman, Michael J., 1986. "Trance States: A Theoretical Model and Cross-Cultural Analysis." *Ethos* 14: 174-203.

Winkelman, Michael J., 1996. "Shamanism and Consciousness: Metaphorical, Political and Neurophenomenological Perspectives." *Transcultural Psychiatric Research Review* 33: 69-80.

Winkelman, Michael J., 2006. "Shamanism and Biological Origins of Religiosity." *Shaman* 14(1/2): 89-116.

Winkelman, Michael J., 2010. *Shamanism: A Biopsychosocial Paradigm of Consciousness and Healing* (second edition). Santa Barbara, CA: Praeger.

Winkelman, Michael J., 2013a. "Shamanism and Psychedelics: A Biogenetic Structuralist Paradigm of Ecopsychology." *European Journal of Ecopsychology* 4: 90-115.

Winkelman, Michael J., 2013b. "Altered Consciousness and Drugs in Human Evolution." In *Entheogens and the Development of Culture: The Anthropology and Neurobiology of Ecstatic Experience*, ed. by John Rush. Berkeley, CA: North Atlantic Books, pp. 23-50.

Winkelman, Michael J., 2013c. "The Integrative Mode of Consciousness: Evolutionary Origins of Ecstasy." In *Ekstasen: Kontexte–Formen–Wirkungen*, ed. by T. Passie, W. Belschner and E. Petrow. Würzburg: Ergon-Verlag GmbH, pp. 67-83.

Winkelman, Michael J., 2015. "Shamanism as a Biogenetic Structural Paradigm for Humans' Evolved Social Psychology." *Psychology of Religion and Spirituality* 7(4): 267.

Winkelman, Michael J., 2021. "An Ethnological Analogy and Biogenetic Model for Interpretation of Religion and Ritual in the Past." *Journal of Archaeological Method and Theory* 28: 1-55.

Winkelman, Michael J. and John R. Baker, 2015. *Supernatural as Natural: A Biocultural Approach to Religion.* London: Routledge.

Withagen, Rob and Anthony Chemero, 2009. "Naturalizing Perception: Developing the Gibsonian Approach to Perception Along Evolutionary Lines." *Theory and Psychology* 19(3): 363-389.

Witherspoon, Gary, 1977. *Language and Art in the Navajo Universe.* Ann Arbor: University of Michigan Press.

Wong, David, 2006, *Natural Moralities: A Defense of Pluralistic Relativism.* Oxford: Oxford University Press.

Woodroffe, J., 1974[1919]. *The Serpent Power*. New York: Dover.

Wylie, Kristine M., Rebecca M. Truty, Thomas J. Sharpton, Kathie A. Mihindukulasuriya, Yanjiao Zhou, Hongyu Gao, Erica Sodergren, George M. Weinstock and Katherine S. Pollard, 2012. "Novel Bacterial Taxa in the Human Microbiome." *PloS One* 7(6): e35294.

Xu, Rui, Narcisse P. Bichot, Atsushi Takahashi and Robert Desimone, 2022. "The Cortical Connectome of Primate Lateral Prefrontal Cortex." *Neuron* 110(2): 312-327.

Yaden, David Bryce, Jonathan Haidt, Ralph W. Hood Jr, David R. Vago and Andrew B. Newberg, 2017. "The Varieties of Self-Transcendent Experience." *Review of General Psychology* 21(2): 143-160.

Yang, Ang and Yin Shan (eds.), 2008. *Intelligent Complex Adaptive Systems*. New York: IGI Global.

Young, David E. and Jean-Guy Goulet (eds.), 1994. *Being Changed by Cross-Cultural Encounters*. Peterborough, Ontario: Broadview Press.

Zahavi, Dan, 1992. "Constitution and Ontology: Some Remarks on Husserl's Ontological Position in the *Logical Investigations*." *Husserl Studies* 9: 111–124.

Zahavi, Dan, 1999. "Michel Henry and the Phenomenology of the Invisible." *Continental Philosophy Review* 32(3): 223-240.

Zahavi, Dan, 2003a. "Inner Time-Consciousness and Pre-Reflective Self-Awareness." *The New Husserl: A Critical Reader*, ed. by Donn Welton. Bloomington, IN: Indiana University Press, pp. 157-180.

Zahavi, Dan, 2003b. *Husserl's Phenomenology*. Stanford: Stanford University Press.

Zahavi, Dan, 2005. *Subjectivity and Selfhood: Investigating the First-Person Perspective*. Cambridge, MA: MIT Press.

Zahavi, Dan, 2007. "Expression and Empathy." In *Folk Psychology Re-assessed,* ed. by Daniel D. Hutto. Dordrecht, Springer, pp. 25-40.

Zahavi, Dan, 2008. "Simulation, Projection and Empathy." *Consciousness and Cognition* 17(2): 514-522.

Zahavi, Dan, 2019. *Phenomenology: The Basics*. New York: Routledge.

Zahavi, Dan and E. Stjernfeld (eds), 2002. *One Hundred Years of Phenomenology: Husserl's Logical Investigations Revisited*. Dordrecht: Springer.

Zhok, Andrea, 2011. "The Ontological Status of Essences in Husserl's Thought." *New Yearbook for Phenomenology and Phenomenological Philosophy* 11: 96-127.

Zigon, Jarrett, 2009. "Phenomenological Anthropology and Morality: A Reply to Robbins." *Ethnos* 74(2): 286-288.

Zigon, Jarrett, 2010. "Moral and Ethical Assemblages." *Anthropological Theory* 10(1-2): 3-15.

Zimmer, J. Raymond, 2000. "Evolutionary Psychology and the Semiotics of Miracles." *Semiotics 2000*, pp. 440-452.

Zippel, Nicola, 2016. "Dreaming Consciousness: A Contribution from Phenomenology." *Rivista internazionale di Filosofia e Psicologia* 7(2): 180-201.

Zoh, Yoonseo, Steve WC Chang and Molly J. Crockett, 2022. "The Prefrontal Cortex and (Uniquely) Human Cooperation: A Comparative Perspective." *Neuropsychopharmacology* 47(1): 119-133.

Zuckerman, Molly K. and Debra L. Martin (eds), 2016. *New Directions in Biocultural Anthropology*. New York: Wiley & Sons.

Index

truing 148n35, 228, 253, 305, 344
 knowledge about our self 279-280
 reality trues out beliefs 256, 343-345
 "self-evident" 255
Trump, Donald 231
Trungpa Rinpoche, Chögyam 23
Turner, Victor 14

unconscious 259, 340, 340n70
 anterograde amnesia and 263n58
 awareness and intuition about the 261
 collective unconscious (Jung) 265
 combining Husserl and Jung 259
 hidden and stratified underground of consciousness 262
 Husserl on the 260-264, 260n57
 Jung on the 264-266
 obdurate nature of the 278, 280
 "passive background" (Husserl) 271
 personal 263
 "psychoid" nature of (Jung) 280
 "sedimentation" ("precipitation") (Husserl) 262
 "spirit" ("spiritual world") and the 280, 290
 trauma and the 271, 299
uroboros 93

value, evaluation
 see axiology
Varela, Francisco 22
Vaughan, Frances 285
Visual Intelligence (Hoffman) 80
von Uexküll, Jakob 24
Vorlesungen über Ethik und Wertlehre (Husserl) 315

Wallace, Anthony F. C. 344
Walsh, Roger 285
Walther, Gerda 307
 Sündenfall or "fall of mankind" 307-308
Watcher, the 84, 92, 267, 338
 a priori subject of the intentional act 267
 as standpoint 84
 defined 50, 370
 distinct from object 97
 "impartial spectator" 91
 transcendental 267

Weber, Max 182
Whitehead, Alfred North 138-139, 313
Wilber, Ken 65
 "you want to know this, do this" 119
Wilson, John 362
What Is Life? (Schrödinger) 69
Wheeler, John 25-26, 93

Yoruba people of West Africa 328
"you see, but you do not observe..." (Sherlock Holmes) 237

Zahavi, Dan 87
Zur Phänomenologie der Intersubjektivität (Kern) 113n28
Zur Phänomenologie der Mystik (Walther) 308

www.ingramcontent.com/pod-product-compliance
Lightning Source LLC
Chambersburg PA
CBHW030633270326
41929CB00007B/64